# Premodern financial systems

*Premodern financial systems: A historical comparative study* describes (in quantitative terms whenever possible) the financial superstructure, such as the method of financing the government, and links it to the essential characteristics of the infrastructure of nearly a dozen societies ranging from Athens in the late fifth century B.C. to the United Provinces in the mid-seventeenth century.

The main features of the financial superstructures discussed are the monetary system, the types of financial instruments and institutions, interest rates, and the methods of financing agriculture, nonagricultural business, households, foreign trade, and government. Aspects of the infrastructures covered include population, urbanization, prices, national output, wealth, and their sectoral and size distribution.

The societies included and treated in detail, varying in line with the availability of information, are Mesopotamia, Athens in the late fifth century B.C., Augustan Rome, the Abbasid caliphate (c. 800 A.D.), the Ottoman Empire in the mid-fifteenth century, Mughal India (c. 1500 A.D.), early Tokugawa Japan, Florence in the early fifteenth century, Elizabethan England, and the United Provinces in the mid-seventeenth century. This study concludes with a chapter summarizing the similarities and differences of these ten regions.

# Premodern financial systems
## A historical comparative study

RAYMOND W. GOLDSMITH

*Yale University*

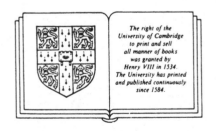

The right of the
University of Cambridge
to print and sell
all manner of books
was granted by
Henry VIII in 1534.
The University has printed
and published continuously
since 1584.

## CAMBRIDGE UNIVERSITY PRESS

*Cambridge*
*New York   New Rochelle*
*Melbourne   Sydney*

CAMBRIDGE UNIVERSITY PRESS
Cambridge, New York, Melbourne, Madrid, Cape Town, Singapore, São Paulo

Cambridge University Press
The Edinburgh Building, Cambridge CB2 8RU, UK

Published in the United States of America by Cambridge University Press, New York

www.cambridge.org
Information on this title: www.cambridge.org/9780521329477

First published 1987
This digitally printed version 2008

A catalogue record for this publication is available from the British Library

Library of Congress Cataloguing in Publication data
Goldsmith, Raymond William, 1904–
    Premodern financial systems.
    1. Finance – History.  I. Title.
HG171.G65   1987    332′.09    86-21558

ISBN 978-0-521-32947-7 hardback
ISBN 978-0-521-06860-4 paperback

# Contents

v

# Tables

ix

# Preface

This study of the financial structure of nearly a dozen of premodern countries, that is, before the eighteenth century, may be regarded as a supplement to the work I have done over the past decades on the financial systems of a number of individual countries in the nineteenth and twentieth centuries (United States, Brazil, India, Japan, and Mexico) and on a comparative basis for a larger number of countries in *Financial Structure and Development* (1969) and in *Comparative National Balance Sheets* (1985). Although it tries, as those studies did, to use as far as possible quantitative data, this obviously can be done only to a much more limited extent, and whatever data are available are much less comprehensive and are subject to larger margins of uncertainty, but such a sometimes hazardous approach has been regarded as preferable to an entirely qualitative description.

Limitations of time, space, energy, and of the available literature have made it necessary to concentrate the study on 10 cases, the selection of which is explained in Chapter 1. Although an attempt has been made to facilitate comparisons by covering the same features of financial structure in the various chapters and in the same order, the limitation of the available literature has led to considerable differences in the detail of their treatment and in the reliability of the descriptions. The absence in almost all cases of time series of relevant data has led to concentration on a short period in the financial history of each case. It is hardly necessary to add that the same factors have forced reliance on secondary sources hoping that not too many relevant ones have been overlooked. Many more publications have been consulted than are cited. The manuscript was written in 1983 and 1984 and illness has prevented me from taking account of later publications.

I am grateful to a few specialists for having read and commented on some of the chapters, particularly Mr. Duncan-Jones (Chapter 3), Professors Ehrenkreutz (Chapter 5), Goldthwaite, Herlihy, and Molho (Chapter 9), and deVries and Montias and Mrs. t'Hart (Chapter 11), who, of course, are not responsible for any remaining errors of fact or questionable interpretations, but I unfortunately have not been able to elicit comments on the other chapters.

Thanks are due to Mrs. Anne Tassi for typing an often difficult to read manuscript and to Mrs. Judi Steinig for her work as production editor.

Raymond W. Goldsmith

New Haven, Connecticut
February 1987

CHAPTER 1

# Introduction

A financial system is the connected universe of financial instruments, financial institutions, and financial markets operating in a given place at a given time, that is, it is the financial superstructure of the economy. Financial systems of different places or dates therefore differ from or resemble each other in the number, character, method of operation, and size of their instruments, institutions, and markets. It is the purpose of this study to describe the financial systems of a number of representative premodern economies and to relate them to the underlying structure of income and wealth. Before proceeding to this task it is necessary to provide a very brief discussion of the purpose and a description of the terms and measures used, the selection of the systems covered, and the sources and limitations of the data, leaving the last chapter to point out the similarities and differences among the systems studied.

In the premodern period financial instruments were almost limited to evidences of debt, that is, to claims and liabilities, which were characterized primarily by their origin, maturity, conditions of service (interest), and repayment, specific security or lack of it, absence or mode of transferability, and issuer. Probably the oldest form of financial instruments were trade and consumer credit usually of a duration of less than one year. The main difference between them is that in the case of trade credit, debtor and creditor are businessmen and the relation is a voluntary and basically equal one, while consumer credit is often if not predominantly the result of necessity and the power of the debtor, usually a peasant or small artisan who is much weaker than that of the lender particularly if he is the borrower's landlord or tax collector. As a result, explicit or implicit interest rates are higher and penalties for default harsher in the case of consumer loans than in that of trade credit. Financial instruments used in trade credit became transferable in various forms culminating in the standardized bill of exchange near the end of the premodern period; consumer

1

credits were hardly ever transferable, some princely obligations being the exception.

Claims against financial institutions, specifically bank deposits and claims arising out of insurance contracts, should be regarded as separate forms of financial instruments. They remained of small importance until near the end of the premodern period.

Long-time instruments took primarily three forms: mortgages secured by real estate (usually rural); bonds or similar instruments issued by some of the numerous types of governmental units, primarily princes and cities; and annuities. While mortgages appeared as early as classical antiquity, though they remained rare, government bonds and annuities were essentially limited to Europe and to the period starting with the thirteenth century.

Corporate stocks with their characteristics of participation in the equity of a business enterprise and generally of limited liability appeared so late and in so few countries that they can hardly be regarded as a premodern financial instrument. They, however, had predecessors in the various less rigid forms of partnerships, often limited to a single venture which are found in the ancient Near East, in classical antiquity, in Islam, and in Europe from the early Middle Ages on.

While full-bodied metallic money is not a financial instrument – though subsidiary coins whose face value exceeds the value of their metallic content are – it is so closely related to other financial instruments and so important to the functioning of premodern financial systems that a description of the monetary regime is an essential part of the financial system. Paper money, in the premodern period found only in China and Japan, is of course a financial instrument, namely, a form of debt, generally issued by a government and not always redeemable.

Financial institutions, if strictly defined as economic units most of whose assets and liabilities are financial instruments and whose activities consist primarily in the handling of such instruments, were rare during most of the premodern period. They are essentially of three types: deposit banks, thrift institutions, such as montepios, and insurance organizations. They became more common only in Italy beginning in the thirteenth century and in other European countries somewhat later. Money changers and pawnbrokers are marginal cases. They have been operating in almost all premodern monetized economies and undoubtedly were much more numerous than financial institutions strictly defined. Unfortunately hardly any concrete information on their number or size exists.

Organized financial markets did not develop in premodern financial systems until near the end of the period and even then operated in only one of the systems studied, in the form of the Amsterdam stock exchange in the mid-seventeenth century.

A financial system may be defined positively or negatively – positively by enumerating the characteristics an economy must possess to qualify as having a financial system and negatively by listing characteristics that by themselves do not suffice to constitute a financial system. As in all definitions outside the sciences a certain degree of vagueness and arbitrariness must be accepted.

To start with the negative aspects of the definition, the presence of full-bodied, usually metallic, money is not sufficient to constitute by itself a financial system, not even in the form of coins and certainly not if limited to the use of metals for pensatory (by weight) payments. Nor does the existence of occasional seed loans or similar necessitous transactions, certainly not if repayable in kind, but not even if repayable in coin. Nor is the collection of taxes payable uniquely or alternatively in coin.

On the other hand the presence of financial instruments (such as fiduciary money, trade credit, bills of exchange, bank deposits, or securities) or of financial institutions (such as banks or insurance organizations) or of financial markets (such as stock exchanges) indicates the existence of a financial system provided they are more than occasional occurrences and represent regular features of the economy.

On the basis of these criteria there were no financial systems in the New World before the sixteenth century and in Africa south of the Sahara as well as in Australia and in Oceania before the nineteenth century, when they were introduced from outside. On the other hand financial systems of different size and complexity can be found in the Near East from the second millennium B.C. on and not much later in Mediterranean Europe, India, and China.

The distinction between premodern financial systems, to which this study is limited, and modern systems is also to some extent arbitrary. It is here seen as the predominance of the monetized sector of the economy and the presence of fiduciary money issued by a central bank, or by a decentralized banking system performing a corresponding function, and of organizations such as corporations enjoying limited liability. This definition puts the beginning of modern financial systems at roughly the early eighteenth century in Western Europe, the late eighteenth century in the rest of Europe and the Americas, the nineteenth century in South and East Asia, Australia, and Oceania, and the early twentieth century in Africa south of the Sahara. As this study does not deal with any of the latecomers, all the financial systems described antedate the eighteenth century.

The advent of the modern financial systems thus seems to antedate that of the Industrial Revolution at least in England if that revolution is assumed to have occurred in the second half of the eighteenth century. But the lag is not long and would disappear or even be reversed in direction if the beginning of the Industrial Revolution were pushed back as is sometimes done, into the seventeenth century. In the rest of the world the appearance of the modern financial system seems to have been simultaneous with that of the Industrial Revolution or even to have followed it. It is therefore not unreasonable to assume that the modern financial system and the Industrial Revolution have appeared at approximately the same time. This is what one would expect if the Industrial Revolution had substantially increased the demand for external funds, at least since the railway age.

The selection among the multiplicity of premodern financial systems of a manageable number must be a compromise between on the one hand including all those systems outstanding either because of their innovations and their effect on other contemporary and posterior systems, or because of the economic importance of the area in which, or the length of the period during which, they operated, and on the other the availability of information, particularly in quantitative form. In some cases fortunately historical importance and availability of data relative to other situations coincide as for Periclean Athens, the Roman Empire, the Caliphate, the Mughal Empire, Elizabethan England, and the United Provinces. In others availability of data was responsible for the choice, namely, the selection of Medici Florence rather than of Venice or Genoa and that of the United Provinces in the mid-seventeenth century rather than of Antwerp in the sixteenth century or of Brugge in the fifteenth. Some systems have been included because of their importance even though the available information is unsatisfactory. This is the case for the Ottoman Empire and, of course, for the few notes on the ancient Near East. Lack of data or relative narrowness or distinctiveness of the financial system – as well as time and space – finally, have led to omitting a few candidates, for example, Sung or Ming China, sixteenth-century Spain, and seventeenth-century France.

A choice is similarly involved with respect to the date at which each system is depicted. One might wish to catch each system at the point of its apogee or its fullest development, but how is this to be determined? In some instances availability of data was the determinant consideration – as for Florence the existence and preservation of the census of 1427 or for the Mughal Empire the information provided by the *Ain-i-Akbari* for the end of the sixteenth century. In the case of Athens, the Abbasid caliphate, the Ottoman Empire, and the United Provinces an earlier date when the country was close to its political and military apogee has been preferred to a later date – the fourth century B.C., the tenth century, the seventeenth century, and the eighteenth century, respectively – when the financial system was more developed, a problem of lag to be touched upon in Chapter 12.

The primary function of a financial system, it will probably be accepted, is to facilitate the exchange of goods, services, and physical and financial assets and thereby to assist, and possibly to permit, economic development and to foster economic welfare. The task of the analysis and comparison of financial systems then would be to show whether, how, and how far such systems have actually discharged their functions, popularly speaking, to determine whether finance has mattered and how much. Unfortunately no method has as yet been developed in theoretical or statistical terms that permits us to decide whether the operation of the financial system of a given place or time has initiated or accelerated economic growth, extensive or intensive, or has increased economic welfare, let alone by how much. If we are lucky, that is, if we have sectorized balance sheets and flow-of-funds accounts or rough substitutes for them for a substantial period or at fairly long intervals, we may ascertain whether the financial superstructure of financial instruments, financial institutions, and financial markets has grown in step with the infrastructure of natural resources, labor, and capital or whether it has lagged behind it or has outpaced it. We may even be able to say whether and to what extent a more rapid growth of the financial superstructure was the result of increasing duplications within it. Since there has been economic growth, even if at a very slow and irregular pace, in situations without a financial superstructure other than metallic coins – over the whole world since the second millennium B.C. and in large parts of it until almost the present time – the existence of a financial superstructure obviously is not a prerequisite of economic development. On the other hand all economies that have grown for protracted periods at substantial speed, say at annual rates of over 1 percent per head, have had a sizable, and with the exception of some centrally planned economies, generally expanding financial superstructure. This fact creates a presumption, but not more than that, that the presence and the expansion of a financial superstructure are a corollary, if not a necessary element, of economic development, at least in market economies. This presumption, moreover, is stronger for the two centuries since the Industrial Revolution than for the much longer preceding period.

The following chapters cannot, therefore, claim to contribute to solving the basic question of the influence of the financial superstructure on the development of the infrastructure of income and wealth before the eighteenth century, that is, before the appearance of modern economies. The best they can do is to permit comparisons between the form and the size of the financial superstructure and some characteristics of the infrastructure in nearly a dozen situations reaching from the second millennium B.C. to the seventeenth century A.D. and stretching from the Near East to India, Japan, and Western Europe. This study of the relations between the financial superstructure and the infrastructure of population, income, and wealth should be helpful in assessing the role of the financial superstructure in a number of premodern cases greatly differing in time, location, and size, even if it cannot suffice to establish causal relationships.

The state of the art now requires us to treat the financial system insofar as it is expressed in quantitative terms as part of a comprehensive system of national accounts, in the flow dimension in the form of flow-of-funds accounts and in the stock dimension in that of national and sectorized balance sheets. To do so for premodern financial systems is, of course, impossible. Indeed it is hardly feasible for any country before the twentieth century and in most cases can be done for only the last two decades. This impossibility, however, is no reason to abandon an attempt to quantify, even if roughly, the main characteristics of a financial system and their relations to the dimensions of the infrastructure of income and wealth. An attempt has therefore been made in all cases to try to determine the order of magnitude of characteristics of the system such as the size and composition of the money stock, of other financial instruments, and of financial institutions, and to inquire into the methods by which the main sectors of the economy – households, business enterprises, and governments – were financed. These figures, however, acquire significance only in relation to basic characteristics of the infrastructure such as population, income and its distribution, wealth, prices, and interest rates. It has therefore been regarded as necessary to include estimates – even if very tentative ones – of these characteristics, estimates that often had to be made for this study as no usable alternatives were found.

A word perhaps needs to be said about the use wherever possible of estimates of national product, in the aggregate or per head, that is, in Chapters 3, 4, and 8 to 11, as a scalar for numerous items, particularly the monetary stock, exports and imports, and government revenues, expenditures, and debt. The prevalent practice of presenting figures in current prices for these magnitudes without providing an indication of their relative size leaves them floating in the air. Expressing them as ratios to national product provides a basis for an appreciation of their economic dimension. This is true even if the estimates of national product are very rough ones. Indeed in comparing the ratios for different magnitudes at the same place and date, the roughness of the national product estimates does not matter. If the use of national product as a scalar is useful for the study of the situation at a given place and date, it is essential if comparisons are to be made of the same items at different dates or for different places.

In the study of modern financial systems use has been made of several ratios to characterize them. One of them, and possibly the single most informative one, is the financial interrelations ratio, the quotient of financial and of tangible assets, which measures the relative size of the financial superstructure. A second is the financial interrelations ratio, the quotient of financial instruments issued by financial institutions to all financial assets outstanding, a ratio that provides an indication of the importance of financial institutions within the financial superstructure and may be supplemented by the ratio of the assets of the banking system to those of all financial institutions. The data, necessarily in quantitative form, available for premodern financial systems are hardly ever sufficient to calculate, or even to approximate, any of these or similar ratios. This makes it difficult to compare in quantitative terms premodern financial systems among themselves or with modern systems. Almost the only quantitative feature of premodern financial systems for which such comparisons can in some cases be made is the ratio of the stock of money to national product, that is, the inverse of the income velocity of money, a figure that provides a rough indication of the degree of monetization of the economy. There is, however, one other important quantitative characteristic of a financial system for which information is available for most premodern financial systems, namely, the level of interest rates on different types of financial instruments. These rates permit some inferences on the scarcity or the abundance of funds and on the risks involved in lending. Price movements, finally, have an intimate connection with the monetary regime, at least over longer periods. For this reason each chapter summarizes the information available on interest rates and price trends.

The task of the comparative study of financial systems is, first, to ascertain the features in which they resemble each other or differ from each other. The second, more difficult, task is to determine to what extent similarities, so far as they exist, permit the establishment of a typology of financial systems and to allocate the systems that have been described in Chapters 2 to 11 and some other system not dealt with in detail to a few broader types. There then remains the third still harder task of deciding whether individual systems or groups of them can be arranged in a sequence in which they not only follow each other in time but justify the establishment of a causal link among them, thus concluding whether or not there has been one path, or a few paths, that all premodern financial systems have followed or whether each of these systems must be regarded as *sui generis*. These questions obviously cannot be approached, let alone answered, before the near-dozen of individual premodern financial systems have been reviewed. A few suggestions will be offered in Chapter 12.

If not an apology at least an explanation is required for the static character of this study, as each chapter represents a snapshot of economic history and does not tell how the financial system whose structure at a given time is described had acquired its form and how it developed afterwards. There are two reasons – one practical, the other conceptual. The main practical reason is the absence in most cases of information that would have permitted a description of the situation backward and forward in time. There is, for example, no source comparable to the Florentine *catasto* of 1427 or to the *Ain-i-Akbari*. As it is the description is already a composite of numerous pieces of information that refer to dates scattered around the reference year. It would have been impossible, or would have required an inordinate amount of additional labor and space, to arrange an enlarged body of information in a time sequence of comparable detail. At the conceptual level the question immediately arises about the length of the period before and after the reference date that should be covered. There is hardly ever enough information to permit a description of changes over a few decades. If on the other hand one asks to see the situation at the reference date within the *longue durée*, a requirement for which the available information may be sufficient, one would have to write a universal history of finance. In the case of the Augustan Empire would one have to go back to the early Roman Republic in the third century B.C. and forward to at least the division of the empire in the fourth century A.D.? Ten snapshots are thus the best that can be offered. This means that the discussion of similarities and differences among systems in the concluding chapter will have to be limited to comparative – that is, interlocally comparative – static. A comparative dynamics remains the goal, but it is as yet beyond reach.

This study, though quantitative wherever possible, does not use econometric methods, and this for two reasons. First, they are beyond the author's competence. Second, and more importantly, they are not regarded as applicable, with few exceptions, to the economic and financial data available for any of the premodern economies with which the study deals.

It has obviously been impossible to base the description of the 10 financial systems covered on primary sources in almost as many Western and non-Western languages. An attempt has, however, been made to use what were regarded as up-to-date and reliable relevant secondary sources in Western languages, not always an easy task as the financial superstructure tends to be relatively neglected by classicists, orientalists, and economic historians. To what extent this attempt has been successful or important materials have been missed will have to be judged in the second case by the list of sources cited, which, of course, do not exhaust those consulted.

## CHAPTER 2

# The financial systems
# of the ancient Near East

The following chapters try to connect the financial system of a country at a given date, that is, its financial instruments and its financial institutions, to its economic infrastructure of national product and national wealth. This is not possible for the ancient Near East, which here includes Mesopotamia and Egypt from the third to the middle of the first millennium B.C. The data are so deficient that hardly anything can be said in quantitative terms about the economic infrastructure, and that description must be limited to the monetary system and to whatever financial instruments and institutions existed. In view of the stability of these economies it is not necessary, nor possible, to try to determine trends in the financial superstructure.

These countries and millennia were essentially nonmonetized, though metals were used to a limited extent in pensatory payments and in the incurrence and discharge of debts, but were never coined, an innovation introduced late in the seventh century B.C. in western Asia Minor. The great majority of the population lived on and from the land. Most rents and taxes to secular and religious authorities were paid in commodities or in labor services. These countries thus had dual economies: A predominant nonmonetized sector of the type of a command economy and a smaller though slowly increasing monetized sector that was important in interlocal domestic trade and predominated in foreign trade.

Mesopotamia, to which most of this chapter will be limited, developed from about a dozen city states in Sumer, its southern part, to great empires, which controlled large areas beyond its borders in the neo-Babylonian and Assyrian periods. Except for its fertile soil, which depended for exploitation on an extensive system of irrigation limiting the cultivable area to not much over 40,000 km², [1] Mesopotamia had few economic resources as it lacked metals, stone, and timber, which had to be imported from its northern or eastern neighbors. Barley was the most important agricultural product and main food, followed by pulses, dates, and sesame, the main source of edible oils. There were substantial herds of cattle, asses, and sheep, the latter providing the basis for the country's most important industry and export product, textiles.

The population of the Near East, including Asia Minor and Iran, has been estimated at about 2.5 million around 3000 B.C. and that of Egypt at about 1 million. The 3.5 million people in these two areas at that time appear to have accounted for about one-fourth of the population of the world. During each of the third and the second millennia B.C. the population of the area is estimated to have doubled, an annual average rate of growth of 0.07 percent, to reach about 12 million around 1000 B.C. and about 15 million around 400 B.C., when their share in world population seems to have declined to about one-eighth (McEvedy and Jones, pp. 124, 226, 344). Population appears to have grown little in Mesopotamia, averaging about 1 million from the beginning of the second millennium B.C. to 400 B.C., its share of that of the Near East being reduced by about one-half.[2]

Though the great majority of the population was engaged in agriculture and lived in villages in Mesopotamia, a substantial proportion lived in cities some of which seem to have had from 10,000 to 15,000 inhabitants as early as the third millennium, while in the early first millennium the largest cities reached 30,000 inhabitants (McEvedy, pp. 34, 44).[3] The degree of urbanization in Mesopotamia was therefore fairly high, probably well in excess of one-fifth. A substantial and apparently increasing share of the populations were slaves, mainly females used in domestic service.[4]

A rough estimate of the order of magnitude of the national product of Mesopotamia in the third and second millennia B.C. uses the scarce reported figures on wages and on the consumption of barley. The wage rate has been put at 6 or 10 shekels of 8.3 g of silver a year (Meissner 1920, p. 189). On the basis of a labor force of 40 percent of a population of 1 million, this indicated a total of 2.4 to 4.0 million shekels, figures which would be on the order of national product if it is assumed that the predominantly nonmonetized income of the agricultural population was equal to the wage rate. The daily consumption of barley can be estimated at about one liter per head[5] or 360 liters per year per head or 3.6 million hectoliters for the entire population. At a price of 125 to 150 liters per shekel (Meissner 1936, p. 5), total barley consumption would have had a value of about 2.5 to 3 shekels per head, or for the entire population of between 2.5 and 3.0 million shekels. There is no information on the share of barley, the main food, in total consumption, but it can hardly have been higher than one-half. On that basis total consumption would have been on the order of 5 to 6 million shekels or somewhat over 5 shekels per head. This is equivalent to fully 45 g of silver or at the Mesopotamian rates of 10 : 1 about 4.5 g of gold, an extraordinarily low value reflecting the high price of precious metals in terms of grains and other commodities. There are not enough data to choose between these two rough estimates, which range from 2.5 to 6 million shekels in the aggregate and 2.5 to 6 shekels per head.

Although no quantification is possible, there is little doubt that foreign trade was of substantial importance as was internal long-distance trade, mostly conducted by boats. Main imports were metals and timber; main exports textiles, the only important nonagricultural product of Mesopotamia (Oppenheim 1970).

Throughout Mesopotamian history most of the agricultural land was owned by temples or the palace, though their shares changed repeatedly and considerably. The share of privately owned land, though generally minor, also underwent considerable variations with a tendency to increase. Only part of the land owned by temples or by the palace was cultivated by servants or slaves; most was rented to individual operators. As a result, although ownership units were large, operating units were small.[6] Rent usually was one-third for grain land and two-thirds for date plantations (Meissner 1920, p. 370). It was originally paid in kind, but in later periods increasingly in silver. For the twenty-third century B.C. land prices of about 3.5 to 10 shekels per hectar are reported (Meissner 1920, p. 367), but this figure is again of limited value because of the rarity of market sales of land. For a total grain area of about three-fourths of the total or of 30,000 km$^2$ the value would then be between 10.5 and 30 million shekels, or about 15 to 40 shekels per head, figures which would have to be considerably increased to include the value of date plantations and garden plots. These figures are not incompatible with the estimates of national product.

In Mesopotamia both barley and silver served as means of payment and standard of value, but silver became increasingly used in the latter function and became predominant from the second millennium on and by the seventh century B.C. had become the sole money.[7] In the absence of coins silver payments were made by weight, the basic unit being the shekel of 8.3 g, 60 of which constituted one mina of 503 g with 60 minas equaling 1 talent of 30 kg silver. From the first millennium on bars of silver weighing 1 shekel or standard fractions thereof came into use and occasionally were stamped to attest purity, thus approaching the character of coins.[8] Originally, 1 shekel of silver was treated as equal to one gur (1.2 hectoliters) of barley, but the relation later became variable (Schneider, p. 75). Gold, which was not a general means of payment but was treated as a commodity, was valued at between 7 and 10 times its weight in silver (Garelli, p. 268). The shekel thus would have been valued at approximately 0.8 g of gold or at a gold price of $20.67 per oz at about $0.50 and at one of $400 per oz at about $10. Throughout Mesopotamian history the degree of monetization, though slowly increasing, remained low reflecting the predominance of nonmarket transactions except in long-distance domestic and foreign trade. The available supply of silver, difficult to divide among amounts hoarded and used as money in circulation, appears to have generally been scarce, in part because Mesopotamia had to rely entirely on imports, mainly from its eastern and northern neighbors, and thus on an excess in the trade in other commodities.

Enough is known about prices to indicate that, though many price relations were fixed by the authorities and persisted over long periods of time, considerable changes occurred in the general price level as well as in individual prices apart even from shorter-term fluctuations reflecting harvest conditions (Curtis and Hallo, p. 111). A considerable, though probably irregular, upward movement in prices is indicated by an estimate that the most important single relation, the silver price of barley, increased from about 200 liters of barley per shekel of silver in the twenty-third century B.C. to about 125 to 150 liters in the eighteenth century B.C. and to about 75 liters in the twelfth and tenth centuries, but then declined to about 150 liters in the sixth century B.C. (Meissner 1936, pp. 5, 34). A substantial increase also is reported for slave prices, namely, from about 20 shekels in the eighteenth century B.C. to 50 shekels in the eighth century when slaves were more numerous (Meissner 1936, p. 34). These figures may be compared to a wage rate of 6 to 10 shekels a year in the eighteenth century (Meissner 1936, p. 37). For that time the price of a slave has been put at 20 shekels – approximately two to three years' wages – that of an ox at 20 shekels, ass at 16 shekels, a sheep at 1.5 to 2 shekels, and a pig at 1 shekel (Meissner 1920, p. 265). A hectar of grain land was valued at about 9 shekels while the price of garden land was nearly 10 times as high. By the sixth century B.C. prices were reported as only slightly higher for grain land but three to five times as high for garden land than a millennium earlier (Meissner 1920).

Temples, royal treasuries, and private landowners and merchants were the main sources of loans, which have been attested since the third millennium.[9] The size of such loans and the share of the three main groups of lenders varied considerably over the following 2,000 years, but it is not possible to quantify any of these developments. It has been asserted that the earliest loans were made by private lenders, but during the second millennium the temples became the most important source of loans when they started making interest-bearing loans; formerly their loans had been interest free. The loans made by temples apparently went mostly to needy poor peasants, partly to provide seeds. Most of the loans of the royal treasuries were connected with their trading activities, particularly in foreign trade. Private lenders supplied merchants, but also made consumption loans. Virtually all loans were made to provide working capital to traders and farmers or for consumption since there was hardly any fixed capital that required financing. As most of the land was owned by temples or by the palace, there was little room for loans financing purchases of real estate. Loans were made either in barley – probably for most consumption loans – or in silver and were repayable in the case of barley loans in kind or in silver. In the first millennium some loans became transferable but indossable bills of exchange never developed. Participation in individual ventures among merchants were common, but long-term associations apparently were not used until well into the first millennium. All lenders used only their own funds. Deposits of barley or silver for safekeeping were known, but not deposits that became commingled with the assets of the recipient and were repayable on demand or at fixed rates. Thus none of the lenders can be regarded as banks. Even the few firms operating in the middle of the first millennium in Babylon (the Egibi family) or in Niniveh (the Murasu family), which have sometimes been called banks, were not banks as they did not receive deposits and combined moneylending with many other economic activities. In the absence of coins there was no need of money changers.

There are no measures of the volume of debt, but the facts that inability to repay led to servitude of the debtor or members of his family for a shorter or longer period and that several kings started their reigns with more or less radical reductions of consumers' debts indicate an often heavy burden of debt on poor peasants.

The level of interest rates on loans was high and reflected the influence of customs on most economic relations; it apparently did not change from the early third to the early first millennium.[10] In Babylonia it was at the rate of 1 shekel per mina per month, that is, an annual rate of 20 percent for loans repayable in silver and at the rate of 5 shekels per mina for three months, corresponding to an annual rate of $33\frac{1}{3}$ percent for grain loans, possibly influenced by the customary share of rent of one-third, although the annual rate appears to have been charged while many loans were repayable after the much shorter period between seeding and harvest time. Rates were higher in Assyria, namely, 25 percent to 33½ percent for silver loans and up to 50 percent for grain loans (Meissner 1920, p. 364). Silver loans among traders seem to have carried higher rates than the standard rates, which essentially concerned consumption loans.[11] Even higher rates appear to have sometimes been charged on small loans to distressed borrowers. In some cases the effective rates of interest were increased by the practice of deducting interest in advance. Compound interest appears to have not been uncommon though forbidden in Hammurabi's law (Leemans 1950, p. 15). On the other hand, some of the loans made by temples were interest free.

Pharaonic Egypt had no financial superstructure to speak of (cf. Helck, Chapter 14). There were no coins and the small volume of market transactions was settled by barter or in copper or silver by weight (Ebert, p. 226). During most of its history, the bulk of the land was owned by the Pharao or by temples that collected and distributed most of the product in kind. In a command economy of this type there was hardly any place for private traders, let alone for money changers, moneylenders, or any type of financial instrument or institution. From the New Empire on (fourteenth century B.C.), however, sales on credit and loans at very high rates of interest existed (Bogaert p. 43).

We must, therefore, conclude that the financial superstructure of the Mesopotamian economy, let alone that of Egypt, including its monetary system, was very small and rudimentary, certainly until well into the first millennium B.C. and cannot be regarded as the model of, or the preparation for, that which developed in the Hellenic world beginning with the sixth or fifth centuries B.C. and which reached substantial size and refinement in the fourth and third centuries.[12]

CHAPTER 3

# The financial system
# of Periclean Athens

Athens, during the period of its greatest political and military power and of its economic dominance over much of the Greek world, the half century between the Persian invasion and the start of the Peloponnesian war, the second half of it under the leadership of Pericles, is characterized by two features. The first is the contrast between the level of art, literature, and science, which was not to be reached again in the Western World until the Renaissance, and its low standard of living, which reflected its generally primitive agricultural, industrial, and financial technology.[1] The second characteristic is the division of functions between, first, the citizens who owned all real estate, cultivated the land, participated in handicrafts, and monopolized the political life; second, the resident foreigners (metics) who shared manufacturing activities with citizens and dominated domestic and foreign trade and finance, but had no political rights; and, third, the mostly non-Greek slaves, who did most of the heavy work and shared domestic chores with the wives of citizens and metics.

## 1    Population

The population of Attica,[2] an area of slightly over 2,500 km², at the beginning of the Peloponnesian War in 431 B.C. has been put at close to 320,000, accounting for not much over one-tenth of the population of Greece.[3] Fully one-half of the population lived in Athens and its port the Peiraios.[4] Citizens are estimated to have constituted only slightly more than one-half of the total population; the resident foreigners (metics), a category which included freedmen, nearly one-fifth; and the slaves, whose ownership was divided among the state, citizens, and metics, fully one-third.[5,6]

Since the early sixth century citizens had been allocated to four classes differing in wealth and political status. Only about 2 percent of the citizens belonged to the first class (*pentakosiomedimnoi*) and 5 percent to the second class (*hippeis*). The bulk of the citizens consisted of the

16

third and fourth class (*zeugites* and *thetes*) who accounted for nearly three-fifths and two-fifths, respectively, of the total.[7] Among the slave population, mostly imported, of which males appear to have constituted about two-thirds, the number of domestic slaves is estimated to have slightly exceeded that of those employed outside the household.

The number and average size of households depends on the allocation of slaves. That of free households has been put at nearly 55,000[8] with an average size of 3.6 persons, which increases to 5 if all domestic slaves are allocated to them and to 6 if industrial slaves are treated in the same way. It is probable, however, that part of the industrial slaves had their own household or lived in groups. The free labor force was close to 60,000, or nearly one-third of total free population, assuming that almost all adult males and only a small proportion of women worked. The proportion was higher for the slave population as it may be assumed that males started working at an earlier age and most women worked. The slave working force may therefore have been near 80,000, bringing the total labor force to 140,000 or somewhat about two-fifths of the population.

There is only indirect evidence to indicate that both birth and death rates were high, that there was a modest rate of natural increase, and that in the half century before the Peloponnesian War both emigration of probably at least 10,000 citizens, who were settled by the state in colonies (*kleruchies*),[9] and immigration of metics and slaves, both from Greece and from foreign countries, were substantial. As a result total population is thought to have increased substantially in this period, though no quantified estimate appears to have been made (Gomme, p. 34), and it is fairly certain that the share of metics and slaves in total population increased substantially at the expense of that of citizens, and that for the same reason the share of the urban population rose. The plague of 429, which may have killed as many as one-third of the inhabitants (Fine, p. 199), and the losses of the Peloponnesian War sharply reduced the population. At the end of the war in 404 B.C. the population of Attica may not have been much over one-half of what it had been a generation earlier. Recovery was slow as the population has been estimated to have been nearly one-fifth below its 431 B.C. level as late as 323 B.C. (Gomme, p. 26).

## 2    National product and wealth

### National product

In view of the wide margin of uncertainty in many of the basic data, national product must be estimated from both the income and the expenditure side using the two independent estimates as mutual checks. The estimate of the income side is made difficult by the fact that wage workers constituted only a fraction of the total labor force while probably similarly large numbers of income earners were self-employed farmers or handicraftsmen and slaves. Domestic slaves pose a special problem as many of them performed services identical to those of housewives whose labor is customarily not included in measuring national product.

The daily wage of an unskilled urban worker is put at 1 drachma a day by practically all investigators from the early nineteenth century to the present, basing themselves on occasional information in the contemporary literature or in inscriptions.[10] It also appears that differences between skilled and unskilled workers were small and that slaves when paid wages received as much as freemen.[11] One may therefore apply a rate close to 1 drachma, say 5 obols, per day to the entire labor force imputing the standard cash wage to self-employed freemen and a slightly lower rate to slaves because of the substantial proportion of domestic slaves. There is no direct evidence of the number of working days per year, but 300 may be regarded as the maximum as there were about 60 holidays (Flacelière, p. 162). In view of the seasonal nature of work in agriculture and in some other sectors, such as shipping, it is, however, unlikely that the effective average working year exceeded 250 days. On that assumption total cash or imputed labor income for a labor force of 140,000 would have been near to 30 million drachmas, or 5,000 talents. This must have been close to national product as rent income and business profits exceeding the level of labor income, indirect taxes, and depreciation allowances,[12] though difficult to estimate, were moderate. It is therefore unlikely that national product would have been in excess of 6,000 talents or somewhat over 100 drachmas per head.[13]

The estimation from the expenditure side is more hazardous. It starts from a generally accepted annual consumption of grain of 6 medimni, that is, about 250 kg per head per year (e.g., Beloch 1885, p. 243; Jardé, p. 130; Mauri, p. 76) and an average price of 3 drachmas per medimn (e.g., Jardé, p. 391) or 18 drachmas. The share of grain in total expenditures of workmen's families in Delos in the third century has been estimated at close to two-fifths (Glotz 1913b, p. 209; Spaventa, p. 28), but should have been slightly lower for the entire population.[14] On that basis total expenditures per head would have come to 50 to 60 drachmas per year and to 200 to 240 drachmas for a family of four[15] and for the total population of Attica to between 16 and 19 million drachmas or between 2,700 and 3,200 talents. To this would have to be added government expenditures of about 1,000 talents (Section 10), resulting in a national product of about 4,000 talents or about 75 drachmas per head.

The difference between the estimates from the income and from the expenditure side is thus fairly large, and the average of the two estimates of 5,000 talents, or nearly 100 drachmas per head, must therefore be used only cautiously.[16,17]

In the absence of a satisfactory method of comparing the purchasing power of the drachma and hence the income per head in Periclean Athens with that of other places and of other times, lacking sufficient information on prices and the distribution of expenditures, the best that can be done is to compare national product per head in terms of two standard commodities, gold and wheat. A national product per year of 100 drachmas is equal to 34 g, or fully one ounce, of gold or to 1,400 kg of wheat. In terms of gold the Athenian value is about the same as that of Augustan Rome, about twice as high as that of India in the mid-nineteenth century, but substantially below the values for England and Wales in 1688 of about 2½ oz or of those of France and the United States in 1820 of fully 3 oz. In terms of wheat the 1,400 kg of Periclean Athens was substantially higher than the 850 kg of the early Roman Empire and only slightly lower than the average of about 1,500 kg in all less developed countries in 1960, but substantially below the 1,800 kg of England and Wales in 1688 and the 2,050 kg of the United States in 1820 (Goldsmith 1984, pp. 280–1).[18]

Whether and to what extent the per head or aggregate nominal or real national product of Attica increased between the Persian invasion and the Peloponnesian War is not known. The population must have grown considerably as the number of citizens has been estimated to have risen from 140,000 to 172,000 (Gomme 1933, p. 26), and it is certain that the number of metics and slaves was much smaller in 480 B.C. than 50 years later. Total population thus should have grown from at most 200,000, and possibly not more than 175,000, to nearly 315,000, or at an annual rate of 0.9 or 1.2 percent, mostly as a result of net immigration and notwithstanding a substantial loss of citizens sent out to form colonies. Aggregate real national product is thus certain to have risen substantially, and the increase in nominal product is likely to have been even larger as prices appear to have tended upwards.[19] An additional boost to real and nominal income was given by the tribute of the allies introduced shortly after the Persian Wars, which before the Peloponnesian War added about one-tenth to Attica's domestic product (cf. Section 10). The increase in aggregate nominal product should have been somehwat larger still. It is therefore, quite likely that the average real income per citizen increased during the period, as usually measured, that is, in terms of commodities and services, though probably only quite moderately. On the other hand, the average real income per inhabitant may not have increased at all (French, p. 157) because of the substantial increase in the share of slaves in the population from a few percent to over one-third. There can be no doubt about a sharp decline in per head and an even sharper fall in aggregate real income as the result of the Peloponnesian War as population declined by nearly one-half. A substantial recovery occurred during the fourth century B.C., but even in 323 B.C. population is estimated still to have been about one-fifth lower than a century earlier, and it is doubtful whether aggregate real income per head had more than regained the level it had reached before the Peloponnesian War. Financial development, particularly that of banking, however, undoubtedly made considerable progress during the fourth century B.C. when much more is known about financial structure than for the fifth century B.C.

### National wealth

The first, and so far the only detailed, estimate of the private wealth of Attica, published as early as 1817, put tangible wealth at 14,000 talents consisting of land (9,000), buildings (2,000), animals (600), and coins and movables (2,400) (Böckh 1817, vol. 2, pp. 23–5; 1886, pp. 575–7). It is not indicated to which date this estimate is intended to apply. It may be that of one of the two property levies of 427 B.C. or of 378 B.C., and indeed it is doubtful that the author was fully aware of the problems involved, and likely that he would have treated the estimates as applicable to both dates, possibly regarding the increase in prices between the two dates as being offset by the reduction in some items as a result of the Peloponnesian War.

The main component, the value of private grain land of about 7,000 talents was obtained by applying an average price of 50 drachmas per plethron (about 550 drachmas per hectar) to an area of over 900,000 plethra (about 80,000 hectares) and deducting 500 talents for state-owned land. The assumed area is too large as later estimates have put the tillable area at nearly 70,000 hectares (Jardé, p. 49), which would have to be reduced to allow for other cultures to about 60,000 hectares. There is hardly any direct evidence on grain land prices, but the scattered information on land prices for the fourth century B.C. (e.g., Büchsenschütz, pp. 84–6) do not make an estimate of 50 drachmas per plethron look unreasonable. The value of private grain lands would then have been on the order of 3,500 talents.[20] The rough allowance for other land, mainly devoted to vines and olive trees, of 2,000 talents has been accepted by later estimators (Beloch 1885, p. 244). The two components of the estimated value of houses in Athens of 1,600 talents, namely, 10,000 houses and an average price of 1,000 drachmas, need revision, the number of houses being much too low and that of their price probably somewhat too high. A rough figure on the order of 1,500 talents seems more reasonable,[21] given the flimsy nature of most dwellings constructed of wood and earth.[22] The estimate for dwellings outside Athens and for nonresidential buildings in Attica of 400 talents appears to be if anything on the low side. There is no material to check the estimate of animals, though the averages for horses at 500 drachmas and for a team of mules at 600 drachmas appear to be high, being equivalent to the price of about three slaves. The situation is similar for the over 2,400 talents for coins and movables, which imply an average of nearly 30 drachmas per head using Böckh's estimate of population, but one of about 45 drachmas per head and one of fully 250 drachmas per household if the more recent estimates of population are accepted. If Böckh's estimate, characterized as extremely low, is raised to at least 3,000 talents and divided equally between coins and movables, the average for the two components would amount to fully 160 drachmas for each of the about 55,000 households. This would be close to one-half of the average household's income. As explained in Section 3, such an estimate of coin, in circulation or hoarded, is regarded as too low and should be raised substantially, possibly to about 3,000 talents. Böckh's adjusted estimates for private tangible wealth then sum to about 14,300 talents. If a figure for total private wealth is wanted, one would have to add the value of slaves of about 2,000 talents[23] and an unknown but certainly small amount – probably not much more than 1,000 talents – for financial assets.

All other estimates of private wealth provide only one aggregate, which includes the value of slaves, as they are derived from contemporary reports on the yield of two property tax levies (*eisphora*) of 427 B.C. and 378 B.C. from which very different figures for private wealth have been derived.[24] The point of contention is whether the reported yield, 200 talents in both cases, and of the tax basis – 6,000 and 5,750 talents – which did not include property owned by thetes, reflect only assessed values or true values. Some authors accepted the assessed values (e.g., Beloch 1885, p. 257) while Böckh and his followers assumed that assessed values represented only one-fifth of total value and thus put private wealth at 30,000 to 40,000 talents for 378 B.C.[25] Others took an intermediate position.[26]

No estimate appears to have been made of the tangible assets of the state. Böckh estimated the value of its grain lands at 500 talents (Böckh 1886, p. 574). The expenditures on public buildings and monuments under Pericles, mainly the Acropolis, the Long Walls between Athens and the Piraeus, and the gold and ivory statue of Athena have been put at 6,000 to 8,000 talents, the lower boundary appearing preferable, divided approximately equally among temples and statues on the one hand and other structures on the other.[27] Most of these expenditures were made in the 440s and 430s B.C. Taking account of the not negligible earlier public buildings and of the fleet, and assuming that the buildings did not require depreciation, the value of state real property at the beginning of the Peloponnesian War should have been in the neighborhood of 7,000 talents. Some allowance should also be made for the Laureion mines; the entry of 1,000 talents is regarded as notional. The approximately 6,000 talents in the treasury[28] would bring total public property to about 13,500 talents and total national wealth to close to 27,000 talents.

These estimates, often very rough but indicative of the orders of magnitude involved, are summarized in Table 3-1 in absolute amounts and as percentages of total national wealth.

Table 3-1 points to several important features of the Athenian economy at its zenith, features that are not too seriously affected by the substantial margins of uncertainty in most of the estimates. The first is the aggregate capital–output ratio of nearly six, a reasonable level. The second is the extraordinarily high share of public property in total wealth of fully one-half. It is doubtful whether as high a ratio can be found anywhere else except in some of the theocracies of the ancient Near East. The ratio of cult buildings and objects in particular is astonishingly high, possibly reaching as much as one-eighth of national wealth.[29] The high ratio of public property is significant because virtually all of it was economically unproductive, even though it may have provided psychic satisfaction to the inhabitants, reducing the capital–output ratio of private wealth to about 2.5. The share of land in private wealth of nearly one-half if slaves are excluded from it and about two-fifths if they are included is not astonishing for an economically undeveloped but highly urbanized economy. It compares with a ratio of about 70 percent in the Florentine Republic in the early fifteenth century, (Chapter 9, Table 9.4), which had about the same population as Attica but was less urbanized. The share of monetary metals in national wealth of about one-third is extraordi-

Table 3-1. *Estimate of national wealth of Attica, ca. 430 B.C.*

|  | Talents | Percent | |
| --- | --- | --- | --- |
| I. *Private Wealth* | | | |
| 1. Grain lands | 3,500 | 28.5 | 13 |
| 2. Other lands | 2,000 | 16 | 7.5 |
| 3. Dwellings | 1,500 | 12.5 | 5.5 |
| 4. Other buildings | 400 | 3.5 | 1.5 |
| 5. Animals | 600 | 5 | 2 |
| 6. Movables | 1,200 | 10 | 4.5 |
| 7. Coined metal | 3,000 | 24.5 | 11 |
| 8. Total | 12,200 | 100 | 45.5 |
| II. *Public Wealth* | | | |
| 1. Grain lands | 500 | 3.5 | 2 |
| 2. Buildings | 7,000 | 48 | 26 |
| 3. Treasure[a] | 6,000 | 41.5 | 22.5 |
| 4. Mines | 1,000 | 7 | 4 |
| 5. Total | 14,500 | 100 | 54.5 |
| III. *National Wealth*[b] | 26,700 | — | 100 |

[a] Disregarding the supposedly "infinitely larger quantity of uncoined treasure" in the temple of Athena (Finley 1973, p. 174).
[b] Not including value of slaves (2,000).

narily high and proved to be transitory as the public treasury was exhausted well before the end of the Peloponnesian War. The only comparable ratios are found in India where gold and silver hoards owned by households rather than by the government also constituted about one-third of national wealth in the mid-nineteenth century (Goldsmith 1983, p. 61).[30]

*Distribution of private wealth*

A rough indication of the concentration of private wealth in 431 B.C. is provided by an estimate of its distribution among the four classes of citizens established in the early fifth century shown in Table 3-2.

This rough estimate suggests that the top 1 percent of households, allocating the slave population to free households and some of the metic households to the top wealth groups, owned about one-fifth of total private wealth, while the following 5 percent held about one-fourth, and thetes and less well-off metics who represented about two-fifths of all free households, but over two-thirds of the total population owned not much over one-eighth of it. This concentration is sim-

Table 3-2. *Distribution of private wealth of Attica, ca. 430 B.C.*

|  | Numbers[a] (households) | Minimum[a] (1,000 drachmas) | Average[b] (1,000 drachmas) | Aggregate (1,000 talents) | Distribution (%) |
|---|---|---|---|---|---|
| 1. Pentakosio-medimnoi | 400 | 20 | 40 | 3.0 | 18 |
| 2. Hippeis | 2,000 | 8 | 12 | 4.0 | 24 |
| 3. Zeugites | 26,000 | 2 | 3 | 6.5 | 38 |
| 4. Thetes | 15,000–20,000 | — | 0.5 | 1.5 | 9 |
| 5. All citizens | 43,400–48,400[d] | — | 3.1–3.5 | 15.0 | 88 |
| 6. Metics[c] | 3,000 | 2 | 4 | 2.0 | 12 |
| 7. Total | 46,400–51,400[e] | — | 3.3–3.7 | 17.0 | 100 |

[a]Cavaignac 1951, p. 19; 1923, p. 58.
[b]Author's estimates.
[c]Only better-off metics; total number of metic households estimated at 9,500 (Gomme 1967, p. 26).
[d]Includes 12,000 kleruchs – mostly thetes – living outside Attica with 4,000 talents. Gomme's estimate is 43,000 citizens' households in Attica, of which 18,000 were thetes.
[e]Including about 6,500 less well-off metics about 53,000 to 58,000 households with total wealth of about 18,000 talents, or an average of 3.1 to 3.4 talents.

ilar to that found in the Florentine property census of A.D. 1427 where the top 1 percent of households owned nearly one-fourth and the top 6 percent about one-half of the total private wealth (cf. Chapter 9, Table 9.5), the differences being well within the margin of uncertainty in such calculations.

A similar result is obtained on the basis of the number of wealthy citizens who had to assume a trierarchy, that is, the maintenance of a warship for one year at least once, in the period between 433 and 401 B.C., which has been estimated at between 800 and 1,200 and nearer to the upper boundary and assuming a minimum wealth of trierarchs at between 4 and 5 talents (Davies, xxiv, xxix). Assuming further that the average wealth of trierarchs was in the order of twice the lower boundary, the total wealth of what may be regarded as the 1,100 richest citizens – nearly 3 percent of all citizen households in 431 B.C. – of about 5,000 talents would have been equal to about one-third of the estimated total private wealth at the beginning of the Peloponnesian War, but a somewhat higher proportion for the average of the 431–400 B.C. period, possibly as much as two-fifths. Such a ratio is compatible with the distribution shown in Table 3-2.

Another indication of concentration of wealth, again in the early

fourth century, is provided by an estimate that a property qualification of 2,000 drachmas would have disenfranchised perhaps more
than two-thirds of the citizens (Finley 1953, p. 255). If it is assumed
that a similar relation obtained for metics and that slaves constituted
about two-fifths of the population of Attica,[31] households with a fortune of over 2,000 drachmas – about 8 years' wages – would have
numbered about 12,000 or one-eighth of all households. Assuming
their average wealth at twice the property qualification at 4,000
drachmas, their total wealth would have been on the order of 6,000
talents[32] or approximately two-fifths of total private wealth of free
households. This would be substantially less than the ratio of fully
one-half that can be inferred for 431 B.C. from Table 3-2, and the
difference is probably large enough to be regarded as significant. A
decrease in the degree of concentration of wealth as a result of the
Peloponnesian War and the loss of the Athenian empire would not be
astonishing.[33]

## 3     The monetary system

Until the Peloponesian War Athens adhered to a pure monometallic
monetary standard. All its coins were of almost pure silver ranging
from 10-drachma pieces (43 g), which were issued only for a limited
period after 480 B.C. apparently as commemorative coins, to the tetra-
drachm (17 g), which by value probably constituted the bulk of the
money in circulation, to the common 2 drachma (stater) and 1 drachma
pieces (8.6 and 4.3 g) and of 3, 2, 1½, 1, ½, and ¼ obols (2.15 g to 180
mg)[34,35] The fractional coins were so small – ¾ cm or less across – that
they were often carried in the mouth (Seltman 1933, p. 109). All the
issues showed the head of Athena on the obverse and her owl on the
reverse. The close adherence of the coins to stipulated weight and
fineness and the uniformity of their design led to their being used
and hoarded far beyond Attica (Seltman 1933, p. 111) and their becoming the second currency over much of the Greek world beyond
the Delian confederacy for which Athens tried to make them the only
legal currency after 445 B.C. when it forbade its allies from continuing
their coinage and required they be exchanged for Athenian coins, an
attempt only partly successful (Robinson, passim; Starr, pp. 68ff; Weil,
p. 55).

The only basis for obtaining an idea of the volume of money in
circulation in Athens is the fact that from the fifth to the second century B.C. the mines of Laureion were the main source of all silver coins
circulating, or hoarded, in most of Greece[36] and had been called as

early as 472 B.C. the "treasure house" of Athens.[37] But this fact is far from permitting an estimate of that magnitude, even assuming the figures suggested for the output of Laureion are correct.[38] First, there was already a substantial volume of silver in circulation around 480 B.C. when large-scale production in Laureion started. Second, considerable amounts of silver, in coins or bars, went into hoards by private holders or by temples or were used in the production of utensils or works of art. Third, Athenian coins circulated in a large and widening area outside of Attica, an area which by the late fifth century comprised most of Greece outside the Peloponnesus. Thus if the silver production of Laureion in the near half-century before 431 B.C. totaled 35,000–45,000 talents, applying the output figures for the 430s B.C. to the entire period, an assumption that probably overstates actual production, only a small fraction of this total of say 28,000 to 36,000 talents could have constituted an addition to the stock of Athenian coins in circulation in Attica. Only one component of the increase in the stock of silver is known, the holdings of the Delian confederacy kept since 454 B.C. in Athens on the Acropolis, which starting from zero in 477 B.C. amounted to about 6,000 talents from about 450 to about 430 B.C.[39] This reduces the increase in silver stock between 480 to 430 B.C. available for all other uses to about 22,000 to 30,000 talents. This sum constitutes an upper limit of the increase in the amount in circulation in Attica, but is so far above it that it can hardly be used to estimate the actual size of that increase or the size in the volume of Athenian coins in circulation or hoarded anywhere. There were at least five important uses of Laureion silver other than coinage; namely, hoarding in the form of bar silver, use in industry, in the arts, and as cult objects,[40] and last but not least wear and tear.[41] If it is assumed that the nominal national product of Attica doubled between 480 and 430 B.C., a generous assumption, the need for additional coins in circulation would have been on the order of 2,500 talents if income velocity of circulation had been unity, probably a minimum, and hence a maximum for increase of coins in circulation in Attica. On the same assumption, the maximum stock of money in circulation in Attica before the Peloponnesian War would have been on the order of 5,000 talents.

## 4    Interest rates

The customary rate[42] for well-secured loans was 12 percent, while for less safe loans it rose to 16 to 18 percent. Rates for unsecured consumer loans in small amounts were much higher, apparently up to 36 percent. For the only important type of commercial loans, bottomry loans, rates varied according to risk, as principal and interest were payable only if the ship safely reached its destination, and ranged from 15 to over 30 percent for a one-way voyage or a round trip which were earned during the half-year of the sailing season or shorter periods. Bottomry loans were regarded as so risky that trustees were not permitted to make them (Bolkestein, p. 113). As land is claimed to have become alienable only after the middle of the fifth century,[43] no rate on mortgages had been established by the beginning of the Peloponnesian War. The yield expected on investments in land was lower, apparently on the order of 6 to 8 percent. There were no legal limitations on interest rates.

## 5    Financial institutions

The only financial institutions operating in fifth or fourth century B.C. Athens were money changers and bankers. Though Athenian coins became increasingly used as the standard currency in the Greek world after the Persian Wars, enough issues of numerous cities as well as Persian gold dareiks remained in circulation to necessitate the operations of money changers. They appear to have been fairly numerous, generally of small size and often metics, and were concentrated in the Piraeus and around the Athenian agora. They charged a commission for their services, apparently on the order of 5 to 6 percent (Bogaert 1968, p. 820).

Bankers (*trapezitai*) who accepted deposits and made loans began to operate only in the late fifth century B.C., being first mentioned in 432 B.C.[44] Their volume of business before the Peloponnesian War must therefore have been negligible. Banks acquired some importance beginning with the early fourth century B.C., but even then there seem to have been only eight of them, and the number of depositors and borrowers remained small and limited to the wealthier classes (Bogaert 1966, pp. 370–71). Loans were usually made to finance consumption or leiturgies and were secured by valuables and thus had little economic significance (Finley 1973, p. 141; Bogaert 1966, p. 822). Organization and methods of operation of the banks have been characterized as primitive and far behind the level reached in the late Middle Ages in Italy.[45]

## 6    Financial instruments

Before the Peloponnesian War financial instruments were rare as virtually all transactions were settled by payment in coins. The volume of mortgages must have still been very small as land had become alienable only around the middle of the fifth century B.C., but there probably were substantial debts of tenants to landlords and some consumer debts. As the first banks apparently began to operate only in the 430s B.C., the amounts of bank deposits and loans must have been negligible. Trade credit seems to have been little used. The only financial instrument of importance was the bottomry loan, discussed in Section 9.

## 7    Financing agriculture

Since land seems to have become alienable only after the middle of the fifth century B.C., the volume of agricultural debt at the beginning of the Peloponnesian War must have still been very small. During the fourth century mortgages on agricultural land became common and the stone markers (*horoi*), which evidenced hypothecation, provide information on the amounts of debt and permit inferences on land values that can probably also be applied to the late fifth century B.C.

At that time large holdings of agricultural land had become rare, and the size of the average holding may have been in the order of 2 to 3 hectares, only one-half of which was cultivated in any one year. The median of the debts inscribed on *horoi* was about 1,000 drachmas, though the amounts ranged from 90 to 7,000 drachmas (Finley 1953, p. 255) but the median of all secured farm debts apparently was substantially greater. Since the value of the mortgaged land was at least twice as large as the debt, the median value of mortgaged farm properties should have been substantially above 2,000 drachmas.[46] The average should have been still larger, but on the other hand it is likely that the mortgaged farms had a higher average value than the unencumbered ones. The average land value of all farms might therefore not be much above 2,000 drachmas for a farm of about 2.5 hectares. The average value of land per hectare would then have been approximately 800 drachmas per hectar or about 70 drachmas per plethron of 0.088 hectar.[47] The 2,000 drachmas would be equivalent to the price of 10 slaves – the average farm probably had only one or two – or, since barley was the main product, to about 800 medimni (nearly 3,400 kg) of grain, or to about 8 years' wages. On the assumption of a yield of 8 percent, the gross output would be about 160 drachmas, hardly a year's wage. The value of land in olives, grapes, or vegetables per hectar was, of course, much higher.[48] Even though in the fourth century B.C. there was no real estate market, sales were sporadic, credit sales the exception, and borrowing was not for productive purposes but reflected the needs of providing dowries or for leiturgies (Finley

1973, pp. 84, 118), these limitations must have been even more pronounced in the decades immediately before the Peloponnesian War.

## 8    Financing manufacturing and domestic trade

Hardly anything is known about how the generally small workshops were financed. Most of these employed only a few workers, though shops with one or two dozen workers were not rare, and there were traders whose enterprises were even smaller and mostly did not distinguish between retail and wholesale operations. Virtually all of them were conducted as sole proprietorships, though at times several members of a family worked together. No distinction was made between household and business finances and no books were kept. The majority of the proprietors were metics and the work force beyond members of the proprietor's family were generally slaves. The only institutional source of credit were the few banks, which operated on a small scale. Trade credit appears to have been in limited use. Most transactions were financed by the proprietors' own funds, and when credit was needed, it was obtained on a sporadic basis from individual lenders. Quantification is not possible.

## 9    Financing foreign trade

Imports and exports were the only activities in which credit played an important role and generated substantial volumes of credit. The reason was that many of the metics or nonresident foreigners who handled most imports and exports did not have enough capital to finance voyages, which often took several months to complete an outward and homeward run, and to shoulder the substantial risks of weather, piracy, and war.

The only component of commodity trade whose value can be approximated with some confidence is the import of wheat, which was of such importance for Athens that it was subject to a considerable degree of control exercised by a special office of 10 corn-guardians (*sitophylakes*) and formed the first subject on the agenda of the 10 meetings per year of the Council of 500. On the basis of a grain consumption of 6 medimni per head per year, 315,000 inhabitants, and a production by Attica of not over 500,000 medimni, about five-sixths of which was barley, the import requirements of an average year would have been on the order of 1.4 medimni,[49] costing at an average price of 3 drachmas per medimn, since imports consisted mainly of wheat, as much as 700 talents.[50,51] This was by far the largest single import and accounted for well over one-half of total imports. There is considerable uncertainty about the value of total imports. The estimates of about 1,000 talents, which are based on a figure given by Thucydides and on the fact that the 2 percent customs duties were farmed out for somewhat above 30 talents per year, refer to the turn of the century. Before the Peloponnesian War the value of imports is likely to have been higher, possibly as high as 1,200 talents.[52] Next to wheat the most important imports were probably timber, iron, copper, hides, and slaves, followed by many individual small luxury items.[53] The cost of slaves should have been in the order of 70 talents, assuming an import of 5,000[54] at an average price of 200 drachmas. There is no doubt that the value of commodity exports was much lower than that of imports as the tribute and other payments of the allies estimated at 600 talents, exports of silver, earnings from shipping services, and expenditures by visitors paid for most of the imports. The only important known commodity exports were olive oil, wool, and ceramics while other manufactured commodities made only a minor contribution.[55] The balance of payments of Athens with the rest of the Greek world thus had the form typical of a developed creditor country, the tribute and other receipts from the allies taking the place of income from foreign investments.

The typical form of foreign trade financing was the bottomry loan (*nautikos tokos*), which was a combination of a loan and an insurance contract. The loan was repayable only on the safe return of the vessel so that the lender bore the risk of shipwreck or loss through action of pirates or enemies.[56] In many cases the risks of fraud by the shipowner or trader were sufficient to have the lender or one of his representatives travel with the cargo.

If it is assumed that two-thirds of commodity imports or exports required credit,[57] the volume of bottomry loans made during a season would have been on the order of 1,000 talents. The amount of such loans outstanding at any one time during the shipping season would be reduced to the extent that on the average a ship made more than one voyage during a season, not likely to less than 500 talents. This is a large amount in comparison to any other financial asset, to money in circulation and even to national product, in the latter case a ratio of about one-tenth. If the average bottomry loan was equal to 2,600 drachmas, the average of the 18 known cases[58] – an aggregate volume of bottomry loans of 500 talents – would have required nearly 2,000 transactions a season. Most of the lenders were apparently private investors who operated singly or in small groups formed for individual loans rather than in enduring partnerships (Finley 1953, p. 264) as bankers did not make bottomry loans (Bogaert 1968, p. 374).

## 10    Financing the government

The crucial characteristic of the finances of Athens[59] from the Persian Wars to late in the Peloponnesian War was the fact that approximately one-half of its expenditures – considerably more than the cost of the navy, which provided the raison d'être of the confederacy – was paid by the contributions of the 200-odd cities that made up the Delian confederacy (the German term *Attischer Seebund* is more expressive) so that only about one-half of the expenditures were raised in Attica. Enough is known about the public finances of Athens in the fifth and fourth centuries from contemporary literary sources and inscriptions to reconstruct the main features of the budget – though the concept did not then exist – with a fair degree of confidence for the expenditures though less so for the domestic revenues.

The two most important fields of expenditures were the military and public works. Military expenditures have been estimated at about 350 talents, mostly for the navy, for 420 B.C. a year between the Archidamian and Dekeleian wars,[60] and it may be assumed that they were of about the same size just before the start of the war. Expenditures on civilian public works appear to have amounted for about 7,000 talents under Pericles, that is, in the three decades before the Peloponnesian War, or fully 200 talents a year.[61] Thus the massive public works expenditures were essentially economically unproductive. Even the gold of the statue of Athena was transformed near the end of the Peloponnesian War into gold coins to defray military expenditures. The only exceptions were the relatively minor expenditures on the Peiraios docks. Essentially, welfare, religious, and political expenditures absorbed about 250 talents, the main item being the payments to citizens to participate in the mass juries, estimated at over 120 talents. Since most officials served without pay, expenditures on salaries appear to have amounted to only about 70 talents, of which the majority was paid to officials serving outside of Attica.

These three major identifiable items of expenditures totaled about 900 talents. This compares with Xenophon's generally accepted figure of 1,000 talents for total expenditures. Some of the difference can be accounted for by a number of minor items of expenditures for which no estimates have been made. The remaining difference may reflect net underestimates on the items for which estimates have been made or an overstatement of the contemporary obviously rounded figure for total expenditures.

The main peculiarity of the structure of expenditures was the extremely high share of religious and political expenditures, which combining current and constructing outlays came close to one-half of total[62] and to most of non-military expenditures, ratios which reflect the nature of fifth-century Athenian democracy illustrated by the estimate that as much as 20,000 citizens, or nearly one-half of all adult males, received some payment from the state (Bogaert 1966, p. 820; French, p. 155). Also remarkable was the high ratio of government expenditures to national product of about one-fifth – far above the ratio of about 5 percent for the Augustan Roman Empire (Chapter 4), though about the same as that for the Florentine Republic in a decade in the early fifteenth century without major warfare (Chapter 9) – a ratio which, of course, was possible only because about one-half of expenditures were financed by the tribute of Athen's allies.

The contemporary and generally accepted reports of total expenditures of about 1,000 talents and of allies' contributions of 600 talents per year[63] before the Peloponnesian War imply internal revenues of 400 talents, but they may have been as high as 500 talents.[64] Probably the most important single source of internal revenue were the silver mines of Laureion, which yielded 50 to 100 talents per year, the methods and rates of assessment being in dispute.[65] The revenues from other productive state properties, particularly substantial holdings of agricultural land,[66] are unknown. Three other important internal revenues were customs duties, the tax on metics, and the tax on slaves. Customs duties, assessed at a rate of 1 percent on imports, exports and reexports and farmed out like other taxes, may be estimated to have exceeded 20 talents a year.[67] Metics had to pay a head tax of 12 drachmas for adult males, somewhat less than half a month's wages. This tax is estimated to have yielded 48 talents a year.[68] A tax of 2 percent was levied on the import, export, and sales within Attica of slaves, yielding an estimate of 38 talents per year.[69] These three taxes then are estimated to have yielded fully 100 talents a year – though their yield may have been as low as 50 talents – together with the harbor tax of 1 percent and the income from public property of 120 to 150 talents.

Among the revenues for which no estimates have been made, the liturgies, the payments for certain festivals and particularly the trierarchy, the maintenance of one warship for one year, were the most important ones. These contributions, which apparently were not graduated, were imposed on wealthy citizens and may be regarded as a substitute for an income tax. They represented a heavy burden on the rich as the cost of a trierarchy, which has been put at 4,000 to 6,000 drachmas (Andréades, p. 358) was equal to about one-fifth of the minimum property, which rendered a citizen liable to this liturgy, even though it was assigned only every second or third year. On the basis of 100 triremes[70] the trierarchy would have been equivalent to a contribution of 70 to 100 talents a year, and the other liturgies would have considerably increased this source of income. The yield from a number of minor indirect taxes, such as market fees, taxes on temporary foreign residents and on prostitutes, and from often substantial fines are hard to evaluate. It is therefore difficult to reach the fairly well-attested total of internal revenues of 400 to 500 talents unless the leiturgies were on the order of 200 to 300 talents, in which case they would have represented 4 to 6 percent of personal incomes and a considerably higher proportion of the upper-income groups liable to them.

There were no direct taxes on citizens until 428 B.C., early in the Peloponnesian War, when the first property tax was levied, which yielded, or was expected to yield, 200 talents, a tax that was repeated several times in the following century.

Before the Peloponnesian War the Athenian state never borrowed internally or externally. During the war, however, it did so on a large scale from the treasury of Athena, exhausting it by the end of the war. However, because this treasury had been constituted by depositing surpluses from the tribute from the allies, this can be regarded as an intragovernmental transaction.

The public finances of Periclean Athens thus were still managed in a rather primitive fashion,[71] and depended to a large extent on the tribute from its allies, which disappeared after the Peloponnesian War. As taxes were farmed out, the government had hardly any financial bureaucracy of its own. Because each source of revenue was administered separately, there was little coordination and, of course, no overall budget. Any systematic financial policy was rendered difficult by the fact that decisions on revenues and expenditures were determined in the volatile mass meetings of adult male citizens and were administered by the council of 500 (*boulê*).[72] The result was a very inefficient system of taxation.

## CHAPTER 4

# The financial system
# of Augustan Rome

## 1    The infrastructure[1]

The early Roman Empire with a settled territory of about 3.3 million km², including all countries bordering the Mediterranean and a population of about 55 million, was the largest political, economic, and monetary unit in the Western World until the nineteenth century, and in these terms probably was not surpassed by its only two competitors, the Chinese and Indian empires, until about A.D. 1000. This chapter will concentrate on the situation at the death of Augustus (A.D. 14). However, because of the slow tempo of changes in most fields, the discussion may in general be read as applicable to the century from the beginning of the principate (28 B.C.) to the death of Domitian (A.D. 96). The discussion may also be regarded as applying to most provinces, except Egypt which had a considerably lower level of prices and nominal incomes and a higher level of interest rates.

### Population

The Roman Empire at the death of Augustus appears to have had a population of between 50 and 60 million people, or only 15 to 18 per km², divided about equally between its western and eastern provinces. There is no evidence of a substantial net change over the first two centuries of the empire as a whole, though there may have been a small increase in the first and a small decrease in the second century. Birth and death rates were high and life expectation short, apparently not over 20 years. Urbanization was low by modern standards, but substantial by earlier standards, given that about one-tenth of the population lived in about 3,000, mostly small, cities, including about 2 million, or 4 percent of the total, in the four largest cities (Rome, Alexandria, Antioch, and Carthage). About 10 to 15 percent of the population of the empire were slaves, but the proportion was much

34

higher – probably on the order of one-fourth – in Italy and even higher in the city of Rome. The working population may be put at aproximately two-fifths of the total, or 20–25 million and the share of agriculture in the labor force at between three-fourths and four-fifths.

### National product

National product per head can be estimated, primarily on the basis of data on food consumption and on wages, at between 350 and 400 sestertii (HS), equal to the same number of dollars at nearly 0.08 g of gold per HS and a gold price per ounce of $400. The total national product of the empire would then have been slightly above HS 20 billion on the basis of a product per head of HS 375[2] and a population of 55 million. Because average income in agriculture was lower than in other sectors, particularly in urban areas, its share in national product seems to have been on the order of three-fifths. It is unlikely that more than one-half of national product was monetized,[3] though the ratio probably had an upward trend during the first two centuries A.D.[4]

In terms of gold the product per head in the Roman Empire of HS 380, or about 1 oz of gold, compares with nearly 2.5 oz in England and Wales in 1688 and about 3 oz in France and the United States in 1820, but with less than 0.5 oz in India and with slightly less than 1 oz in Brazil in the mid-nineteenth century. The wheat equivalent of HS 375, namely, about 850 kg, of national product per head in the early Roman Empire was equal to somewhat less than half of that of England and Wales in 1688 or the United States in 1820, but somewhat above one-half of that of all less developed countries in 1960. Other indicators of the standard of living point to a level similar to that of medieval Europe. Comparison in terms of purchasing power, which are necessarily very rough, suggest that national product per head in the early Roman Empire was similar to that of the average of less developed countries in the mid-twentieth century but above that of the poorer among them, for example, India (Goldsmith 1984, pp. 280–81).

As in the case of population there is no evidence of an upward trend in income per head, and hence in total national product, over the first two centuries of the empire, either in real terms or since no substantial change in the price level has been observed in nominal terms. But again real income per head may well have increased very slowly up to the early second century A.D. but to have lost any gain by the beginning of its fourth quarter. This absence of any net growth over the first two centuries is in accord with an apparently very low rate of gross capital formation – probably not over 2 percent of national product – and the near absence of net capital formation in directly productive assets, though the stock of public buildings and of some other types of public structures such as roads and aqueducts increased.

Concentration of income was pronounced (Goldsmith 1984, pp. 276–78). Augustus' income may have been in the order of HS 15 million or about 0.1 percent of national product. That of the 600 senators, out of about 15 million families, has been put at an average of HS 150,000, or a total of nearly HS 100 million, or 0.5 percent of national product. That of the top 3 percent of income recipients probably was on the order of one-fourth of the total, their share in personal wealth was of course considerably higher, possibly as high as one-half of the total.

## 2    The monetary system

Augustan Rome, as it has been asserted of the whole Graeco-Roman world, had no fiduciary money, no credit creation, no negotiable instruments, no business loans except bottomry loans (though consumer or political loans were common), and no long-term partnerships or corporations (Finley, pp. 141–44). Its legal system did not proceed beyond providing for discontinuous occasional capital investments (Weber 1956, p. 46).

Very little is known about the financial superstructure, particularly in quantitative terms, and many of its features are in dispute. Thus no estimates exist of a crucial figure such as the size and the structure of the stock or money and of its velocity of circulation (Pekary, p. 101). In this situation a fairly detailed discussion of the monetary system, which is better known than the rest of the financial superstructure, is unavoidable.

Its "sound money," accepted over an area larger than any before and after until the nineteenth century, together with its army and its legal system may be regarded as the three main contributions to the stability of the Roman Empire during its first two centuries.[5]

The monetary system was of great simplicity. It was reorganized by Augustus shortly after the establishment of the principate, which starting with Caesar's issues has been called "the greatest progress in the standardization of money forms that the ancient world had ever seen" (Heichelheim, vol. III, p. 212) although it did not involve a radical change. It was essentially a symmetallic system with two basic coins, the gold aureus of nearly 8 g[6] and the silver denarius of nearly 4 g, which were supplemented by the sestertius (HS) of copper with an admixture of zinc or tin (*aurichalcum*) and the copper as, semis, and quadrans, which were not legal tender as the gold and silver coins were. The distinctive feature of the system was that though it did not involve hylophantism, that is, an obligation of the government to redeem its coins at a fixed rate for bullion,[7] fixed rates between the different coins were decreed and accepted through the second century A.D.[8]

Since the monetary authorities did not exchange one type of coin for another, this essential service was provided by money changers, private or in some cities municipal, who charged a substantial fee, apparently one as per denarius, or fully 6 percent.[9]

This system remained in force without change until the reign of Nero when the weight of the aureus was reduced from one forty-second to one forty-fifth Roman pound, that is, from 7.8 to 7.25 g without change in fineness – it had been coined at one fortieth lb or 8.20 g under Caesar – while the silver content of the denarius was reduced by one-eighth. A second debasement occurred under Trajan when the fineness was reduced by another 5 percent. From the late second century on the silver content of the denarius (then about 50 percent) was almost continuously reduced until by the time of Diocletian's edict in A.D. 301 it had fallen to about 50,000 per pound of gold[10] or over 130 times the number under Augustus. The consecutive debasements of silver coins were not accompanied by a recall of outstanding coins and their reminting until under Trajan in A.D. 107 (Bernhart, vol. I, pp. 17ff). It is astonishing that notwithstanding the substantial debasement of the silver coins it apparently took until the late second century A.D. for gold coins to disappear from circulation.[11] Silver-money illusion seems to have persisted for over a century.

The official parity rate of 25 denarii to 1 aureus implied a relation of about 12 to 1 between gold and silver, one of about 30 : 1 for *aurichalcum* to silver and one of about 60 : 1 for copper to silver. As the silver content of the denarius was reduced, while the parity rate remained unchanged, the ratio declined to about 10.5 : 1 under Nero, to about 10 : 1 under Trajan, and to about 8 : 1 near the end of the second century A.D.[12] The maintenance of the official parity relations resulted in the simultaneous circulation at the same official value of denarii with different silver content. The large seignorage charged on the minting of silver coins – and the absence of hylolepsy – apparently made it unprofitable to melt down the denarii of higher silver content.

Accounts were kept mostly in denarii or sestertii rather than in aurei (Burns, p. 409; Jones 1953, p. 294), probably because the latter were inconveniently large in comparison to most transactions.

Table 4-1 shows the weight, metal, and fineness of the various coins together with their equivalent in gold, in wheat, and in labor days. It is clear that aurei can only rarely have been used in consumer purchases or in wage payments as one of them bought about 220 kg of wheat, over two months' consumption of a family of four, and was equal to well over one month's income of a common laborer and to about one-half of one of a legionnaire's three yearly remunerations (cf. Goldsmith 1984, p. 269). Gold coins were probably used primarily for purchases of some luxury goods and slaves in wholesale and foreign trade, for large tax payments, and for financial transactions and were rarely seen outside cities. Even the denarius was equal to about half a day's expenditures of an urban family and was probably rather uncommon in the countryside except for rent and tax payments. Most retail transactions must have been settled in subsidiary coins.

Minting of gold and silver coins was reserved to the emperor and was done at the large Rome mint supplemented by several provincial mints, all operated by imperial officials. The mint at Lugdunum (Lyon) established in 15 B.C. under Augustus was the most important (Pauly and Wissowa, vol. XVI, part 1, p. 484). In the western provinces minting of subsidiary coins was increasingly left to the senate evidenced by the letters SC (senatus consulto) on most of them (Handwörterbuch der Staatswissenschaften, vol. V, p. 917) and chiefly done in Rome. In the eastern provinces it was in numerous hands, mostly of cities[13] and provincial governors.

The imperial gold and silver coins were legal tender and circulated throughout the empire except in Egypt (Mattingly, vol. I, p. 11), whereas subsidiary coins generally had only a local area of circulation. Availability of subsidiary coins seems often to have been insufficient, leading to the use of substitutes. Egypt formed a separate monetary area with a circulation of subsidiary coins, which were not accepted in the rest of the empire, while the import of imperial gold and silver coins for circulation in Egypt was prohibited.[14]

Most of the newly minted gold and silver coins apparently were reminted older issues the government had received as taxes. The bullion used by the mints for other coins was furnished by the gold and silver mines of which an increasing and finally dominating proportion were imperial property.[15] The mines were operated by the govern-

## Table 4-1. Characteristics and equivalents of coins of Augustan Rome

| | Aureus[a] | Denarius[b] | Sestertius (HS) | Dupondius | As | Semis | Quadrans |
|---|---|---|---|---|---|---|---|
| Metal | gold | silver | aurichalcum[f] | | copper | | |
| Fineness (‰) | >990 | 980–990 | | | 1000 | 1000 | 1000 |
| Weight (grains) | 7.85 | 3.98 | 27.30 | 13.65 | 11.30 | 5.65 | 2.83 |
| Equivalent | | | | | | | |
| gold (g) | 7.79 | 0.31 | 0.08 | 0.04 | 0.0195 | 0.0098 | 0.0049 |
| wheat (kg)[c] | 2.23 | 8.92 | 2.23 | 1.12 | 0.5600 | 0.2800 | 0.1400 |
| labor days[d] | 33.33 | 1.32 | 0.33 | 0.17 | 0.0825 | 0.0413 | 0.0206 |
| (dollar)[e] | | | | | | | |
| 20.57 | 5.15 | 0.21 | 0.05 | 0.025 | 0.0125 | 0.0063 | 0.0031 |
| 400– | 100.15 | 4.01 | 1.00 | 0.50 | 0.0250 | 0.1250 | 0.0625 |

[a] Also few half-aurei and fourth-aurei (Bernhart, vol. I, p. 18).
[b] Also, rare, half-denarii.
[c] On basis of HS 3 per modius, i.e., HS. 0.44 per kg.
[d] On basis of HS 3 of daily wage of common laborer.
[e] On basis of gold content.
[f] Copper with about one-fourth zinc and/or tin.
Sources: Mattingly and Sydenham, vol. I, pp. 2/4; Sydenham, p. 187.

ment or by lessees mostly with slave labor.[16] The metal for the subsidiary coins was purchased in the market by the issuers.

Seignorage apparently was high, partly because the cost of producing coins was high. It has been estimated at about one-fourth for gold coins, more for silver coins, and possibly as much as 50 percent for subsidiary coins, leaving a substantial profit to the imperial treasury and other issuers (Regling et al., p. 106; Bolin 1958, pp. 97ff).

There is no reliable information on the volume of minting of the different types of coins, on the movements across the empire's boundaries, or on their stock at any point of time, and hence on their velocity of circulation. The only statistical evidence available concerns the metal content of the numerous coin hoards, which have been found beginning with the eighteenth century within the territory of the empire and outside its boundaries (Bolin 1958, pp. 53, 336ff). The distribution of the hoards among gold, silver, and subsidiary coins and among issuing emperors and authorities permit some precarious deductions about the structure of the stock of money in circulation at the date the hoards were abandoned and about the length of time different types of coin remained in circulation.

The volume of silver coins in circulation in A.D. 150 has been estimated at 100 g or HS 100 per head (Patterson, p. 216)[17] The corresponding figure for A.D. 14 should have been substantially lower because, to judge by the periods of issue of the denarii found in hoards, there were substantial issues under Hadrian, Trajan, and Vespasian though not under the Julian emperors. A substantial decrease in the stock is also suggested by the estimate that the world stock of silver, most of which is attributed to the Roman Empire, was considerably higher – apparently by about two-thirds – in A.D. 150 than in 50 B.C. (Patterson, p. 218). The stock in A.D. 14 may therefore have been in the order of 60 to 70 g per head or a total of about HS 3.5 billion.

Another estimate puts the volume of silver coins in circulation at HS 1.6 billion in 50 B.C., down from HS 1.9 billion in 75 B.C.[18] No figures are available for the following century, and the information for the next two centuries is limited to indices of coinage derived from the distribution of coins in hoards. The fact that denarii minted by the Republic constituted about two-thirds of the hoards deposited in the later part of the first century A.D. suggests that minting in the intervening century was small and that losses through wear and other factors may have been substantial.[19] On the other hand, between 50 B.C. and A.D. 14 the stock was increased by the Ptolemaic coins circulating in Egypt. Unless the volume of new coins issued between 50 B.C. and A.D. 14 was much larger than now appears to have been the case, the stock at the death of Augustus may not have exceeded HS 2 billion. Such a small increase in the stock in the face of a substantial increase in the size of the empire – particularly by the addition of Gaul and of Egypt – and of a probable increase in the degree of monetization is compatible with the apparent absence of an increase in the price level and a moderate increase in the velocity of circulation. Averaging these two estimates points to a circulation of silver coins of nearly HS 3 billion, or about HS 50 per head.[20]

In the case of gold coins a rough estimate of gold production within the Roman Empire (half of it from Iberia), which puts it slightly above 2,000 talents for the period from 50 B.C. to A.D. 500, is the only basis for an estimate of the stock.[21] If gold production is assumed unrealistically to have proceeded at a steady pace during this eventful long period, the annual average output of 3.7 tons would be equivalent to nearly HS 50 million per year. In view of the disappearance of gold coins from circulation during the second century A.D., the cessation of gold mining in most areas in the third century, and the decline of the economy in the third to fifth centuries, it is likely that the bulk of the 2,000 talents was produced during the first 250 years of the period. On this assumption, annual output during that period might have been as high as 80 tons per year or HS 100 million. For the period from 50 B.C. to A.D. 14 output would then have totaled fully HS 6 billion. This figure would have to be reduced by the amount of gold not used in the production of coins, a substantial net outflow across the boundaries and small amounts for wear, and increased for minting, out of Caesar's war booty from Gaul[22] and Augustus's from Egypt.[23] The stock of aurei at the death of Augustus might then have been in the order of HS 4 billion compared to that of denarii of close to 3 billion, in line with assertions by classicists that gold coins constituted the bulk of money in circulation or hoarded.[24]

Nothing is known abut the quantities of subsidiary coins minted or in circulation, but complaints about shortages and the use of substitute tokens (*tesserae*) in the contemporary writings are numerous.[25] This fact together with the constitution of hoards suggests that the value of subsidiary coins was small in relation to that of aurei and denarii.

Thus the total stock of money at the death of Augustus may have been in the range of HS 6 to 8 billion. This would imply ratios of three-tenths to four-tenths of total and of three-fifths to four-fifths of monetized national product and velocities of circulation of 2.5 to 3 for total and of 1.5 to 2.5 for monetized national product. In evaluating these figures it must be taken into account that a substantial proportion of the coins, particularly of aurei, was kept not as means of exchange but as stores of wealth, and were rarely turned over. The velocity of circulation of the coins not thesaurized, particularly of subsidiary coins, was therefore considerably higher. Disregarding this problem, a velocity of circulation, compared to total national product, of 2.5 to 3.0 was comparable to those found for some countries in Europe in the fifteenth to seventeenth centuries.[26,27] (For Florence compare Chapter 9; for England in 1688 see King, p. 34.)

Given the supply-side limitation on the money stock by the output of the gold and silver mines operated by the imperial government and the virtual absence of money substitutes like bank deposits, the scope for monetary policy was narrow.[28] The authorities undoubtedly could vary the production of gold and silver and the amount of bullion coined, but there is no evidence of a conscious policy in this field. One may rather assume in view of the substantial seignorage, the external drain, and the apparent tendency of a shortage of currency to satisfy transactions demand that the production of gold and silver was kept as close as possible to the technological maximum. Since there is no record of the opening of important new mines, it may be assumed that output had a downward trend reflecting gradual exhaustion of deposits, which would be compatible with the absence of any sustained upward movement of prices for the first two centuries of the empire. The authorities, of course, had control over the speed with which they minted and distributed metal from war booty. However, in the three important cases, Caesar's Gallic, Augustus' Egyptian, and Trajan's Dacic treasure, distribution appears to have been rapid and to have led to a temporary rise in prices, at least in Italy. The authorities had greater latitude in the case of subsidiary coins. Here they seem occasionally to have permitted issues regarded as excessive, which could hardly ever endanger the stability of the price level given the small proportion of subsidiary coins in the monetary stock.[29]

The second possibility of monetary policy was debasement of the currency, particularly in view of the apparent money illusion of a rather unsophisticated public until the violent inflation of the third century. For over two centuries the imperial government made only sparing use of this possibility: Weight and fineness of the aureus remained unchanged, and the silver content of the denarius declined by only one-fourth between the monetary reform of Augustus and the death of Marcus Aurelius, that is, at the practically insignificant average rate of 0.15 percent a year and in no case by more than about 0.20 percent a year, and in three steps separated by about 80, 50, and 60 years, that is, by at least two generations. During and for half a century after the reign of Augustus stability was complete.

## 3      Financial instruments

In the absence of government and corporate securities, the range of
financial instruments was narrow. The most important ones were
mortgage loans on agricultural land, consumer loans to the poor or
to upper-class borrowers living beyond their means or needing funds
for political expenditures, and debts of tenants to landlords. Trade
credit appears to have been small except bottomry loans. The mortgage lenders were mostly wealthy individuals who made such loans
more or less regularly. Some mortgage loans were also made by religious or benevolent institutions and occasionally by municipalities.
There is no evidence that would permit even a rough estimate of the
volume of financial instruments outstanding, but whatever evidence
there is points to low ratios of income and wealth. Financial transactions were sporadic and there was no organized market for any financial instrument.

The private sea-borne trade gave rise to one of the few financial
instruments, bottomry loans which were generally made by groups of
lenders to reduce the substantial risk of shipwreck and other losses.
Only few details are known about loan conditions and interest rates.[30]

## 4      Financial institutions

The only entities resembling financial institutions were money changers (*numularii*), moneylenders (*feneratores*), bankers (*argentarii* or *trapezitai*), and tax farmers (*societates publicanorum*). There were no insurance organizations or mortgage banks.

Money changers were ubiquitous as the nature and diversity of ancient coins called for examination and attestation for genuineness and
for exchanges between gold and silver coins and particularly between
silver coins and the numerous local subsidiary coins for which they
charged a fee on the order of 1 in 16.[31] They also facilitated money
transfers by putting their seal (*tessera*) on bags of coins attesting to the
value of content (cf. Heichelheim, pp. 19, 819–20; Laum; Marquardt,
vol. V, pp. 61–9; Oehler, passim). Money changers operated as single
proprietorships and had to be licensed by the authorities who also
fixed the rate of commission on exchanges and occasionally taxed their
income from them.

Moneylenders limited themselves to short-term consumer loans either
in substantial amounts to people living beyond their means or in small
amounts and at usurious rates to small farmers or city dwellers in
distress or in arrears with rent or tax payments.

Bankers were more common and more important in Italy and in the eastern provinces, particularly in Egypt where they had been operating on a substantial scale since at least the fourth century B.C. (cf. Preisigke, passim) than in the western provinces, in which they had been little known before these became part of the Roman Empire in the second or first century B.C. Indeed in the eastern provinces they seem to have been less important under Roman rule than before. The *argentarii* often combined money changing and testing and acting as auctioneers with the more specific banking functions of receiving deposits, with or without interest, making loans, and transferring coins within the empire since transfers by *giro* were apparently rare except in Egypt (Preisigke).[32] Nothing is known about the size of these deposits, which probably were smaller than their likewise unknown own capital. They cannot have been negligible as a banker in Pompeii, a medium-sized provincial city, had one deposit as large as HS 38,000 (Breglia, p. 53), equal to about 30 average family yearly incomes, though only about one-fourth of that of an average senator. However, the deposits seem to have been generally of small size and isolated and did not constitute an "effective credit system" (Duncan-Jones, p 2). The bankers' loans probably were mostly made for consumption or political expenditures (Bogaert, p. 838).

There were numerous *argentarii* in Rome, some of which had their tables in a separate section of the forum, the *tabernae argentariae*. Most other cities seem to have had at least one banker, such as Pompeii. Like *numularii* they operated as single proprietorships.

The nearest approximation to financial organizations of importance were the tax farmers, discussed in Section 9.

The most important suppliers of external funds thus were not financial institutions but private wealthy citizens, and the largest of them, it has been claimed, was the emperor.


5     Interest rates

In comparison to the ancient Near East or Greece, and less so in comparison to the Republic, the early empire was characterized by rather low interest rates.[33] Rates on long-term loans on good security, primarily land, which are fairly well attested, were in the western part of the empire in the range of 4–6 percent while 6 percent apparently was the level of yields expected on long-term investments, again predominantly in land. Less secured and short-term loans carried somewhat higher rates but apparently did not approach the legal maximum of 12 percent. The exceptions were unsecured consumer loans to needy borrowers for which much higher rates, reputedly up to 48 percent were charged.[34] Rates appear to have been higher in the eastern provinces, where good long-term loans cost 8–9 percent[35] and were still more expensive in Egypt with about 12 percent (Billeter, p. 110). Rates on bottomry loans varied according to length and risk per voyage. Values on the order of 20 percent per voyage, usually taking only a few weeks, have been reported (Homer, p. 49).

## 6 Financing agriculture

Although agriculture sustained about four-fifths of the population and generated about two-thirds of national product, it used few external funds. This is obvious for the large segment of self-sufficient independent small farmers or tenants. If they borrowed, it was because of emergencies or because they fell behind in the payments of rents or taxes, and they usually had to pay usurious interest rates to moneylenders or their landlords. Medium-sized and large landlords, though creditworthy and though there was a developed law on mortgages, traditionally did not borrow to purchase land or to improve their properties.[36] If they borrowed, it was generally for daughters' dowries and similar purposes or because they were living beyond their means. The lenders usually were wealthy individuals. Nothing is known about such mortgages as existed except their interest rate of 4–6 percent, for example, about the ratio of mortgaged to total properties or about loan-to-value ratios. An indication of the small volume of mortgages is the absence of an organized real estate market or of real estate agents (Finley, p. 118).[37] However, as the total value of land in the empire should have exceeded HS 100 billion (Section 10), even very low ratios of mortgaged land and of loan-to-value ratios would have produced a not negligible total amount of mortgage loans that probably were smaller than the much more numerous rent and tax arrears, which should not be regarded as voluntary financing.

## 7 Financing domestic trade

Though the empire was a predominantly agricultural and only partly monetized economy, the facts that a large part of its area was close to the Mediterranean and hence profited from relatively low costs of transportation, that traffic was safe and internal duties were low provided the basis for a substantial volume of trade that appears to have increased substantially during the first and second centuries A.D.[38] However, no estimates of its size or its expansion seem to have been attempted.

The largest single component of sea-borne domestic trade was the export of wheat from Egypt and North Africa to Rome.[39] It was managed by the imperial government on the basis of Egyptian and North African grain, provided mainly by the tax in kind imposed on the cultivators and employed about 300 ships of 150 to 200 tons each (Oliva, p. 231). Rome's grain imports have been estimated for the early empire at 130,000 talents per year from Egypt and 156,000 talents from North Africa, in addition to 64,000 talents from Sicily, Sardinia, Spain, and Syria (Oliva, p. 231), representing a value of about HS 160 million at an average wheat price of HS 3 per modius or HS 450 per ton. This flow, which represented nearly 1 percent of national product without requiring a substantial amount of private financing must have constituted a substantial proportion of total domestic sea-borne trade. Total grain trade by sea and by land, of course, was considerably in excess of these flows, though it is impossible to say by how much.

After grain the most important domestically traded commodities probably were olive oil, wine and – the only important manufactured item – pottery products, but no estimates exist about their absolute or relative volume.

Most domestic trade, other than urban retail trade, arose in connection with providing the urban population with the basic foodstuffs and raw materials. With an urban population of about 6 million and an average expenditure on foodstuffs and raw materials per head of at most HS 200, this trade could have been not much in excess of HS 1 billion. Urban exports were much smaller since a substantial proportion of the upper strata of the urban population lived as absentee landlords. Total domestic trade other than urban retail trade should then have been in the order of HS 2 billion. Urban retail trade may have added another HS 2 billion, equal together to less than half the total monetized national product. The volume of trade in the still largely nonmonetized countryside appears to have been small.[40]

Information is deficient about the financing of domestic overland wholesale and retail trade. In the absence of instruments such as bills, book credit would be the only possible form of financing. While it is likely that in some cases producers extended such credit to wholesalers and wholesalers to retailers, there is no evidence about how common such transactions were in different trades and different regions, how they were handled and what terms – duration and interest rates – were customary.

## 8     Financing foreign trade

The main import and export products of the empire and their origins and destinations are fairly well known, but there is virtually no information on the quantities and values involved as no records have been preserved of the income from customs duties.[41] Classical authors agree that usually the balance of trade was passive, an assertion confirmed by the finds of Roman coins beyond the boundaries of the empire, particularly in India and central Europe.[42] The only estimate is that made late in the first century A.D. by Plinius[43] who put the excess of imports over the eastern frontier at least at HS 100 million a year. The balance of trade over the other boundaries probably was also negative, but to a considerably lesser extent. A negative balance of somewhat over HS 100 million would not be extraordinarily high in relation to the empire's national product, namely, slightly over 0.5 percent, but as it was settled mostly in gold, it would be high in relation to, and indeed approximately equal to, gold production within the empire. No alternative estimate has been made by modern scholars.[44]

Total imports must, of course, have been in excess of the negative balance of trade by the amount of exports, on which there is no information. If exports covered as little as one-half of imports, total imports would have been in excess of HS 200 million or fully 1 percent of national product. This is not an unreasonably low ratio for a large country in a period in which trade was essentially limited to luxury products. India's imports as late as 1840 were probably not in excess of 2 percent of national product, and Japan's were below 4 percent as late as 1885, though in both cases not concentrated on luxury products.[45] A much higher figure for imports in unlikely as it would imply a relatively high ratio of exports to imports.

The empire's international trade was conducted entirely on a cash basis, there being no evidence of credit extended across its boundaries if only because of the absence of financial instruments that could have been used for such purposes. In the eastern trade, settlements were primarily in gold coins, but chiefly in silver for trade across the Rhine and Danube.

## 9    Financing the government

In line with his policy in most fields of limiting himself to the institutional changes made inevitable by the transformation of the republican senatorial government[46] into that of his principate, Augustus introduced few changes in the field of public finance, continuing the practice of the Republic of taking over the preexisting system of taxation of the conquered territories. However, the level of expenditures was increased considerably by shifting from a citizen to a professional standing army and by increasing the number, functions, and pay of salaried civil servants, increases which were made possible by the addition of Gaul and Egypt as important sources of revenue.

The Republic had had only one treasury (*aerarium populi romani* or *saturni*), which was under the direction of the senate.[47] Augustus added a special treasury for the payment of veterans' separation payments (*aerarium militare*), which was fed by the receipts of the new sales and inheritance taxes. He also began to administer the tributum from the imperial provinces (particularly Egypt, Syria, and most of Gaul and Spain), which contributed the bulk of tax revenues rather than farming them out as had been universal under the Republic, though the formal constitution of an imperial treasury (*fiscus*) appears to have been delayed until the reign of Claudius. Such transfers continued until the imperial treasury had become dominant by the end of the second century A.D. The gradual shift from tax farming[48] to direct collection reduced the margin between the sums levied on the population and those reaching the treasury, which had been very large under the Republic due to the notorious exactions by tax farmers and by officials.

*Expenditures*

At the time of Augustus total expenditures of the imperial government amounted according to two recent estimates to either HS 600 or 825 million[49] or between 3 and 4 percent of gross national product. The expenditures of local governments are not known, but were certainly well below those of the central government. It is therefore unlikely that the expenditures of all levels of government exceeded in the early first century A.D. HS 1 billion or 5 percent of gross national product, even allowing for the fact that because most taxes were farmed out the burden on the population was somewhat higher than the government's revenues. Such ratios are somewhat below the comparable figures for, for example, England in 1688, the United States and France in 1820, and the less developed countries in 1960, and, of course, are far below the ratios in developed countries since World War II,[50] a reflection of the limited fiscal capacity of a predominantly agricultural and only partly monetized economy as well as the economically liberal policies of the early Roman Empire, which in fact, though not dogmatically, were close to what could be called laissez-faire.

Expenditures increased during the remainder of the first century A.D., though probably only moderately, and more rapidly during the second century, both in absolute terms and in relation to national product. Under Antoninus Pius total expenditures have been estimated at over HS 1,200 million of which the military accounted for about one-third (MacMullen 1985). If these figures were accepted, total expenditures would have almost doubled while the costs of the armed forces would have hardly increased, a rather unlikely state of affairs.

*Revenues*

There is agreement on the three main sources of revenue of the Roman Empire, as of the Republic, the *tributum* (or *stipendium*), the customs duties and the rents from public land, but not on their relative size and hardly any information exists on their absolute size.[51]

The regional distribution of revenues as well as the ratio of revenues to income was very unequal because Italy was exempted from direct taxation and a disproportionate share of direct taxes was levied in two provinces acquired after the middle of the first century B.C., Gaul and Egypt.

The *tributum*, which did not apply to Italy, was levied as it had been under the Republic in two forms, a tax on agricultural land (*tributum solis*) and a head tax (*tributum capitis*).[52] The base rate and method of assessment of the land tax varied among provinces and smaller areas because the Roman administration generally continued the practices in force when the various territories became part of the empire. The tax was levied as a quotient of the crop, for example, one-tenth, or at a fixed rate for units of land depending on culture or quality of soil, in some provinces such as Egypt on the basis of detailed catasters based on periodic censuses and kept up to date between them.[53] The tax often was imposed on communities, which divided the burden among individual cultivators. Under the Republic it was collected throughout the empire by groups of wealthy individuals organized into tax-farm companies (*societates publicanorum*) among whom knights (*equites*) predominated because senators were prohibited from participating, bidding at fixed totals on the usual 5-year contracts for the collection of specific taxes in entire provinces or other areas. The *societates publicanorum* apparently had active and silent partners holding shares, which could be transferred and sometimes were actively traded. The tax-farming contracts were extremely profitable under the Republic as the tax farmers were practically free to exact as much as they could and supervision by the government was very limited. In this situation one must assume collusion among the potential bidders for the contracts to avoid erosion of their monopoly profits. Augustus continued the farming of the *tributum*, at least for the senatorial provinces, but beginning in the later part of Tiberius' reign or at the latest under Claudius, tax farmers were gradually replaced by imperial officials (Hirschfeld, p. 69), which generally resulted in some reduction of the tax burden. Except for Egypt hardly anything is known about the methods of assessment or the rates of tax. In most provinces cash payments seem to have predominated, except in Egypt and North Africa where the tax on grain lands was levied in kind.

Customs duties (*portoria*) were collected not only at the frontiers of the empire but also at numerous points of the boundaries or within 10 customs districts within it.[54,55] As a result merchandise might have to pay customs duties several times while moving from its place of origin to its ultimate destination. Collection was farmed out and was handled by a large number of employees estimated at over 20,000 (de Laet, p. 449), often slaves or freedmen of the tax farmers. The rate of tax on the eastern frontier, where most the imports entered the empire, was 25 percent but apparently was lower elsewhere. There also were some lower export duties about which less is known (Cagnat, pp. 140–43), supplemented by occasional export prohibitions, particularly on armaments. Internal customs rates varied between 2 and 5 percent, and there were some additional local sales taxes, particularly in Rome (Cagnat, pp. 153–74).

A tax of 5 percent was levied, as it had been since the fourth century B.C., on giving slaves their freedom (*vicesima libertatis* or *manumissionis*).[56] The tax was paid by the slaves if they bought their freedom but by the owner if manumission was free. Augustus added a tax on 4 percent of the sale of slaves.

Augustus also introduced two new taxes that were to provide the funds for paying separation payments to veterans, an inheritance tax (*vicesima hereditatium*) and a sales tax (*centesima rerum venalium*). The inheritance tax[57] was levied at the rate of 5 percent on inheritances from the estates of Roman citizens, but not on provincials, except for inheritances by close relatives. This tax was collected in nine districts and in Rome. The exemption level is not known, but must have been low as only "poor" heirs did not have to pay the tax.[58] Some doubt exists about the scope of the 1 percent tax on sales. It is generally treated as payable only on sales by public auction, but some classicists regard it as due on a wider range of sales.[59] Both taxes were farmed out under Augustus, but later were increasingly collected by imperial officials.

There were a number of other sources of revenue about which little is known. These seem to have contributed little under Augustus though they became more important later on, such as "gifts" to the emperor on his accession or other occasions (*aurum coronarium*).[60]

The imperial government owned extensive lands, mostly acquired on the occasion of the conquest of the various provinces, which were farmed out. The rent, paid in cash or in the case of grain lands in kind, was customarily one-third of the product in Egypt (Neesen, pp. 100–2) and probably was between one-third and one-half in the other provinces. Notwithstanding the importance of these properties for the finances of the empire or its rural economy, very little is known about their extent, location, and administration.

The revenue system, which Augustus had taken over from the Republic, continued with only minor changes for the next two centuries and was substantially altered beginning with the third century A.D. It weighed considerably more heavily on agriculture than on other sources of income and on the provinces than on Italy and was moderately regressive. It was also fairly inelastic as tax rates and methods of assessment appear to have remained unchanged for a very long period.

### A *tentative quantification*

Poor as the data are, expenditures can be estimated with a smaller margin of error than revenues, thanks to work done by classicists on military expenditures based on fairly reliable data on troop strength and pay rates. Thus military expenditures (excluding separation payments) for the time of Augustus have been estimated about 40 years ago at HS 275 Million (Frank, pp. 4ff) and more recently at HS 350 million (MacMullen 1985, n. 4) and about HS 380 million (Hopkins, p. 125). Estimates, trustworthy as to the order of magnitudes, have also been made for the separation payments to veterans based on the known amounts paid per veteran and estimates of the proportion of the troops entitled to such payments retiring each year. Two, apparently independent, estimates put these expenditures at HS 75 million per year.[61] In the case of the *annona*, the grain and occasionally oil and other foods, distributed gratis to the Roman plebs, the two estimates made are close, namely, HS 60 and HS 75 million (Marquardt, p. 117; Frank, p. 5). The sum of the estimates of these five types of expenditures thus range from HS 410 to HS 530 million. The higher figure is more compatible with the much rougher estimates of revenues to which resort must be had. Of other substantial expenditures any estimate has been made only for civil servants, namely, about HS 50 million (Frank, pp. 5–6), which are low in line with the limited scope of direct civil imperial administration under Augustus and the farming out of almost all taxes. The remaining expenditures must have been relatively low because a good part of all expenditures on public buildings were defrayed by wealthy citizens or the emperor himself out of his private fortune and most expenditures on roads were included in the military budget or had to be borne by the municipalities served by the roads.[62] Most of these expenditures are likely to have increased during the first and second centuries, but not very substantially, for example, by the increase in military pay by one-third under Domitian and by the gradual replacement of tax farmers by imperial officials.

Only part, though very likely the majority, of expenditures were made in cash. Probably the largest item of expenditures in kind was the *annona*, grain coming from taxes in kind, particularly in Egypt, or from imperial domains, particularly in the province of Africa. Part of the grain furnished to the troops as part of their pay may also have come from these sources.

Because about one-half of total expenditures were military and most of the army was stationed along the frontiers, mainly along the Rhine and Danube and on the Parthian frontier,[63] and another substantial part of expenditures were spent by plebs and the court in Rome, large amounts of currency and grain raised as revenues in other provinces, particularly in Egypt, North Africa and Gaul, must have been transferred over long distances.[64] Within provinces, on the other hand, the provincial treasuries used revenues to pay for expenditures and transferred only the excess to Rome (Hirschfeld, p. 76).

As the government did not borrow nor generally accumulate surpluses,[65] revenues must have been very close to expenditures. The estimates of expenditures of about HS 600 and HS 825 million are therefore the starting point and the anchor of any attempt to estimate the yield of the different sources of revenue. In the absence of almost any estimates by contemporaries or by classicists, all that can be attempted is to try to establish orders of magnitude and to see whether the resulting figures are reasonable in comparison with relevant better known magnitudes. It may thus be assumed that the bulk of revenues, namely, HS 450 or 600 million was contributed by the three major sources, and leaving about HS 75 million to inheritance and sales taxes and between HS 75 and 50 million for all other revenues.

In the case of *tributum* one may start from the contemporary estimates of revenues of HS 40 million for Gaul and HS 40 to 60 million for Egypt.[66] Since these two provinces, which accounted for not much over one-fifth of the population of all provinces (Beloch, p. 507), were much more heavily taxed than the others, total *tributum* must have been well below five times the collections in Gaul and Egypt. If *tributum* per head in the other provinces was half that in Gaul and Egypt, the total for the Empire would have been in the order of HS 300 million; if the ratio was only one-third, it would have been about HS 225 million.[67] This would have been equal to fully one-third to one-half of total expenditures in the first and to fully one-fourth and nearly two-fifths in the second case.

An estimate, even a rough one, of the revenues of custom duties is more hazardous,[68] particularly as there is no indication of the division of the total between internal and external duties. On the basis of the estimate of a value of imports of not much over HS 200 million (Section 8) and an average duty of close to 25 percent, the yield of external customs duties would have been in the order of HS 40 million. The residuals of not more than HS 100 or 150 million, making some allowance for custom receipts on exports, a figure that should be regarded as a maximum, implies a value of internal trade subject to customs of HS 2.50 to 3.75 billion at an average rate of duty of 4 percent, which allows for the fact that part of the merchandise was subject to customs more than once. These amounts would have been equal to between one-eighth and one-sixth of total and below one-fourth and three-eighths of monetized national product, not unreasonable ratios, but figures that are likely to overstate than to underestimate the value of internal trade subject to customs and hence the yield of internal *portorium*.

Firmer ground exists for an estimate of the yield of the two taxes allocated by Augustus in A.D. 6 to finance veterans' separation payments, which have been put at about HS 75 million (cf. footnote 61). If an estimate of the yield of the sales tax of HS 20 million[69] is accepted, about HS 50 million are left for the inheritance tax. At a rate of the sales tax of 1 percent, a yield of HS 20 million implies a tax base of HS 2 billion or of one-fifth of monetized national product. Such a ratio is difficult to accept unless the term "auction sales" is interpreted broadly, and it is difficult to understand that a tax limited to public auctions should have been regarded as "oppressive" or "very unpopular" or should have led to sufficient public pressure to lead the parsimonius Tiberius to reduce it by one-half (cf. footnote 59). On the other hand to interpret it as a general sales tax not only runs counter to its name – it was also known as *centesima auctionum* – but is unlikely because such a tax would have required a large body of officials to collect it about whom no contemporary reports exist and administrative techniques not available except possibly in Egypt, and because the implied tax basis of HS 2 billion cannot have referred to all or a large proportion of even retail sales.

There are also difficulties with a yield of fully HS 50 million of the inheritance tax.[70] At a rate of 5 percent a devolution rate or estate tax multiple of 25[71] and the assumption that close relatives whose inheritances were exempt from the tax, accounted for one-half of total estates,[72] the tax base would have been of the order of HS 50 billion. It is very difficult to accept that the estates of Roman citizens above the exemption level could have been as large as, or even close to, such a sum, which represents about one-third of all private wealth in the Roman Empire as estimated in the following sections. Thus it is hard to explain a total yield of HS 75 million for the two taxes, even though the total of the two taxes seems well attested.

It is even more difficult to obtain an idea of the yield of the 5 percent tax on the manumission of slaves. Although it may be justified to use the HS 2,000 value per slave for purposes of legal compensation[73] and an estimate of the total number of slaves of about one-sixth of the population or 9 million, there is no evidence on the ratio of manumissions. To yield HS 50 million per year, a rather high figure in comparison to other minor taxes, there would have to have been about 500,000 manumissions per year or 6 percent of the slave population.[74] It is equally hard to estimate the yield of the tax on slave sales (Cagnat, p. 244), which probably was small.

The reasonableness of any estimate of the revenues from the government's agricultural, and primarily cereal, lands can be established only indirectly.[75] On the basis of the share of rent payments of at least one-third, a revenue of HS 100 million would imply a value of production of at most HS 300 million. Even if wheat constituted as much as four-fifths of total production, or about HS 250 million, this would represent at most 80 million modii of wheat. This is not much more than the wheat supply of the city of Rome of 350,000 talents or 50 million modii, and is equal to only about 3 percent of the empire's wheat crop of about 2,750 million modii.[76] Even a higher estimate of HS 150 million corresponds to a share in the empire's wheat crop of less than 5 percent. Such ratios look very low in view of the scattered evidence of the extension of public lands in the empire, particularly in the main wheat producing provinces of Egypt and Africa, but appear to be close to the maximum that can be accommodated within total revenues of HS 825 million.

Piling Ossa on Pelion we then get the indications of the orders of magnitude of the main components of the revenues and expenditures of the Roman imperial administration at the death of Augustus shown

Table 4-2. *Alternative estimates of revenues and expenditures of Roman Empire, ca.* A.D. *14*

|  | Amounts (HS million) | | Distribution (%) | |
|---|---|---|---|---|
|  | A | B | A | B |
| *I. Revenues* | | | | |
| 1. *Tributum* | 200 | 250 | 33 | 30 |
| 2. Customs duties | 150 | 200 | 25 | 24 |
| 3. Revenues from public lands | 100 | 150 | 17 | 18 |
| 4. Inheritance tax | 55 | 55 | 9 | 7 |
| 5. Sales tax | 20 | 20 | 3 | 3 |
| 6. Manumission tax 7. Others*a* | } 75 | 150 | 13 | 18 |
| 8. Total | 600 | 825 | 100 | 100 |
| *II. Expenditures* | | | | |
| 1. Armed forces | 350 | 370 | 58 | 45 |
| 2. Separation allowances | 75 | 75 | 13 | 9 |
| 3. Dole (*annona*) | 75 | 75 | 13 | 9 |
| 4. Civil service | 50 | 75 | 8 | 9 |
| 5. Others | 50 | 230*b* | 8 | 28 |
| 6. Total | 600 | 825 | 100 | 100 |

*a* Includes, e.g., tax on slave sales, rent from mines and revenues from coinage.
*b* Probably too high.

in Table 4-2 based on two sets of estimates that may be regarded as lower and upper boundaries.

How does this structure of revenues and expenditures compare with the better known distributions for other countries and periods, which may be regarded as even roughly comparable?[77] The earliest period for which such a comparison is feasible is England in the early eighteenth century. In 1720, a year without major military operations, excise taxes constituted over two-fifths of revenues, and customs and land (including other assessed) taxes about one-fourth each (Mitchell and Deane, pp. 386ff). Thus the share of indirect taxes with about three-fourths was substantially higher than in the early Roman Empire, though the difference was small in the case of customs duties. The structure of expenditures, however, showed wide differences. Debt charges, absent in Rome, absorbed over two-fifths of the expenditures of the British crown, and civil service expenditures accounted for one-sixth against well below one-tenth of the total, but the share of military expenditures (including separation payments) of not much over one-third was far below that of about two-thirds in the Roman Empire.

### Municipal finances

Virtually no quantitative information has been preserved on the income and expenditures of municipalities.[78] Classicists seem to agree that they were small (cf. Marquardt, p. 101). It is known that both types of expenditures and sources of revenue were multifarious and varied substantially among and within provinces because the imperial government left the municipalities considerable latitude in the organization of their finances with the result that they remained under the empire in many respects what they had been before they passed under Roman rule. Because taxes were to a large extent preempted by the imperial government, the municipalities had to rely on other sources, such as the sometimes substantial income from the ownership of real estate; the hiring out of municipally owned slaves; fines; water rates and port charges; and, generally an important item, payments for holding municipal offices.[79,80] Borrowing apparently was resorted to only rarely and limited to some oriental provinces. Even more varied were the fields of expenditures for municipal services as well as for public buildings, a field to which wealthy private citizens often contributed, for circus and other entertainments for the population, and last but not least for the cult of the emperors and gifts to imperial officials.

## 10    A national balance sheet

Is it possible to construct a national balance sheet of the Roman Empire that would show the position of financial instruments among all assets? Not if a comprehensive reasonably trustworthy estimate is demanded. It seems, however, possible to establish the orders of magnitude of the main components of such a document.

There is no doubt that land, and particularly agricultural land, was the dominant item in the national balance sheet. On the basis of a share of agriculture of three-fifths national product, a share of rent in agricultural income of one-half, the most uncertain component, and a capitalization factor of 17, corresponding to an average yield of 6 percent, and a small allowance for nonagricultural land, the value of land would have been equal to about 5.5 times gross national product. For a national product of slightly over HS 20 billion, the value of land would then be in the order of HS 110 billion.

The value of reproducible tangible assets was undoubtedly much smaller. On the basis of a net capital formation rate of 2 percent, no upward trend in national product, and an average length of life of 50 years, all assumptions leading to an over- rather than an underestimate, the value of reproducible tangible assets would be in the neighborhood of one year's national product or about HS 20 billion. This figure may be regarded as also covering inventories and monetary metals. National wealth, therefore, should have been in the order of 6.5 years' national product or HS 130 billion.

The value of slaves was small in comparison – for a slave population of not more than 9 million and an average price of about HS 2,000 – probably too high – not over HS 18 billion or about one-eighth of tangible assets.

For financial assets even rough estimates are beyond reach. There is no doubt, however, that their value was very small compared to that of tangible assets. In the absence of government or corporate securities and in view of the small size of bank deposits, only three types of financial assets need to be considered: mortgages, trade credit (including bottomry loans), and consumer credit. It seems unlikely that the total of these three types of financial instruments should have been equal to half a year's national product, that is, HS 10 billion, or about one-twelfth of tangible assets, that is, the financial interrelations ratio is unlikely to have been as high as 0.10 and it may have been as low as 0.05. The financial intermediation ratio (assets of financial institutions : all financial assets) was undoubtedly minimal.

How do these ratios – for the ratios are more significant than the absolute figures – compare to those existing in other at least broadly comparable situations?

In England in 1688 the value of tangible assets was 5.5 times that of gross national product. The value of land accounted for fully three-fifths of that of all tangible assets or for 3.5 times national product while reproducible tangible assets were equal to about twice national product. Financial assets amounted to about eight months' national product or one-eighth of tangible assets. In comparison the wealth – income and the land value – income ratios were somewhat higher in Augustan Rome, while the ratio of land to reproducible tangible assets was much higher and the ratio of financial to tangible assets probably was substantially lower. These relationships are to be expected as the level of capitalization rates was comparatively low in the Roman Empire, resulting in a high ratio of land values to income, and the empire was still more agrarian and less developed than late-seventeenth century England.

Table 4-3. *National balance sheet components as multiples of gross national product; Rome and six countries*

| | Rome A.D. 14 | England 1688 | USA 1805 | France 1815 | Germany 1850 | India 1860 | Japan 1885 |
|---|---|---|---|---|---|---|---|
| Land | 6.5 | 3.5 | 1.2 | 3.5 | 4.3 | 0.8 | 2.9 |
| Reproducible tangible | 1.0 | 1.9 | 1.1 | 2.9 | 5.1 | 1.4 | 3.4 |
| Monetary metals | 0.2 | 0.2 | 0.0 | 0.2 | 0.2 | 0.9 | 0.0 |
| Assets | | | | | | | |
| Tangibles | 7.7 | 5.6 | 2.3 | 6.5 | 9.4 | 3.2 | 6.3 |
| Financial | 0.5 | 0.7 | 0.7 | 1.0 | 1.7 | 0.5 | 1.9 |
| National | 8.2 | 6.3 | 3.0 | 7.5 | 11.2 | 3.7 | 8.2 |
| Financial | | | | | | | |
| interrelations ratio[a] | 0.08 | 0.15 | 0.30 | 0.14 | 0.18 | 0.23 | 0.30 |

[a] Line 5 divided by lines 1 + 2.
*Sources:* Col. 1, cf. text; cols. 2–6, Goldsmith 1985, Tables A-7, A-22, A-5, A-6, A-7 and A-12.

For the comparison of the position of slaves in the national balance sheet, there is only one case available, a case for which the estimates are more reliable, the United States before the Civil War. Here the ratios of the value of slaves to either land or to all national assets are not too different from those in the early Roman Empire, namely, in 1805 and 1850 about one-fourth of the value of land and about one-twelfth of national assets (Goldsmith 1985, p. 297) against about one-sixth and one-eighth in Augustan Rome, the share of slaves in the total population (17 percent in 1805 and 14 percent in 1850) probably being approximately the same as the early Roman Empire.

Comparisons in Table 4-3 with the United States in 1805, France in 1815, Germany in 1850, India in 1860, and Japan in 1885, all before the start of modern economic growth, show a similar picture with respect to the financial interrelations ratio, namely, a much lower level for Augustan Rome than for the other countries. The ratios of the value of reproducible tangible assets to that of land or to national product were also relatively low in imperial Rome. On the other hand, the Roman ratio of the value of land to national assets and to national product was much higher than that in any of the other countries.

Compared to the Hellenistic monarchies, and particularly Egypt, the financial system of the Roman Empire did not in general represent progress, even in the first two centuries of its long existence. Indeed, particularly in the western provinces, its banking system played probably a smaller role in the economy than had been the case in the successor states of Alexander's empire. There were two important exceptions. The monetary system of the early Roman Empire was probably the most stable that had ever been seen in such a large area and its legal system, even if not primarily developed for use in finance, was superior to any predecessor. The financial superstructure, however, remained small in comparison to the infrastructure of national wealth and relatively simple.

CHAPTER 5

# The financial system
# of the early Abbasid caliphate

Within a generation of their crossing the border of the peninsula in
A.D. 632, the Arab armies conquered most of the territories of the
Byzantine Empire and destroyed the Sassanid Empire.[1,2] In the following century they added substantial territories in the East and particularly in the West so that their empire in the early eighth century
extended from the Indus to the Provence. As a result of the replacement of the Omayyad by the Abbasid dynasty in A.D. 752, most of
North Africa as well as Spain became independent, in fact reducing
the population of the caliphate by about one-fourth and shifting its
political and economic center from Syria to Mesopotamia and Iran
and the capital from Damascus to Baghdad. The conquest had been
so rapid, the number of conquerors so small, and the economic and
cultural level of the conquered territory so much higher than that of
Arabia that the caliphate in most fields took over the existing Byzantine or Sassanid institutions with only little change, the most important one being the conversion of a substantial part of the population
to Islam and from the eighth century on the use of Arabic as the sole
official language. This was done to such an extent that the Omayyad
caliphate has been called the neo-Byzantine Empire and the Abbasid
caliphate the neo-Sassanid Empire.[3] The caliphate remained in es-
sence a military dictatorship based on the sharia, the islamic religious
law, though the extent of centralization and of the harshness of administration varied and the role of cities and of nonagricultural activities slowly increased. The first century of the Abbasid caliphate may
be regarded as the peak of the empire's military and political power
and of its economic prosperity.[4]

## 1    Population

The population of the Abbasid caliphate around A.D. 800 has been
estimated at about 26 million, down from about 33 million half a cen-

Table 5-1. *Estimates of population* A.D. *600 to 800* (*millions*)

| | McEvedy and Jones | | Issawi | Russell | | Synthetic Estimate |
|---|---|---|---|---|---|---|
| | A.D. 600 (1) | A.D. 800 (2) | A.D. 750 (3) | A.D. 600 (4) | Others (5) | A.D. 800 (6) |
| 1. Sind | — | — | 2.0–3.0 ⎤ | | | 2.5 |
| 2. Turkestan | 1.0[a] | 1.1[a] | 0.5–1.0 ⎥ 4.6 | | | 1.0 |
| 3. Afghanistan | 2.5 | 2.4 | 1.0–1.5 ⎥ | | | 2.0 |
| 4. Iran | 5.0 | 4.0 | 3.0–4.0 ⎦ | | | 4.0 |
| 5. Iraq | 1.0 | 2.5 | 5.0–6.0 | 9.1 | 4.0[f] | 4.0 |
| 6. Syria[b] | 1.9 | 2.3 | 3.0–4.0 | 4.0 | | 3.0 |
| 7. Arabia | 5.3 | 5.0[c] | 1.5–2.0 | 1.0 | | 2.5 |
| 8. Egypt | 3.0 | 3.8 | 4.0–5.0 ⎤ | 2.7 | | 4.0 |
| 9. Libya | 0.3 | 0.4 ⎫ 3.0–4.0 ⎦ | | 1.9 | | 0.5 |
| 10. Tunisia | 2.5[d] | 2.7[c] ⎭ | | | | 2.5 |
| 11. Caliphate | 24.5[e] | 26.8 | 23.0–30.5 | 25.8[e] | | 26.0 |

[a] One-half of estimate of present Russian Turkestan.
[b] Includes Lebanon, Palestine, and Jordan.
[c] Of which Yemen 2.5.
[d] Includes one-half of Algeria (1.8).
[e] Including 2.5 for Sind.
[f] Ashtor 1976, p. 89.
*Sources:* Cols. 1 and 2 – McEvedy and Jones, pp. 133ff; col. 3 – Issawi, p. 381; col. 4 – Russell, p. 89.

tury earlier, reflecting the accession to factual independence of much of North Africa and of Spain each of which is credited with a population of about 3.5 million (see Table 5-1).[5] Density of population for the entire area was very low – about 3 per km² – but since only about one-tenth of the area may have been cultivated as slightly in excess of 40 per km² of land under cultivation.[6] Both the eastern and the central provinces accounted for nearly 10 million or fully one-third of the total and the African provinces for about 7 million or fully one-fourth. What may be regarded as politically and economically the heartland of the Abbasid caliphate – Iran and Iraq – contained about 8 million inhabitants or less than one-third of the total, and Arabia, the home of the conquerors, only about 2.5 million or not much over one-tenth. Looked at historically, both the provinces that had formed part of the Byzantine Empire and those that had constituted the Sassanid Empire contributed about 10 million or together about three-fourths of the total population of the caliphate of the early ninth century A.D. By that date the population of Arab descent must have become a relatively small minority.[7] The proportion of the population that had not adopted Islam is not known, but must have been substantial particularly in the formerly Byzantine provinces.[8]

Population in most provinces increased slowly from the conquest to the tenth century when the tendency was reversed (Ashtor 1969, p. 544). The only available set of estimates puts the increase between A.D. 600 and 800 at slightly below 10 percent and that in the two following centuries at only 3 percent, all of the total increase of nearly 3 million being attributed to Egypt and Iraq, followed by a decline by 3 percent between A.D. 1000 and 1200.[9] At an average annual rate of increase of less than 0.05 percent, birth and death rates must have been about equal, and probably very high, since net immigration or emigration were negligible. Expectation of life at birth was very low, probably around 20 years.

There are no estimates of the degree of urbanization or of the share of the slave population. As Baghdad is supposed to have had a population of 500,000 around A.D. 800 and there were about half-a-dozen cities of over 100,000 inhabitants (Basra, Kufa, Wasit, Damascus, Kairouan, and Samarkand),[10] the urban population should have been well above 1 million and may have been close to 2 million, that is, between 5 and 8 percent of the total. Most of the population outside the cities was engaged in agriculture (including livestock raising). The share of agriculture in total population and labor force could therefore hardly have been below three-fourths and probably exceeded four-fifths.

Since slaves were rare in the countryside,[11] though common in the cities,[12] it is unlikely that they would have constituted as much as one-tenth of the total population. The ratio is likely to have increased over at least the first three centuries after the conquest and probably understates the economic and social importance of slaves and in particular their political influence from the ninth century A.D. on when they constituted an increasing proportion of the military.[13] A substantial proportion of the agricultural population, however, lived under conditions that in fact, though not in law, were similar to serfdom and adscription to their village (for Iraq, Forand, p. 36).

## 2     National product

It is an advantage of national accounting that the value of national product can be derived from two independent sources, income and expenditures, which should yield the same result. For the Abbasid caliphate, as for most countries through at least the Middle Ages, the data available for either approach are very scarce and sometimes contradictory. For a country in which over nine-tenths of the population lived on the land, the crucial figures are the incomes and the expenditures of the rural population, and about these virtually nothing is known quantitatively. The few data available for a few points in time and a few places all refer to the urban population, whose incomes and expenditures were on the average undoubtedly considerably higher, though to an unknown extent, than those of the rural population.

An unskilled worker in the late eighth century may be estimated to have had on the average a wage income of one dirham per day[14] of four to six hours (Beg, p. 156). The average for the urban population was considerably higher as the average wage of skilled craftsmen was about twice as high as that of a common laborer (Ashtor 1969, p. 70; Beg, p. 165). The salaries of many officials (Ashtor 1969, pp. 65–66, 93) and the incomes of many merchants and of landlords living in the cities were still higher. On the other hand the incomes of the rural population were substantially lower. Hence the assumption that the average income of the entire population was equal to 1 dirham per day and to 300 dirhams per year should be regarded as an upper limit of an estimate of national product, and a figure of 250 dirhams may be preferable. There is no evidence regarding the number of income recipients, but on the basis of the usual relation in countries where few women earn income, it may be put at about one-third to two-fifths of the total population, that is, approximately 9 to 10 million. On that basis the national income of the Abbasid caliphate at the beginning of the ninth century A.D. would have been on the order of 2.25 billion dirhams or at most 3 billion dirhams or at the rate of 15 dirhams per dinar have amounted to 150 to 200 million dinars.

Turning to the expenditure side, the minimum at the beginning of the ninth century A.D. has been put at 0.2 dinar, or 4 dirhams, per month, supposedly per person (Ashtor 1969, p. 62) or 16 dirhams for a family of four. The other estimates are considerably higher. One puts the "annual requirement of a married couple in a humble station of life" at 300 dirhams (Mez, p. 379; the figure probably includes children). The second estimates food expenditures alone of a worker's family at 300 to 480 gold marks (Hinz, p. 54), which is equivalent to about 60 to 100 g of gold or about 15 to 24 dinars or 225 to 360 dirhams, which assuming food to account for two-thirds of total expenditures would imply total expenditures of about 350 to 550 dirhams. These three estimates thus suggest a total expenditure for the 26 million inhabitants, assuming in each case four persons per household, of fully 1, 2, and 2.25 to 3.5 billion dirhams, only the two highest estimates from the expenditure side being close to that derived from the income side.

Combining these very rough estimates and making some allowance for items not included, the national product may then be put on the order of 3 billion dirhams or 120 dirhams per head (8 dinars) or 34 g of gold at 4.25 g of gold per dinar, compared to slightly over 30 g for the early Roman Empire (Chapter 4).

Information on prices is not sufficient to estimate the average real income per year in the early Abbasid period except in terms of gold, namely, 25 to 30 g. For Egypt in the eleventh century when more data are available, the annual minimum salary of a worker has been estimated at 24 dinars, or 6 dinars or 25 g of gold per member of a four-person household, and the consumption of the two main foods – bread and meat – per head at nearly 1,100 calories (Ashtor 1959, p. 97), which compares to 1,700 calories for total average food consumption in India in 1948–49 (Food and Agriculture Organization, p. 245), though probably considerably less in medieval India. All the available evidence suggest a quite low standard of living in the Abbasid caliphate, though the variety of food increased for the middle and upper classes (Ashtor 1959, p. 77). The standard of living in Egypt in the eleventh century, however, seems to have been considerably lower than in the early ninth century.[15]

As at least nine-tenths of the population lived on the land, agricultural income must have constituted the bulk of national product. If it is assumed that average urban income, including that of absentee landlords, was three times as high as that of the agricultural population and the latter accounted for 90 percent of the total, their share in national product would have been equal to three-fourths. Total rural or agricultural income, now including that of absentee landlords, was probably on the order of nine-tenths. How the total was divided among the peasants, the landlords, and the government is not known, but the share of either the land tax and other government exactions or rent of between two-fifths and one-half is an indication of the division (Cahen 1970b, p. 518). If the share of the peasants was as high as three-fifths, their total consumable income would have been on the order of 65 dirhams per head or 260 dirhams for a family of four. If it was as low as one-half, it would have been only about 50 dirhams per head or 200 dirhams per family, a truly miserable level (Ashtor 1969, p. 37).

There are no figures permitting an estimate of the degree of inequalities of income. The fairly numerous data on the incomes of the

military and of high public officials in comparison to those of common laborers and artisans point, however, to very large income differences. Thus even common soldiers received three times (infantry)
and six times (cavalary) the wages of common laborers (*Encyclopaedia
of Islam*, vol. I, p. 730). In the eighth and ninth centuries department
heads and judges in Iraq received about 7,000 dirhams per year –
more than 20 times the wage of a common laborer even if employed
for 300 days. Officials of ministerial rank touched between 25,000
and 120,000 dirhams and chief ministers (viziers) 120,000 to 480,000
dirhams, the latter figures equal to about 1,600 laborers' income. Possibly more relevant are the estimates of a cost of living of the middle
bourgeoisie of 3,600 dirhams per year and of the upper bourgeoisie
of 5,400 dirhams, or about 12 and 18 times, respectively, a common
laborer's wages.[16,17]

## 3    The monetary system

In the first years after their conquests the Arabs, having no coins of
their own, used those in circulation in the occupied territories, that is,
in the formerly Byzantine provinces principally the gold nomisma of
about 4.5 g and in the former Sassanid Empire the silver dirham (the
Greek δηναριον) of about 4 g.[18] When the caliphs started issuing their
own money around the middle of the eighth century, they not only
retained the weight and fineness of the Byzantine and Sassanid coins
but also their design, even though these showed the portraits of Byzantine emperors and Sassanid kings and Christian or Persian religious symbols, with the addition of only a few Arabic words (Miles, p.
364). It was only in the very last years of the century that the caliph
Abd-el-Malik issued the two coins that were to remain the standard
throughout Islam for centuries (Grierson, passim). These were the
gold dinar of about 4.25 g and a fineness of 96 to 98 percent and the
silver dirham of nearly 2 g and similar fineness. It is not known how
rapidly and how the old coins disappeared from circulation, supposedly by recoinage. While the dinar retained its quality and became the
leading international currency for centuries, the dirham began to de-
teriorate in the ninth century. As the dinar was inconveniently large
for most transactions, representing about two weeks' earnings of a
common laborer, the mints also issued pieces of one-half and of one-
quarter dinar, and other fractions circulated without official sanction
(Cahen 1970b, p. 86; Lombard 1971, p. 177). Small change was provided by fulus of copper and bronze of which many types were in
circulation.[19]

Gold, silver, and copper coins were issued and circulated simultaneously at rates varying over time and to some extent among regions
as determined by the market. Originally, a dinar was valued at 10
dirhams, but it soon rose to 14 dirhams, which approximately corresponded to the weight of the two coins and a gold–silver ratio of 10 : 1,
and by the early ninth century was valued at 15 to 20 dirhams.[20] In-
tertemporal and interlocal variations in the value of the fals partly
reflected differences in the weight of its various types, the ratio ranging between 24 to 48 fulus per dirham, that is, about 0.10 to 0.05 g of
silver and about 2 and 4 percent of a common laborer's daily wage.[21]
Through the eighth century gold coins continued to predominate in
the western, formerly Byzantine, provinces of the empire and to be
required in payment of taxes and silver coins in the eastern provinces,
both being current in Iraq. But from the ninth century on gold became more and more the standard. If the 624 coins listed in an old
numismatic study (Lane-Poole, p. 84) could be regarded as a random
sample of all coins issued between A.D. 695 and 955, one would conclude that by value gold coins constituted about seven-eighths of the
total; that average issues per year increased by nearly one-half between the reigns of the Umayyad and the first five Abbasid caliphs
and then declined by nearly one-half in the following 150 years; and
that issues of silver coins practically ceased after the end of the reign
of al Mamun in A.D. 840. These figures do not help to explain the
apparently slow, but continuous, substantial increase in prices observed during the ninth century A.D. (Ashtor 1969, p. 465).

The absence of legally fixed relations between gold, silver, and copper coins and the variations in their weight required the operations
of official or unofficial money changers (*djabadhs* and *sarafs*) who were
present in even small cities.[22,23]

The Abbasid caliphs, like their predecessors, had four main sources
of the metals required for the issuance of coins. The first was booty,
which had been particularly important in the case of silver, large
amounts of which came into their possession upon the fall of the Sassanid capital of Ktesiphon in A.D. 642. The acquisition of large amounts
of gold from Christian religious establishments in the former Byzantine provinces may be regarded as falling in the same category.[24]
The second was the voluntary or forced recoinage of old coins, and
the third the production of precious metals within the caliph's realm,
in the case of silver largely in Iran, in that of gold from Afghanistan,
Turkestan, Arabia, and Egypt. Finally gold could be acquired from
producers beyond the boundaries, mainly the Sudan and West Africa
(Quiring, p. 198).

Our ignorance about the quantities involved is almost complete. Contemporary accounts accepted by modern Islamists assert that gold coins were plentiful,[25] though this does not appear to have been the case for silver coins. There seem to have often been shortages of copper and bronze coins, new issues of which appear to have stopped early in the ninth century (Udovitch 1979). The only quantitative evidence are estimates of the production of gold within the territory of the Abbasid caliphate or in regions known to have been sources of gold imports. Output within the caliphate has been estimated for the period of A.D. 501 to 900 at about 120 tons, or 0.3 tons per year, mostly from Afghanistan and Turkestan, while that of the known African suppliers has been put at about 230 tons or nearly 0.6 tons per year (Quiring, p. 198). Thus the amount of new gold available for minting can hardly have been in excess of 0.5 ton per year or about 120,000 dinars or at a rate of 15 dirhams per dinar of about 1.75 million dirhams, a very small sum compared to a national product of the order of 3 billion dirhams. Hence either the plethora of gold was much less than reported (Ehrenkreutz 1959, p. 130; Miles, p. 377) or new gold contributed only a small proportion to the minting of dinars and to their volume in circulation.

Issuance of gold and silver coins was limited to the caliphal mints. Gold coinage was concentrated in Baghdad, Fostat, and Kairouan, but silver was coined in about 30 places. Copper and bronze coins, on the other hand, were issued by numerous provincial and city mints, apparently without control by the central government (Ehrenkreutz 1977a, p. 77). The amount of seignorage, if any, realized by the mints does not seem to be known, but it is fairly certain that the mints practiced neither hylophantism or hylolepsy, that is, did not exchange coins for metal at fixed rates.

The only estimate of the volume of minting that has been found is a conjecture that in the second half of the ninth century A.D. the output of coins of the Cairo mint did not exceed 100,000 dinars (Ehrenkreutz 1977a, 277), or 1.5 million dirhams. If Egypt had at that time been representative of the entire caliphate, its output of coins would, on the basis of Egypt's share in population, have been on the order of about 10 million dirhams. This figure may be compared with a national product of the caliphate in the second half of the ninth century A.D. of about 3 billion dirhams, a relation of less than one-half of one percent.

If the stock of coins is assumed to have been 20 times the annual coinage, it would have been on the order of 2 billion dirhams, or about two-thirds of national product. The ratio of coins in circulation to total national product would have been even lower because of the often asserted large extent of thesaurization (Becker, p. 235). The ratios to monetized national product would, of course, be higher, but by how much it is difficult to estimate. Where Islamists mention the problem, and they rarely do, they declare that the economy was "highly monetized," (Ehrenkreutz 1976, p. 209). In an economy in which about three-fourths of the national product originated in agriculture, one would expect a low ratio of monetization, but in the Abbasid caliphate with its heavy taxes mainly payable in money, the ratio may well have been above one-half. If so, the apparently low ratio of money in circulation to national product and the correspondingly high velocity of circulation and the contradictory reports of the abundance or shortage of gold and silver coins pose unsolved problems. As the Scotch dominie said: "Brethren, there is a great difficulty here; let us look it straight in the face and move on."

## 4    Financial institutions

The only common financial institution,[26] if it can be called such, were the ubiquitous money changers and assayers, often Christians or Jews, most of whom operated locally on a small scale charging a commission of one percent, though more for small transactions.[27] Some, however, also undertook the interlocal transfer of funds, sometimes for substantial amounts, particularly in the case of the transfers of tax revenues from the provinces to Baghdad, through letters of credit and orders of payment. This was done through an informal network of money changers and merchants based on personal relations. Occasionally, individual money changers were given a monopoly for a city or province as compensation for making loans to the government. From the ninth century A.D. on a few larger firms developed, chiefly in Baghdad and Cairo, that regularly made loans and accepted deposits for safekeeping (*depositum regulare*), the best known of which was that of Joseph ibn Phineas and Aron ibn Amram (cf. Fischel, passim). Since these firms operated only with their own funds and always combined credit extension and money transfer with retail or wholesale trade, the whole system has been characterized as "bankers without banks" (Udovitch 1979, p. 255).

There were no insurance organizations since Islamic law regarded insurance as a type of gambling, which was forbidden (Labib, p. 94).

While not a financial institution, a specific Islamic institution, the wakf, similar to trusts in Western countries, was of some importance in the financial structure. One type of wakf set aside some property, generally real estate, for the maintenance of a religious, beneficial, or educational institution; another provided for using the income for a specific group of persons, mostly members of the family of the donor or his descendants. Both types of wakfs, which could be set up only by and for the benefit of Muslims, were inalienable and supervised by the religious or judicial authorities. Their attraction was that their Koranic sanction, and in the case of public wakfs the character of the beneficiaries, protected them at least to some extent from confiscation by the government and from dispersal among heirs.

Wakfs were rather rare in the first centuries after the conquest, but by the tenth century they had become widespread. Most of them apparently were small, with annual revenues generally on the order of 500 to 1,000 dirhams,[28] or two to four times a common laborer's wage, though their importance later increased greatly.

## 5 Financial instruments

Probably the most common financial instrument[29] was trade credit, the use of which has been described as widespread both at the wholesale and retail levels. The prohibition of interest was circumvented by quoting a difference in price of 2 to 4 percent between immediate and delayed payment (Udovitch 1979, p. 265). Interest-bearing loans were rare particularly for longer terms, as they could legally be made only by non-Muslim lenders. The supply of funds, therefore, generally took the form of the participation of the supplier in the profits of the venture, an arrangement similar to the Western commenda. There were no bills of exchange, but several forms of letters of credit issued for substantial fees, and not negotiable, permitted the interlocal transfer of funds. Although evidence is lacking, there are likely to have been arrangements about arrears in rents between landlords and tenants and probably about arrears in taxes between tax farmers and taxpayers.

## 6 Interest rates

Islamic law forbids interest (*riba*) among Muslims, a prohibition originally applied only to loans but gradually extended to many types of transactions that were regarded as involving an interestlike gain of the lender, including exchange rate differences.[30] As a result there were no long-term loans among Muslims for which the prohibition of interest could hardly be circumvented. The remuneration of capital, therefore, had to take the form of profit sharing in commercial transactions or of rental arrangements in agriculture. While non-Muslim, mostly Christian and Jewish, lenders could and did provide some interest-bearing loans, apparently at quite high rates, their volume cannot have been large in comparison to national product, and were made mainly to caliphs or high government officials and for consumption rather than for productive purposes.[31]

## 7    Financing agriculture

In both the Byzantine and Sassanid empires a large part of the land was owned by the sovereign and members of his family and court, by nobles of various ranks, and by religious organizations, but virtually all of it was operated in small plots by tenants, peasants living in village communities, who were tied to the land (*adscripti glebae*) in a semiservile status. The Arab conquerors left the peasants in possession, as the small number of their warriors and their policy of settling them in cities did not require land for settlement, and changed ownership only for the holdings of the crown, religious institutions, and the high Byzantine and Sassanid nobility, who left or were executed,[32] land which became the property of the caliph. By the time of the early Abbasids some of these holdings had been bestowed on Arab and converted notables who had become absentee landlords, sometimes on a large scale (Ashtor 1969, p. 74; Cahen 1970b, p. 519). There were, of course, substantial regional differences in the distribution of the land among the different types of owners and in the size distribution of holdings. Nothing is known in quantitative terms about these matters.

There is agreement among scholars, though little quantitative evidence, of an increase in rural population and in agricultural production over the first two centuries after the conquest.[33] Progress took the form both of an increase in the area under cultivation and in output per unit of land, the latter reflecting in particular improvements of irrigation and in methods of cultivation. An important aspect of agricultural progress was the increasing dispersion of crops, usually originating in India, over large parts of the caliphate (Watson 1981, p. 39).

The main forms of cooperation between capital and labor in agriculture were reflected in the character of tenancy arrangements rather than in a supply of funds originating outside of agriculture. At the one extreme, when the landlord furnished implements as well as working animals, the share of the tenant in the product might be as low as one-fifth; at the other, when the tenant developed a plantation on the landlord's raw land, he became the owner of half of it. In most cases the tenant's share appears to have been one-half or somewhat less of the product (Cahen 1970a, p. 111; Rodinson 1961, p. 182).

There apparently was little credit used in agriculture. Long-term loans were precluded by the prohibition of interest and by the restrictions on alienation of land. There undoubtedly were short-term debts, particularly in the form of tax and rent arrears in which the lender's compensation was arranged in a form avoiding a direct interest charge – and at very high effective cost to the borrower – but little is known about them. Investments, mainly in land improvement and irrigation, were financed by the peasants' labor or the landlords' surpluses, or in the case of part of the irrigation works by the government. The only flow of outside funds into agriculture came from the increasingly important class of urban absentee landlords, but it took the form mostly of the acquisition of land rather than of the provision of funds for improvements.

## 8    Financing the nonagricultural private economy

Credit was regularly used only in the financing of domestic retail and wholesale trade and in international trade. In other sectors, primarily handicrafts and housing, the funds needed for fixed and working capital were essentially provided by the owners of the shop or house or in the relatively rare case of rental housing by the landlord, partly again because of the prohibition of interest on loans, a provision more difficult to circumvent here than in trade transactions.[34]

Domestic interregional trade is asserted, though on the basis of scarce and nonquantitative evidence, which generally refers to the period beginning with the ninth century, to have been quite active (cf., e.g., Sourdel 1968, p. 314), partly because the caliphate created a large and varied area within which the same coins and the same language could be used and within which travel and transportation were fairly safe and, though some internal duties existed, fairly free. Because most of the domestic trade was overland, except in Mesopotamia and Egypt, transportation was expensive, limiting trade essentially to commodities of high value, particularly textiles. Trade in bulky goods, particularly grains and building materials, was generally limited to short distances between urban centers of consumption and their fairly close neighborhood. In domestic interlocal trade short-term credit was apparently commonly used and in connection with it letters of credit.

These transactions were, however, limited to personally acquainted merchants and rested on their personal trust and did not involve financial intermediaries. These operations apparently were considerably more intensive from the ninth century A.D. on than under the Umayyad and early Abbasid caliphs.

Financing international trade, which was subject to a complex system of duties about which very little is known, posed a microeconomic problem (the settlement of individual transactions) and a macroeconomic one (the balance of transactions of the caliphate as a whole with the rest of the world). Though no information exists on the relation between the value of transactions settled in coins, often in the form of purses, by barter,[35] and by credit, it is likely that credit settlements were not dominant, though their share was probably higher in trade across the Mediterranean and with the Byzantine Empire than in the trade across the Sahara and with India. There is substantial, though entirely nonquantitative, information on the commodities traded.[36] Slaves certainly constituted the single most important import article, supplied mainly from Slavic Europe, Turkestan, and sub-Saharan Africa, followed by gold mainly from West Africa and the Sudan, and by spice and precious stones from India. The most important single export probably was textiles, mostly from Egypt. It is difficult to see how textiles and the other export commodities can have balanced the large imports of slaves and Eastern luxuries. Hence most of the gold imports apparently did not stay within the caliphate but were used to settle part of the unfavorable balance of trade with eastern Europe evidenced by massive finds of Islamic coins,[37] and with India. Islamists have not even recognized the problem involved, a problem that became much more important from the ninth century A.D. on, as the volume of both imports and exports was much more moderate in the seventh and eighth centuries,[38] when the metal of the Sassanid booty and that taken from the Christian institutions in the formerly Byzantine provinces may have been sufficient to settle the trade deficit.

## 9    Financing the government

The revenue system of both the Byzantine and the Sassanid empires rested on a land tax and a poll (head) tax.[39] These were taken over with initially only small changes by the caliphate for its non-Muslim subjects, while the Muslim population was liable only to a much lighter system of tithes, which had been instituted in Arabia by Muhammad, and was not subject to poll tax. When the large-scale conversions to

Islam threatened to erode the tax basis, conversion no longer carried with it exemption from land tax. Henceforth only the minority of the agricultural land owned since after the conquest by Muslims or covered by special treaties made at that time continued under the tithe system, though in practice the caliph seems to have had wide authority to allocate any piece of land to either of the two categories. Due to regional differences within a very large area in legal arrangements, in methods of assessment, and administration and in tax rates and to changes over time, the revenue system had become very complex by the eighth century A.D. (Dennett, p. 22; Løkkegaard, p. 117).

The land tax was certainly the most important source of revenues. Though it is not possible to determine its share in the total, it probably was well in excess of one-half. The assessment was based either on the size of the plot, the land being classified by quality and use and need of irrigation, or on the yield. The rates varied regionally and over time. One schedule of the first type, referring to Iraq in the ninth century, may be seen as an example as it may be assumed to reflect relative yields (dirham of 3 g silver per *djarib* of 0.16 hectars):

| | |
|---|---|
| Barley | 2 |
| Wheat | 4 |
| Vegetables, sesame, cotton | 5 |
| Sugar cane | 6 |
| Date palms | 8 or 10 |
| Vineyards | 10 |
| Olives | 12 |

Rates appear to have increased, particularly from the ninth century on, when the price level rose.[40]

Land taxes were payable either in kind or in money, the latter method harder on the peasants since often they did not have enough cash and had to borrow at usurious though illegal rates. Until the mid-eighth century payments in money seem to have prevailed, at least in the central and eastern provinces, but from then on payment in kind became more common, at least for grain, and particularly in Mesopotamia. Originally the tax was levied by government officials who were responsible to the treasury, but under the Abbasid caliphs tax farming based on contracts for several years awarded by auction began to spread, a method that put additional burdens on the peasants. In either case the village community was responsible for the tax liabilities of all members, even the often substantial number of those who had fled the land (Becker 1924, p. 173 for Egypt; Løkkegaard, p. 97ff).

Little is known about the rate of the land tax in relation to the owners' and operators' income. It seems to have amounted to at least two-fifths but often exceeded one-half.[41]

The poll tax on non-Muslims was an important source of revenue in the first one or two centuries after the conquest when a substantial proportion of the population still adhered to their old faiths. The tax was levied only on adult free males and excepted the very poor. The rates apparently varied over time and among regions. Under the Abbasid caliphate three wealth classes were distinguished. These paid 1, 2, and 4 dinars per year, respectively, generally payable in cash (*Encyclopaedia of Islam*, vol. II, p. 560). The tax constituted a considerable burden on the non-Muslim population, though one less heavy than the land tax.[42] The poll tax was in theory to be devoted to charities and pensions, but in practice was often put to other uses. With increasing conversions the poll tax lost importance, but in the early Abbasid caliphate it must still have been of substantial size, particularly in Egypt. By the mid-twelfth century, however, it had become negligible even in Egypt, yielding a mere 130,000 dinars (*Encyclopaedia of Islam* vol. II, p. 56a), probably well under 5 percent of total revenue.

Muslims were subject to the *ushr*, in principle a tax of one-tenth of the income from land but also for some other types of assets levied at lower or higher rates, for example, at half the standard rate for artificially irrigated land. They were also subject to the *zakat*, originally an alms tax introduced by Muhammad, which was due on agricultural products, animals, precious metals, and merchandise at varying rates, for example, one-tenth for agricultural product, and was in principle to be used only for charitable purposes. In practice, however, there apparently was no strict distinction between *ushr* and *zakat*, except possibly that the former title was applied to the tax on agricultural land and the latter to that on other assets. The yield of the two taxes was much lower than would correspond to the formal rates, partly because payments were mostly based on self-assessment and were to some extent regarded as voluntary. The receipts were used in the way the authorities preferred, often locally without being transferred to the central treasury. No information on the yield of *ushr* or *zakat* has been preserved and no estimate of it made.[43,44]

In addition to the four main taxes – *kharadj, djyzia, ushr*, and *zakat* – there existed numerous minor levies (cf., e.g., Kremer, vol. I, p. 278), including arbitrary ones such as confiscations of legally or illegally acquired large fortunes – known collectively as *mukuz* and regarded as illegal by Islamic theologians – which varied locally and over time. Little is known about their character and rates and nothing about their yield. In the aggregate they probably added substantially to the burden of the main taxes.

Although the main features of the taxation of agricultural land and the income from it are reasonably clear, there is not enough information to assess the character and the effective level of taxation of other types of income and wealth. It is, however, evident that it was much lower for nonagricultural wealth and incomes in law and still more in fact, particularly for movable property, and incomes from wages and salaries, self-employment, and profits. As a result the average effective rate of taxation was much higher for agricultural incomes, though less so for those drawn from *ushr* lands, than for urban incomes, with the result that the revenue system resulted in a large-scale transfer of incomes from the rural sector, particularly the peasants, to the urban sector, particularly the court, government officials, and the military. As the leading authority on the subject concluded, "It can scarcely be doubted that the fiscal regime was oppressive if no more than that of neighboring non-Muslim states" (cf., e.g., Kremer, vol. I, p. 278).

Under the Abbasid caliphs the administration of public revenues and expenditures was centralized in the treasury in Baghdad, which in about half a dozen departments (*diwan*) employed a large number of officials and clerks, operated on bureaucratic principles, and kept systematic records, including detailed budgets, none of which has been preserved. Similar though smaller offices were maintained in the provinces, the head of which was the most important local official next to the governor and the army commander. The public treasury was kept separate from the caliph's private purse, but financial transactions between the two occurred.

It is fortunate that in the absence of complete budgets the total of cash revenues for the caliphate as well as for its provinces have been preserved for 5 years in the very late eighth and early ninth centuries. They range from 417 million to 530 million dirhams,[45] averaging 460 million dirhams. The figures are not entirely comparable as there are some variations in the extent to which taxes in kind are included, small differences in geographic coverage, and some doubts about whether they refer to actual receipts of the treasury in Baghdad or the amounts budgeted to be received. It is, however, certain that the figures are below the total amount of government revenues, as they do not include the receipts from some of the taxes, particularly *djizya* and *zakat* as well as local duties (Cahen 1970b, p. 534), and what may be more important apparently do not include that part of tax receipts used locally, but only that part transferred to the treasury in Baghdad.[46] How large the understatement was is not known, but it must have been substantial.[47] Finally the burden of the taxpayers was further increased by the difference between the amounts exacted by the tax farmers and those paid to the government. This was in the aggregate probably still moderate under the early Abbasid caliphs as most of the taxes were collected by government officials, but became very sizable later when the scope of tax farming expanded and it became general.

Table 5-2 shows the cash revenues of the treasury for a year near A.D. 780 as reported by Ibn-Khaldun about A.D. 1380 on the basis of contemporary sources,[48] the numerous individual provinces having been combined into nine regions.[49] The figures do not include revenues in kind, which apparently amounted to about one-fourth of the cash revenues[50] because their value has not been reported by provinces. The cash revenues of each region are compared to its estimated population around A.D. 800 and for most regions to the present cultivated area, the latter a hazardous procedure since it assumes that there have been no substantial changes over 1,200 years. By coincidence, or otherwise, for one region, Mesopotamia, the only one for which a contemporary estimate has been found, it is practically the same as the present figure.

Table 5-2 suggests that for the entire caliphate the cash revenues of the treasury in Baghdad averaged about 17 dirhams per inhabitant, which should have been equal to about one-sixth of product per head. It also suggests, and this with a much greater degree of probability, that the differences in cash revenues reaching the central treasury were very large and much larger than the differences in nominal or real product per head can have been. It is, for example, out of the question that income per head should have been more than three times as large in Mesopotamia and Iran as in Egypt and about seven times as large as in Sind, Syria, Arabia, and North Africa. The differences rather reflect, in addition to those in product per head, factors such as differences in the burden of taxation, in the ratio of taxes in kind, and in revenues retained locally to those remitted to Baghdad, in the ratio of *ushri* to *karadj* land, in tax rates, and finally in price levels. It is in general not possible to disentangle these factors. In a few cases an explanation suggests itself, most obviously in the case of the low cash revenue per head of Arabia, where all land benefited from the *ushr* regime and where there were no non-Muslims to pay

Table 5-2. *Central government revenue, population, and cultivated area by regions in Abbasid Caliphate, ca. A.D. 800*

| | Revenue (million dirham) (1) | Population (million) (2) | Cultivated area (1,000 km²) (3) | Revenue per Inhabitant (dirham) (4) | Revenue per Km²; (1,000 dirham) (5) | Distribution (%) Revenue (6) | Distribution (%) Population (7) |
|---|---|---|---|---|---|---|---|
| 1. Sind | 12 | 2.5 | — | 5 | — | 3 | 10 |
| 2. Afghanistan and Turkestan | 44 | 3.0 | — | 15 | — | 10 | 12 |
| 3. Iran | 135 | 4.0 | 160 | 34 | 0.9 | 31 | 15 |
| 4. Mesopotamia | 149 | 4.0 | 55[c] | 37 | 2.7 | 35 | 15 |
| 5. Syria[a] | 24 | 3.0 | 80 | 8 | 0.3 | 6 | 12 |
| 6. Arabia | 10 | 2.5 | 40 | 4 | 0.3 | 2 | 10 |
| 7. Egypt | 44 | 4.0 | 29 | 11 | 1.5 | 10 | 15 |
| 8. Libya | 1 | 0.5 | 21 | 2 | 0.1 | 0 | 2 |
| 9. Tunisia[b] | 13 | 2.5 | 75 | 5 | 0.2 | 3 | 10 |
| 10. Caliphate | 432 | 26.0 | —[d] | 17 | 0.7[e] | 100 | 100 |

[a] Including Lebanon, Palestine, and Jordan.
[b] Including one-half of Algeria.
[c] Estimated at 51–58 in mid-seventh century (Kremer, vol. I, p. 258).
[d] On the order of 600.
[e] Approximately.

*Sources:* Col. 1 – cf. text; col. 2 – footnote *d*; col. 3 – 1980 values (*FAO Production Yearbook*, 1981, pp. 45ff).

*djizya.* The position of Mesopotamia and Iraq[51] at the top of the list corresponds to what one would expect on the basis of the available nonquantitative information, particularly in the case of Mesopotamia, which was generally regarded as the richest province of the caliphate,[52] particularly its central part (the *sawad*) in which cash revenue per inhabitant may have been as high as 50 dirhams. There is no explanation for the astonishingly low cash revenue per inhabitant from Egypt, which has generally been regarded as the most oppressed province of the caliphate[53] and had a higher than average proportion of *djizya*-paying inhabitants, even though its price level has been estimated to have been about two-fifths lower than that of Iraq (Ashtor 1969, p. 81). Similar problems are posed by the extremely low averages for North Africa, Sind, and particularly for Syria – certainly not favored by the Abbasids – though in the first two cases distance from Baghdad may have been a factor.

The amount of 17 dirhams per inhabitant, it has already been indicated, seriously understates the total burden of taxation in cash and kind levied in the provinces. This was certainly well above 20 dirhams and may have been as high as 30 dirhams, equal to between one-sixth and one-fourth of national product. A rate of all government revenues in the neighborhood of one-third of national product would not be astonishing – though extraordinary when compared with a rate of about 5 percent in the early Roman Empire – if it is remembered that the rate of the tax on agricultural income was between two-fifths and three-fifths, though actual collections may have been somewhat below the stipulated rates. While the total tax burden in relation to product was higher than that indicated in column 4 of Table 5-2, in all regions the differences among regions were probably smaller.

Column 6, which shows the regional distribution of the cash revenue received by Baghdad, is of importance because it emphasizes the dependence of the central treasury on Mesopotamia and Iran, which together accounted for two-thirds of the total, the *sawad* alone for about one-fourth.

The differences in the cash revenue per unit of area shown for most regions in column 5 must be treated with even more caution because the estimates of cultivable area are more hazardous than those for population. The average for the seven regions for which figures for the present cultivable area are available, which account for three-fourths of the population of the caliphate and for about seven-eighths of the cash income of the treasury, was about 850 dirhams per km² and ranged (excluding Libya) from about 170 dirhams for North Africa to 1,500 dirhams in Egypt and to 2,700 dirhams in Mesopotamia.

The relatively high values for Egypt and Mesopotamia are to be expected as the economy of both countries was based on irrigation agriculture. The difference between them and the other regions nevertheless remains astonishingly large.

All that is known about the structure of expenditures of the central treasury is that by far the single largest item was the costs of the army. For the early Abbasid caliphate the total army budget has been put at 14 million dinars, of which about two-thirds for the standing army of 50,000 men (*Encyclopaedia of Islam*, vol. I, p. 1145, vol. II, p. 508). The total of about 200 million dirhams would have been close to one-half of the total cash revenue of the central government but probably would have represented only about one-third of total government receipts. This was the result of the relatively high pay of the soldiers – at that time mostly natives of Khorasan in Afghanistan rather than Arabs – which on the average amounted to about five times a common laborer's wages (Grünebaum, p. 138), while the number of soldiers in the regular army equaled less than one percent of the adult male population. The next largest item probably was the extravagant expenditure of the court, [54] followed by the salaries of the numerous bureaucrats. Expenditures for welfare and public works apparently were small because they were defrayed largely out of local receipts from *zakat* and *djizya*. There was no long-term government debt. The central treasury as well as some of its provincial offices occasionally borrowed for short periods in anticipation of tax receipts, illegally paying high interest rates or rewarding the lenders by various lucrative privileges or other compensations (Shimizu, pp. 16ff; Lotz, p. 18).

The system of public finance as a whole thus was regressive on the revenue as well as the expenditure side; discriminated against the rural and non-Muslim population; was to a substantial degree arbitrary and unpredictable; did little to foster economic development; and in the form of tax farming provided the main avenue for the accumulation of wealth by officials, merchants, and large landlords (e.g., Becker, pp. 213, 236; Labib, p. 93), most features becoming accentuated from the ninth century on.

## CHAPTER 6

# The financial system of the Ottoman Empire at the death of Suleiman I

Though separated by over seven centuries the Ottoman Empire at the death of Suleiman the Magnificent and the Abbasid caliphate at the death of Harun al Rashid were very similar in location, population, and political, economic, and financial structure. Eastern Anatolia, Mesopotamia, Arabia, Syria, Egypt, and the eastern part of the Maghreb were common to both empires. Although the Ottoman Empire did not include Iran and Sind, it did include Western Anatolia, the Balkans, and Hungary. Both empires had close to 30 million inhabitants and hence a similar density of population. Both were predominantly Muslim, but tolerant of religious minorities, and the Koran and the Sharia, the canon law of Islam, provided the framework for daily life. Arabic was the lingua franca in both. Politically, both were autocracies, the monarch being the religious as well as the civil head of the state. Both were primarily agricultural with a low degree of urbanization. Foreign trade played a minor role in their economy and their financial system was rudimentary. Finally, the level of real national product probably was not very different, though possibly somewhat higher in the Ottoman Empire. Changes in the techniques of agriculture, manufacturing, transportation, trading, and government as well as private finance were small for a distance of three-fourths of a millennium (cf. Inalcik 1969, p. 135).

A characteristic of the Ottoman Empire, important also for its financial administration, was a method of recruitment (the *devshirme*), which applied to the civil servants as well as to the numerous court personnel and to a part of its armed forces, particularly the infantry (*janissaries*). This was the conscription at an early age of Christian subjects, mostly from the Balkans, who were forcibly converted to Islam, the more promising of them trained in specialized institutions in Istanbul and then assigned to the different branches of the administration in the capital or the provinces, opening careers which included the highest civilian and military positions in the empire. The con-

80

scripts became slaves of the sultan (*kapi kullari*) with the result that their estates reverted at their death to their master, in principle in their entirety, in practice in their majority. This method of recruitment created a military and bureaucracy of life-long members, entirely dependent on and loyal to the sultan; free of familial attachment – the positions were not inheritable – without local roots, as they were often reassigned to different places; very well paid, particularly in the upper reaches; and apparently at least as efficient and probably not more corruptible than their parallel in contemporary Europe. The system, however, rapidly deteriorated after the middle of the sixteenth century.[1]

## 1    Population

At the death of Suleiman I – to Westerners "the Magnificent," but to his subjects "the Lawgiver" (*kanuni*) – in 1556 the Ottoman Empire (excluding vassal states like Valachia, Moldavia, and the Chanate of the Krim tatars) covered a surface of about 9 million $km^2$ – about as much as Christian Europe. However, most of it, particularly in Arabia and North Africa, was desert, reducing its cultivated area to below 1 million $km^2$.[2]

In the middle of the sixteenth century the empire's population was slightly above 25 million – about one-third that of Christian Europe – of which about one-fourth each lived in Europe (Balkans and Hungary), in Anatolia, in the Near East (Syria, Lebanon, Palestine, Iraq), and in North Africa, mainly in Egypt. On the basis of cultivated area, density averaged about 25 per $km^2$.[3]

Suleiman's realm was not only a multinational but also a multireligious empire. In the Balkan provinces in 1520–35, Christians constituted four-fifths of the population and in the capital of Istanbul nearly one-half.[4] In Anatolia, in contrast over 90 percent of the population were Muslims, and their share is likely to be similarly high in the other provinces, though statistical evidence is lacking. For the empire as a whole Muslims should have constituted about four-fifths of the total population.

The proportion of slaves in the population was low, put at "at least 5 to 10 percent in some cities" (Matran 1962, p. 45), but their political and economic importance was substantial as they constituted a large proportion of the sultan's civil servants and armed forces and were concentrated in the capital.

The degree of urbanization was low, though it increased rapidly during the sixteenth century. The population of Istanbul is estimated to have risen from less than 100,000 in 1478 to about 400,000 in 1520–30 and to 700,000 in 1571–80, equal to approximately 1.5 and 2.5 percent of the population of the empire. Cairo, the second largest city, appears to have had about 400,000 inhabitants throughout the sixteenth century. The population of a good dozen of other cities in Europe and Asia Minor, down to places of 5,000 inhabitants, increased from about 260,000 to 360,000 inhabitants between 1520–30 and 1571–80 (Raymond, pp. 27, 170), or about 1 to 1.5 percent of the population of these provinces. It is therefore unlikely that the total urban population substantially exceeded 6 percent of that of the empire even in 1571–80, approximately the same ratio as in Europe (McEvedy and Jones, p. 38).

There is little doubt that the population in the area of the empire of Suleiman's death increased substantially during the sixteenth century. One set of estimates leads to an increase by about 5 million[5] or 20 percent or nearly 0.2 percent per year. Most of this increase must have remained in the countryside, probably putting pressure on resources, as cities can hardly have absorbed even as much as one-fifth of it.

## 2     National income and wealth

### Aggregates

In view of the importance of an estimate of national product as a measure of the size of the economy as well as a scalar for many relevant magnitudes such as government revenues, taxes, foreign trade, money in circulation, and financial assets, it is unfortunate that the information to be found in the literature, at least in that in Western languages, does not permit a calculation, even a rough one, from either the income or the expenditure side. One is, therefore, reduced to indirect approaches, which at best provide an idea of the order of magnitude involved.

A far-out upper limit on the size of national income is provided by the basic wage of the *janissaries* of 4 akches per day,[6] or nearly 1,500 akches or 25 ducats per year in the 1570s. This, of course, was far above the average wage of a laborer or the average income of a peasant, but by how much is not known. Even if the *janissaries'* wage had been three times as high as the average household income throughout the empire, its aggregate personal income would have been on the order of 2,500 million akches or 40 million ducats[7] or about 1.5 ducats per head, and national product would not have been much higher.

A more promising approach is to start from the government revenue of Egypt of 50 million paras (excluding arrears) near the end of the century (cf. Section 6). The amount should have been of similar size at the middle of the century, then corresponding to about 100 million akches.[8] On the basis or rates of land tax of one-tenth to one-half (cf. Section 6) of product, the income of Ottoman Egypt might then be put, allowing for nonagricultural income, at approximately 400 million akches. Egypt contained about one-fifth of the population of the empire.[9] A combination of these assumptions leads to an estimate of the national product of the empire at the middle of the sixteenth century on the order of 2,000 million akches or somewhat over 30 million ducats in the aggregate and of about 80 akches or 1.5 ducats per head.

Another estimate may be based on the land tax in the provinces under the fief system, which contained about two-thirds of the population of the empire. This may be put at over 350 million akches (315 million from fiefs and 50 million from lands of the sultan) in the seventeenth century[10] and probably not much less in the mid-sixteenth century. Assuming a ratio of one-fourth to one-third between land tax and agricultural product and making allowance for the much smaller nonagricultural product, one obtains an estimate for the national product of the empire – at 1⅓ times that of the fief provinces – in the mid-sixteenth century on the order of 2,000 to 2,500 million akches, or 32 to 40 million ducats or 1.3 to 1.6 ducats per head.

Finally, a similar estimate can be reached by starting from the sum of revenue of the central government [183 million akches in 1564 (Hammer-Purgstall 1827, vol. 3, p. 182)] and of the land tax in the fief provinces (about 350 million akches) on the assumption of a ratio of total revenues to national product of one-fourth to one-third. This yields a figure of 1,600 million to 2,100 million akches, or 27 million to 35 million ducats, or 1.1 to 1.4 ducats per head.

The resulting estimates of national product per head of 1¼ to 1¾ ducats, or 4½ to 6 g of gold, are extraordinarily low in terms of gold – the comparable well-attested figure for England and Wales in 1688 of £10 corresponded to 75 g, and it has been estimated at about 30 g for the Roman Empire at the death of Augustus (Goldsmith, p. 280). To what extent this reflected a low real product per head or a low price of gold in terms of commodities[11] is difficult to say.

"Whether there was a growth in per capita income or not is a question until now not even tackled by Ottoman historiography" (Gerber, p. 317) and one entirely beyond the data now available. The answer is likely to be "no" or "to a very small extent."

There is no possibility of estimating the value of national wealth except to say that it probably amounted to five times or somewhat more of national product.

## Distribution

Thanks to the preservation and recent analysis of some of the registers of estates filed with the legal authorities in two large cities, something is known about the size distribution and the structure of estates.[12]

On the basis of these data it may be estimated that in Bursa, one of the wealthiest cities of the Ottoman Empire, of somewhat over 700 estates filed in 1467–68 and 1487–88, which averaged slightly less than 20 ducats (then about 900 akches), about 25 percent were valued at less than 10 ducats, nearly 60 percent at between 20 and 200 ducats, about 15 percent at between 200 and 2,000 ducats, and a little over 1 percent at over 2,000 ducats. Of the aggregate value of these estates those below 20 ducats accounted for not much over 1 percent, those of 20 to 200 ducats for about 20 percent, those of 200 to 2,000 ducats for about 50 percent, and the few estates of over 2,000 ducats each for nearly 30 percent. Concentration of wealth was therefore very pronounced with a Gini ratio of about 0.70. The largest fortunes were left by money changers/goldsmiths, merchants, and silk weavers – the leading industry in Bursa.

In Edirne (Adrianople), the previous capital of the empire, of 93 estates of over 30,000 akches left between the middle of the sixteenth and of the seventeenth century one-fourth were valued at over one million akches. In the sixteenth century the estates of the rich averaged between 8,000 and 9,000 ducats (about 500,000 akches before the devaluation of 1584). Among 175 estates averaging 280,000 akches real assets constituted about three-fifths: namely, houses and shops and household goods, 14 percent each; land and livestock, 17 percent; inventories, 12 percent; and slaves, 3 percent. Of the two-fifths in the form of financial assets, approximately one-half consisted of cash, mostly gold coins, the other half included accounts receivable, interest-bearing loans, and partnerships (*mudabara*, similar to the Western commenda).

There is no way of determining to what extent these two small samples of estates are representative of the size distribution and structure of private wealth of the urban population of the Ottoman Empire. Concentration of wealth is likely to have been more pronounced in Istanbul than in Bursa or Edirne because it was the residence of the richest subjects of the sultan, members of the court, officials, and businessmen, but less pronounced in most smaller cities.

No comparable information is available on the size distribution or the structure of the wealth of the great majority of the population who lived in the countryside, but some indication is given by the data on fiefs, which accounted for a large part of the agricultural properties in the European and Asia Minor provinces.[13] In 18 provinces, of about two dozen in the area, nearly 40,000 fiefs were reported in the mid-seventeenth century with an assessed annual revenue, based on cadastral surveys, of about 250 million akches or slightly over 6,000 akches per fief. Of them about 2,500 were classified as large fiefs (zia- met) each of which was supposed to yield a revenue of 20,000 to 100,000 akches. Assuming an average revenue of 45,000 akches, their total revenue would have been on the order of 110 million, leaving about 140 million akches for the remaining small fiefs (timar), or an average of about 4,000 akches. In addition the few hundred governors of provinces and smaller areas had similar revenues (chass), each exceeding 100,000 akches and totaling about 65 million akches, suggesting an average of over 200,000 akches. There were in addition rural properties of the sultan of large though unknown extent. These 18 provinces had a rural population on the order of one-half of that of the empire or about 13 million and hence approximately 2.5 million households. The total income of these 2.5 million households is not known, but it is not likely to have been in excess of 1 billion akches. In that case the revenue of the fully 1.5 percent of householders represented by the sultan, governors, and holders of large fiefs of over 350 million akches would have represented about one-third of total agricultural revenue. Even if the latter should have been as high as 1.5 billion akches the share of the top 1.5 percent of rural income recipients would still have been as high as one-fourth. In evaluating these figures, it is necessary to take account of the fact that the holders of fiefs had to do military service and to provide retainers whose number depended on the size of their revenue. Even then the concentration of net revenues remains pronounced. It was probably larger than that in the early Roman Empire or in Elizabethan England, though smaller than that in the Mughal Empire (Goldsmith 1984, p. 285 and Tables 7-3 and 10-2).

Although there is no information about the structure of the wealth of the rural population, there is no doubt that it consisted to an overwhelming extent of land, livestock, plantations, agricultural buildings, and household goods. It is only among the top wealth holders that urban properties and financial assets may have constituted a modest proportion of their total assets.

The estimates of fief revenues are based on figures referring to the middle of the seventeenth century. They should, however, not have been very different in the reign of Suleiman, particularly with respect to relations if not to absolute figures, as the assessed revenues of fiefs apparently remained fairly stable.

## 3     The monetary system

The reign of Suleiman was one of the few periods of stability of the monetary system in Ottoman history. The country was, as throughout its history, on a symmetallic system, silver and gold coins of domestic and foreign origin being accepted at varying rates reflecting the value of their metallic content.[14]

The most common coin, particularly for small transactions, was the silver akche (little white one), known to Europeans by its Greek name of asper. This was a small coin with a diameter of about 1.25 cm, a weight of slightly over 1 g containing from the 1510s to the 1570s about 0.65 g of silver, about one-half of its original silver content of the fourteenth century. Some of the about two dozens of provincial mints also issued pieces of 4 or 6 akches. Because the akche was inconveniently small for many commercial or fiscal transactions or for hoarding, sealed bags of 20,000 akches were often used. An apparently large, though unknown, part of the silver money in circulation consisted of two larger pieces that were minted abroad and imported, namely, the *esedi kurus*, that is, the Dutch Leeuwendaalder, weighing 26.5 g and containing 15.5 g of silver, and hence equal to about 25 akches, and the slightly heavier *kara kurus*, that is, the Spanish piece of eight reales, both known to Westerners as piastres. The Ottoman authorities often put their stamp on these foreign coins, but they seem to have been accepted without it. In Egypt the standard silver coin was the para, which weighed about 2 g, and in the sixteenth century was equal to 2 akches but in the seventeenth century to 4 akches.

The situation was similar in the case of gold coins. Besides the domestically minted ashrefi of 2.3 g of gold, several foreign gold coins were in circulation, particularly the Venetian ducat of about 3.6 g, which was probably regarded as the standard coin of stable metallic content.

Copper coins of between 1/16 and 1/8 akche apparently were rare (Matran 1962, p. 247), though the akche pieces must have been inconveniently large for many retail transactions.

There are no data on the volume of output of the Ottoman mints or of imports and exports of foreign coins. It is therefore impossible to estimate, even roughly, the volume of money in circulation or its velocity. It is not even known how the mints obtained the metal they coined, particularly in the case of silver coins since the empire did not have large silver mines. The gold minted probably came mostly from the Sudan. Complaints about shortages of currency were common, but too vague to permit significant conclusions (cf. Inalcik 1969, p. 138). Similarly vague are the guesses that the empire had a positive balance of payments with Europe, but a negative one with its eastern neighbors (Matran 1979, passim).

Soon after Suleiman's death the monetary system started a process of deterioration that continued through most of the seventeenth and eighteenth centuries. Its clearest evidence is the decline in the silver content of the akche. As a result the gold ashrefi rose from an average of 60 akches in 1550–80 to 120 akches as early as 1584 and a century later was worth 360 akches (Matran 1962, Table 2).

## 4    Price movements

The price level increased substantially even while the silver content of the akche remained unchanged, in part reflecting the plethora of silver imports. Between 1490 and 1555 the increase in food prices in Istanbul, the only available series, has been put at slightly over 40 percent in terms of akche, a still modest rate of 0.5 percent per year. In the following 40 years the index rose by 275 percent in terms of akche and by 100 percent in terms of silver, increases of 3.3 percent and 1.7 percent, respectively, per year. During the first half of the seventeenth century, however, the index declined moderately, so that in 1655 it was only by 225 percent in terms of akche and by 35 percent in terms of silver above its level of a century earlier, implying annual average rates of inflation of about 1.2 percent and 0.3 percent, respectively (Barkan 1973, pp. 65ff).

## 5    Financial instruments and institutions

The range of financial instruments available in the Ottoman Empire in the sixteenth century was very narrow. There were no paper money, no bank deposits, no government securities, and, of course, no private bonds or stocks. Long-term loans were ruled out by the prohibition of interest. This left only short-term loans, for which ways around the prohibition could be found, in the form of trade credit and of loans among individuals,[15] particularly by landlords and others to peasants. These apparently were common, though there is no indication about their volume. Short-term business loans seem to have carried interest at 10 to 15 percent,[16] but the rates were much higher on consumer loans, particularly in the countryside.

There were no financial institutions in the narrow sense. Private banking houses, developed only beginning in the seventeenth century, were mostly operated by members of national minorities and concentrated on transactions with the treasury. The extension of credit remained an activity ancillary to trading and to property administration of wealthy individuals or of religious foundations (wakf) without reliance on external funds. Money changers must have been numerous, but very little is known about their number, distribution, or operations.

## 6     Financing the private economy

The published information on how the main sectors of the private economy of the Ottoman Empire of the sixteenth century, or for that matter the fifteenth or seventeenth centuries – agriculture, handicrafts, housing, internal and foreign trade – were financed is extraordinarily limited and in quantitative terms almost nonexistent. It is more limited, in fact, than in two comparable cases, the Abbasid caliphate and the Mughal Empire, and more limited also than for classical antiquity and for medieval Europe. This limitation is astonishing in view of the fact that the Ottoman Empire was a bureaucratic state producing extensive records. Of the numerous Europeans who visited it, lived in it, and did business with it, those of them who wrote about their experiences unfortunately were more interested in the affairs of the seraglio, folklore, and possibly the sultan's armed forces than in the country's economy.[17] There are indications, however, that many relevant documents have been preserved in archives in Istanbul and in other cities belonging to the empire, such as Cairo and Bursa, which may at some time permit a less inadequate treatment of the subject.[18]

One is therefore limited to a few vague generalities. Possibly the most important among them is the generally acknowledged fact that commercial techniques and particularly the use of credit were backward[19] compared with those of Europe, not only of the sixteenth century but even as far back as the thirteenth century, and those of contemporary India, and were hardly ahead of those of the Abbasid caliphate. The reasons for this backwardness are not entirely clear. Among them are the rigid interpretation of Islam, such as the prohibition of interest, which guided the government, and the apparent disinterest of the politically dominating Turkish population in commercial activities, which were mainly left to minorities such as Greeks, Armenians, and Jews (Matran 1979, pp. 172–3).

It is typical of the lack of information that we have no quantitative information of the volume or structure of imports and exports.[20] It is supposed on the basis of fragmentary evidence that the balance of trade with Mediterranean Europe was positive and that this trade was predominantly financed by the European parties, primarily by Italian merchants, while that with the East – mainly Persia, India, and China – which was overwhelmingly conducted on a cash basis, was definitively negative due to substantial imports of luxury goods, such as spices, jewelry, indigo, fine textiles, and silk and the scarcity of export commodities. The Ottoman Empire lacked a coherent policy in the field of foreign trade except for the prohibition of exports of commodities regarded as of military importance. Import and export duties were low, in principle 3 percent of value, with apparently many local variations.

## 7    Financing the government

### The Empire

Because the Ottoman government[21] in general took over the systems of taxation that had been in force in the conquered territories, with some obvious exceptions such as the imposition of the head tax on non-Muslims in the territories that had been part of the Byzantine Empire, and made no attempt to establish uniform methods of assessment and collection or tax rates throughout the realm, the multiplicity and diversity of taxes and other revenues increased. Contemporary and modern descriptions of many details of the system exist, but as no budget or other quantitative information has been preserved for the sixteenth century, it is not possible to form an overall view of the system and of its structure.[22]

Although apparently no detailed accounts have been preserved before the middle of the sixteenth century, a Turkish author put total revenues of the treasury at 183 million akches and expenditures at 190 million akches, or about 3 million ducats each.[23] Such a figure is not incompatible with the contribution of Egypt, which contained about one-sixth of the population of the Empire of about 0.5 million ducats (cf. Section 6).

There is little doubt that the land tax constituted the backbone of the system and provided the largest single component of revenue and possibly furnished as much as three-fourths of the total. The land tax was in most of the empire collected by holders of noninheritable fiefs, who in return owed specified military or other services, by high officials, or by foundations (wakfs) rather than by officers of the treasury in Istanbul, headed by the finance minister (*defterdar*) and by other local representation except for the lands owned by the Sultan. The main exception was Egypt where in the absence of fiefs the land tax was collected by local treasury officials as were all other revenues, and the treasury in Istanbul received only a fixed contribution, near the end of the sixteenth century of about 20 million paras or 0.5 million ducats. Rates of the land tax varied greatly depending on the presumed yield and among provinces. Their range has been estimated at between 10 and 50 percent of product (Gibb and Bowen, vol. I, p. 240). On the basis of the revenue of the holders of fiefs, of high officials, and the sultan, the yield of the land tax in the provinces outside of Egypt and a few other areas treated similarly, may be estimated at about 350 million akches. This should probably be considered as a maximum since the land tax yielded about 70 million akches in Egypt whose population was approximately one-fourth of that of the provinces in which the tax was collected by the landowners.

The peasants were also subject, at least in some provinces, to a small fixed tax, which for the standard size plot of 6 to 15 hectares amounted to 22 akches and for agricultural workers to 3 or 6 akches and was collected for the sultan's treasury (Inalcik 1978, p. 238).

No quantitative information exists for the sixteenth century of the yields of the numerous other sources of revenue, particularly those from urban areas, those levied on trade, and the head tax on non-Muslims.[24] These revenues, in contrast to the land tax, were received by the treasury in Istanbul either as a result of direct collection or from tax farmers.

In the absence of a budget for the mid-sixteenth century, little can be said about the structure of expenditures except that they were dominated by the cost of the military forces and of the court in Istanbul.[25]

Under Suleiman revenues, including booty, tributes, and confiscations, seem to have exceeded expenditures substantially until the early 1560s with the result that a large surplus was accumulated, supposedly averaging about 2 million ducats a year, or about one-third of the annual revenue. The treasure, kept in coins in the "Seven Towers," is reported to have amounted to about 16 million ducats, or over two years' revenue, as late as 1596 (Morawitz, p. 4), probably well below its size in the mid-sixteenth century, but was rapidly dissipated in the early seventeenth century.[26]

### Egypt

The only part of the Ottoman Empire for which a complete budget for the sixteenth century has been preserved is Egypt.[27] The budget of this province, which accounted for about one-fifth of the population of the empire and was of particular importance as its granary and main grain supplier of the capital, for the year 1596–97, is summarized in Table 6-1. From a fiscal point of view Egypt differed from the provinces in Europe and in Asia Minor in three basic respects:

Table 6-1. *Budget of Ottoman Egypt, 1596–97*

| | Amount | | |
| --- | --- | --- | --- |
| | Total (million para) | Per head[c] (para) | Distribution (%) |
| I. *Revenues* | 66.1 | 13.2 | 100.0 |
|   1. Land tax | 40.8[a] | 8.2 | 61.8 |
|   2. Customs | 5.5[b] | 1.1 | 8.3 |
|   3. Tithe on spices | 3.6 | 0.7 | 5.4 |
|   4. Poll tax | 1.6 | 0.3 | 2.4 |
|   5. From tax farmers and office holders | 4.0 | 0.8 | 6.1 |
|   6. Profit on coins | 2.6 | 0.5 | 3.9 |
|   7. Others | 8.0 | 1.6 | 12.1 |
| II. *Expenditures* | 44.7 | 8.9 | 100.0 |
|   1. Payments | 5.0 | 1.0 | 11.2 |
|   2. Salaries of high officials | 6.8 | 1.4 | 15.2 |
|   3. Wages | 26.6 | 5.3 | 59.5 |
|   4. Other | 6.3 | 1.3 | 14.1 |
| III. *Balance* | 21.4 | 4.3 | 100.0 |
|   1. To Istanbul | 19.8[d] | 4.0 | 92.5 |
|   2. To Holy Cities | 1.4 | 0.3 | 6.5 |
|   3. Left in Egypt | 0.2 | 0.0 | 0.0 |

[a] Of which 6.1 is arrears.
[b] Of which 3.6 is in Alexandria and Rosetta.
[c] Of which 17.9 is in cash.
[d] Based on population of 5 million (McEvedy and Jones, p. 227).
*Source:* Shaw 1968, pp. 21, 86ff.

The system of fiefs did not apply to Egypt; government expenditures in Egypt, including the pay of the armed forces, were financed by revenues raised within the province; and an amount fixed in monetary terms had to be remitted to the treasury in Istanbul, predominantly in coins in a large heavily guarded annual convoy.

In 1596–97, 80 years after the conquest of the country by Selim I, the father of Suleiman, total revenues were reported at 66 million paras equivalent at that time to 264 million akches or about 50 akches per head. The land tax was the main source of revenue, yielding slightly over three-fifths of the total, of which one-seventh represented tax arrears. Three districts in the delta accounted for over two-thirds of the total, while Upper Egypt contributed not much over one-tenth.

The rate of the land tax depended on presumed yield. Where it was collected in kind, the minority of cases, the rates ranged from one-tenth of the produce from the poorest lands to one-half to the most fertile areas, generally those in the Nile delta. The second largest source of revenues were customs duties – international, interprovincial, and intraprovincial – with 8 percent of the total. The poll tax on non-Muslims furnished only 2.5 percent of total revenue. At a yield of 40,000 gold pieces – from one piece for poor to four gold pieces for rich non-Muslims – it implies only 20,000 non-Muslim households, or about 2 percent of the population. The remaining one-fourth of revenues came from a multitude of sources, including many excises, some of the more important items being shown in Table 6-1.

In the absence of even rough estimates of the value of product of Egypt, it is not possible to evaluate the burden of taxation. From a recent estimate it appears that in the sixteenth century the tax per unit of area and the share of the land tax in peasants' income differed greatly among districts depending on fertility. It constituted less than 20 percent of income in Upper Egypt but nearly 50 percent in Lower Egypt, but left the farmer and his family about the same amount of wheat, namely, 0.6 to 0.8 kg per day per consumer unit (Hansen, pp. 478–83). Given the predominance of agriculture in Egypt's income and the likelihood that the burden of taxation was not lower on the urban than on the rural population – revenue from urban areas has been put at fully one-eighth of the total (Shaw 1962, p. 183), well above the share of the urban population, though probably not above its share in income – the overall burden of taxation is not likely to have been below one-third of the province's total income and may well have approached one-half when the numerous semilegal and extralegal levies of the authorities and of tax farmers are taken into account.

By far the largest component of expenditures were those for the pay of troops, which required somewhat more than one-half of the total. The 6,200 members of active military corps, the most highly paid element, received 20 million paras, an average of 3,300 paras, that is, over 40 pieces of gold, equivalent to nearly 5 oz of the metal. The salaries of 50-odd high officials absorbed no less than 15 percent of total expenditures, averaging an extraordinary 125,000 paras – fully 3,000 gold coins or 10 kg of gold – per recipient, equal to the income of more than 2,000 households, and ranging to over 800,000 paras for the governor (pasha) of Egypt (Shaw 1962, p. 210).

The excess of revenues over expenditures within Egypt of fully 21 million paras was equal to nearly one-third of total revenues and to nearly one-half of expenditures within Egypt. The bulk of it was delivered to the treasury in Istanbul, nine-tenths of it in the form of coins. The remainder was transferred to the Holy Cities. It is again impossible to evaluate with precision the burden of this "external drain," but it is not likely to have been below one-tenth of the national income of Ottoman Egypt, a high level of an unrequited transfer.

## CHAPTER 7

# The financial system of Mughal India at the death of Akbar

At the death of Akbar "the Great" in A.D. 1605 Mughal India with a population of about 110 million and an area of about 2.5 million km², covering the entire peninsula down to about 19° North, contained about one-fifth of the population of the world, was only one-fourth below that of Ming China, and was slightly ahead of the total of the several dozen states into which Europe was then divided. This was a dramatic change from the situation at the accession of Akbar in 1556 when his domain was limited to about 0.3 million km² and probably had no more than 30 million inhabitants. The empire, enlarged as the result of about half a century's warfare, had become unified in some important respects – *pax Akbarica*, a common monetary system, free movement throughout the empire, and a basically similar system of taxation and land allocation – but it still showed many regional differences in the details of political and financial arrangements.

Although the size of the empire somewhat increased during the seventeenth century under Akbar's three successors (Jahangir, Shahjehan, and Aurangzeb, particularly in the Dekkan) and while urbanization, real national product per head, internal and particularly foreign trade increased, and the financial system developed, the empire at the death of Akbar was probably at the peak of its political power and coherence and close to its economic zenith.

Another, more mundane reason for centering this chapter on the turn of the sixteenth to the seventeenth century is the existence of the *Ain-i-Akbari* written in the 1590s by or under the direction of Abul Fazl, one of the closest associates of the emperor, a document that provides more quantitative information on most political and economic aspects of the empire than any similar source before the eighteenth century, except for the Florentine property census of 1427 or the Domesday Book of 1086.

1       Population

With about 110 million inhabitants at the beginning of the seventeenth century,[1] Mughal India was the second most populous country, considerably behind Ming China but slightly ahead of the total of
the several dozen countries of Europe. Indeed some of the empire's
provinces had as many inhabitants as the two most populous European countries, the Kingdom of France and Muscovy.[2] Over its area
of about 2.5 million km² density averaged 44 per km² with great regional variations.

   Area and population were much smaller at the accession of Akbar
half a century earlier. At that time the empire had an area of only
about 0.3 million km², covering a narrow strip of territory extending
from Kabul to Agra,[3] and its population was probably not in excess
of 30 million concentrated in the upper Ganges Valley and the Punjab.[4]

   Moslems, though politically and economically dominant, constituted only a minority of the population. Their share has been put at
20 to 25 percent (Maddison 1971, p. 30) though it was probably higher
in the larger cities. Most of them were converts, as it has been estimated that only about one-tenth of them descended from the original
invaders that had come from the northwest (Maddison 1971, p. 30).
In contrast of the 415 leading nobles only 57 were Hindus, mainly
Rajput chiefs and few Hindustani Moslems, while most of them were
Persians or Afghans, who had come to India under Akbar or his father.[5]

   Population growth was slow and irregular. For the sixteenth and
seventeenth centuries the average annual rate of growth has been estimated at 0.24 percent.[6]

   There is no information on birth and death rates. In the virtual
absence of growth and migration, both must have been nearly equal,
and undoubtedly both were very high, probably close to 5 percent per
year of the population.[7] Expectation of life was low, probably well
below 25 years.[8]

   The number of households was in the neighborhood of 22 million,
assuming an average family size of five persons.[9] That of the male
labor force may have approached 35 million, while that of the female
labor force, essentially limited to part-time agricultural workers, must
have been much smaller in terms of full-time members of the labor
force.[10]

   There are no contemporary indicators or modern estimates of the
labor force. Application of the corresponding estimates for the 1857–

Table 7-1. *Area and administrative units of provinces in Mughal India*

| | Area (in 1,000 km²) (1) | Districts (*sarkars*) (2) | Subdistricts (*parganas*) (3) | Villages (1,000) (4) | Area per village (km²) (5) |
|---|---|---|---|---|---|
| 1. Agra | 120 | 13 | 203 | 30.2 | 3.97 |
| 2. Ajmer | 314 | 7 | 197 | 7.9 | 39.75 |
| 3. Allahabad | 90 | 10 | 177 | 47.6 | 1.89 |
| 4. Awadh | 69 | 5 | 38 | 52.7 | 1.31 |
| 5. Behar | 144 | 7 | 199 | 55.4 | 2.60 |
| 6. Bengal | 182 | 24 | 787 | 112.8 | 1.61 |
| 7. Delhi | 173 | 8 | 232 | 45.1 | 3.84 |
| 8. Gudjerat | 202 | 9 | 198 | 10.4 | 19.42 |
| 9. Lahore | 141 | 5 | 234 | 27.8 | 5.07 |
| 10. Kabul | 340 | 6 | 125 | 6.7 | 50.75 |
| 11. Malwa | 298 | 12 | 201 | 18.7 | 15.94 |
| 12. Multan | 170 | 3 | 88 | 9.3 | 18.28 |
| Twelve old provinces | 2,243 | 109 | 2,779 | 424.5 | 5.28 |
| 13. Berar | 129 | 16 | 142 | 10.9 | 11.83 |
| 14. Kandesh | 20 | 1 | 32 | 6.3 | 3.17 |
| 15. Orissa | 50 | 5 | — | — | — |
| 16. Thatta | 66 | — | — | — | — |

*Sources:* Cols. 1 and 4, Habib 1963, p. 4; figures refer to mid-seventeenth century; cols. 2 and 3, *Ain-i-Akbari,* (Jarrett, vol. II, pp. 115ff.); figures refer to 1590s.

1900 period yields a total labor force of about 50 million (nearly 35 million male; fully 15 million female), divided into an agricultural one of about 40 million and a nonagricultural one of about 10 million, much of which was urban (Heston, p. 394). On the basis of a total urban population of 16 million, the urban labor force at Akbar's time could hardly have been in excess of 7 million, mostly male. This would leave about 40 million for the agricultural labor force, allowing at most 2 million for the nonagricultural labor force in rural areas.

Though there are no estimates of the regional distribution of the population, that of the number of villages, of cultivated area, and of land tax revenues (compare Tables 7-1 and 7-5) indicate that the population was concentrated in the Ganges Valley. The seven provinces in that area (Lahore, Delhi, Agra, Awadh, Allahabad, Bihar, and Bengal) contained nearly four-fifths of all villages and accounted for over one-half of the cultivated land and of the land tax revenue, although they occupied not much over one-third of the empire's area.

Urbanization was fairly high, the proportion of the urban population having been estimated at about 15 percent,[11] corresponding to about 16 million. The three largest cities – Agra, Delhi, and Lahore – had a population of about half a million each; the next six cities together about 1.0 million,[12] and all cities of 100,000 or more inhabitants probably between 3.5 and 4.0 million inhabitants. A considerable, though unknown, proportion of the urban population were slaves (Moreland 1920, p. 85), mainly imported from Africa.

The bulk of the population – about 85 million or over three-fourths of the total – lived in the countryside in about 470,000 villages,[13] an average of about 180 inhabitants or 35 families per village, but apparently with large variations in size.[14] Most of the villagers were engaged in agricultural and related activities, but there was also a substantial number of artisans, merchants, and officials, particularly in the larger villages. They can hardly have numbered less than 5 million, leaving about 80 million of agriculturists, representing somewhat over 15 million households of which probably not more than 12 million[15] owned or rented land. Most of the agricultural population lived in a semiservile situation required to cultivate the land but secure in its occupation, prohibited to leave their village, though in fact escapes were common.[16] The tribal population has been estimated at about 10 million, probably ignored in most other statistics (Maddison 1971, p. 33).

## 2    National product

The available data unfortunately do not permit an independent estimate of gross national product from the product, income, and expenditure sides, which would provide important checks.[17] The only approach as yet possible is from the income side. Here

$$Y_m = \bar{y}_r p_r + \bar{y}_u p_u + \bar{y}_n p_n + \bar{y}_t p_t$$

where $y$ is aggregate income and $\bar{y}$ income per head, while the subscripts $m$, $r$, $u$, $n$, and $t$ identify, respectively, the Mughal Empire, the rural and urban sectors, the nobility including the court, and the tribal population, and $p$ the respective populations. Of the components of this equation the populations of the four sectors are the figures least in doubt. As explained in Section 1 they are put at 85, 16, well below 1, and 10 million, respectively. Among the estimates of average incomes per head the most important one, that of rural income, can be based on land revenue payments, the only macroeconomic contemporary well-attested economically relevant quantity; that for average urban income is difficult to estimate and is subject to a considerable margin of uncertainty; that of the nobility and court is known to be about equal to the yield of the land tax; and, finally, that of the tribal population is so small that the error in any reasonable guess is without substantial effect on total national product.

In 1596 the assessed value of the land tax (*gama*) was R 129 million.[18] It is, however, known that actual collections (*hasil*) were lower, though no contemporary or modern comprehensive estimate of the difference appears to have been made. On the basis of the relation between *hasil* and *yama* in about one-sixth of all the villages in the middle of the seventeenth century,[19] it may be put as on the order of one-fifth, leading to an estimate of between R 100 million and R 110 million for the amount actually collected from the peasants from this tax. There is greater uncertainty about the ratio of tax collections to agricultural income, a ratio that differed among provinces and collection districts. Near the end of Akbar's reign, around A.D. 1600, the standard rate in the provinces under the *Zabt* regime was one-third, but apparently was higher in the other provinces. (For a discussion of the ratio compare Section 9.) For the empire as a whole a ratio on the order of two-fifths appears to be reasonable, leading to a gross agricultural product for the area subject to land tax of R 250 million to R 275 million.

This must be increased, first, by 3 to 4 percent for the product of land tax exempt for religious purposes[20] – the occupiers being called by Shahjehan the "army of prayer" (Raychaudhuri 1982, p. 178), or by about R 10 million. It would have to be increased, second, for the product of the tax-exempt land of the zamindars or other tax collectors, which formed part of their remuneration, but is more conveniently included in their total gross income, which has been estimated at between one-fourth and one-third of the land tax revenue or between R 25 million and R 35 million (cf. Section 9). To obtain an estimate of the total income of the rural population two more items must be taken into account. The first is the pay of the troops and other men the zamindars had to keep, which has been put at one-sixth of the land tax revenue,[21] about R 15 million. The second is the income of the nonagricultural village population, which may be put very roughly at about R 20 million on the basis of one million households and an average annual income of R 20, slightly above the wage of unskilled urban workers.

The total income of the rural population, including the zamindars, part of whom probably lived in smaller cities, would then have been between R 320 million and R 355 million, or about R 4 per head. Of this, however, the peasants (including the zamindars' retainers) received only about R 265 million to R 290 million gross and between R

120 million and R 165 million net of taxes and collectors' take, or about R 3.5 per head gross and R 1.5 to R 2 net or about R 18 gross and R 7.5 to R 10 net per household.

The estimates of the income of the urban population, excluding court and nobles, must be built up separately for unskilled laborers, skilled workers and artisans, and middle-class residents. In this case the difficulties are equally serious in dividing the total urban population of 16 million and its labor force of about 7 million[22] among these three groups as in estimating the average income of each of them.

There is no quantitative material to divide the urban labor force among its three main components: unskilled workers, which may be presumed to include the entire female labor force; skilled workmen, including artisans; and merchants, professionals, military, and other more affluent groups. It is, therefore, to some extent arbitrary, if three-fifths of the urban labor force of about 7 million is regarded as unskilled and three-tenths as skilled, leaving one-tenth for the third group. There is agreement that the daily wage for an unskilled worker was on the order of 2 dams, or R 0.05.[23] This figure reported in the *Ain-i-Akbari* referred to the capital (Agra) in the last decade of the sixteenth century and is likely to have been somewhat above the average for the entire country. There is no information on the length of the work year, that is, the number of days for which the workers were actually paid, but it is unlikely that it could have been in excess of 300 days. On that basis the wage bill for the unskilled urban force would have been on the order of R 15 per head and about R 60 million in the aggregate.

The margin of uncertainty is much wider for the second and particularly the third group. The daily wages for skilled workers appear to have ranged from about 3 to nearly 10 dams per day (Blochmann, p. 225). Assuming an average of 5 dams per day and again a work year of 300 days, annual earnings would have been somewhat below R 40 per head and R 80 million in the aggregate. The range for the third group is much wider, going up to at least R 125 per year for the members of the cavalry of the emperor and the nobles, regarded as "professional gentlemen troopers" (Habib 1969, p. 56) who had to provide their own horses. It is therefore extremely difficult to decide on an average income for this group and to put it at R 75 per head is fairly arbitrary, leading to an aggregate income of R 50 million.[24] On the basis of these partly very hazardous estimates, the total annual income of the urban population, excluding the court and the nobles, would have been on the order of slightly less than R 200 million.

As the court and the nobles received almost all of the land revenue, their annual income should have been close to R 100 million. The division of the total between the emperor and the nobles is not known. On the basis of an estimate (Table 7-4) that near the end of Akbar's reign approximately one-fifth of the land tax came from imperial lands (*khalisa*) and that the emperor received most of the revenue from minor taxes, the emperor's annual income might have been on the order of R 25 million, leaving about R 80 million for the nobles.

Combining the estimates for the four main sectors and adding a small allowance – say R 20 million[25] – for the essentially nonmonetary income of the tribal population, the following tentative picture emerges[26,27]:

1. Rural population:   R 340 million = 53 percent
2. Urban population:  R 190 million = 29 percent
3. Court and nobles:  R 100 million = 15 percent
4. Tribal population:  R 20 million = 3 percent
5. Total population:  R 650 million = 100 percent

On this basis annual national income per head around A.D. 1600 would have been on the order of R 6 per head for the entire population, about R 4 for the rural population and R 12 for the urban population and very much more for the nobles, probably more than R 50,000.

Since taxes on the urban population were low – here put fairly arbitrarily at R 10 million – the distribution of disposable income was considerably more favorable to the urban population than that of gross income. On the other hand the heavy expenditures on their military retainers sharply reduced the share of court and nobility in spendable income. On that basis average spendable income per head was about R 6 for the entire population, R 2.5 for the rural population, R 11 for the urban population, R 13,000 per noble, and about R 10 million for the emperor.

There are no measures of the absolute or relative size of capital expenditures. Most of the monuments for which the period is famous, except Fahtepur Sikri – such as the great mosque and the Red Fort in Delhi and the Taj Mahal – were built after the death of Akbar and did not serve economic purposes.[28] As the urban population grew, there must have been a substantial amount of housing construction, and there was some investment in irrigation and in gardens and orchards. That the share of the net capital formation was very small is evidenced by the very low rate of growth of national product. Even with a rate of growth of 0.25 percent a year and a capital output ratio of 3, the net capital formation ratio would have been only 0.8 percent of national product. Indeed the country had hardly any stock of productive reproducible capital except housing in general of very poor quality, hardly any consumer durables, a small merchant fleet, substantial but only slowly growing livestock herds, and similarly slowly increasing inventories since equipment used in agriculture and handicrafts was minimal, the whole economy being extremely labor intensive.

An income per head of about R 6 for the Mughal Empire in 1600 compares with considerably more reliable estimates of about R 24 in 1860 and R 68 in 1912 for undivided India (Goldsmith 1983, pp. 5, 69). To acquire significance these figures must be shifted from a current to a constant price basis by the use of national product deflators. Such deflators exist only since the mid-nineteenth century. For the period between 1600 and 1860 only rough price indices based on a small number of commodities, mainly foodstuffs, are available. One such index puts the purchasing power of the rupee in 1600 at four times the 1851–70 average and at seven times the value for 1911 (Mukherjee, p. 47). Another older estimate is very similar, indicating a ratio of six between the purchasing power of the rupee in 1600 and 1912.[29] On this basis the average income per head of R 6 in 1600 would have had a purchasing power of R 24 in 1851–71 prices, equal to the observed value of income per head in current prices in 1860 suggesting that real income per head was the same in 1600 as in 1860. Between 1857 and 1912 real income per head is estimated to have increased by fully 25 percent (Goldsmith 1983, p. 56) so that in 1600 it would have been about one-fifth below that of 1912, as shown in Table 7-2. Continuing the calculation, real per head income of 1600 would have been nearly 30 percent below that of 1950, shortly after India became independent, and nearly 55 percent below that of the Republic of India in 1980.[30] Thus the average rate of growth of real income per head was zero in the two and one-half centuries following the death of Akbar – probably slightly increasing during most of the seventeenth century and declining thereafter to the early nineteenth century[31] – and not much above one-half of one percent per year (0.62 percent) between 1857 and 1980 though it rose to 1.30 percent per year since independence.

An attempt is made in Table 7-2 to compare real national product per head in India around 1600 and its development over the following four centuries with that of three leading Western economies. This

Table 7-2. *National product per head in Mughal India, Great Britain, France, and the United States, 1600-1980*

| | 1950 = 100 | | | 1970 dollars | | | |
|---|---|---|---|---|---|---|---|
| | | Great | | United | | Great | | United |
| India | Britain | France | States | India | Britain | France | States |
| (1) | (2) | (3) | (4) | (5) | (6) | (7) | (8) |
| 1600 | (73) | 9 | — | — | (178) | 178 | — | — |
| 1700 | (80) | 13 | 17 | 8.5 | (195) | 255 | 268 | 274 |
| 1800 | (65) | 18 | 22 | 12 | (170) | 354 | 330 | 387 |
| 1857 | 73 | 38 | 37 | 22 | 178 | 785 | 583 | 709 |
| 1913 | 92 | 69 | 73 | 56 | 224 | 1,335 | 1,134 | 1,805 |
| 1927 | 103 | 74 | 77 | 69 | 251 | 1,453 | 1,213 | 2,225 |
| 1950 | 100ᵃ | 100 | 100 | 100 | 244 | 1,964 | 1,575 | 3,224 |
| 1980 | 156 | 186 | 297 | 185 | 380 | 3,660 | 4,675 | 5,960 |

ᵃ 1948 assumed equal to 1946.
Sources: Col. 1, 1860–1927, Goldsmith 1983, pp. 5, 69, 142/43; 1950–1980, Summers, Kravis, and Heston, 34ff; for 1980 extrapolated from 1977 on basis of *IFSYB*, 1983. Cols. 2 and 3, 1700–1927, Maddison 1983, 169ff; col. 2 rough estimate for 1600; 1950–1980, as for col. 1. Col. 4, 1700–1927, based on Lebergott, pp. 60–61; 1950–1980, as for col. 1. Cols. 5–8, 1950, Summers, Kravis, and Heston, pp. 34ff.

comparison starts from the detailed calculations of the real national product per head in 1950 in terms of 1970 U.S. prices and obtains estimates for earlier dates by applying to the 1950 values indices of real national product per head in each of the four countries, indices which use the prices of each country for a base period. The problems and risks of such comparisons are well known, but they remain valuable if used cautiously and checked against other evidence.

It then appears that in 1700 real national product per head in India at about $200 1970 dollars was about one-fourth below that of Great Britain, France, and the United States.[32,33]

Since real national product per head was certainly lower in most other European countries, the difference between India and Europe as a whole appears to have been small. In the case of Great Britain the comparison can be carried back to 1600 when its national product per head in U.S. 1970 prices is put at nearly $180, identical with that of Mughal India. A radical change, however, occurred in the following century and a half. While the average real income per head in India in 1857 was only slightly above that of 1700 – probably not above $200 in 1970 prices – the figures had now risen to about $580 for France, $785 for Great Britain, and $710 for the United States, and even for Italy to $490, or to between 2.5 and four times that of India. In the following century, the difference widened dramatically. By 1950 India's real national product per head had declined to about one-eighth of that of Great Britain and France and to less than one-twelfth of that of the United States. The decline continued until the present but at a much slower rate and with the result that in 1980 India's real national product per head stood at between 10 and 6 percent of that of the three Western countries compared to ratios of between 75 and 80 percent in 1700 and close to 100 in 1600.

By the same methods and with similar reservations, it is possible to compare India's real national product per head in 1600 with that of a number of less developed countries in 1950, countries that in 1600 probably had a considerably lower product per head than India. The approximately $180 in 1970 prices of India's national product in 1600 then compares with figures for 1950 of about $320 for Egypt, $350 for Syria, $380 for Morocco and Iran, $430 for Turkey, $450 for Iraq, $630 for Greece, and $650 for Mexico and Peru (Summers, Kravis, and Heston, pp. 34ff). The level of real national product of Mughal India in 1600 was thus below that of most less developed countries in the mid-twentieth century.

There are not enough data to compare Mughal India's real national product per head in 1600 with that of now still less developed countries at the same or a neighboring date. The only comparison that can be made is with Brazil whose real national product per head in 1850, when it probably was not much different of that of 1800, has been estimated at 30 percent of its 1950 level (Goldsmith 1986, pp. 22, 83, 224) of nearly $580 in 1970 prices (Summers, Kravis, and Heston, p. 36), that is, about $180. Thus India's real product per head in 1600 was about the same as Brazil's in 1850 or 1800.

A possibly more informative picture may be obtained by comparing a number of economically relevant features of the Indian and the English economy in 1600 and 1688 shown in Table 7-3. In aggregate terms, of course, Mughal India was much larger than Elizabethan England, approximately 20 times in terms of area and population, but population density was only moderately higher in India as probably were the birth and death rates. On the basis of exchange rates, however, wages and prices were much lower in India, but the purchasing power of the rupee was much higher than its exchange rate. If productivity per man is assumed to have not differed greatly in 1600, as is suggested by the approximate equality of real product per head,

Table 7-3. *Comparison of the economy of Mughal India and England in the seventeenth century*

| | Year | India | England and Wales | India ÷ England |
|---|---|---|---|---|
| 1. Area (1000 km²) | 1600 | 2,500 | 150 | 16.7 |
| 2. Population ⎫ | 1600 | 110 | 4.3 | 25.6 |
| 3. (millions) ⎭ | 1688 | 125 | 5.7 | 21.9 |
| 4. Population ⎫ inhabitants | 1600 | 44 | 29 | 1.52 |
| 5. density ⎭ per km² | 1688 | 50 | 38 | 1.32 |
| 6. Gross national product ⎫ | 1600 | R 600 | £25.0 | 2.70[a] |
| 7. per year (million) ⎭ | 1688 | R1,000 | £55.4 | 1.50[a] |
| 8. Gross national product ⎫ | 1600 | R 5.5 | £ 5.8 | 0.11[a] |
| 9. per head ⎭ | 1688 | R 8.0 | £ 9.5 | 0.07[a] |
| 10. Unskilled wage ⎫ | 1600 | R .05 | d 8.0 | 0.17[a] |
| 11. per year ⎭ | 1688 | R .09 | d 13.0 | 0.14[a] |
| 12. Exchange ⎫ | 1600 | R 1.0 | d 27 | — |
| 13. rate ⎭ | 1688 | R 1.0 | d 20 | — |
| 14. Gold price, ⎫ | 1600 | R 1.39 | d 32 | 1.00 |
| 15. per grain ⎭ | 1688 | R (1.90) | d 32 | (1.19) |
| 16. Wheat price ⎫ | 1600 | R 1.20 | sh 8.20 | 0.33[a] |
| 17. per 100 kg ⎭ | 1688 | R 3.40 | sh 7.05 | 0.80[a] |
| 18. Government ⎫ | 1600 | 19.0 | — | — |
| 19. revenues ⎬ percent of | 1688 | 28.5 | 16.8 | 1.70 |
| 20. Land ⎬ national | 1600 | 17.2 | — | — |
| 21. tax ⎭ product | 1688 | 26.0 | 5.8 | 4.48 |
| 22. Interest ⎫ Percent | 1600⎫ | 18 | <10 | >1.80 |
| 23. Rate ⎭ | 1688⎭ | | 5 | 3.60 |
| 24. Prices ⎫ 1688 | | — | 1.13 | — |
| 25. Wages ⎭ 1600 | | 1.80 | 1.63 | 1.10 |

[a] Using exchange rates of 27 d in 1600 and 20 d in 1688; use of purchasing power parity rates would greatly increase the ratios for lines 6 to 11 at least tripling them.
*Sources:* For India: rows 1, 2, 6, 10, and 12 – Cf. text; rows, 3 and 7 – rough estimates; row 11 – based on increase between 1616 and 1690—93 (Habib 1982a, p. 379); row 12 – e.g., Mukherjee, pp. 29–30; rows 14 and 15 – Habib 1961, pp. 15–16; rows 16 and 17 – Habib 1963, p. 83, value for 1688 is average for 1670 and 1702; rows 18 to 21 – land tax revenue estimated at 80 percent of assessed value (Habib 1963, pp. 399–400), rough estimate for other taxes; rows 22 and 23 – *hundi* rate (Pelsaert, p. 33); row 24 – food grains, based on Habib 1982a, pp. 372–3; row 25 – derived from rows 10 and 11. For England and Wales: rows 1 to 3 – McEvedy and Jones, pp. 41, 43; row 6 – 1600 rough estimate, based in part on movements in prices and wages (Phelps-Brown and Hopkins); row 7 – 1688 Lindert and Williamson, p. 393; rows 10 and 11 – Phelps-Brown and Hopkins, p. 11; rows 12 and 13 – as for rows 12 and 13; rows 14 and 15 – based on 7.3 g gold per pound sterling; rows 16 and 17 – Winchester college; 100 liters (Mitchell and Deane, p. 479); rows 19 and 21 – for government revenue Mitchell and Deane, p. 286; for national product, Lindert and Williamson, p. 393; row 21 includes other assessed taxes; row 22 – legal limit for private loans (Homer, p. 131); row 23 – midpoint of range for good commercial loans (Homer, p. 131); row 24 – Phelps-Brown and Hopkins, p. 28, price of unit of consumables; row 25 – derived from rows 10 and 11.

the rupee's purchasing power would have been about six times its exchange value, which is about twice as large a difference as exists now (Kravis, Heston, and Summers, p. 342).

The relationships changed considerably during the seventeenth century. Population grew somewhat more rapidly in England as probably did real national product per head. On the other hand wages and particularly prices increased more in India, and the exchange value of the rupee declined by about one-fourth.

Differences were large and increased in two financially important measures. The share of government revenues in national product was substantially higher in India, and the difference would be even larger than that shown in Table 7-3 if the Indian ratio included the exactions of the tax collectors. In that case the Indian ratio at the end of the seventeenth century with well over one-third would be at least twice as high as that in England. Because of the great difference in the structure of taxation, the difference would be even larger for the land tax, about one-third of national product in India (including collectors' take) against only 6 percent in England. Finally interest rates were much higher in India than in England, and the difference widened during the seventeeenth century.

## 3    Income distribution

Because of the peculiarity of the Mughal economy that most of the armed forces (other than the rural gendarmerie kept by the zamindars) were maintained and paid not by the central government but by a small number of nobles (mansabdars) out of the revenues of agricultural lands (jagirs) assigned to them by the emperor, a distinction must be made between the distribution of gross income and of net income after the mansabdars' or zamindars' expenditures on their troops.

As the total of the land tax revenue accrued to the emperor and the mansabdars, their total income in 1595–96 would have been equal to about R 130 million in terms of the assessed value of the tax and to fully R 100 million in that of the actual collections. The latter amount is equal to about one-sixth of national product. Both the emperor and the nobles are likely to have had some other incomes, but they are likely to have been small in comparison to the income from the land tax. The share of the nobles in total assessed land tax revenue has been estimated at 82 percent (Moosvi 1980, p. 340), the remaining 18 percent supposedly representing the emperor's share derived from the tax on his own lands. If it is assumed that the shortfall of actually collected, behind assessed, tax revenues was uniformly about one-fifth for all recipients, the total would be slightly above R 100 million divided between about R 20 million for the emperor and about R 85 million for the nearly 1,700 mansabdars.[34]

The sum of fully R 100 million cannot be regarded as the aggregate gross income of the nearly 1,700 highest income recipients in the empire since a substantial number of commoners, particularly many zamindars and some merchants and professionals, must have had incomes well above the income of the majority of the mansabdars.[35] The share of the 1,700 largest income recipients must therefore have been about 16 percent but by how much it is impossible to say. The concentration of incomes indicated in Table 7-4 must therefore be regarded as the minimum.

It then appears that the emperor and the 122 top ranking nobles – something like $6 \cdot 10^{-6}$ of all 22 million households – received on a gross basis nearly one-eighth of total national product and that their total average gross income was slightly above R 600,000, or the annual wage of about 40,000 unskilled workers (for the 122 nobles alone about R 450,000, or fully 30,000 annual wages). For the nobles the cost of the armed forces they were required to maintain apparently absorbed about three-fourths of their gross income. The net income of the 122 top nobles, however, still came to fully 2 percent of national product and averaged about R 110,000, or the annual wage of over 7,000 laborers. If it is assumed that the ratio was the same for the emperor, who also maintained a large military establishment, the net income of the 122 top income recipients in national product would have been on the order of 3 percent. On the same assumptions the share of the net income of the emperor and all nobles would have approximated 4 percent.

In addition, concentration of income was extreme within the group of 1,672 mansabdars and the emperor. The emperor alone accounted for over one-sixth of the total net income of the group – about the same as the share of Augustus in the income of the 600 senators – (Goldsmith 1984, p. 277) while the 25 mansabdars with the highest gross income, 1.5 percent of their number, received nearly two-fifths of the total net income of the group.[36]

How does this concentration of income in Mughal India compare with that in other countries or in modern India? If a measure of concentration of incomes over their entire range is wanted, in the form of, for example, a Lorenz curve or a Gini index, the question cannot be answered. For the very top of the income pyramid, however, a comparison is possible with a few other countries.

In the Mughal Empire around 1600 the share of the net income of

Table 7-4. Gross and net income of emperor and nobles in Mughal India ca. A.D. 1600

| Rank group | Contingent[a] | Number | Aggregate expenditures (million rupees) | | | | | Expenditures per mansabdar (R 1,000) | Percent of national product[d] | |
| | | | Zat[b] | Animals and carts | Salaries[c] | Total | Share (%) | | Col. 6 | Col. 8 |
|---|---|---|---|---|---|---|---|---|---|---|
| I | 5,000 | 12 | 5.1 | 1.8 | 13.1 | 20.0 | 18.5 | 1667 | 3.1 | 0.256 |
| II | 2,500–5,000 | 13 | 2.8 | 1.1 | 21.5[f] | 25.4[f] | 23.5 | 1954[f] | 3.9[f] | 0.307[f] |
| III | 500–2,500 | 97 | 5.8 | 2.5 | 2.6 | 10.9 | 10.1 | 112 | 1.7 | 0.017 |
| IV | 100–500 | 465[e] | 4.6 | 2.1 | 14.1 | 20.8 | 19.3 | 45 | 3.2 | 0.007 |
| V | 10–100 | 1,084 | 2.5 | 1.8 | 7.3 | 11.6 | 10.7 | 11 | 1.8 | 0.002 |
| Mansabdars | 10+ | 1,671[e] | 20.7 | 9.3 | 58.7 | 88.7 | 82.1 | 53 | 13.6 | 0.008 |
| Emperor | | 1 | — | — | — | 19.3 | 17.9 | — | 3.0 | — |
| Total | | 1,672 | 20.7 | | | 108.0 | 100.0 | 65 | 16.6 | 0.010 |

[a] Number of horsemen supposed to be maintained and paid by mansabdars.
[b] Personal salary of mansabdars.
[c] Salaries of contingent, derived as difference between col. 5 and sum of cols. 1 and 2.
[d] Based on a national product of R 650 million.
[e] Derived from Moosvi (1980) pp. 333 and 335; on p. 340 the figures are given as 365 and 1571.
[f] These figures seem strange.
Source: of basic data: Moosvi 1980, pp. 333, 335, 340.

the top one-ten-thousandths of all families, that is, 2,200 of them, was probably on the order of 5 percent of national product and practically the same in total personal income. In the Roman Empire at the death of Augustus in A.D. 14 the share of the same fraction of all families, that is, 1,400 of them, may be put at somewhat above one percent (Goldsmith 1984, p. 285). In England in 1688 the comparable share of the top 136 families (temporal lords) was slightly above 2 percent.[37] By 1979–80 the same ratio for the top 1,750 families had declined sharply to below 0.2 percent on a gross and to as little as 0.08 percent on a net (after tax) basis (U.S. Bureau of Commerce 1983, Table 15.2 and p. 265). In the United States in 1979 the income of the top 6,000 income recipients amounted to fully 0.40 percent on a gross and to nearly 0.25 percent on a net basis (U.S. Bureau of Commerce 1982–83, p. 256). In these developed economies the share of the top one-ten-thousandth of all households in national product thus is less than one-tenth as large as it had been in Mughal India.

In present-day India the top 12,500 taxpayers, or the top one-ten-thousandth of all families, had in 1977–78 an assessed income of about R 2,000 million before and R 750 million after income tax, equal to nearly 0.3 percent and 0.1 percent of total personal disposable income.[38] These ratios are far below those of Akbar's India of fully 5 percent of total net (spendable) personal income – about 50 times the present share. A more restricted group, the 275 taxpayers with an assessed income of over R 500,000, the top group for which the figures have been published, had in 1977–78 an assessed income of R 464 million before and of only R 76 million after income tax, or about 0.01 percent of total personal disposable income. The net income (after expenditures on military retainers) of the group comprising the same proportion of all families, numbering 45, including the emperor in Akbar's days, accounted for fully 3 percent of total freely spendable personal income, a share more than 300 times as high as that in contemporary India.

*Tempora mutantur*

All these estimates involve a substantial margin of uncertainty, but even so they leave little doubt that the share of the small very top of the income pyramid in Mughal India was the highest known to man with the possible exception of a few theocracies such as pharonic Egypt and ancient Mesopotamia.

A second indicator of the inequality of income is the ratio between the average annual income of the top income group and the average family income for the entire country and the annual wage of an unskilled laborer. In Akbar's empire the average net income of the mansabdars and the emperor, $0.75 \times 10^{-4}$ of all families, of over R 12,000 was more than 600 times as large as that of R 20 of the average family and equal to the annual wage of R 15 of about 800 common laborers. In Augustan Rome the 600 senators, about $0.4 \times 10^{-4}$ of all families, have been estimated to have had an average income of about HS 150,000, or about 100 average family incomes and the annual wages of about 170 unskilled workers (Goldsmith 1984, p. 277). In England and Wales in 1688 the average annual income of the 200 temporal lords, $1.5 \times 10^{-5}$ of all families, of £6,060 per year was equal to that of 155 average families (Lindert and Williamson, p. 393), and that of about 360 common laborers.[39] In present-day Great Britain, on the other hand, the average annual income of the 2,000 people with a taxable income of over £100,000 in 1979–80, $7.7 \times 10^{-4}$ of all families, of £157,000 before and £74,000 after income tax equaled the average disposable personal income of about 15 families on a gross and of 8 families on a net basis and the wages of about 40 unskilled workers.[40] In the United States the average income of the 3,570 taxpayers reporting in 1979 an income of more than $1 million – $0.6 \times 10^{-4}$ of all families – of $2.25 million before and $1.50 million after income tax equaled the average income of about 70 families before and of about 50 families after taxes and the wages of about 130 unskilled workers.[41]

In present-day India, finally, the 7,000 top income recipients with an income of over R 100,000, or $0.6 \times 10^{-4}$ of all families, had an average gross income of R 220,000 and a net income of R 76,000, equal on a net basis to that of about 14 families and to the wage of about 40 common laborers (U.S. Bureau of Commerce 1979, p. 448; International Monetary Fund 1983, p. 275).

We thus get the following relations of the average net income after income tax of the top group to that of the wage of common laborers.

| | | |
|---|---|---|
| India,1600 | 1672 persons = $0.8 \times 10^{-4}$ families | : 800 |
| 1977–78 | 7000 persons = $0.6 \times 10^{-4}$ families | : 40 |
| Rome,14 | 600 persons = $0.4 \times 10^{-4}$ families | : 170 |
| England,1688 | 200 persons = $1.5 \times 10^{-5}$ families | : 360 |
| 1979–80 | 2000 persons = $0.8 \times 10^{-4}$ families | : 40 |
| United States,1979 | 3570 persons = $0.6 \times 10^{-4}$ families | : 130 |

Mughal India again leads the list.

## 4 The monetary system

Like many other economic features of his empire, Akbar also reorganized its monetary system.[42] The rupee of about 11 g of silver of about 96 percent fineness became the standard coin and the unit in which accounts were kept. Because it was too large for most everyday transactions – it was equal to about 20 days' wages of a common laborer – it was supplemented by silver coins of one-half, one-fourth, one-eighth, one-tenth, and one-twentieth rupee.[43] Even the smallest of these still represented a day's wage. The most common coins, therefore, were the dam of about 21 g of copper worth one-fortieth of a rupee and the pieces of 2, one-half, one-fourth, one-eighth, and one-tenth dam.[44] Even these coins were not sufficient for small change or for wage payments. In many parts of the country cowrie shells, imported mainly from the Maldive Islands, were used. About 3,500 of them were worth one rupee or 90 a dam.[45] Mohurs of about 11 g of pure gold were the most important gold coins and were used mainly for thesaurization,[46] which is understandable as they were equal to about half a year's income of the average family. There were also numerous other gold coins, larger and smaller than a mohur,[47] most of which were probably rarely seen, the large ones being struck only for special occasions and kept mostly in the emperor's treasure.[48]

There was no legally fixed relation between the gold, silver, and copper coins, and of course the cowries, but during the reign of Akbar 40 dams were customarily accepted for one rupee. The relations rather fluctuated as a result of supply and demand conditions. At the end of the sixteenth century a mohur was worth about 9 rupees, but its price rose during the following century to about R 15 in the 1660s. The rupee depreciated even more with respect to the copper coins, its value falling below 20 dams from the 1660s on (Habib, 1982, pp. 367, 370). A peculiarity of the system was that one-year-old rupees were taken by the treasury only at a discount of 3 percent against *sikka* (fresh) rupees, and one of 5 percent for two-year-old rupees, older coins being valued by weight. This was apparently done to encourage recoinage to the mint's profit.

The mint was ready to issue new coins for any of the three monetary metals brought in by the public – in general the *shroffs* – charging a seignorage of 5 percent and 0.6 percent for the cost of minting, but did not redeem coins in bullion. Mohurs were coined during the latter part of Abkar's reign only in four mints, silver coins by over a dozen and copper coins in about 40 provincial mints (Blochmann, p. 31). Coinage was an imperial privilege, though coins issued in territories more recently incorporated into the empire continued in circulation valued by weight, as apparently did a limited amount of coins issued by semi-independent rulers within the empire. Under such a system there was not room for monetary policy except changing the weight or fineness of coins.

The gold bullion offered to the mint came partly from rivers and mines situated in India, the latter during Akbar's reign still outside the empire's boundaries, and partly from abroad. Silver bullion was partly provided by Indian mines and partly by imports as a result of customarily active balance of commodity trade, largely by circuitous routes from Peru (Habib 1982, p. 363). There is no evidence of copper imports, but most or all cowries were imported. In good mercantilist fashion exports of gold and silver were prohibited.

There are unfortunately no statistics of the economically most important facts, the volume of minting and of coins in circulation. The only relevant figure is the estimate by a contemporary British visitor that money in circulation around 1610 was no less than R 250 million (Hawkins, cited in Habib 1960, p. 1), probably not including the R 100 million of silver coins in Akbar's treasure, implying an income velocity of circulation of about 2.5 for total national product and one of about 5 for monetized product. These values are much lower than the velocity of about 10 in 1860 (Goldsmith 1983, p. 13) in relation to total national product, possibly because a larger proportion of the coins, particularly the dominating rupee coins, were hoarded (Smith, p. 411). Nevertheless the figure of R 250 million appears to be on the high side.

After silver coins had almost disappeared from circulation as a result of debasement, the volume of currency in circulation has been estimated to have almost tripled between the 1590s and 1640, most of the increase occurring before 1610.[49,50] As the price level did not triple during the period,[51] the difference would have to have been absorbed partly by an increase in the income velocity of circulation, partly by slow growth of real national product, and partly by an increase in the degree of monetization.[52]

At the beginning of the seventeenth century the rupee was traded at a rate of 27 pence.[53] This was equivalent to 0.72 g of gold or at the Indian rate of gold to silver of 9 : 1 to 6.5 g of silver while a rupee contained about 11 g of silver. It is not clear how this divergence could persist over decades as it was much in excess of transportation, insurance costs, and seignorage. Later in the century when the exchange rate had risen to 33 pence while 0.72 g of gold in England at the now prevailing Indian gold–silver ratio of 15 : 1 were equal to 10.8 g of silver, the difference had almost disappeared. In view of the small volume of Indian trade with Europe at the beginning of the seventeenth century the market must have been very narrow.

## 5    Financial instruments

In the absence of government debt, corporate securities and mortgages, with the exception of some urban home mortgages and some secured by zamindars' revenues, the only two types of financial instruments in common use were open trade credit and hundis.

Hundis were similar to European bills of exchange, usually were payable after two months, involved a small charge (one percent), and could be transferred and discounted. Information on rates of discount, which apparently varied according to places of issue and payment and included insurance of the goods underlying the hundi, is sketchy. They probably were somewhat above the rates on commercial credit, which were in the neighborhood of 1.5 percent per month.[54] Hundis were widely used both for financing domestic trade and for the interlocal transfer of funds.

In the seventeenth century a new instrument developed, the bottomry loan, a combination of loan and maritime insurance, which carried high and varying rates up to 60 percent (Raychaudhuri 1982, p. 374).

## 6    Financial organizations

By far the most common, and possibly the most important, organizations were the *shroffs* found in all towns and in most villages,[55] which combined their original activity of assaying and money changing with moneylending to the peasants. Less numerous but of larger size were the urban establishments that made loans to artisans, merchants, nobles, and occasionally even to the treasury, arranged interlocal transfer of funds, and dealt in hundis. Some of them, one may presume the larger and better known ones, also accepted demand and time deposits – in mid-seventeenth century in one instance at a monthly rate of 5–8 percent – and may therefore be regarded as bankers of the modern type.[56] The very large bankers, who played an important role in financing the imperial government, developed only after the middle of the seventeenth century (Leonhard, passim).

The establishments were generally operated by one individual, possibly aided by members of his family. Most of these individuals were Hindus belonging to a few castes that specialized in these activities and operated at only one location. There existed, however, extensive interlocal correspondent relationships among the different types of firms. There is no quantified information on these matters.

## 7 Financing agriculture

The use of credit in agriculture was determined by the character of ownership and cultivation of land and the resulting demand for and supply of agricultural credit. Theoretically, the emperor was the owner of all land, and the occupiers only something like tenants at will. As a result possibilities of sale or mortgaging of land hardly existed. Any credit to agriculturalists therefore had to be unsecured or secured by other assets.

The low level of investment in improvements limited the demand for medium and long-term credit. The modest improvements made by the emperor, nobles, zamindars, and the better-off peasants were financed by their own funds. The government, however, in case of need made loans for the acquisition of seed and cattle and for developing additional acreage and organizing new villages (*takavi*) (Habib 1964, p. 397), though the main incentives appear to have been tax reductions or temporally limited exemptions. There undoubtedly was some demand for short-term credit to buy seeds and similar purposes and to carry crop inventories. The main demand for credit by the peasants, however, was for consumptive purposes – as it has been in India well into the nineteenth and even the twentieth centuries (Goldsmith 1983, pp. 43ff, 125ff, 213ff) – such as for food and seed grain in case of crop failures and other calamities, for the payment of taxes and even more importantly for the relatively large expenditures required by custom for marriages and funerals. Some credit was also required on the occasion of sales or mortgaging of zamindari rights, but the amounts involved cannot have been large compared to the aggregate income of the zamindars.

Whatever demands for credit there arose were apparently met within the village or in the nearest town. The main groups of lenders were the local moneylenders, the village headmen, the wealthier peasants, some merchants, and the zamindars. The effective interest rates were undoubtedly very high, though in many if not most cases interest was not paid in cash but in produce or labor services and sometimes by sale of the debtor's children.[57]

There is no possibility of estimating the volume of agricultural credit. For the mid-1890s agricultural indebtedness has been put at between one-fourth and one-third of agricultural income (Goldsmith 1983, p.

44). The ratio may not have been much different, though probably somewhat lower, in Mughal India since the methods of agricultural finance changed substantially only in the course of the twentieth century. On that basis agricultural debt may have been in the order of R 50 million, or on the average about R 3 per peasant household, though certainly very unevenly distributed among them and in many cases constituted an extremely heavy burden on the borrowers.

## 8    Financing the nonagricultural private economy

As in the case of agriculture very little credit was used to finance long-term investments and moderate amounts for working capital in manufacturing, but most credits were employed in financing consumption. The difference, however, was the existence of a well-developed system of credit in domestic interlocal trade.

Urban artisans used credit for materials supplied to them by merchants under the putting-out system, particularly in some textile trades, and for working capital borrowed from moneylenders. The largest specialized workshops of the emperor and of some nobles (karkhanas) (cf. e.g., Moreland 1920, p. 174; Raychaudhuri 1982, p. 287), which produced luxury goods for their own use or for gifts but not for sale, did not use credit.

In domestic trade credit was used for interlocal commerce rather than for the activities of the bazaars that existed in all towns and many villages and dealt mostly in agricultural commodities and textiles produced locally or in the neighborhood except possibly in areas close to large cities. The volume of interlocal trade is supposed to have been substantial and to have increased considerably during the seventeenth century,[58] though quantitative information is entirely lacking. Thus trade should have required a substantial volume of credit extended by the suppliers as well as by moneylenders and by nobles and made extensive use of hundis.[59] It is, however, probable that most of the funds required in interlocal trade were provided by the merchants themselves. Since interlocal trade can have handled only a moderate proportion of total agricultural output – certainly well below the proportion corresponding to the output sold by the peasants primarily to obtain cash to pay their land tax – though a larger one of manufactures, which, however, constituted only a fraction of urban output because of the high share of services, the volume of interlocal trade cannot well have exceeded R 100 million.[60] The volume of credit employed must have been well below that level, partly because some of the most important customers, the government and the nobles, generally did not require credit, and probably was not above that of agricultural credit though its nature was different – commercial and regular rather than necessitous and sporadic.

Interest rate on commercial credit varied greatly and the reasons for the reported wide differences are not clear. The reported rates refer to a period well after Akbar's death, specifically to dates between 1624 and 1665 and range from 0.5 percent to 1.25 percent per month (disregarding one reported upper boundary of 2.5 percent) (Habib 1964, pp. 402–03). The unweighted average of the 35 rates quoted is 0.76 percent per month. One-half of these rates refer to Surat and the other half to Ahmadabad and Agra and most of them to transactions of British merchants. They should probably be regarded as minimal for the country as a whole and for the late sixteenth century. The usual bazaar rate seems to have been one percent per month.

The volume of credit used in foreign trade must have been minimal until well into the seventeenth century because most transactions were on a cash basis, particularly in trade with the Near and Far East, if only because of the absence of the necessary financial instruments and because of the small volume of exports and imports, notwithstanding the colorful descriptions of its extent and variety (cf. e.g., Chaudhuri 1982). Thus the imports of the East India Company from India averaged only R 150,000 per year in 1601–10, or 0.025 percent of India's national product, and even in the 1620s had risen to only about R 700,000 per year.[61] Total commodity exports and imports in the early seventeenth century therefore are not likely to have exceeded R 1 million or about 0.2 percent of national product, though the ratios were higher for a few manufactures (fine textiles), and the volume of credit used in foreign trade was, of course, much smaller still.

The volume of consumption credit appears to have been substantial. The nobles frequently overspent their large incomes and had to borrow for shorter or longer periods from moneylenders. These loans must have been very risky as the political power of the higher ranking nobles made it difficult to enforce claims against them and the effective interest rate must have been high (Habib 1964, p. 407ff). In hardship cases nobles, however, could borrow from the treasury for up to 10 years and at the very modest rates of between 6 and 11 percent (Habib 1964, p. 409).

## 9      Financing the government

Reflecting the rapid expansion of the Mughal Empire during Akbar's reign – from less than 0.3 million km$^2$ to about 2.5 million km$^2$ and from about 30 million to 110 million inhabitants – the financial system of the government[62] at the emperor's death still showed substantial regional differences although reforms introduced in the mid-1580s had considerably reduced them, and it remained of great complexity. The system was characterized on the revenue side by the predominance of the land tax (more correctly a tax on crops) and on the expenditure side by military outlays and by the fact that the majority of land tax assessments were collected and most of the expenditures on troops were not paid by officials of the emperor but by nobles (mansabdars) who were allocated the revenues of specific pieces of land (jagirs) as sources of their income and by their revenue collectors, the zamindars.

The central government's financial administration was headed by the wazir, the highest official who reported directly to the emperor and was the head of the ministry of finance (*diwan-i-kul*), which had a substantial staff of officials and clerks in the capital. The ministry had an office in each of the 12 and later 15 provinces, which in turn controlled the revenue offices in every one of the 3,000 districts (*pargana* or *mahal*). These district offices, each of which on the average was in charge of fully 1,500 villages with more than 5,000 farm families spread over an area of over 800 km² were headed by an amil, who was assisted by officers in charge of revenue collection (*chaudhuri*), records (*quanungo*), and accounts (*patwari*) and their staffs (cf. organization chart in Schwartzberg, p. 45), an extensive and apparently fairly efficient bureaucratic organization that constituted the backbone of the empire's economic administration (Habib 1963, p. 294). The senior officers received a fixed cash salary and/or some tax-exempt land. The first sentence of the *Ain* demands that the revenue collector "should be a friend of the agriculturalist" (Blochmann, p. 43); in fact the relationship is likely to have been rather an adversary one with the advantages on the side of the revenue authorities.

The central financial administration fixed the methods of assessment, the rates of tax, and the modalities of collection throughout the empire, which were applied by a combination of its own district offices, the zamindars, and the village headmen with more or less uniformity, efficiency, and harshness. Nonpayment of tax by the peasants or their village was regarded as rebellion and severely punished.

Close to one-half of the land tax was collected under what has been called the regulation system formulated in the 1580s, which applied to most of the *zabt* provinces of Multan, Lahore, Delhi, Agra, Awadh, and Allahabad (Moreland 1929, p. 110ff), an area within Akbar's original domain. Here the rates for each crop and land of different quality for units of area were fixed for long periods in terms of money, although abatements from the standard rates were granted in case of crop failure. The rates were in principle set at one-third of the crop but actually appear to have averaged somewhat higher. The tax could be paid in several installments. The system had the advantage that the peasant knew in advance his tax liability for different crops and could arrange his planting accordingly, but it left the risk and the chance of fluctuations in crop size and in commodity prices on him. On the other hand it assured the recipients of the tax, that is, the emperor and the nobles, of a fairly predictable income. The tax, though levied at flat rates, was regressive as it absorbed a higher proportion of the product exceeding subsistence requirements of the smaller peasant than of the larger peasant.

In the other provinces arrangements were less uniform. In particular in some of them assessments were based on average yields over the preceding 10 years or set as a percentage of the actual crops or on another basis. Here too payment in money was prevalent, but to some extent payment in kind was acceptable. The effective tax burden appears to have been in the order of at least two-fifths of gross product.

The assessed value of the land tax for the empire in 1595–96 is reported at R 130 million, up from R 91 million in 1580 and slightly below the R 146 million of 1605 (Habib 1963, p. 399), the increases mostly reflecting the continual extension of the empire. Actual tax collections fell somewhat short of assessments for the empire as a whole, apparently by about one-fifth (cf. footnote 19). For 1595–96 the actual land tax revenue should therefore have been between R 100 and 110 million. This would have been equal to nearly one-sixth of total national product, to nearly one-third of total rural income, and to about two-fifths of the peasants' gross product.

Approximately one-fifth of the total land tax revenue went to the emperor (see Table 7-4) on the basis of his own lands (*khalisa*), which were distributed throughout the realm, but are supposed to have been concentrated in more fertile and more easily accessible districts. The remaining four-fifths went, very unequally distributed (Section 3), to about 1,700 nobles on the basis of their jagirs, that is, the lands the revenue of which was granted to them by the emperor at his pleasure and discretion. The jagirs, which in general consisted of a number of noncontiguous pieces of land, were granted for short periods, usually for only about three years, apparently in order to prevent the development of a close association of the nobles with a given territory such as existed in medieval Europe and in the later caliphate. The short tenures obviously were an incentive for the holders to squeeze as much as possible out of their jagirs without consideration of the long-term effects of such policies and discouraged any investment in improvements. A system less likely to lead to an increase in agricultural productivity would be difficult to devise. Jagirs were not inherited, but it seems to have been not uncommon for the emperor to grant a noble's heirs other jagirs. The main obligation of the holders was the maintenance of a stipulated number of troops on foot, horse, and elephants, the ranks of the nobles being expressed by the number of troops they were supposed to keep, down from 10,000, a number which, however, was substantially above the number actually maintained.[63]

In most villages the collections of the land tax was in the hand of the zamindars who had the right – inheritable, salable, and even mortgageable – to charge the peasants for their service and/or were compensated for it by the allocation of tax-free land. In return they had to maintain foot soldiers and cavalrymen – the former in fact a part-time rural gendarmerie – which could be called upon by the emperor.[64,65]

Notwithstanding the crucial role of the zamindars in the financial structure of Mughal India, little is known about them, not even their number. They should have numbered well over 3,000, the number of revenue districts, and well below 200,000, a figure obtained by applying the average number of zamindars in seven revenue districts in Bengal in the late eighteenth century, namely, 70 (Cohn, Table II) – the only such figure that has been found – which is likely to have been far above the average for the empire during Akbar's reign. There are no data for a choice within this unhelpfully wide range except a consideration of the average net income per zamindar. Assuming, as discussed below, a total net income of all zamindars of at least R 10 million, a number of 3,000 would involve an average income of over R 3,000 while one of 200,000 would imply an average income of only 50. The first figure is unacceptably high as it would put a zamindar's average net income at about one-fourth that of a noble of which there were less than 1,700 in the empire (Table 7-4) while the second one is unacceptably low as it is equal to the average net income of only about five peasant families. If their number had been equal to the geometric average of the two extremes, that is, in the order of 25,000, their average net income would have been R 400 or equal to about 45 farm families' net income, a not entirely unreasonable figure. A figure in the order of 25,000 would mean that a zamindar collected the revenue of nearly 20 villages and that the average revenue district had about eight zamindars.

There is no direct evidence for zamindars' total or net aggregate income. Their expenditures on maintaining their troops, however, have been estimated at 16 percent of the yield of the land tax, and at "a pretty large amount relative . . . [to their] . . . net income" suggesting a net ratio of at least 10 percent and a gross ratio (Moosvi 1978, pp. 364–65) of over 25 percent of the land tax, that is, about R 10 million and R 25 million, respectively. These charges would have increased the total burden on the peasants of the land tax to about R 130 million, or one-half their gross income and to about one-half of national product.

Village headmen apparently received a compensation of 2.5 percent of the land tax either in cash or in the form of the allocation of tax-free land (Moosvi 1978, p. 360). This added a few million rupees to the peasants' burden.

For 14 provinces which accounted for well over nine-tenths of total assessed land tax, the tax averaged R 135 per km$^2$ of taxable land, about R 200 per village, and about R 5.5 per peasant family. There were, however, substantial differences in these averages among provinces, which can be followed in Table 7-5 – the data coming in general from the *Ain-i-Akbari*. The *Ain* provides similar information for most of the about 125 subprovinces (*sarkars*) and the about 3,000 revenue districts (*parganas*), but these do not seem to have been comprehensively collected or analyzed.

The assessed tax per village varied from about R 100 in Allahabad, Awadh, and Behar to about R 1,000 in Ajmer, Berar, and Gudjerat. Since there is no information on population by provinces, the variations of assessed land tax per village cannot be used to infer differences in tax per head. These differences were certainly smaller than those in tax per village, but by how much it is impossible to say.

The more relevant figure of tax per unit of assessed area showed much smaller though still substantial interprovincial differences. Compared to an average of about R 130 per km$^2$, it was as low as about R 70 in Awadh and Malwa, between about R 100 and 110 in five provinces (Ajmer, Allahabad, Bengal, Bihar, and Delhi), and around R 130 in Agra and Gudjerat – these seven provinces with an average of about R 100 to R 130 accounted for about one-half of the total assessed revenue – but reached slightly over R 200 in Behar and Lahore, R 260 in Multan, and nearly R 350 in Berar. Some of these differences reflect differences in the quality of the soil and the avail-

Table 7-5. *Land tax assessments in Mughal India, ca. 1600*

| | Assessed area (1,000 km²) (1) | Total (million rupee) (2) | Per km² (3) | Per village (4) | Tax exempt percent (5) |
|---|---|---|---|---|---|
| 1. Agra | 106 | 13.7 | 129 | 454 | 3.9 |
| 2. Ajmer | 65 | 7.2 | 111 | 911 | 0.8 |
| 3. Allahabad | 49 | 5.3 | 108 | 111 | 5.1 |
| 4. Awadh | 71 | 5.1 | 72 | 97 | 3.3 |
| 5. Behar | 49 | 5.6 | 114 | 101 | 2.8 |
| 6. Bengal | (59) | 6.4 | 108 | 57 | — |
| 7. Delhi | 149 | 15.0 | 101 | 333 | 3.9 |
| 8. Gudjerat | 80 | 10.9 | 136 | 1048 | 1.7 |
| 9. Lahore | 66 | 13.9 | 211 | 500 | 1.7 |
| 10. Kabul | (4) | 0.0 | — | 300 | 0.2 |
| 11. Malwa | 83 | 6.0 | 72 | 321 | 0.5 |
| 12. Multan | 21 | 3.8 | 181 | 409 | 2.6 |
| Twelve old provinces | 802 | 94.9 | 118 | 226 | — |
| 13. Berar | 48 | 16.7 | 348 | 982 | 7.6 |
| 14. Kendesh | 47 | 7.6 | 162 | 120 | — |
| 15. Orissa | (20) | 4.3 | (215) | (500) | — |

*Sources:* Col. 1 – Habib 1963, p. 4, applying average size of measured villages to total number of measured and unmeasured villages. The ratio is 1.43 for the 12 old provinces but varies greatly from hardly over 1.00 for Agra, Delhi, and Lahore to about 72 for Bengal. The figures refer to the middle of the seventeenth century when the number of villages in the old provinces should have been higher than in 1595–96 to which cols. 2 and 5 refer. The figures shown in col. 4 should therefore be regarded as minima. Col. 2 – Habib 1982b, Table 1. Col. 5 – Antonova, p. 107. The figures refer to the percent of land tax that would have been assessed on tax exempt (*suyurgal*) land.

ability of irrigation, but a substantial part of the range in the assessed tax per square kilometer remains to be explained, particularly for Berar and Multan, in part possibly by differences in the efficiency of tax administration and collection and by historical accidents.[66]

Little is known, and almost nothing in quantitative terms, about other regular revenues of the central government, both rural and urban. These included customs duties levied in principle at rates of 2.5 or 5 percent, though actually apparently sometimes higher,[67] some duties on internal trade and on urban artisans' activities. The total revenue from these levies undoubtedly was quite small in comparison to the yield of the land tax. The burden of taxation thus was sharply lower on the urban population and on the rural nonagricultural workers than on the peasants. It probably did not exceed 5 percent of the former's income and yielded possibly R 10 million, but any estimate is hazardous in view of the absence of contemporary data and of studies by modern economic historians comparable to those available on rural taxation.

The emperor had in addition a substantial income from the escheat of all estates left by nobles, or by such wealthy commoners as he chose, except wives' jewelry and what assets the decedent might have managed to hide, although the emperor might grant a small proportion to the heirs.[68] The discouraging effects on saving and investment of this policy are obvious. It was also the custom, not lightly disregarded by his nobles, to offer the emperor substantial gifts on many occasions, notably on his birthday. These two types of revenues probably constituted a substantial proportion of the emperor's total net income, and it was these rather than saving out of tax revenues that permitted Akbar to leave a large treasure, even if it was considerably smaller than the reported nearly R 350 million (de Laet, 107), or more than half a year's national product, or about 15 years' regular gross income of the emperor.

In comparison to the information on the revenues of the Mughal Empire, very little is known in detail about its expenditures except that, since there was no government borrowing and apparently no substantial saving out of regular revenues, these must have been approximately equal to revenue. It is also known that the bulk of expenditures were for the armed forces, for the emperor, as well as for the nobles and for the zamindars.

In the case of the nobles it has been estimated that about three-fifths of the income they received in the form of the land tax of their jagirs were used to pay their armed retainers and for the maintenance of their forces, a total of about R 60 million (Table 7-4). It is likely that the share of military expenditures in the emperor's regular revenues was not much lower adding another R 15 million. Thus about three-fourths of the land tax revenue and over two-thirds of the total regular revenues of the government were spent on the maintenance of the armed forces even after Akbar's major campaign had ended.

After maintaining their troops the mansabdars are estimated to have had nearly R 21 million to spend, or over R 12,000 for each of them, equal to about 800 common laborers' wages. There are no statistics about how they spent these large sums, but contemporary reports leave no doubt that almost all went for luxury expenditures, particularly on harems, stables, jewelry, and thesaurization insofar as it could be done in ways escaping the attention of the emperor's revenue agents after their deaths, and for gifts to the emperor. Expenditures on land improvements, except on gardens and orchards and for other productive purposes, were minimal.

The emperor's expenditures out of his regular revenue not absorbed by his armed force – in 1647 nearly 90,000 men (Raychaudhuri 1982, p. 179) – are unlikely to have exceeded R 10 million. Most of them went to maintain his very large court, including a harem of supposedly 5,000 ladies (Blochmann, p.44) and many times as many of their servants and guardians. A contemporary report according to which the daily expenditures in the 1630s in the capital amounted to R 30,000 for the harem and R 50,000 for maintaining the imperial court and stables (de Laet, pp. 110–11)[69] is obviously exaggerated as it implies annual expenditures on the order of nearly R 30 million, but the relation between the two main items of nonmilitary expenditures is interesting.

Very little is known about the finances of provincial and local governments, particularly the nature and size of their revenues (cf. Moreland 1923, pp. 283–96). They were very numerous, considerably interferred with internal trade, and resisted the attempts of several administrations to abolish or reduce them. There is no possibility of evaluating their yield, but it was certainly not negligible, though fairly small in relation to the revenues of the imperial government, and therefore added only fractionally to the burden of the latter of well over one-fifth of national product, excluding and fully one-fourth including the zamindars' charges on the peasants.

## CHAPTER 8

# The financial system
# of early Tokugawa Japan

In any analysis of the economy of early Tokugawa Japan[1,2] under its first three shoguns (Ieyasu, Hidetada, and Iemitsu) from 1600 to 1651, and hence of its financial structure, half a dozen characteristics of Japan during that period, and indeed until the mid-nineteenth century, must be kept in mind.[3]

1. By seventeenth century standards Japan was in terms of population a large and rapidly growing country. With about 20 million inhabitants at the beginning and about 30 million at the end of the century, Japan was larger than any European country – it had, for example, slightly more inhabitants than France and about five times the population of England and Wales – and outside of Europe was surpassed only by the Ming Empire of China and by Mughal India.

2. Tokugawa Japan was a more highly centralized and controlled country than any in Europe and from 1615 on enjoyed external and internal peace.

3. The description of Japan's political structure as *bakuhan* indicates the coexistence of territories directly owned by the shogun, which covered about one-fourth of the country, with about 250 fiefs awarded by the shogun to vassals (daimyo) who had substantial freedom of action within their fiefs, but in fact were not much more than governors serving at the shogun's pleasure and under his orders.

4. Tokugawa Japan was a hierarchical society characterized by the continued existence – a relic from earlier centuries – of a large warrior caste (samurai or bushi), which is estimated to have accounted with their families and servants for between 5 and nearly 10 percent of the total population, but soon lost their original function.

5. By seventeenth century standards Japan was not a poor coun-

try. Though the primary occupation of over four-fifths of the population was agriculture, in particular the cultivation of rice, most farmers supplemented their farm income, often to a substantial extent, by other activities, mainly in handicrafts, trade and, transportation.

6. Urbanization increased rapidly during the seventeenth century. For places with over 3,000 inhabitants the share in total population has been estimated to have doubled from about one-twelfth to one-sixth.

7. From the 1640s on to the mid-nineteenth century Japan was practically isolated from the rest of the world as a result of a conscious policy. Trade and other economic contacts with foreign countries were minimal and strictly controlled.

8. The degree of monetization of the economy was still low at the beginning of the seventeenth century, particularly in the rural areas, and rice continued to play an important role as a sort of money of account, but monetization made rapid progress during the century, particularly its second half.[4]

# 1     Population

## Size and growth

The population of Japan, ethnically homogeneous, has been estimated in 1600 at between 18 million and 22 million, then larger than that of any European country, even though only about one-fifth as large as that of the Chinese empire. It was at that time in the midst of a phase of fairly rapid growth for premodern periods, averaging nearly 0.3 percent per year during the sixteenth and seventeenth century, a movement that came to a halt in the eighteenth century.[5] In the absence of international migrations this increase was the result of a small excess of birth- over death-rates, both relatively low at approximately 2 percent – very similar to those of 1872–75 (Ishii; Bank of Japan, p. 17) – the result of widespread population control, particularly female infanticide evident in a male–female ratio of about 1.3, a mean age at first marriage of 19 to 25 years, an average number of children born per family of only 3.5, and a share of population of working age of over 60 percent. Life expectancy was in the forties, the same as in the late nineteenth century (Hanley and Yamamura 1955, pp. 323–4; Saito, p. 34).

For the entire territory of Japan density was about 57 per km$^2$ in the early seventeenth century, but since probably only about one-tenth

Table 8-1. *Regional distribution of population and urbanization in Japan, early eighteenth century*

| Region | Total (1) | Urban population (millions) Total (2) | Large[a] cities (3) | Small[b] cities (4) | Places Large[a] cities (5) | Small[b] cities (6) | Urbanization (%) Total (7) | Large[a] cities (8) | Small[b] cities (9) |
|---|---|---|---|---|---|---|---|---|---|
| Tohoku | 3.5 | 0.46 | 0.19 | 0.27 | 4 | 76 | 13.1 | 5.4 | 7.7 |
| Chubu | 7.0 | 0.98 | 0.28 | 0.70 | 4 | 99 | 14.0 | 4.0 | 10.0 |
| Kanto | 6.0c | 1.30 | 0.80d | 0.50d | — | | 21.7 | 13.3 | 8.3 |
| Kinki | 5.5 | 1.33e | 0.88e | 0.45 | 5 | 132 | 24.2 | 16.0 | 8.2 |
| Chigoku | 3.5 | 0.48 | 0.18 | 0.30 | 4 | 97 | 13.7 | 5.1 | 8.6 |
| Shikoku | 2.0 | 0.28 | 0.07 | 0.21 | 2 | 65 | 14.0 | 3.5 | 10.5 |
| Kyushu | 4.0 | 0.58 | 0.22 | 0.35 | 4 | 124 | 14.5 | 5.5 | 9.0 |
| Japan | 31.5 | 5.20 | 2.62 | 2.58 | 23f | 593f | 16.5 | 9.0 | 7.5 |

[a] 30,000 and over.
[b] Below 30,000 (excluding about 1,200 class 7 cities with average population of well under 1,000 inhabitants).
[c] Based on figure for East Japan (Rozman, p. 272).
[d] Rough division of urban total.
[e] Includes Osaka.
[f] Excluding Kanto.

*Source:* Rozman, pp. 252, 257, based except in col. 5 and 6, on rounded figures for classes of cities.

of it was cultivated[6] the more relevant density of rural areas was much higher, for the cultivated area on the average possibly on the order of 500 per km², then certainly one of the highest in the world.

The two most densely populated regions were the Kanto plain with Edo (Tokyo) and the Kinsai plain around Osaka. In the early eighteenth century, it has been estimated that the country's population was about equally divided between the eastern and the western part of the country as shown in Table 8-1. In 1600 when total population was about one-third smaller the distribution probably was similar, though possibly slightly more favorable to the western part. About four-fifths of the population lived on the main island (Honshu).

### Occupational distribution

The primary occupation of the great majority of the population was agriculture, chiefly rice cultivation, probably for well over four-fifths of the total.[7] Many farmers, however, were engaged for part of their time in nonagricultural activities, particularly spinning and weaving, some handicrafts, petty trading, and transportation (cf. Smith 1969). The share of strictly agricultural activities in total labor input was therefore substantially smaller, possibly as low as two-thirds.

A characteristic feature of the Japanese economy was the large number of a hereditary class of warriors (samurai or bushi). Their number together with that of their valets, two to each samurai, and of their families, has been estimated at between 5 and nearly 10 percent of the population.[8] The share probably was higher in the early than in the late Tokugawa period. They were privileged in many ways in comparison to the rest of the population, in particular the exemption from direct taxes. Originally most of the samurai lived on and operated their little fiefs. Under the Tokugawa regime, however, most of them were resettled in the new castle towns and became rentiers living on the rice stipends they received from the shogun or their feudal lords (daimyo). At the same time since military activities, except representational ones, practically ceased after 1615 some of the samurai became in fact civilian officials of the shogun or of their overlords or they were idle and their economic situation deteriorated.[9]

Full-time artisans, merchants, and other nonagricultural workers were not very numerous, though constituting a large part of the urban population and some groups of merchants, particularly rice traders, became very rich and powerful mainly in the later part of the Tokugawa period.[10]

*Urbanization*

Near the end of the sixteenth century Japan had only four real cities
with an estimated total population of about 400,000 (Smith 1959, p.
4), the two largest being Kyoto and Osaka followed by Sakai and Fu-
shimi, or a little over 2 percent of the total of Japan. There were in
addition castle towns, port cities, and market towns, which may have
brought the total urban population, including that of quite small towns,
to about 8 percent of the total (Rozman, p. 285), and almost the entire
population lived in about 60,000 villages (Smith 1937, p. 6) with an
average of about 300 inhabitants and about 40 families.[11]

The increase of urbanization during the following century was ex-
plosive – it has been called "perhaps the most remarkable period of
urban development in any premodern country."[12] As a result of the
foundation of numerous castle towns by the shogun and by many
daimyos, most of the samurai had to move to one of these towns or
the new capital Edo where all daimyos had to establish large and elaborate residences for their families and where they had to live themselves part of the time, the *sankinkotai*, that is, alternative attendance
system, which was perfected in the 1630s.[13]

In 1600 according to one estimate about 110 castle towns existed,
mostly small and of recent origin, but nearly half of them ceased to
function as such during the seventeenth century. An additional 175
were founded after 1600, but nearly 50 soon declined (Taeuber, p.
25). The most rapidly growing and soon the largest city was Edo whose
population around 1725 is estimated to have exceeded 500,000 or
even having reached one million (Smith 1959, p. 67), larger than any
city in Europe at that time, and equal to over 1.5 or 3 percent of the
country's population. By the end of the seventeenth century Osaka
and Kyoto appear to have had populations of about 300,000 each
(Rozman, p. 228). Though no other city seems to have reached 100,000
(except Kanazawa), there may have been a dozen towns with 30,000
to 60,000 inhabitants.[14] The share of all towns with over 10,000 inhabitants around 1700 has been estimated at about 10 percent of the
total population (McClain, p. 1) or about 3 million people, a rate of
urbanization in excess of all European states except the Low Countries and a number of city dwellers larger than in any of them.

Another estimate (Rozman, p. 285) puts the number of urban places,
including very small ones, in early Tokugawa Japan at 330. Of these
the six largest had a total population of about 500,000 or nearly 3
percent of the national total, about one-half of which were accounted

by Osaka. The about 300 smaller places were credited with a total population of 700,000, or 4 percent of the total, and an average of only about 2,300. The 25 cities of intermediate size are estimated to have had 300,000 inhabitants, that is, 12,000 each and somewhat below 2 percent of the country's population. All 330 places in classes 1 to 6 thus had an aggregate population of 1.4 million, or 7 percent of the national total of 20 million. The 500 class 7 cities apparently had on the average well below 1,000 inhabitants, the mean of class 6, and hence often must have resembled large villages.

A more detailed estimate for the early eighteenth century, reproduced in Table 8-1, which also covers quite small towns, put the share of the urban population in about 700 places at fully 5 million or one-sixth of the total population. Of the total urban population nearly 2 million, or almost 6 percent of the country's total population, lived in Edo and Osaka, compared to less than 2 percent in 1600. The other two dozen larger cities had a total population on the order of 1 million, an average of approximately 40,000, and together 3 percent of the national total. The total population of nearly 700 smaller places was about 2.4 million. The average of only about 3,500 indicates that the estimate must include many very small places.

The urbanization ratio was highest, with somewhat over 20 percent, in Kanto and Kinki, which included Edo and Osaka, respectively. The ratio was in the narrow range of 13 to 15 percent in the other five regions. The differences are due mostly to those in the shares of larger cities, which ranges from less than 4 to 17 percent of the total, to that of the smaller cities is shown as between 8 and 11 percent of total population, possibly due to the method of estimation.

The increase in urbanization can be followed in more detail in Table 8-2. Within the century before 1720 the number of places of over 3,000 inhabitants is estimated to have increased from about 130 to over 300, while total population rose from 1.5 million to about 6 million. The ratio of total city population doubled from 8 to 16 percent. Among the urban population the share of cities with over 10,000 inhabitants rose from slightly below one-half to nearly three-fifths or from about 4 percent to nearly 11 percent of the country's population.

A long-time comparison indicates that in 1898, 30 years after the end of the Tokugawa rule, about 225 places with a population of over 10,000 each, a total of 8 million, or 18 percent of the country's total, the degree of urbanization had further increased considerably as the number of places with more than 10,000 inhabitants about tripled

Table 8-2. *Number and population of places of different size*

| 000 | | Number | | Population (1,000) | |
|---|---|---|---|---|---|
| | | Early Tokugawa | Around 1720[a] | Early Tokugawa | Around 1720[a] |
| 1. | Over 1,000 | 0 | 0 | — | — |
| 2. | 300–900 | 0 | 2[b] | — | 0.75[b] |
| 3a. | 70–300 | 3 | 5 | 0.40 | 0.45 |
| 3b. | 30–70 | 3 | 15 | 0.10 | 0.62 |
| 4. | 10–30 | 25 | 53 | 0.30 | 0.75 |
| 5. | 3–10 | 100 | 220 | 0.50 | 1.10 |
| 6. | 1–3 | 200 | 420 | 0.20 | 0.42 |
| 7. | <3 | 500 | 1010 | 0.20[c] | 0.40[c] |
| Total (number) | | 831 | 1725 | | |
| (millions) | | | | 1.7 | 3.9[d] |
| Japan (millions) | | | | 18.0 | 31.5 |
| (%) | | | | 9.5 | 12.4[e] |

[a] Excluding Kanto.
[b] Excluding Edo (0.80).
[c] On basis of 400 per place.
[d] Including Kanto 5.20.
[e] Including Kanto 16.5.
Source: Rozman, pp. 252ff; 285.

and their aggregate population and their share in the country's population approximately doubled.[15]

*Income distribution*

Although no figures on the distribution of personal income and wealth exist, the information on the size of the assessed rice (or equivalent) income of the approximately 200 daimyos in 1598 and in 1602 after the redistribution of Ieyasu after his victory of Sekigahara, shown in Table 8-3, should approximate the distribution of over two-thirds of the country's rice (and other grain) crop, which in turn accounted for probably about one-half of total personal income (cf. Section 2) and for an even higher share of total personal wealth. The figures, it is important to remember, reflect the daimyos gross income. A substantial proportion was absorbed by payments to retainers. That proportion is not known[16] and undoubtedly varied substantially among daimyo and may have been correlated positively or negatively with the

Table 8-3. *Cumulative size distribution of fiefs of over 10,000 koku*[a] *in 1598 and 1602 (%)*

| 1,000 kokus | Number | | Amount (million kokus) | |
|---|---|---|---|---|
| | 1598 | 1602 | 1598 | 1602 |
| 10 | 33.3 ⎫ | | 3.7 ⎫ | |
| 20–49 | 64.7 ⎬ | 81.5 | 15.6 ⎬ | 21.5 |
| 50–100 | 82.4 ⎭ | | 28.8 ⎭ | |
| 101–200 | 92.2 | 87.3 | 47.5 | 30.3 |
| 201–500 | 95.6 | 93.7 | 57.1 | 49.9 |
| 501–1,000 | 98.5 | 98.9 | 73.6 | 80.3 |
| Over 1,000 | 100.0 | 100.0 | 100.0 | 100.0 |
| Total, absolute figures | 204 | 189 | 18.63 | 19.11 |

[a]The lower limit defining daimyonal rank (one koku = 145 kg = 180 hectoliters).
*Source:* Derived from Sansome, pp. 413–16.

size of their gross income and may also have differed among *fudai* and *tozama* daimyo, the former more closely associated with the house of Tokugawa, that is, having fought on the side of Ieyasu at Sekigahara. In addition, exactions by the shogun, for example, for public works, differed among daimyo. Finally the share of the daimyo in his peasants' crops varied somewhat around the common rate of two-fifths. The distribution of net income may therefore have differed somewhat though probably not very substantially from that shown in Table 8-3.

In 1598 near the end of Hideyoshi's reign the total assessed revenue of the 204 fiefs with gross revenue of 10,000 koku or more of rice – the sources do not indicate whether unhulled or hulled – equal to the annual consumption of about 10,000 people, was 18.7 million koku, an average of 92,000 koku per fief. This was about 70 percent of the estimated national total of about 27 million koku.[17,18] How the difference of about 8 million koku was divided among fiefs of less than 10,000 koku, the holdings of the imperial family – probably not over 1 million koku – the temples and others does not seem to be known.

After the victory of Sekigahara, which made Ieyasu at 60 the undisputed, though in parts of the country only grudgingly accepted, master of Japan, he confiscated 90 fiefs with a revenue of 4.3 million koku, of which 12 exceeding 100,000 koku accounted for 2.43 million koku or 56 percent. He also reduced four fiefs by 70 percent or 2.22 million koku to 0.92 million koku. These 6.5 million koku Ieyasu used to increase 115 fiefs by an average of about 60,000 koku. As a result in 1602 there were 189 fiefs with over 10,000 koku totalling 19.1 million koku or just over 100,000 koku per fief, not quite one-tenth above the average of 1598.[19]

The cumulative size distribution of daimyonal fiefs shown in Table 8-3 and the number and holdings of the several size classes show a very high degree of concentration, with a Gini ratio of about 0.8. The distribution of 1602, after the large-scale redistribution by Ieyasu, affected about one-third of the total area; but in this tabulation Ieyasus personal fiefs appear in both years with 2.56 million koku or 13 percent of the total of 1,000 koku (Sansome 1963, 4).

The share of the about 82 percent of the daimyos with revenues between 10,000 and 100,000 koku declined between 1598 and 1602 from 29 percent to 22 percent. That of the daimyos with revenues between 100,000 and 500,000 koku – 27 in 1598 and 23 in 1602 – was reduced fractionally from 13.2 to 12.2 percent of the total. As a result the share of daimyos with revenues over 500,000 koku each, or about 2.5 percent each of all daimyonal fiefs – 9 in 1598 and 12 in 1602, including Ieyasu – rose from 43 to 50 percent, in both cases including 13 percent of holdings of Ieyasu.

Apparently approximately one-third of the fief area was held by the Tokugawa family, one-fourth by tozama daimyos who were less closely associated with the shogun, and the remainder mostly by fudai daimyos.

Although no similar data have come to attention for later dates, it is likely that additional confiscations, probably mostly of fiefs of tozama daimyo, by Ieyasu and his successors greatly increased the holdings of the Tokugawas. These additions have been estimated at 3.83 million koku by Ieyasu (1602–16), 4.53 million koku by Hidetada (1616–23), and 3.85 million koku by Iemitsu (1623–51). These confiscations increased the Tokugawa holdings by the time of Ieyasu's death to 6.4 million koku, or about one-fourth of the national total, and by the middle of the seventeenth century about 12 million koku or fully one-half of the total for Japan, were in the hands of the Tokugawas (Sansome 1963, p. 4).

Since the size distribution of the land not allocated to daimyos and its revenues are not known, it is not possible to estimate the distribution of all land in Japan and hence to approximate that of total personal income and wealth. In view of the heavy concentration among the approximately 200 fiefs, which accounted for about two-thirds of the agricultural land, the national Lorenz curve of personal income and wealth must have been far from diagonal; even if income and wealth of land not held by the Tokugawas and the daimyos was not highly concentrated and that of the urban population was less concentrated than that of land, their share in the respective national totals should have been as high as one-third.

## 2     National product

### *Total product in current prices*

Apparently no attempt has been made to estimate the size, or even the order of magnitude, of the national product of Tokugawa Japan, in current or constant prices, although this figure is of great importance as the handiest summary of the size of economic activities, as the scalar for many economic activities, and as a basis of comparison over time or with other countries.

In this situation a very rough estimate could be made either from the expenditure side on the basis of the expenditure of the basic food (rice) or from the income side on the basis of the wages of unskilled workers using a formula developed by Bairoch according to which average annual national product per head is equal to 200 times the daily wage of an unskilled worker (Bairoch, p. 777). The wide margin of uncertainty in either approach is evident given the scarcity of the relevant data, the considerable annual price fluctuations, and the substantial though decreasing regional differences in prices and wages (Yamamura 1981, p. 369).

Assuming an annual consumption of rice (including other grains) of nearly one koku (145 kg) per person, a retail price of rice of about one-half ryo per koku[20] and a share of rice and other grains in total expenditures of between two-fifths and three-fifths, all for the first quarter of the seventeenth century,[21] national product per head would have been between 0.7 and 1.2 ryo. Provisionally the round figure of one ryo, or 15 g of gold, will be used.

Although there is no possibility of quantification, there is little doubt that the capital formation ratio in Japan was high for a premodern economy in the early Tokugawa period and throughout the sixteenth century. The need to provide housing for an increase in population by about one-half during the century, or approximately 300,000 persons per year, the construction of numerous new towns with often extensive castles and other public buildings, and the creation of a large new capital with a vast palace for the shogun's court and many elaborate residences for daimyos alone ensure a relatively high rate of capital formation. This was increased by extensive irrigation works and land reclamation projects, road construction, and agricultural improvements (cf. particularly Yamamura 1981). These expenditures were financed primarily out of the tax revenues of the shogunate, the daimyos, or the labor services (*corvées*), which they exacted from the peasants, and by the wealthier peasants themselves. In the case of irrigation and reclamation works city merchants seem to have participated to a substantial extent (Hirschmeier and Yui, p. 15). It is fairly certain that the contribution of borrowed funds was negligible. This relatively high rate of capital expenditures is compatible with a fairly low rate of growth of total real product – probably well below one percent per year – because a substantial part of the expenditures, for example, those on castles and luxury residences, were not directly productive.

### *International and intertemporal comparisons*

Although it is very difficult to determine even the order of magnitude of national product of Japan in the early Tokugawa period – or before the 1870s – in current prices or in comparison in terms of purchasing power with that of Japan in modern times or of other countries at approximately the early Tokugawa period, comparisons in terms of gold are feasible although less significant economically because of the differences in the value of gold in terms of commodities.

An estimate of national product per head in Tokugawa Japan early in the seventeenth century of about one ryo was the gold equivalent to about 15 g of fine gold or almost one-half of an ounce, or slightly above $10 at the pre-1935 parity. This was not much below the gold value of the national product per head in 1878, which has been estimated at about 13 yen (Table 8-4) when the foreign exchange value of the yen was $0.92 (Bank of Japan, p. 318). This, of course, does not mean that the purchasing power of national product per head was about the same in early Meiji Japan as it had been two and one-half centuries earlier in early Tokugawa Japan since the purchasing power of gold in terms of commodities probably had risen considerably though it is difficult to estimate by how much. The most important single price, that of rice, had increased from about two-fifths of a ryo per koku, or about 6 g of gold early in the seventeenth century (Iwahashi, pp. 239, 274), compared to nearly 7 yen or 10 g of gold in 1868–72 (Bank of Japan, p. 90). Both the values for the early seventeenth century and the early Meiji period of about 15 g of gold are,

Table 8-4. *Nominal and real product per head in Japan, 1868–1913*

| Gross national product (billion yen) (1) | Population (million) (2) | Product per head | | | |
|---|---|---|---|---|---|
| | | Nominal (yen) (3) | Real (yen of 1934–6) (4) | $ (5) | Gold (g) (6) |
| 1868 | 0.32 | 34.0 | 9.4 | 55 | 9.4 | 14.1 |
| 1878 | 0.48 | 36.2 | 13.3 | 67 | 12.2 | 18.5 |
| 1885 | 0.81 | 38.4 | 21.1 | 101 | 17.8 | 26.7 |
| 1900 | 2.41 | 43.8 | 55.0 | 143 | 27.1 | 40.7 |
| 1913 | 5.01 | 51.3 | 97.7 | 158 | 48.2 | 72.3 |

*Sources:* Col. 1 – 1868, estimated on basis of 1878 using changes in population and in wholesale price index of Asahi Shimbun (Bank of Japan, p. 78); 1878, extrapolated from 1885 value on basis of Ohkawa's estimates (*Bank of Japan*, p. 32); 1885–1913, Ohkawa and Shinohara, pp. 251ff. Col. 2 – 1868, rough estimate; 1878–1913, *Bank of Japan*, pp. 12ff. Col. 4 – 1868–1878, rough estimates; 1885–1913, based on Ohkawa and Shinohara, pp. 256ff. Col. 5 – 1858–1913, col. 3 divided by $ price (*Bank of Japan*, pp. 318–22). Col. 6 – 1868–1913, col. 5 × 1.5.

of course, quite small compared to figures for later dates shown in Table 8-4. In 1913, for example, the national product per head of nearly 100 yen was equal to fully 70 g of gold.

The estimated gold value of national product per head in early Tokugawa Japan can also be compared with those for a few other countries at approximately the same period:

| Japan | ca. 1616 | 15 g | |
|---|---|---|---|
| Mughal India | ca. 1600 | 7 g | (Chapter 7) |
| England and Wales | ca. 1600 | 67 g | (Chapter 10) |
| United Provinces | ca. 1650 | 100 g | (Chapter 11) |

Here again the relations between the gold value of national product per head of the different countries cannot be used to measure differences in purchasing power because of differences in the purchasing power of gold over commodities, or over silver, except over the then rare internationally traded commodities.

While a quantitative comparison in terms of real product per head is not possible, Japan in the seventeenth century apparently was not "a very poor country even by contemporary European standards" (Hanley and Yamamura 1977, p. 70).

If real national product per head was about equal to both half an ounce of gold at the beginning of the Tokugawa era and early in the Meiji era (by monetary regulations the gold content of one Meiji yen was equal to that of 10 ryo at the end of the Tokugawa period), then real national product per head was higher than that at the beginning of the Tokugawa era, if and to the extent that the current price level had risen by less than 10 times. Unfortunately, as has already been indicated, there is no commodity price index directly linking the early seventeenth century and the late 1860s.

If the current price level increased by about 400 percent in these two and a half centuries, real national product per head would have doubled. This would imply an annual average rate of growth of about 0.28 percent for the period of about two and one-half centuries, undoubtedly unevenly distributed over the interval and probably more rapid during the sixteenth than during the eighteenth and early nineteenth centuries. This is *prima facie* not an unreasonable rate for a premodern economy, but it will take a great deal of work on production, consumption, rural incomes, and wages during the Tokugawa era and prices, particularly in the seventeenth century, before one may venture a judgment of even the order of magnitude of the figure, though it is not unlikely that it will be found to fall between 0.2 and 0.3 percent per year.[22]

## 3    The monetary system

One of the first economic measures undertaken by Ieyasu after his decisive victory of Sekigahara was the issuance beginning in 1601 of a new set of gold and silver coins to constitute the sole precious metal money in the territory controlled by him, that is, all of Japan beginning in 1615.[23] The coinage of gold and silver generally had been a monopoly of the central government, which since the mid-seventeenth century also controlled the gold and silver mines.

The gold coins were thin oval-shaped pieces of gold with an admixture of silver. Methods of production were apparently rudimentary. Dimensions and weight of the coins, which had no milled edge, varied slightly. Gold coins were issued in denominations of 10, 1, one-half and one-fourth ryo. The 10-ryo pieces (*obun kin*), ellipses with axes of about 15 and 9 cm, weighed about 165 g and contained 110 g of fine gold and 55 g of silver. It is reported that only 16,565 10-ryo pieces were minted – without indication over which period – containing about 1.8 tons of gold ($1.2 million at pre-World War parity). The large unit value of the 10-ryo pieces – about a dozen unskilled workers' annual wage – as well as the small number minted, approximately one for every 180 families in the country, suggest that their possession was limited to the shogun, his court, and some daimyos, and that the coins like decorations were issued as rewards for services to the shogun.

Even the one-ryo piece (*roban-kin*), a thin elongated ellipse with axes of about 7 and 0.4 cm weighing about 17.8 g of which 15.2 g was fine gold, was much too valuable to be used in retail transactions or for wage payments being equal to about a year's wage of an unskilled worker. It was probably mainly used for thesaurization and for some wholesale and credit transactions. Total coinage for the period 1601– 1695 (including recoinage) has been reported (including one-half ryo pieces) at slightly below 15 million ryo (Shinjo, p. 5; Rathgen, p. 159). This would be equal to about half a year's total national product, but a considerably higher proportion of monetized national product and a still higher proportion of monetized income in Eastern Japan where gold was the precious metal used. Only a part of this amount is likely to have been used in economic transactions and the ordinary Japanese is unlikely ever to have used a gold coin. The smallest gold coin was the rectangular (about 1.8 by 1.0 cm) one-quarter ryo piece, which weighed 4.4 g, 855/1000 fine, and hence contained about 3.8 g of gold. This again was hardly suited to retail transactions or wage payments as its value was on the order of three-months' wages of an unskilled worker.

No quantitative information has been found of the issuance of gold coins after Ieyasu, but as the Japanese gold and silver mines appear to have been exhausted fairly early in the seventeenth century (Ohkawa and Shimbo, p. 17), it is possible that no furthur net issues took place. The amount of gold coins in circulation in 1695 has been estimated at 10.6 million ryo or well below half a year's national product. Recoinages with same weight but lower fineness, however, occurred fairly frequently in the eighteenth and early nineteenth centuries with the result that the gold content of the ryo had been reduced by about nine-tenths at the end of the Tokugawa period.

Silver money did not have a fixed value but was valued by weight. Under Ieyasu two types of fine silver pieces were issued one of which (*cho-gin*) weighed approximately 160 g and therefore at the exchange rate of the early seventeenth century of 50 momme per ryo was worth 0.8 ryo. About 30 million of these heavy pieces, worth 1.2 billion momme, or 24 million ryo, are reported to have been minted over an unspecified period (Shinjo, p. 5). These pieces were probably mostly used among merchants. The other silver piece (*mameita gin*) weighed only between about 3.2 and 4.2 momme or 12 and 16 g containing 80 percent silver. Even this piece of which also 24 million ryo worth are reported to have been minted (Shinjo, p. 5) was too large for most retail transactions and wage payments.

There are no estimates of the output of Japanese silver mines in the early Tokugawa period. The amount of silver transferred to the government has been put at an annual average of 6.2 tons or 1.65 million momme or 33,000 ryo (Sado cited Yamamura and Kamiki 1983, p. 345). This figure, however, cannot be used as a measure of silver minted and still less as one of silver in circulation because only a fraction of silver minted was surrendered to the government, but on the other hand not all silver was used as money and there was a substantial outflow of silver particularly to China (Yamamura 1983, pp. 343–5). Finally an estimate puts silver in circulation in 1695 at 3.3 million ryo – less than one-third of gold pieces – or 200 million momme or 7 momme per head (Ohkawa and Shimbo, p. 107) a figure difficult to reconcile with the other estimates as silver constituted the standard precious metal in the western half of Japan, which included its commercial and financial capital, Osaka. The size of silver in circulation in early Tokugawa Japan must therefore be regarded as uncertain.

The common currency of Tokugawa Japan was copper coins (*mon*) as they had been for centuries before. Until the late seventeenth century, however, even copper coins seem to have been rare (a "curiosity," Smith 1959, p. 73) in the countryside. A large part of the circulation, whose size appears to be unknown, was of Chinese origin. But beginning in 1606 new copper coins were minted and the Chinese coins gradually eliminated. Details of the process are lacking in the literature in Western languages. The ratio between copper, silver, and gold coins fluctuated. In the early seventeenth century one ryo was worth between 3,000 and 4,000 copper coins and one momme between 60 and 80 copper coins. The ratio between gold and silver was about 12 : 1 (Shinjo, p. 7).

Tokugawa Japan thus had a trimetallic monetary system – in addition to which rice served as a medium of exchange in rural areas – in which the ratios between the three metals were subject to frequent fluctuations. The volume of coinage was apparently determined primarily by the output of the mines. The government practiced neither hylophantism nor hylolepsy. Monetary policy was essentially limited to changes in the weight and fineness of the gold coins, repeated recoinages and debasements starting in the late seventeenth century.

In addition to the metallic coins minted by the central government many of the feudal lords issued paper money of different denominations (*hansatsu*) mostly during the later part of the Tokugawa period (Sakudo 1955, pp. 18ff). These issues circulated probably only within a small territory. No information on the volume of the circulation of these issues, which became more common during the later part of the Tokugawa period, appears to have been collected. By the end of the period over 1,600 types of such notes are reported to have been in existence (Andréades, p. 23). The central government apparently resorted only rarely and late to the issuance of paper currency in unknown amounts.

One characteristic of the Tokugawa monetary system was its regionalization, continuing previous practices. Gold coins were used in eastern Japan, particularly the Edo area, and silver coins in the west, particularly the Osaka area, while copper coins were in use throughout the realm. As the Edo area had a substantial balance of payments surplus, primarily because the tax-financed expenditures of the court and the nobles, large exchange transactions transferring gold to the Edo area were necessarily, handled primarily in Osaka.

## 4    Prices, wages, and interest rates

Quantitative information during the seventeenth century is almost nonexistent. The only exception is the price of rice in a few cities. They indicate no trend between 1606 and the early 1630s at an average of 20 momme or 0.40 ryo or nearly 6 g of gold. By the middle of the century the price had moved up to somewhat over 30 momme, and by the end of the century it had reached 80 momme per koku (1698–1702 average for Osaka), a rise much sharper than earlier in the century, although the market is supposed to have been increasingly integrated over the whole country. In view of the high share of rice in total national expenditures, the general price level is likely to have shown a similar upward trend after the 1630s, although probably a somewhat more moderate one and certainly one showing considerably less pronounced year-to-year fluctuations.

The apparently total absence of wage data, at least in the literature in Western languages,[24] is possibly the most important single obstacle to a quantitative analysis of the economy of the early Tokugawa period. In view of the notorious stickiness of wages in traditional societies, it is unlikely that wages rose as rapidly as prices when the upward price movement started in the 1630s, though such a lag may not have occurred in farmers' and businessmens' income. A lag is, however, well documented even if not in quantitative terms for the samurai whose rents were fixed in terms of rice or money (Yamamura 1974).

Determination of interest rates was left to the market. Advances by money changers and bankers in commercial transactions are reported to have been in the order of 12 to 20 percent nominal, but considerably higher if additional charges are included (Crawcour, p. 349). The small loans in rural areas probably carried considerably higher, though not well-known rates. Deposits earned no interest.

## 5    Financial instruments and organizations

While the financial structure[25] of Japan at the beginning of the seventeenth century was still rudimentary and the degree of monetization low, both developed rapidly, mostly during the second and third quarters, so that it could be claimed that at the end of the seventeenth century its credit system was "not inferior to those existing in Europe at that time" (Crawcour, p. 342). Quantitative data to illustrate this development are unfortunately almost completely lacking, at least in the literature in Western languages.

There were even before the seventeenth century numerous money changers and local moneylenders and pawnbrokers[26] who advanced small amounts at high interest rates and usually for periods of less than one year to farmers and artisans. But for many of them this was not their only or even their main activity, and most of these transactions took place within a village or small town. Book credit among merchants was also not uncommon. The creation of more elaborate credit instruments and of units specializing in financial transactions was, however, essentially a development of the seventeenth century, particularly its second half.

Among financial instruments book credit among merchants became much more common and in wholesale trade dominant. In addition various forms of bills of exchange were developed, usually for 30 to 60 days, and from the middle of the century became transferable and often changed hands. The need for cash was reduced by the introduction of clearing-type settlements at fixed dates. As rice was the most important object of trade, particularly the storage of the tax rice received by the daimyo in Osaka and its sale, particularly in Edo, warehouse rice delivery orders became an important financial instrument, sometimes used as an object of speculation. Notwithstanding some legal obstacles mortgages on agricultural land and on urban structures developed, but apparently only for small amounts and on a limited sale.

There were no government or corporate securities.

Probably the most important financial innovation was the development, chiefly during the second half of the century, of bank-type institutions, which started either as money changers, merchant houses, or the financial agents of daimyos and many of which continued their original activities together with their banking operations.

By the third quarter of the century a group of 10 large banking houses had developed in Osaka, the commercial as well as financial capital of Japan (the *junin ryogae*), who were recognized as a sort of central bank by the government. They held what was in effect the country's cash reserve and acted as lenders of last resort. There were about another 150 smaller bankers in Osaka who were directly or indirectly affiliated with one of the Big Ten, kept most of their cash with them, and enjoyed overdraft privileges to agreed amounts.

The assets of the banks, other than cash, consisted essentially of loans to or bills of merchants, mostly of the wholesale type and, to an increasing extent, the daimyos [in one known case about nine-tenths of total loans near the end of the seventeenth century (Crawcour in Hall, p. 195)], generally to finance stored tax rice or future rice crops. The usual rate of interest charged appears to have been between 12 and 15 percent.

Nothing is known in quantitative terms about the sources of the banks' funds, particularly the ratio of their own capital to their deposits on which no interest was paid, and among the deposits the ratio of those of other banks, merchants, and daimyos. Part of the liabilities were, in the later part of the century, in different forms of transferable deposit certificates and checks, which to some extent could be regarded as part of the money supply.[27]

Bank-type institutions were less numerous and important in Edo, where their main business was with the government for which they acted as fiscal agents in tax collection and other activities. They were probably rare in other cities, in which the credit system was much less developed and most transactions were on a cash basis.

Because western Japan used silver and eastern Japan gold and Edo had a substantial positive balance of payments with Osaka, there was a large volume of transfers requiring the exchange of silver into gold. These were handled by the banks and money changers who daily fixed the exchange rates between the two metals; the transfers were effected by bills or similar instruments at a charge, excluding the exchange charge, of $\frac{2}{3}$, 1, to 2 percent.

There were no insurance organizations, mortgage banks, or other financial organizations.

## 6    Financing agriculture

In view of the predominance of agriculture in the Japanese economy – over four-fifths of the population living on the land and about three-fifths of national product originating in agriculture – it is unfortunate that very little is known quantitatively, or at least published, except in Japanese, about the sources and methods by which agricultural production, expansion, and improvement of arable land and the distribution of agricultural products were financed.[28] Even in the absence of more than occasional figures for small areas, there is little doubt that the labor of farm operators was the most important single source of permanent improvements. In short-term financing of crop production, other sources, both within and from outside the village, played a substantial and increasing role. On the other hand the information on methods of production and land ownership is more extensive than for many premodern societies.

There are, of course, no comprehensive statistics of the size distribution of farms by crop area or by rice production. In the English language literature only three sets of data have been found, one for six villages for one year each between 1593 and 1796, another for eight villages for one year each between 1587 and 1750 (Smith 1968, pp. 295ff), and one for a single village for four dates between 1595 and 1870 (Smith 1959, p. 162).

The average number of households in these three groups was 63, 38, and 51 (averaging the number for the three dates 1595, 1663, and 1771 for the single village). The average crop area for the first group was about 73 cho or about 1.15 cho per household (1 cho ~ 1 hectar). In the second group for which no information of crop area is given, the rice crop averaged about 8.2 koku (1,190 kg), which would mean at an assumed average household size of eight about 1.0 koku per person. This figure is somewhat higher than that obtained from the estimates of total rice crop and total population.

While the available figures do not provide a direct comparison of average crop area or yield per cho among the three samples, they permit a few interesting conclusions.

1.  The range of average number of households per village, average crop area per household, average rice crop per household, and average rice yield per cho was wide. The number of households ranged among the 15 villages from 13 to 148 with an average of 48. The average area per household of the

6 villages for which this information is available varied from
0.7 to 3.6 cho. The average rice crop per household in the 9
villages ranged from 2.5 to 15.5 koku (360 to 2,250 kg). These
figures are of only limited value as differences among villages
in the number of average persons per household or of the
share of the rice crop in total income are not known.

2.  There was no obvious relation between the dates of the re-
    ports and average crop area or rice crop per household in the
    two groups of villages.

3.  Possibly the most interesting result is that the size distribution
    of either crop area or rice crop, as shown by Lorenz curves
    for the aggregate six or eight villages, were very similar, not-
    withstanding the differences in location or dates. Both distri-
    butions were very unequal. The lower half of households ac-
    counted for only about one-tenth of total crop area or rice
    crop. At the other extreme the top 5 percent of households
    owned over three-fifths of the total crop area and harvested
    an equally high proportion of the total rice crop. The inequal-
    ity might have been slightly less on a per head basis. There
    were, however, large differences in the distribution among
    individual villages.

# 7    Financing the government

Taxes in kind or money and in labor services (*corvée*) were levied not
only by the shogunate, essentially as the owner of a substantial proportion of the land, but also by 200-odd daimyos and on a limited
scale by a few cities. Although the number and variety of levies were
very large, the bulk was contributed by the land tax collected at the
standard rate of 40 percent of product for rice and lower rates for
other products, predominantly in kind but as the seventeenth century
progressed to an increasing extent in money. It was collected by officials of the shogun or the daimyo through the village authorities who
allocated the total assessed among the peasants and were responsible
for deficiencies.[29] The total yield of the land tax may have been equal
to one-fifth to one-third of national product, as the actual rate of the
levy appears to have been slightly below the standard. No data are
available on the yields of other levies.

The assessed yield of each piece of land had been fixed on the basis
of its quality by an elaborate survey undertaken late in the sixteenth
century under Hideyoshi Toyotomi and apparently was not substantially changed during the Tokugawa period except for land improved

or newly brought into production.[30,31] As result, the yield of the land tax does not seem to have increased substantially, notwithstanding the apparent rise in production. Hence the ratio of land tax yield to national product is likely to have declined. In the absence of time series (or approaches to them) of yields, tax receipts, and national product, these statements must remain conjectural.

The daimyos, the samurai, and the city dwellers (*chonin*) paid no direct taxes. The daimyos could, however, at the shogun's pleasure be requested to undertake at their expense public works, particularly the construction or maintenance of roads, bridges, and castles, often of substantial size in comparison to their income. More burdensome were the expenses of maintaining establishments in Edo for their families and retinues, an item which increased in importance after the middle of the seventeenth century. The largest item of the daimyo's expenditures were the maintenance (rice stipends) of their numerous samurai and their families, most of whom lived in one of the castle towns of their daimyo, their number reportedly varying in proportion to the daimyo's land tax income (supposedly one samurai per 35 koku of rice or equivalent per year) (Sansome 1961, Appendix 11; 1963, p. 26). The different types of expenditures of the daimyos apparently increased during the Tokugawa period. As a result their financial position deteriorated, and many of them were forced to borrow from urban moneylenders, particularly in Osaka, at rates from 12 to 15 percent, often on the security of future rice crops (Hanley and Yamamura 1977, p. 345). The lenders often were the daimyo's agents for collecting, storing, and distributing their tax rice (Honjo, p. 258). These developments appear to have occurred mostly from the late seventeenth century on. There do not seem to exist any statistics of the finances of the daimyo.[32]

As the administrative machinery of the shogunate was not heavy and there were no substantial military operations after 1615, the main expenditures were the maintenance of the court, which increased greatly as time went on, and the rice stipends of the shogun's samurai (*hatamoto*). As a result of parsimonious management as well as of confiscations, the first shoguns accumulated reserves. Thus Ieyasu is reported to have left about 2 million ryo and his son Hidetada about 3 million ryo (Honjo, p. 270). From the late seventeenth century on, however, the treasure was rapidly dissipated and the shogunate's financial position became often precarious, requiring increasing requests for "thank money" from city merchants and occasional resort to moneylenders, particularly the Big Ten organized in 1672. As it has been said by a nineteenth century observer, "Financial management was the weakest point of the Tokugawa regime" (Rathgen, p. 43), at least after the mid-seventeenth century. In the absence of budgets before the mid-eighteenth century nothing can be said in quantitative terms.

The samurai, who soon were "transformed from rural fief holders to landless urban-living stipendiaries" (Hall et al. 1981, p. 207) owed their lords certain increasingly ceremonial obligations for which they received fixed rice rents for the consumption of their family or for sale to defray their other expenditures. As a result of price rises and presumably increasing standards of living of the rest of the population, the financial situation of most samurai deteriorated notwithstanding their exemption from direct taxes and many of them became impoverished.

Urban citizens were subject to many minor indirect taxes and in some cities to real estate taxes. The major burden on the wealthier citizens, however, were the amounts due to the shogun at his discretion formally as gifts or compulsory low-interest loans, about which no quantitative information seems to exist. The prosperity of the merchant class during most of the Tokugawa period indicates, however, that their effective burden of taxation cannot have been unduly heavy.

## CHAPTER 9

# The financial system
# of Medici Florence

Florence was the most important financial center during most of the fourteenth and fifteenth centuries[1] not only in Italy but also in Western Europe (de Roover 1963 p. 125). Within that period concentration on the first half of the fifteenth century is indicated by the preservation and recent tabulation[2] of the about 60,000 schedules of the property census (*catasto*) of 1427, a document with a scope and detail rarely equaled, certainly not before the nineteenth century.

Any consideration of the financial system of the Florentine Republic in that period will have to take account of at least four basic facts. First, the Republic was one of the smaller Italian states. Even after a considerable extension of its territory during the first quarter of the fifteenth century, it covered only 11,000 km$^2$ (Herlihy and Klapisch-Zuber, p. 110), or 4 percent of the area of Italy, and with a population of about 300,000 inhabitants accounted for the same small proportion of its population[3] ranking behind Venice, Milan, Genoa, the papal states, and the kingdom of Naples. Second, while Florence was the leading financial center of the peninsula and an important commercial and industrial city, it was surpassed by Venice and Genoa in overseas trade and in contrast to them had no colonies. Third, the first half of the fifteenth century was for Florence, as for most of Italy, a period of slow growth or even of stagnation following the sharp recession set off by the Black Death of 1348, a period which reached its trough near the end of the fourteenth century. How pronounced the setback was is indicated by the fact that the population of the city of Florence in 1427 of a little over 40,000 was at least one-half lower than it had been a century earlier (Herlihy and Klapsich-Zuber, p. 176); that the production of its most important industry, woolens, in the early fifteenth century was only about half as large as at its fourteenth-century peak;[4] and that the resources of its leading bank, the Medici, were far below those of the Bardi and Peruzzi in the mid-fourteenth century.[5] The city's national product in 1427 thus must

Table 9-1. *Price and wage movements in Florence, 1401–50*
(*1401–10 = 100*)

| Year | Wheat | Gold | Wages | |
|------|-------|------|-------|-----|
| | | | Unskilled | Skilled |
| 1401–10 | 100 | 100 | 100 | 100 |
| 1411–20 | 87 | 104 | 94 | 101 |
| 1421–30 | 69ᵃ | 111 | 85ᵈ | 101ᵉ |
| 1431–40 | 102 | —ᶜ | 93 | 103ᶠ |
| 1441–50 | 92ᵇ | 118 | 101 | 107 |
| 1427 | 69 | 109 | 90 | 101 |
| 1401–10 | 20.4 | 77.3 | 10.9 | 17.9 |
| | | soldi per | | |
| | staio<br>(18 kg) | florin | | day |

ᵃ9 years.
ᵇ8 years.
ᶜ105 for 3 years.
ᵈ8 years.
ᵉ6 years.
ᶠ9 years.
Source of basic data: Goldthwaite 1980, pp. 492ff.

have been well below that of a century earlier. Fourth, Florence was engaged throughout most of the fifteenth century, with the exception of the decade from 1414 to 1423, in wars with most of its neighbors. Because they were conducted by mercenaries, these wars absorbed a substantial proportion, extraordinarily high for the period, of national product in the form of taxes or forced loans.

It is fortunate for the user of statistics spread over the first half of the fifteenth century that neither population nor wages nor, it seems, prices showed a definite trend. This is suggested by the movements of the wages of unskilled and skilled laborers and of the prices of gold and wheat – the latter certainly fluctuating considerably more than the general level of commodity prices – shown in Table 9-1. Hence the level of nominal national product in 1427 should not have differed much from an average for the first half of the fifteenth century. However, the year of the *catasto* seems to have had a slightly lower price and wage level than the preceding or the following decades.

Table 9-2. *Population of the Florentine Republic in 1427 according to the* catasto

|  | Florence | Six cities[a] | Fifteen towns | Country-side | Republic |
|---|---|---|---|---|---|
|  | *Numbers (in 1,000)* | | | | |
| 1. Households | 9.9 | 6.7 | 6.0 | 37.2 | 59.9 |
| 2. Persons | 37.2 | 26.3 | 24.8 | 175.8 | 264.2 |
| 3. Persons per household | 3.74 | 3.91 | 4.14 | 4.72 | 4.41 |
|  | *Distribution (%)* | | | | |
| 1. Households | 16.6 | 11.2 | 10.0 | 62.2 | 100.0 |
| 2. Persons | 14.1 | 10.0 | 9.4 | 66.5 | 100.0 |

[a] Arezzo, Cortona, Pisa, Pistoia, Prato, and Volterra.
*Source: Catasto* of 1427 tabulated by Herlihy 1977, Table 1.1.

# 1  Population

According to the supposedly comprehensive property assessment of 1427, the Florentine Republic had a population of 264,000 of whom 37,000 lived in the city of Florence, about 25,000 each in six cities and in 15 towns, and 176,000 in the countryside (Table 9-2). It is, however, likely that the population of the city was somewhat above 40,000 and that of the Republic was in excess of 300,000.[6] While no comprehensive records appear to exist of birth and death rates and of migration, it is likely that both rates were high and that the slightly negative balance was made up by immigration from the countryside whose population declined.[7]

# 2  National product

An estimate of national product, even a rough one, which is essential not only as a measure of economic activity but also as a scalar for many other magnitudes such as government receipts and expenditures, money in circulation, debt, and wealth, must be built up piecemeal from numerous sources of varying reliability as no contemporary or modern estimates exist.

One important, and indeed the largest, component of income that can be based on comprehensive and fairly reliable primary data is property income (excluding imputed rent) because the property values in the *catasto* of 1427 were generally derived by capitalization of income at a rate of 7 percent.[8] This yields an estimate of declared property income of about f 1.05 million. This estimate must be increased first, because only one-half of owner-operators' agricultural income was capitalized; second, because of the omission of imputed rents on residences and of the property income of the church and other nonprofit organizations; and third, because the estimates of income that underlie the wealth figures in the *catasto* were substantially underestimated, according to one authority by as much as 20 to 40 percent (Conti, p. 58). These adjustments can be made only quite roughly, but it may be estimated that they would bring property income to over f 1.5 million and possibly to close to f 2 million.

Wage income, the second largest component, was relatively low as only about one-third to one-half of the employed population of Florence appears to have earned wages (Cohn, p. 206). The proportion was certainly lower for the Republic, particularly in the countryside.[9] It is unlikely, therefore, that there were more than 6,000 wage earners in Florence and more than 30,000 in the Republic. The wage bill for the wage workers in Florence would have been on the order of f 0.30 million, using an average of the data on wages for unskilled and skilled workers of 14 soldi (f 0.15) per day[10] and an average work year of 250 days, that is, about f 45 per year. Though there are no data on wages outside of Florence, they are certain to have been lower than in the city,[11] particularly in the countryside, and the share of skilled workers must have been considerably smaller. If they were on the average one-half of the Florentine level, their wage bill would have been in the order of f 0.60 million, bringing the wage bill for the Republic to f 0.90 million. This ratio of wage income to property income of about one-to-two is low, but not unreasonable in historical perspective.[12] There remain indirect taxes of about f 0.2 million (Molho 1971, p. 54) and small allowances for capital consumption.

On the basis of these estimates, fairly reliable for about two-thirds of the total, the gross national product of the Florentine Republic in 1427 can be put at about f 3 million, or about f 45 per household or about f 10 per person.

The only basis for a distribution of this total among the city of Florence and the rest of the territory is that of assessed wealth, which puts the share of Florence at two-thirds. This figure is likely to overstate the share of Florence in national product because of its lower share in wage income, the exemption of one-half of agricultural operators' income, and the probable larger extent of underreporting outside of Florence. The actual share of Florence in the national product of the Republic is therefore likely to have been between 50 and 60 percent.

Average income per household would then have been in the order of f 140 to f 170 in Florence but only of f 21 to f 27 in the rest of the Republic. The difference in per head income would have been even larger, namely, about f 38 to f 45 in Florence compared to about f 5 to f 6 elsewhere.[13] These estimates need to be checked against available data from the expenditure side.

The first of these is the personal exemption of f 200 per person, except servants and slaves, in the *catasto* as it represented the capitalization at the usual 7 percent of f 14, which apparently was regarded as an adequate minimum level of consumption (Fiumi 1965, p. 280). If this figure is regarded as applicable to the entire population, it would imply total consumption expenditures of at least f 0.6 million for Florence and of f 4.2 million for the Republic. If, however, it was based on the level of expenditures in the city, as is likely, since the property tax was levied only in Florence, the figure applicable for the entire territory would be substantially lower, but probably not less than f 3.0 million.

A second estimate starts from a contemporary figure for average expenditures for an adult in 1395–1405, of f 11½ per year for the three basic foods (bread, wine, and meat) (Goldthwaithe 1980, p. 344). Using expenditure patterns regarded as applicable to fifteenth century Florence, this would indicate total expenditures per adult of f 15 to f 18, or expenditures per head of the entire population, given the considerably lower expenditures of women and children, of f 12 to f 15. Applying these figures to total population yields an estimate of f 3.6 to f 4.5 million for the Republic. These figures are considerably too high for 1427, first, because prices appear to have declined between 1400–05 and 1427 – wheat prices fell by about one-third though the decline in the general price level is likely to have been considerably smaller – and second, and more important, because expenditures in the countryside are certain to have been below those in Florence. These sources thus point to total consumption expenditures in the Republic of f 3.0 to 3.5 million. Another estimate puts annual expenditures per head for four basic foods around 1445 at f 6½ per head for the Republic (Goldthwaithe 1980, p. 346), which points to total consumption expenditures for a population of 300,000 of about f 3 million. The figure for 1427 should be slightly lower as wages and prices were slightly higher in 1445 than two decades earlier.

Use of a further near-contemporary estimate yields a similar result. It states that around 1480 a family of five or six could live respectably (*civilmente*) in Florence on an income of no more than f 70, implying an expenditure per head of f 13 (Goldthwaithe 1980, p. 350). The figure is certainly considerably higher than the average for the Republic because it seems to refer to a middle-class family in Florence. It implies at most total consumer expenditures of about f 2.5 million given the absence of evidence of a substantial price trend in the intervening half century.[14]

In the absence of comprehensive price information, these figures cannot be satisfactorily compared with national product per head or household for other cities or countries, contemporary or modern. The best that can be done is to express the Florentine figures in terms of two key commodities, gold and wheat. At about f 9 per ounce and a gold price of $400 per ounce, the per head product of average personal consumption in the Florentine Republic of about f 10 would have been equal to slightly above 1 oz of gold or $400, though for the city of Florence, the equivalent would be as high as 4 oz or $1,600. This compares with about 1 oz for the early Roman Empire and 1.5 oz in England and Wales in 1688, and with nearly 4 oz in the United States in 1820. In terms of wheat the average product of the Florentine Republic of about 1,000 kg compares with 850 kg in the early Roman Empire, 1600 kg in England in 1688, and 2,050 kg in the United States in 1820 (Goldsmith 1984, pp. 280–81).

A sectoral breakdown of national product is not yet possible. Nevertheless, the still predominantly agrarian character of the population of the Republic is indicated by the estimate that more than three-fifths of all families "lived principally from the land" (Herlihy and Klapisch-Zuber, p. 268). Their share in the accrued wealth of the Republic, however, was probably in the order of only one-fifth,[15] the same share as in the United States in the early nineteenth century. The share of agriculture in national product is difficult to estimate but is not likely to have been in excess of one-fourth, excluding rent to city dwellers. An idea of the social and occupational structure of the city of Florence is provided by the fact that about 9 percent of all households belonged to the 7 major guilds, and 23 percent to the 14 minor guilds, including tradesmen and artisans, while 20 percent were classified as employees, leaving 44 percent without indicated profession including rentiers, such as absentee landlords, and the relatively numerous households headed by widows. About 21 percent of all households and 38 percent of those with declared professions belonged to the textile trades (Herlihy and Klapisch-Zuber, pp. 289, 295).

## 3    Wealth

Taxable real property in the Florentine Republic (which did not include residences) was put at just over f 8 million in the *catasto* of 1427

Table 9-3. *Taxable wealth of the Florentine Republic in 1427 according to the* catasto

| | Florence | Six cities | Fifteen towns | Country-side | Republic |
|---|---|---|---|---|---|
| *I. Aggregate amounts (million f)* | | | | | |
| 1. Real property | 4.13 | 1.14 | 0.61 | 2.18 | 8.06 |
| 2. Movables | 3.47 | 0.59 | 0.17 | 0.22 | 4.45 |
| 3. Public debt | 2.57 | 0.00 | 0.00 | 0.00 | 2.58 |
| 4. Gross wealth | 10.17 | 1.73 | 0.79 | 2.40 | 15.09 |
| 4. Deductions | 2.50 | 0.33 | 0.14 | 0.32 | 3.29 |
| 6. Taxable wealth | 7.67 | 1.39 | 0.65 | 2.08 | 11.79 |
| *II. Amounts per household (f)* | | | | | |
| 1. Real property | 415 | 169 | 103 | 59 | 135 |
| 2. Movables | 349 | 87 | 28 | 6 | 74 |
| 3. Public debt | 259 | 2 | 0 | 0 | 43 |
| 4. Gross wealth | 1,022 | 257 | 131 | 65 | 252 |
| 5. Deductions | 252 | 50 | 23 | 9 | 55 |
| 6. Taxable wealth | 770 | 207 | 108 | 56 | 197 |
| *III. Structure (%)* | | | | | |
| 1. Real property | 40.4 | 65.9 | 78.2 | 90.6 | 53.4 |
| 2. Movables | 34.1 | 33.9 | 21.6 | 9.3 | 29.5 |
| 3. Public debt | 25.3 | 0.2 | 0.2 | 0.1 | 17.1 |
| 4. Gross wealth | 100.0 | 100.0 | 100.0 | 100.0 | 100.0 |
| 5. Deductions | 24.6 | 19.3 | 17.2 | 13.4 | 21.8 |
| 6. Taxable wealth | 75.4 | 80.7 | 82.8 | 86.6 | 78.2 |
| *IV. Geographical distribution (%)* | | | | | |
| 1. Real property | 51.2 | 14.1 | 7.6 | 27.0 | 100.0 |
| 2. Movables | 78.0 | 13.2 | 3.8 | 5.0 | 100.0 |
| 3. Public debt | 99.7 | 0.1 | 0.1 | 0.1 | 100.0 |
| 4. Gross wealth | 67.4 | 11.4 | 5.2 | 15.9 | 100.0 |
| 5. Deductions | 76.0 | 10.1 | 4.1 | 9.8 | 100.0 |
| 6. Taxable wealth | 65.0 | 11.8 | 5.5 | 17.7 | 100.0 |

*Source of I:* Herlihy 1977, Table 1.1.

(Table 9-3), representing mostly the value of land, a considerable amount of which though located outside the city was owned by residents of Florence.[16] This figure seems to have been substantially understated in the declarations of the taxpayers and excluded one-half of the value of owner-operated agricultural real estate – possibly as much as f 1 million – as well as real property owned by the government and by nonprofit organizations, particularly by religious institutions. The value of the latter has been estimated at f 1.1 million, apparently substantially understated, and actually was probably close to f 2.0 million.[17] The adjusted figure for nonresidential nongovernment real property thus probably should be put at between f 14 and f 15 million.[18]

The value of three other items – residences, their contents, and government real property – can only be very roughly estimated. Rents and house prices appear to have been low, not astonishing in view of the fact that population was considerably lower than a century earlier. The value of residences may therefore not have exceeded f 2 million,[19] including at least f 0.5 million for contents,[20] of which at least one-half was within the city of Florence on the basis of the distribution of the value of all real property. The extent of the government's real property appears to have been small with a notional value of possibly f 0.5 million.

The margin of error in the estimation of inventories, which in the *catasto* were included in movable property, is even larger; however, a figure on the order of f 1.2 million, equal to about one-tenth of tangible assets and about one-half of national product, appears to be reasonable.[21]

The value of all tangible assets within the Republic, including a rough estimate for monetary metals, as shown in Table 9-4, should then have been within a range of f 17 to f 18 million, or nearly six times national product. A figure of this order is similar to ratios for Western European countries between the late seventeenth and the early twentieth centuries (e.g., 6.0 for England and Wales in 1688), though higher than those for the United States until the late nineteenth century and those for India until the mid-twentieth century (Goldsmith, 1985, Table 16).

Financial assets other than claims against the Monte were assessed at nearly f 4.5 million, of which f 3.5 million were in the city of Florence. Underreporting was probably highest in this item, and its correct value may easily have been as high as f 6 million. On the other hand, the nominal value of the claims against the Monte of 2.6 million, practically all in Florence, is likely to be exact as it could easily be checked by the tax authorities. However, since the claims were generally assessed at 50 percent of nominal value, while the market value was only around 35 percent, the assessed figure should be reduced to f 1.8 million, bringing the market value of all financial assets to nearly f 9 million or nearly three-fifths of that of tangible assets. For the citizens of Florence alone financial assets were probably nearly equal to tangible assets. Deductions, mainly debts, are likely to have been somewhat understated,[22] but are not likely to have been substantially lower than f 3 million for private citizens and f 1.8 million for the government.

Table 9-4. *Wealth of the Florentine Republic in 1427*

| | Florence | Rest of territory | Republic |
|---|---|---|---|
| *I. Amounts ($f$ million)[a]* | | | |
| 1. Private real property[b] | 5.0 | 6.0 | 11.0 |
| 2. Residential structures | 0.8 | 0.7 | 1.5 |
| 3. Furnishings | 0.3 | 0.2 | 0.5 |
| 4. Inventories | 0.8 | 0.4 | 1.2 |
| 5. Public and institutional real property[c] | 1.2 | 1.0 | 2.2 |
| 6. Coins | 0.8 | 0.2 | 1.0 |
| 7. Total | 8.9 | 8.5 | 17.4 |
| *II. Amounts per head[d] ($f$ 1,000)* | | | |
| 1. Private real property[b] | 1.13 | 0.17 | 0.30 |
| 2. Residential structures | 0.20 | 0.03 | 0.05 |
| 3. Furnishings | 0.08 | 0.01 | 0.02 |
| 4. Inventories | 0.20 | 0.02 | 0.04 |
| 5. Public and institutional real property[c] | 0.30 | 0.04 | 0.07 |
| 6. Coins | 0.20 | 0.01 | 0.03 |
| 7. Total | 2.11 | 0.27 | 0.51 |
| *III. Distribution (%)* | | | |
| 1. Private real property | 53 | 64 | 58 |
| 2. Residential structures | 10 | 10 | 10 |
| 3. Furnishings | 4 | 3 | 3 |
| 4. Inventories | 10 | 6 | 8 |
| 5. Public and institutional real property[c] | 14 | 14 | 14 |
| 6. Coins | 10 | 3 | 6 |
| 7. Total | 100 | 100 | 100 |

[a] Compare discussion in text.
[b] Includes livestock; excludes row 2.
[c] Includes church property.
[d] Based on population of 40,000 in col. 1 and 260,000 in col. 2.

Wealth was very unequally distributed, as was property income since its value in the *catasto* was generally derived by capitalization of income. The Gini coefficient was as high as 0.79 for Florence and 0.75 for the other six cities in the Republic.[23] Since the value of residences and their contents were excluded from the *catasto*, concentration for a more comprehensive concept of wealth may have been somewhat lower. No comparable figures appear to have been published for the countryside, but concentration was probably lower than in the cities. This is suggested by the fact that concentration was lower in the cities

Table 9-5. *Size distribution of net assessed wealth of four quarters of Florence according to the* catasto *of 1427 (%)*

| Top | Top 150 families | | | | |
| --- | --- | --- | --- | --- | --- |
| | S. Croce | S. Giovanni | S. M. Novella | S. Spirito | Florence |
| 1–15 | 38.5 | 39.2 | 45.1 | 37.0 | 39.9 |
| 16–30 | 16.2 | 20.2 | 14.6 | 18.4 | 17.9 |
| 31–45 | 10.5 | 9.0 | 9.4 | 12.0 | 10.6 |
| 46–60 | 7.7 | 6.6 | 7.3 | 8.6 | 6.9 |
| 61–75 | 6.3 | 6.0 | 5.5 | 6.5 | 5.9 |
| 76–90 | 5.4 | 4.9 | 4.7 | 4.8 | 5.0 |
| 91–105 | 4.6 | 4.2 | 4.1 | 4.0 | 4.2 |
| 106–120 | 4.1 | 3.8 | 3.7 | 3.5 | 3.8 |
| 121–135 | 3.6 | 3.3 | 3.0 | 2.8 | 3.1 |
| 136–150 | 3.1 | 2.8 | 2.6 | 2.4 | 2.7 |
| 1–150 | 100.0 | 100.0 | 100.0 | 100.0 | 100.0 |
| Rest | — | — | — | — | — |
| Total | — | — | — | — | — |
| f. 1,000, total | 731 | 1,267 | 806 | 951 | 3,755 |
| Number population | 150 | 150 | 150 | 150 | 600 |
| f per head | 4,875 | 8,445 | 5,375 | 6,340 | 6,260 |

*Source of basic data:* Martiñes, pp. 353ff for top wealth holders, Herlihy and Klapisch-Zuber, p. 123 for number of households. Assessed wealth of each quarter derived on the assumption that average of assessees below the top 150 was equal to the city average.

for real property than for total wealth and particularly for financial assets. The Gini ratio for the Republic is therefore unlikely to have been lower than 0.75 and the share of the top decile lower than two-thirds.

In the city of Florence, which accounted for two-thirds of the declared wealth in the Republic, the wealthiest 1 percent of households held 27 percent of the total and the following 9 percent fully 40 percent.[24] The poorest one-half of the households declared only 3 percent of total wealth. Concentration was highest for public debt (Gini ratio about 0.90), 57 percent of which was held by the top 1 percent and 86 percent by the top 10 percent, followed by other financial assets (Gini ratio about 0.80), and was lowest for real property (Gini ratio about 0.70), the top 10 percent of wealth holders owning fully three-fourths of all assessed other financial assets but only about 45 percent of real estate (Herlihy and Klapisch-Zuber, pp. 250–51).

Variations in declared wealth by age were irregular and rather moderate, wealth averaging about f 940 for declarants of 18 to 42

| Total population | | | | |
|---|---|---|---|---|
| S. Croce | S. Giovanni | S. M. Novella | S. Spirito | Florence |
| 20.0 | 19.0 | 23.3 | 16.8 | 19.6 |
| 8.4 | 9.9 | 7.5 | 8.4 | 8.7 |
| 5.5 | 4.4 | 4.8 | 5.5 | 5.2 |
| 4.0 | 3.2 | 3.7 | 4.9 | 3.4 |
| 3.3 | 2.9 | 2.8 | 2.9 | 3.0 |
| 2.8 | 2.4 | 2.4 | 2.2 | 2.4 |
| 2.4 | 2.0 | 2.1 | 1.8 | 2.1 |
| 2.1 | 1.9 | 1.9 | 1.6 | 1.8 |
| 1.9 | 1.6 | 1.5 | 1.3 | 1.5 |
| 1.6 | 1.4 | 1.3 | 1.1 | 1.3 |
| 52.0 | 48.7 | 51.3 | 45.5 | 49.0 |
| 48.0 | 51.3 | 48.7 | 54.5 | 51.0 |
| 100.0 | 100.0 | 100.0 | 100.0 | 100.0 |
| 1,405 | 2,600 | 1,570 | 2,090 | 7,665 |
| 1,731 | 3,278 | 1,952 | 2,820 | 9,781 |
| 811 | 793 | 805 | 741 | 784 |

years compared to an average of f 1,220 for those over 42 years (Herlihy 1977, Table 1.3).

Differences in declared wealth per head in the four quarters of Florence, shown in Table 9-5, were moderate, indicating that on this scale there were no *beaux quartiers* and slums.[25] Those in the size distribution of wealth were more pronounced, but can be partly explained by the differences in population. Compared to an average declared net wealth of f 784 per head for the city, the averages for the four quarters ranged only from f 741 to f 811. The share of the top 150 wealth holders in total declared wealth varied from 46 to 52 percent and that of the top wealth holders from 17 to 23 percent. If the limit is drawn for better comparability at the top 5 percent of the population of each quarter, the shares for the four quarters were about 43 percent for S. Croce, 50 percent for S. Giovanni, 57 percent for Santa Maria Novella, and 45 percent for S. Spirito.[26]

There were also wide differences in wealth among occupations. Compared to an average of about f 770 of assessed net wealth in the city of Florence, bankers (no numbers of members given) ranked first with an average of f 8,750 followed at a long distance by traders in wool with f 3,300 and in other textiles with f 1,700, and by lawyers and spice dealers with slightly over f 1,000. All other 19 specified professions showed averages from f 600 for paper dealers to f 80 for city employees.[27] The ranking was similar in the three largest cities outside Florence (Pisa, Pistoia, and Arezzo), though the levels of wealth were much lower for the highest ranking occupations.

The structure of wealth differed not only between Florence, the cities and towns, and the countryside, but also between households of differing wealth in each of these areas (Herlihy and Klapisch-Zuber, pp. 253–55). In Florence real property (excluding residences) constituted with little variation nearly one-half of total wealth for the bulk of households with wealth between f 50 and f 2,500 but was considerably lower for the poorest households as well as for the richest households for whom the share fell below one-third. In contrast the share of movable assets other than public debt was highest for households with less than f 50 wealth, possibly largely currency, but did not change for other households for which it stayed between 30 and 40 percent. Public debt was below 5 percent of total wealth for the poorest half of households but rose to over one-third for the top 5 percent of households. Differences were much less pronounced for the six other cities. Here real property represented with little variation four-fifths of total wealth for three-fourths of households, leaving in the virtual absence of public debt holdings about one-fifth for other financial assets, and still accounted for nearly one-half for the top 5 percent of households. In the countryside real property was completely dominant.

On the average deductions, mostly for debt, because the tabulations disregard the personal exemptions of f 200 per adult male, amounted to fully one-fifth of declared wealth, nearly one-fourth in Florence and one-sixth in the rest of the Republic. In absolute figures the difference was much larger, about f 250 per household in Florence, against only f 13 elsewhere. These figures, together with a similar difference for average financial assets of f 610 for Florence against f 22 for the rest of the Republic, indicate clearly that financial activities within the Republic were practically limited to the city of Florence and within the city to a small minority of the population as nearly three-fourths of financial assets and a probably similar proportion of debt were accounted for by the top tenth of wealth holders.[28]

## 4    The monetary system

Beginning in the mid-thirteenth century the monetary system[29] of the Florentine Republic was symmetallistic.[30] Gold coins – the florin of

3.53 g, until 1402 and 3.33 g thereafter, that is, at a gold price of $400 per ounce about $44 or $42 – circulated alongside silver coins whose metallic content fell progressively below the original ratio of 20 soldi to the florin and various copper coins whose value represented only a small fraction of that of total circulation. During the first three decades of the fifteenth century the ratio kept close to 80 soldi per florin, rising from 76 soldi in 1400–02 to 83 soldi in 1428–30 (Goldthwaite 1981, p. 430 after Bernocchi, vol. III). Most retail transactions and wage payments within the Republic were settled in silver and copper coins, while gold florins, which had become one of the main international currencies, and in the fourteenth century the most common one (Cipolla, XIIII), were used within the Republic mainly for business transactions and larger tax payments but also for some wage payments and retail sales and were dominant in international trade insofar as coins were used (Cipolla, p. 37). To ensure full weight of the coins, which could be clipped as they had no milled edge (an invention of the seventeenth century), they were often put by the mint in sealed bags and circulated in that form (as *fiorini di suggello*) in larger transactions.[31] This system necessitated the services of money changers who charged a small fee.[32] Business records were kept in a separate currency of account (pounds *affiorino*), which was divided into 20 *soldi affiorino* and 240 *deniers affiorino*, and was based on gold.

In the absence of statistics of money in circulation, four possible approaches to at least a rough estimate of the magnitudes involved have been explored: contemporary estimates,[33] mint statistics,[34] a residual from the *catasto*,[35] and finally analogies with other places and dates.[36] Unfortunately the range of these estimates is so wide that the figure provisionally accepted of f 1.2, which implies a velocity of circulation of 2½ and is equal to 8 percent of national wealth and to about one-sixth of financial assets, remains judgmental.[37]

## 5    Financial institutions

Though the fifteenth century has been described as the "silver age of Italian banking," Florence was still the "financial capital of Western Europe," (Miskimin 1976, 151), and the Medici bank was the dominant factor in its banking system (de Roover 1963, p. 75). The bank, organized in 1397, reached its zenith under Cosimo de' Medici in the second quarter of the fifteenth century, declined after Cosimo's death in 1464 and was liquidated 30 years later when the Medici were temporarily expelled from Florence. Thanks to the conservation of many of their records and their analysis by R. de Roover, more is known about the Medici bank than about any other financial institution before the seventeenth or even the eighteenth century.

What is known about the operations of the Medici bank, as well as other banks in Florence and Tuscany, justifies the conclusion that they were technically the most advanced financial institutions before the late sixteenth and possibly the late seventeenth century and were definitely surpassed in these respects only in the nineteenth century.[38]

The Medici bank was an international organization with branches in Italy and Western Europe. At one time or another it had branches in 11 cities and correspondents in several others, but it never had more than nine branches at any one time and most of the time less than half a dozen, the most important of which were in Florence, Rome, Venice, and Geneva. Each of the branches was organized as a legally separate partnership between originally a holding-company-type partnership controlled by members of the Medici family, and after the mid-fifteenth century directly between family members and some outsiders, generally the branch managers. The organization was unified by some members of the Medici family, Cosimo for the period from 1424 to 1464, being the largest partners in the Florence holding company and in all of the branches. This permitted a high degree of centralization of decision making, particularly under Cosimo.

Though the Medici bank was the largest and most influential financial organization in Florence – indeed in Western Europe – except for the Monte, there were numerous other bankers (de Roover 1963, pp. 75, 95), the Pazzi probably being the second in size (de Roover 1963, p. 366), and many money changers. There are no data permitting an estimate of the share of the Florence branch of the Medici bank in the assets of all financial institutions.[39] In 1422 there were 72 firms engaged in international banking (*banchi grossi*) but only 33 in 1470 (de Roover 1963, p. 374), and the number of moneylenders and money changers must have been much larger. However, it is unlikely that the share of the Medici bank was lower than one-sixth or higher than one-third.

In 1427 the assets of the three main branches of the Medici bank, as shown in Table 9-6, totaled f 315,000, equal to fully one-tenth of the national product of the Florentine Republic, a ratio above that existing in modern countries. Of total assets nearly one-fourth were claims against other Medici companies, reducing consolidated assets to about f 235,000. Cash represented only 7 percent of consolidated assets, but credit balances with correspondents added 27 percent to liquid assets. Loans were the largest component with fully two-fifths

Table 9-6. *Balance sheet of the Medici banks in 1427 (%)*

|  | Structure | | | | Local distribution | | | |
|---|---|---|---|---|---|---|---|---|
|  | Florence (1) | Rome (2) | Venice (3) | Total (4) | Florence (5) | Rome (6) | Venice (7) | Total[a] (8) |
| I. *Amounts*, 000 f | 100 | 169 | 46 | 315 | 31.8 | 53.6 | 14.6 | 315 |
| II. *Assets* | | | | | | | | |
| 1. Cash | 4.2 | 6.6 | 1.0 | 5.0 | 26.8 | 70.7 | 2.5 | 16 |
| 2. Correspondents | 4.9 | 20.9 | 53.3 | 20.6 | 7.6 | 54.6 | 37.8 | 65 |
| 3. Loans | 43.6 | 31.9 | 15.7 | 33.2 | 41.7 | 51.4 | 6.9 | 105 |
| 4. Trade credits | 4.9 | 3.8 | 1.1 | 3.8 | 41.5 | 54.3 | 4.2 | 12 |
| 5. Other Medici companies | 27.2 | 26.6 | 18.6 | 25.7 | 33.7 | 55.8 | 10.5 | 81 |
| 6. Partners | 11.3 | — | — | 3.6 | 100.0 | — | — | 11 |
| 7. Other assets | 3.9 | 10.2[c] | 10.3 | 8.2 | 15.1 | 66.7 | 18.2 | 26 |
| 8. Total assets | 100.0 | 100.0 | 100.0 | 100.0 | 31.8 | 53.6 | 14.6 | 315 |
| III. *Liabilities and net worth* | | | | | | | | |
| 1. Correspondents | 6.7 | — | 25.2 | 5.8 | 36.8 | — | 63.2 | 18 |
| 2. Accounts payable | 17.5 | 90.6 | 40.2 | 59.9 | 9.3 | 80.9 | 9.8 | 188 |
| 3. Trade debt | 2.4 | 1.8 | 1.5 | 2.0 | 38.7 | 50.0 | 11.3 | 6 |
| 4. Other Medici companies | 51.3 | — | — | 16.3 | 100.0 | — | — | 51 |
| 5. Partners | 3.8 | 0.3 | — | 1.4 | 88.4 | 11.6 | — | 4 |
| 6. Other liabilities | 0.9 | 1.1 | 6.6 | 1.8 | 15.5 | 32.8 | 51.7 | 6 |
| 7. Total liabilities | 82.6 | 93.8 | 73.4 | 87.3 | 30.1 | 57.6 | 12.3 | 274 |
| 8. Capital | 12.0 | — | 19.0 | 6.6 | 58.0 | — | 42.0 | 21 |
| 9. Undistributed profits | 5.4[b] | 6.2 | 7.7 | 6.1 | 27.1 | 54.7 | 18.2 | 20 |
| 10. Net worth | 17.4 | 6.2 | 26.6 | 12.7 | 43.4 | 26.2 | 30.4 | 41 |
| 11. Total | 100.0 | 100.0 | 100.0 | 100.0 | 31.8 | 53.6 | 14.6 | 315 |

[a] f 1,000
[b] Includes excess assets 2.5.
[c] Includes "silver plate" 3.1.
*Source of basic data:* de Roover 1963, pp. 206–07, pp. 226–27, pp. 246–7

of total consolidated assets, leaving one-fifth for other assets that included about 5 percent each for trade credits and claims against partners. There were, however, considerable differences in the asset structure of the three branches. The liquid assets (cash and correspondents) constituted less than one-tenth of the assets of the Florence branch, but nearly one-third in the Rome branch and one-sixth in the Venice branch. In the Florence branch the 150 loans to outsiders averaged fully f 250 or 8 years' wages of an unskilled workman. In Rome, in contrast, the six loans of over f 1,000 each of a total of 222 averaged f 2,320 and accounted for over one-fourth of the total while the smaller loans averaged f 170. Most of the larger loans were probably made to persons connected with the curia. Loans were of very small importance in the Venice branch. The character of the loans of the Medici bank was such that "they contributed little to economic growth," but "were mainly used to finance either conspicuous consumption of royal courts or military campaigns in Italy or abroad" (de Roover 1963, p. 374), as had been the case with the loans of the Bardi and Peruzzi (Sapori 1926, pp. 74ff).

Total liabilities to outsiders of the three branches totaled about f 220,000, almost all in deposit and similar form. Their character differed greatly among the branches. In the Florence branch the 105 accounts averaged f 170 – almost as much as the average loan – which indicates that the firm's clientele was limited to wealthier households and enterprises. Deposits were insignificant in the Venice branch. In Rome the average of the 320 accounts of about f 420 was 2½ times as high. What is more significant is that the 24 accounts of over f 1,000 each – of which there can have been only a few in the Florence branch – averaged f 4,350 and together accounted for nearly three-fourths of the total. The deposit of the Apostolic Camera alone with f 24,500 constituted one-sixth of the total, and most of the other large depositors were ecclesiastics. The Rome branch evidently depended for its funds on its position as the official banker of the curia, which it lost when Eugene IV became pope.

The net worth of the three branches of about f 40,000, over two-fifths attributable to Florence, was equal to one-eighth of combined assets and to nearly one-fifth of liabilities to outsiders. It was divided about equally between capital and udistributed profits.

In contrast to the completeness of the accounts for 1427, derived from the schedules submitted to the *catasto*, information on assets and liabilities at other dates is scarce. It is, therefore, impossible to follow their development over time except for the capital of the three branches, which increased from f 24,000 in 1402 to f 27,570 in 1420 and to

Table 9-7. *Profits of the Medici banks, 1397–1450 (%)*

|  | Local distribution | | | | Distribution over time | | | |
|---|---|---|---|---|---|---|---|---|
|  | 1397 to 1420 | 1420 to 1435 | 1435 to 1450 | 1397 to 1450 | 1397 to 1420 | 1420 to 1435 | 1435 to 1450 | 1397 to 1450 |
| Florence | 17.7 | 9.9 | 9.4 | 11.6 | 37.4 | 26.3 | 36.3 | 100.0 |
| Rome | 55.5 | 64.7 | 33.9 | 48.6 | 27.8 | 41.1 | 31.1 | 100.0 |
| Venice | 15.9 | 13.6 | 24.2 | 18.0 | 20.5 | 22.8 | 59.3 | 100.0 |
| Naples | 10.9 | 0.4 | — | 2.8 | 97.7 | 2.3 | — | 100.0 |
| Geneva | — | 11.4 | 18.0 | 11.6 | — | 30.5 | 69.5 | 100.0 |
| Others[a] | — | — | 14.5 | 6.5 | — | — | 100.0 | 100.0 |
| Total |  |  |  |  |  |  |  |  |
| Percent | 100.0 | 100.0 | 100.0 | 100.0 | 24.4 | 30.9 | 44.7 | 100.0 |
| 000 f | 143 | 181 | 261 | 585 | 143 | 181 | 261 | 585 |
| 000 f per year | 6.1 | 11.7 | 16.3 | 10.8 | 6.1 | 11.7 | 16.3 | 10.8 |

[a] Avignon, Ancona, Basel, Bruges, London, and Pisa.
*Source of basic data:* de Roover 1963 pp. 47, 55, 66.

f 75,000 in 1451 (including f 17,000 attributed to the wool and silk shops) of which the Florence holding company owned nearly three-fourths, an increase at an annual rate of 2.8 percent in the first and one of 3.3 percent in the second period.

The Medici bank was a quite profitable institution until the middle of the fifteenth century. From 1397 to 1450 its profits averaged nearly f 11,000 per year, or somewhat above 10 percent of its net worth, equal to about 0.4 percent of the national product of the Florentine Republic or nearly 400 man-years' wages of an unskilled laborer. Profits rose from about f 5,000 in the first two decades of operation to f 11,700 in the years 1420–35 and to f 16,300 in the following 15 years, an average annual rate of growth of 1.8 percent. Most of the profits originated in loans and foreign exchange. The operation of two wool and one silk shops in Florence contributed only 7 percent for the period as a whole, rising from 5 percent in 1397–1420 to 11 percent in 1435–50. The Rome branch was the most profitable one, contributing nearly one-half of the firm's total profit for the period as a whole and as much as two-thirds in 1420–35. Venice contributed nearly one-fifth and Geneva and Florence fully one-tenth each. The changes in the distribution or profits during the three subperiods can be followed in Table 9-7.

Most of the total profits of the three branches during the period from 1402 to 1451 of about f 550,000 were apparently distributed to the partners since net worth does not seem to have increased by more than about f 50,000, chiefly representing retained earnings (de Roover 1963, p. 371). Most of the distributions went to members of the Medici family. Between 1397 and 1451 they received from the Florence holding company an annual average of about f 8,200 while the general managers received over f 3,700 a year, both extraordinarily high incomes being equal to about 270 and 120 years' wages of an unskilled worker (at present U.S. rates about $2.7 million and $1.2 million).

## 6    Financial instruments

The most important financial instruments, apart from coins, were bills of exchange, trade (book) credit, and claims against the commune, supplemented by loans to households by other households or by other lenders. Their total value was declared for the *catasto* of 1427 at f 7 million, including business inventories, of which f 2.6 million, or about one-third of all financial assets, consisted of the assessed value of public debt. The remaining nearly f 4.5 million were probably underreported to a substantial extent, and may be assumed actually to have had a value of at least f 5 million and possibly as much as f 6 million. Their components, though ascertainable from the original schedules that have been preserved, do not seem to have been tabulated. Since deductions, mostly debts, were reported, and evidently not understated, at f 3.3 million and net foreign claims or debts must have been relatively small, it may be assumed that claims including mortgages were of about equal size, which would leave about f 1¾ million for money and business inventories, a not unreasonable but rather low amount of which possibly one-half each might be allocated to inventories and two-thirds to coins.

The claims against the Monte were the object of an active market characterized by some contemporaries and historians as speculative (Kirshner, p. 341; Barbadoro, p. 666, already for 1371), at prices far below their book value. There is no information on the volume of transfers.

While Florence had not been a leader in their development the bill of exchange (Melis 1966–67, pp. 110ff; 1972, pp. 89, 103) the checklike *"ordine scritto"* had been in common use and fully developed since the mid-fourteenth century, and the former was the dominant instrument in the financing of foreign trade. Book credit was even older and prevailed in domestic trade. Most of the sales within the textile industry, by far the most important one in Florence, were on credit (de Roover 1968, p. 298). How common trade credit was is indicated by the fact that a stonecutter listed in his *catasto* schedule 130 debtors for f 2,178, an average of 17 – half a year's wage of an unskilled worker – including 90 accounts of less than one florin (Goldthwaithe 1980, p. 313).

Though there was a limited amount of activity in maritime insurance, a field in which Florence obviously lagged and ranked well behind Italian port cities, particularly Genova, the volume of claims outstanding at any one time was negligible, and life insurance was practically nonexistent (Edler, pp. 188ff; Melis 1966–67, ch. IV). In the absence of corporations there were no corporate stocks or bonds or other obligations. Partnerships, often of short duration, were the common form of business organization of more than small size but did not issue financial instruments evidencing ownership.

# 7 Interest rates

No financial system can operate without interest. Florentine bankers and merchants, like those all over medieval Europe, therefore took advantage of permitted exceptions to the church's prohibition of interest on loans, for example, by charging penalties for late payment or used semilegal circumventions, particularly in foreign trade by incorporating interest in the exchange rates applied.[40] Interest rates on commercial transactions appear to have ranged from 12 to 15 percent.[41] The fact that the valuation in the *catasto* capitalized property income on the basis of 7 percent indicates this was regarded as a typical yield of long-term investments. The commune promised 5 percent for most of its long-term debt, though it did not always pay them, but for its short-term debt had to pay much higher rates. Six to 8 percent was paid on time deposits by banks (de Roover 1963, pp. 41, 237). Rates on consumer credit were considerably higher as indicated by the fact that when Jewish moneylenders were readmitted to Florence in 1430 they were permitted to charge 20 percent (Molho 1971, pp. 157–60), which certainly must be regarded as well below actual effective rates. Indeed, in 1420 a regulation provided for a maximum interest rate of 25 percent (Molho 1971, p. 34).

# 8 Financing business and households

There is unfortunately little information, and hardly any in quantitative form, that would permit one to describe how capital expenditures were financed, nor is there quantitative information on the volume and composition of these expenditures. To judge from possibly comparable situations, for example, England in the late seventeenth century, gross capital expenditures are unlikely to have exceeded 5 percent of national product so that they probably were below f 150,000 a year and were devoted mainly to residential, civic, and religious structures.

Because fixed capital used in business was very small, financing was needed mostly to carry inventories and pay wages. To what extent this was done by trade or bank credit or by the owners themselves is not known. Since total debts were reported in the *catasto* at only f 2.5 million, business debts must have been considerably smaller, probably in the order of f 1 million. It can be inferred from the loans made by banks – total loans of the Florence branch of the Medici bank were only slightly above f 40,000 (Table 9-6) – that they contributed only the minority of business borrowings.

Many households were in debt that probably had essentially been incurred either for the purchase of a home or for consumptive purposes. As the value of residential property has been estimated in Table 9-4 as being in the order of f 1.5 million, home mortgage debt is unlikely to have been as high as f 0.5 million so that most of household debt appears to have been incurred to finance current consumption.

## 9    Financing the government

### Income and expenditures

The finances[42] of the Florentine Republic were characterized throughout most of the fifteenth century by very heavy military expenditures, traceable to the relatively high pay of the mercenaries used to fight the Republic's wars,[43] and were in a state of crisis for most of the fifteenth century. For the first three decades of the century, the only long period for which data are available (Table 9-8), military charges, spent largely within the Republic, accounted for about two-fifths of total expenditures. In 1427, a year of large-scale hostilities, they were close to 45 percent. Total expenditures during these three decades averaged fully f 800,000, though in years of peace they were in the order of only f 500,000, but even then were about twice as large as tax receipts. Government expenditures thus were equal in 1427 to over one-fourth of national product and during the first three decades of the century were hardly even below one-fifth of it.[44] These

Table 9-8. *Government receipts and expenditures of the Florentine Republic, 1401–30*

|  | Amounts (f 1,000 per year) | | | Distribution (%) | | |
|---|---|---|---|---|---|---|
|  | 1401 to 1410 (1) | 1411 to 1420 (2) | 1421 to 1430 (3) | 1401 to 1410 (4) | 1411 to 1420 (5) | 1421 to 1430 (6) |
|  | *I. Receipts*[a] | | | | | |
| 1. Taxes | 324 | 298 | 241 | 54.3 | 67.9 | 31.4 |
| a. Sales taxes | 205 | 198 | 159 | 34.3 | 45.1 | 20.7 |
| b. Taxes on countryside | 119 | 100 | 82 | 20.0 | 22.8 | 10.7 |
| 2. Forced loans (*prestanze*) | 273 | 141 | 526 | 45.7 | 32.1 | 68.6 |
| 3. Total | 597 | 439 | 767 | 100.0 | 100.0 | 100.0 |
|  | *II. Expenditures*[a] | | | | | |
| 1. By administration | 583 | 434 | 669 | 71.2 | 63.5 | 70.3 |
| a. Civilian[b] | 200 | 200 | 200 | 24.4 | 29.2 | 21.0 |
| b. Military | 383 | 234 | 469[c] | 46.8 | 34.3 | 49.3 |
| 2. By Monte | 236 | 250 | 282 | 28.8 | 36.5 | 29.7 |
| 3. Total[d] | 819 | 684 | 951 | 100.0 | 100.0 | 100.0 |

[a] Based on seven years in col. 1 and on five years in cols. 2 and 3.
[b] Rough estimate, probably too high.
[c] Average of three years. If the estimates for the other years (Molho 1971, p. 11) are accepted the decadal average would be between 700 and 1,000 correspondingly increasing rows 1 and 3 and changing the distribution in cols. 4 to 6.
[d] Average deficits, excluding expenses of civilian administration are given by Molho (1971) as 273, 141, and 526, respectively for cols. 1 to 3.
*Source of basic data:* Molho, 1971, p. 61.

are ratios hardly ever seen for long periods before the mid-twentieth century.[45]

The Republic had two main sources to finance its expenditures. The first was current taxes consisting of sales taxes (*gabelle*) and of taxes levied on the territory outside Florence. The receipts of sales taxes averaged nearly f 190,000 a year during the first three decades of the fifteenth century but showed a slightly declining trend. In 1427 they yielded f 185,000 or about 6 percent of consumer expenditures in the Republic, though a higher proportion of those in Florence, cities, and towns since they were not levied in the countryside. The taxes on salt and wine constituted over one-third of the total and the gate tax, mostly on foods and textiles, over one-half, while a tax on contracts contributed 7 percent (Molho 1971, p. 54). The tax on the territory outside the city brought in on the average f 100,000 a year, which constituted a substantial proportion of the total income of the countryside, probably as much as one-fifth. Its yield declined from a maximum of over f 150,000 in 1407–09 to less than f 80,000 in 1429–30, reflecting the depopulation and impoverishment of the countryside and some reduction in tax rates.[46] On the average, however, the share of sales taxes remained at about two-thirds of the total. If personal income showed no secular trend, the burden of these two taxes declined by about one-fourth from the first to the third decade of the century.

The second main source of financing the government were the *prestanze*, a property levy in the form of forced loans, which was assessed at irregular intervals, sometimes several times a year,[47] mainly to defray military expenditures, at a flat rate of 0.5 percent of net wealth plus a small amount per head. The levies showed sharp fluctuations, yielding about f 2.70 million in the first decade of the century, f 1.40 million in the second most peaceful decade, but over f 5.20 million in the third decade.[48] On an annual basis the *prestanze* ranged from f 400,000 in 1416 to f 703,000 in 1424. If changes in the value of national product, which were probably small given the relative stability of wages and prices, are disregarded, the property levy with slightly over f 300,000 per year absorbed about one-fifth of personal income of the inhabitants of Florence. From 1424 to 1430, however, with an average of about f 520,000 the levy was equal to over one-third of their personal income. Because the levy fell only on property income, its impact was even heavier. In 1427, for instance, the f 544,000 of the levy was equal to 7 percent of taxable wealth, to about 5.5 percent of taxpayers' total property, and about 100 percent of their property income (except the uncertain interest on their claims against the Monte), assumed to average 7 percent of taxable property. For the average of the first two decades of the century the impact of the levy was, of course, considerably less severe, but still probably in the order of 3 percent of taxable property, about two-fifths of property income and about one-eighth of total income. Because of the high personal exemption of f 200 per person, only a minority of families – apparently less than one-in-four[49] – were liable to pay the property levy, and most of the payments were made by a relatively small number of taxpayers. For the actual taxpayers the levy therefore absorbed a large proportion of their total income and all or more than all of their property income. In years of high levies some taxpayers apparently had to liquidate assets or to borrow in order to pay the levy. The fact that the levy increased the taxpayers' holdings of government debt and hence yielded a low and irregular income constituted only a small offset.

The expenditures of the Republic consisted essentially of three items, civilian administration, interest and amortization of the public debt, and military expenditures. Statistics of current civilian expenditures are lacking, but they may have been as high as f 200,000 a year or about 7 percent of national product. The expenditures of the public debt administration averaged a little over f 250,000 a year during the first three decades of the fifteenth century, or 8 percent of national product, with a slight upward trend. The crucial and sharply fluctuating expenditures were military, which averaged over f 350,000 a year, that is, about two-fifths of total expenditures or about one-eighth of national product, but were much higher in the first and third than in the second decade. They fluctuated for the 15 years for which they are known between f 94,000 in 1420 and f 550,000 in 1426, that is, between about 3 percent and nearly 20 percent of national product.

### Public debt

The public debt of the Republic, administered by the Monte Commune, constituted a crucial element in its financial structure.[50] It is therefore unfortunate that quantitative information is very scarce because the records, though many of them have been preserved, have not yet been organized, summarized, and published.

The Monte – called an example of "this genial creation of our city states" (Barbadoro, p. 673) – goes back to the thirteenth century, but at the beginning of the fourteenth century was very small owing less than f 50,000. It then grew rapidly, the debt reaching f 0.6 million in 1343, f 1.5 million in 1364, and f 3.0 million in 1400, the figures presumably referring to face value,[51] and hence progressively overstating the market value of the debt. In the *catasto* of 1427 holdings in the Monte were reported at f 2.6 million, which implies a face value of about f 5 million since holdings were generally assessed at one-half their face value.[52]

The public debt consisted of numerous classes with differing maturities and interest rates. The main long-term debts promised an interest rate of 5 percent, which, however, was only irregularly paid. The claims against the Monte were freely transferable, though in general only among citizens of the Republic, and by 1427 appear to have had a market value of only one-third of face value, a level which seems to have prevailed during most of the first half of the fifteenth century (Becker 1965, p. 455). There is not enough information on prices and interest payments available to calculate the effective yield on the various classes of claims against the Monte. Since most of the claims originally represented not voluntary purchases but resulted from property levies, the effective yield was important for taxpayers to decide whether to sell the claims acquired through such levies or to retain them and for others when using such claims as a short- or long-term investment.

Sales to foreigners required special authorization and were apparently rare except for sales to condottieri and mercenaries. In the decade from 1423 to 1433 only 35 such authorizations were sought, involving a face value of f 515,000 of mostly 3 percent claims and an actual value of f 305,000 (Molho 1971, p. 147) or nearly 60 percent of par. It must be assumed that foreign buyers expected the stipulated interest to be actually paid.[53]

If there were about 5,000 creditors of the Monte in 1380 (Becker 1968, p. 158), every second household in Florence and almost every middle- and upper-class family would have been, but because some houses had several accounts the unduplicated number may have been much smaller.[54] As the *prestanze* fell most heavily on these groups, the holdings in the Monte were considerably more concentrated than total wealth. Thus the top decile of wealth holders owned about seven-eighths of the total claims against the Monte compared to a share of somewhat over two-thirds in total assessed wealth and the Gini index was about 0.90 for claims against the Monte against 0.79 for the total population. Similarly, claims against the Monte constituted nearly one-third of their total assessed wealth compared to about one-eighth for the rest of the population. Finally, the holdings in the Monte of the top decile of assessees averaged about f 2,200 against the f 40 for the other households.

Another fund, the Monte delle Doti, was set up in the 1420s to enable fathers and other relatives to provide dowries (Kirshner and Molho, passim; Molho, 1971, pp. 138–43). This was done by promising depositors very high implicit interest rates – between 15 and 21 percent – on deposits for terms between 5 and 15 years. If the girl died or entered a convent, which happened in over one-fifth of the cases, only the deposit was returned (Kirshner and Molho, p. 414). The fund started very slowly. After 7 years' operations it had received only 46 deposits for a total of less than f 5,000 and even in 1442 hardly 1,800 deposits totaling f 125,000 and averaging f 71 had been offset to the extent of f 93,000 by 379 payouts averaging f 250 leaving a balance of only f 34,000. As the fund had to pay more in accumulated interest or maturing deposits than it could earn, outpayments increasingly exceeded income. By 1458 the fund had paid out f 566,000 or slightly over f 300 per depositor, $4\frac{1}{2}$ times what it had received from depositors, and thus had come to constitute a drain on the commune's resources and thereby had in effect transferred general tax revenues to the beneficiaries who generally belonged to the upper income groups as suggested by the fact that the average payout was equal to about eight times average annual household income.

## 10    A national balance sheet

A summary of the financial structure of the Florentine Republic in 1427 is provided by the tentative balance sheet shown in Table 9-9. The figures for the different components of the assets and liabilities are of course subject to a considerable margin of error, and more so for the separate estimates for the city of Florence and the rest of the territory than those for the Republic, though the main items are based on the *catasto*. Sources and details of the estimation are provided in the notes to Table 9-9.

Of the four most important ratios that can be derived from a national balance sheet, the first, the financial interrelations ratio (financial assets : tangible assets) is shown to have been on the order of two-fifths if coins are included with tangible assets, but of nearly one-half if they are treated as financial assets. This is in historical perspective a very high ratio, indicating a relatively large size of the financial superstructure, considerably higher than the ratio for England and Wales for 1688 (0.17) and that for now developed countries except Great Britain in the middle of the nineteenth century (Goldsmith 1985, Table 19). The second ratio, the financial intermediation ratio (claims against financial institutions : all financial assets) on the other hand was low, though it can only be estimated with a wide margin of error, probably on the order of only 0.05, which compares with values of 0.09 for Great Britain in 1800 and an average of 0.12 for less developed countries in the mid-twentieth century (Goldsmith 1985, Table 47). This indicates a still relatively low degree of institutionalization of the financial structure. The debt-to-assets ratio of over one-fifth was fairly high, as was the ratio of government debt to national wealth of about 15 percent on the basis of the face value of the debt, though only about one-tenth at its market value. These are levels rarely found before the nineteenth century. The share of land in total tangible assets, finally, can be estimated only very roughly as the *catasto* does

Table 9-9. *National balance sheet of the Florentine Republic in 1427*

| | Florence (1) | Rest of territory (2) | Republic (3) |
|---|---|---|---|
| | *I. Amounts[a] (f million)* | | |
| 1. Tangible assets[b] | 8.1 | 8.3 | 16.4 |
| 2. Coins | 0.8 | 0.2 | 1.0 |
| 3. Financial assets[c] | 4.0 | 1.2 | 5.2 |
| 4. Claims against Monte[d] | 1.8 | 0.0 | 1.8 |
| 5. Total assets | 14.7 | 9.7 | 24.4 |
| 6. Debt | 4.4[e] | 0.8 | 5.2 |
| | *II. Amounts per head (f 1,000)* | | |
| 1. Tangible assets[b] | 2.03 | 0.32 | 0.55 |
| 2. Coins | 0.20 | 0.01 | 0.03 |
| 3. Financial assets[c] | 1.00 | 0.05 | 0.17 |
| 4. Claims against Monte[d] | 0.45 | 0.00 | 0.06 |
| 5. Total assets | 3.68 | 0.38 | 0.81 |
| 6. Debt | 1.10[e] | 0.03 | 0.17 |
| | *III. Distribution (%)* | | |
| 1. Tangible assets[b] | 56 | 84 | 68 |
| 2. Coins | 5 | 3 | 4 |
| 3. Financial assets[c] | 27 | 13 | 21 |
| 4. Claims against Monte[d] | 12 | 0 | 7 |
| 5. Total assets | 100 | 100 | 100 |
| 6. Debt | 30[e] | 8 | 21 |

[a] Cf. text.
[b] Table 4.
[c] Excluding rows 2 and 4.
[d] Market value (as in row 6).
[e] Includes total debt of Monte.

not separate land and structure values in the real property classification and omits residential and institutional structures. It is unlikely to have been below three-fourths, compared to ratios of about two-thirds for England and Wales in 1688 and for still about one-half for most now developed countries in the early nineteenth century (Goldsmith 1985, Table 39).

## CHAPTER 10

# The financial system
# of Elizabethan England

Economically, and even more financially, England at the death of Queen Elizabeth, and certainly at her accession in 1558, was closer to the situation in the later Middle Ages of the fifteenth century[1] than to that in the mid-eighteenth century after the overseas expansion and the "financial revolution"[2] involving in particular the creation of a large tradeable public debt, a central bank issuing paper currency, and a number of joint stock companies of substantial size.

## 1 Population

The population[3] of England continued the fairly rapid growth, which had started around 1400 after the reductions reflecting the Black Death, throughout the Elizabethan period and until the mid-seventeenth century. Between 1558 and 1603 it increased by 35 percent or at an annual average rate of nearly 0.7 percent to reach at the death of Elizabeth a level of about 4.5 million or about 30 inhabitants per km². The increase by about 1.2 million was the result of crude birth rates of about 3.5 percent, death rates of about 2.5 percent, and a small net outward migration of about 0.1 percent. Expectation of life at birth averaged slightly over 35 years. In 1601, 60 percent of the population are estimated to have been in the 15–60 years group with 33 percent below 15 years and only 7 percent above 60 years and a dependency ratio of 0.7.

The population was distributed rather unevenly over the realm. Density was considerably higher in a belt stretching from Norfolk to Somerset, including the most densely populated home counties, than in the rest of the country, particularly in Wales, the Midlands, and the North.[4]

Urbanization was fairly high for a preindustrial country. London alone with 200,000 inhabitants around 1600 – compared to only 45,000 in 1500 (Palliser, p. 203; for 1500 Miskimin, p. 185) – accounted for

Table 10-1. *Occupational distribution of households, 1688 (%)*

| Occupation | | Households (1) | Members (2) | Income (3) |
|---|---|---|---|---|
| I. Aristocracy[a] | | 0.1 | 0.5 | 5.9 |
| II. Agriculture[b] | } excluding | 17.6 | 33.8 | 33.3 |
| III. Other occupations | }      IV | 31.4 | 12.9 | 48.3 |
| 1. Officeholders | | 0.7 | 1.3 | 3.3 |
| 2. Professionals[c] | | 2.4 | 2.3 | 4.9 |
| 3. Merchants | | 1.9 | 1.2 | 11.6 |
| 4. Shopkeepers and tradesmen | | 7.3 | 3.3 | 8.4 |
| 5. Artisans[d] | | 18.4 | 4.4 | 18.8 |
| 6. Military and naval officers | | 0.7 | 0.7 | 1.2 |
| IV. Laborers, outservants, common sailors and soldiers, cottagers, paupers, and vagrants. | | 50.8 | 52.7 | 12.5 |
| V. Total | | 1391[e] | 5500[e] | 54.4[f] |

[a] Lords, baronets and knights.
[b] Includes esquires and gentlemen (1.2 in col. 1, 10.8 in col. 2).
[c] Includes clergymen.
[d] Includes miners.
[e] Thousands.
[f] Million pounds.
*Source:* Gregory King's estimates as revised by Lindert and Williamson, p. 393, for cols. 1 and 3; King's estimates (p. 31) for col. 2 which differ slightly from those that would be obtained by applying King's figures of members per household to Lindert and Williamson's for numbers of households.

nearly 5 percent of total population, its growth due entirely to net immigration from the countryside since the excess of death over births has been estimated at over 50,000 for the second half of the sixteenth century alone (Wrigley and Schofield, p. 168). The three next largest cities of more than 10,000 inhabitants each (Bristol, Norwich, and York) accounted for another 1 percent, and the remaining 15 cities with more than 5,000 inhabitants each added fully 2 percent for a total ratio of about 8 percent (Palliser, p. 203). There were in addition about 80 county centers and about 500 generally quite small market towns with a population between 600 and 1,500.[5] If these are included, the urbanization ratio should have been on the order of 20 percent. The share of foreigners was small – probably well below 1 percent – but their importance in commerce and handicrafts was substantial.[6]

While there are no estimates of the social or occupational distribution of the population and its income during the reign of Elizabeth, that for 1688, shown in Table 10-1, should approximate it with the exception that the share of agriculture (group II and most of group IV) should have been somewhat higher at the beginning of the seventeenth century than near its end and that of most other occupations somewhat lower.

In 1688 agriculture, here including only esquires, gentlemen, freeholders, and farmers but not farm laborers, cottagers, and rural poor, accounted for fully one-sixth of all households, for one-third of total population, and for one-third of total personal income. These ratios are, of course, far below the share of the total rural population, which should have been on the order of about three-fifths of all households (cf. Section 1) and well over one-half of total income (cf. Section 2).[7] Among other occupations artisans (including manufacturing, handicrafts, building trades, and mining) and shopkeepers and tradesmen dominated, together accounting for one-fourth of both the number of households and of their total income. These ratios are probably as high as may be found for these groups in premodern economies. What might be regarded as the bourgeoisie (officeholders, professionals, merchants, and officers) numbered about 5 percent of households but received fully 20 percent of total personal income. If esquires and gentlemen are included, though most of them lived in the countryside, the share of the group rises to 6 percent of households and to 30 percent of personal income. At the bottom, what would later be called the proletariat (group IV) constituted one-half of all households but received only one-eighth of total personal income.

An indication of the occupational distribution of the urban population outside of London during the sixteenth century, mostly during its second half, can be derived from the data for seven cities (Table 10-1).[8] The most numerous were the food and drink and the leather crafts with nearly one-fifth each of the total, followed by the textile and clothing trades with one-eighth each, and by the metal working and building trades with about 5 percent each. Since no figures are provided for gentry and professions at the upper end of the income scale and for inactive persons and paupers at the other, these ratios overstate the share of the enumerated trades in the total population. It has been estimated that in the early sixteenth century wage earners constituted at least one-half of the urban and about one-fourth to one-third of the rural labor force (Clarkson, pp. 47–8).

## 2    National product and wealth

In the absence of any serious contemporary or modern estimates of national product and wealth, the only feasible if hazardous approach

Table 10-2. *Estimate of gross national product of England and Wales, 1565 and 1603*

|  |  | 1565 (1) | 1603 (2) |
|---|---|---|---|
| 1. Population ⎫ |  | 63 | 86 |
| 2. Price level ⎪ |  | 53 | 81 |
| 3. Real product per head ⎬ 1688 = 100 |  | 79 | 85 |
| 4. Gross national ⎱ Aggregate ⎪ |  | 26 | 59 |
| 5. product ⎰ per head ⎭ |  | 42 | 69 |
| 6. Gross national ⎱ Aggregate (million £) |  | 14.1 | 32.1 |
| 7. product ⎰ Per head (£) |  | 4.2 | 6.9 |
| 8. Gross national ⎱ Aggregate (million £ of 1688) |  | 27.0 | 39.7 |
| 9. product ⎰ Per head (£ of 1688) |  | 7.9 | 8.5 |
| 10. Gross national ⎱ Aggregate (tons of gold) |  | 135 | 310 |
| 11. product ⎰ Per head (g of gold) |  | 41 | 67 |

*Sources:* Line 1 – Wrigley and Schofield, p. 528, with addition for Wales of about 0.20 million; line 2 – compare text below; line 4 – lines 1 × 2 × 3; line 5 – lines 2 × 3; lines 6 and 7 – lines 4 and 5 × 1688 values (£54.4 million and £10.0, respectively) of Lindert and Williamson, p. 393; lines 8 and 9 – product of lines 1 and 3 or line 3 × 1688 values; lines 10 and 11 – lines 6 and 7 × 0.965 g gold per £, i.e., £36 per pound troy of 373 g.

is to start from the estimates of Gregory King for 1688 (King, pp. 30, 32) and to extrapolate them backwards to 1603, the year of the death of Elizabeth I and to 1565 just after the recoinage and only seven years after the Queen's accession. The various steps taken in this estimation can be followed in Table 10-2.

National product in 1688 has been put in a recent revision of King's estimates at £54.4 million (Lindert and Williamson, p. 393) (compared to his figures of £43.5 million) or £9.9 per head (compared to King's £7.9). These figures may be regarded as reasonably reliable. The population of England in 1565 and in 1603 according to the most recent estimates was 14 and 37 percent, respectively, below that of 1688 (Wrigley and Schofield, p. 528), and it has been assumed that the inclusion of Wales, which had only about 5 percent of the population of England did not affect the ratios (Pollard and Crossley, p. 83; Wrigley and Schofield, p. 566). The margin of uncertainty is wider for the increase in the price level, which was undoubtedly substantial (cf. Section 3). An estimate that puts the price level of 1603 at nearly one-fifth below that of 1688 and that of 1565 at only slightly above one-half of that level has been accepted. Combining the changes in population and price level yields a gross national product in 1565 of 42 percent and in 1603 of 69 percent of that of 1688. There are no firm data on which to base an estimate of the movements in real product per head. It seems, however, reasonable to assume a small increase, here put at 0.2 percent per year, for the seventeenth century,[9] as well as for the period of 1565 to 1603. Aggregate real product per head in 1603 and in 1565 would then be 15 percent and 21 percent below that of 1688, while the estimate of aggregate national product in current prices would be about 40 percent below that of 1688 in 1603 and in 1565 would stand at about 25 percent of the 1688 level, the corresponding figures for product per head being about 30 and nearly 60 percent below those of 1688. The estimates of national product in current prices of about £32 million in 1603 and of about £14 in 1565, equal to 67 and 41 g of gold per head,[10] will be used throughout the chapter as a scalar for many other magnitudes,[11] fully realizing the substantial margin of uncertainty involved.

Lacking the possibility of estimating the sectoral distribution of national product in 1603 or in 1565, some indication of the situation can be obtained by the distribution of 1688. While King does not provide figures for the most important characteristic of sectoral distribution, the share of agriculture, an estimate of 56 percent has been derived from his data.[12] The shares in 1603 and particularly in 1565 should be somewhat higher, probably in the order of three-fifths in 1603 and close to two-thirds in 1565.[13]

King's estimates also provide some insight into the shares of the income of some nonagricultural sectors in total personal income, which in 1688 was very close to total national product. Thus, the income of the 128,000 families in commerce, which constituted 13 percent of all families, amounted to one-fifth of total personal income and that of the 94,000 families of seamen, soldiers, and officers to only 4 percent.[14] This would be about two-fifths of total nonagricultural personal income.[15]

There are no data to allocate total product among regions. It is, however, very likely that average income per family or person was higher in London and the few other larger cities than in the rest of the country, and that it was generally higher in the flatter and better watered eastern and southern counties than in the hillier and drier western counties of England and in Wales (cf., e.g., Coleman, pp. 32–4).

King estimated the "increase of the nation," to be interpreted as investment or saving, probably on a gross basis, in 1688 at £1.8 million (King, p. 47) or 4 percent of income, an astonishingly high figure as

Table 10-3. *Estimates of distribution of personal income*

| Average annual income (£) | Number | | Income | |
|---|---|---|---|---|
| | Percent of families | | Percent of families | |
| | Class | Cumulated | Class | Cumulated |
| < 15 | 48.3 | 48.3 | 13.0 | 13.0 |
| 16–50 | 36.0 | 84.3 | 34.0 | 47.0 |
| 21–100 | 10.5 | 94.8 | 17.2 | 64.2 |
| 101–500 | 4.8 | 99.6 | 27.3 | 91.5 |
| 501–1,000 | 0.3 | 99.9 | 4.0 | 95.5 |
| > 1,000 | 0.07 | 100.0 | 4.5 | 100.0 |

it implies at an average reproducible capital–output ratio of 2,[16] an annual rate of growth of about 2 percent. There are no data available for an alternative estimate or for a modification applicable to 1603 or 1565.

More confidence can, on the other hand, be placed in the revised estimates of the distribution of personal income based on King's figures which are summarized in Table 10-3 (Lindert and Williamson, p. 393).

Thus the lower half of income recipients accounted for not much over one-eighth of total personal income, while it took only about one-seventh of all families to account for one-half of all personal income. The 1,026 families with income of over £1,000 per year – about 25 times the average family income – representing only 0.073 percent of all families – received nearly 5 percent of all personal incomes. Finally the 200 temporal lords with an average income per family estimated at £6,060 appropriated 2.2 percent of total personal income. This represented a high degree of concentration of income with a Gini ratio of about 0.55.[17]

Although there are no statistics to confirm the hypothesis, it is likely that income was somewhat but probably not much less concentrated in 1603 and in 1565, at least at the very top of the income pyramid, as the accumulation of large fortunes depending on royal favors during the seventeenth century[18] may have been offset by the inroads of the Commonwealth.

A contemporary estimate of the rent income of the temporal and spiritual lords can be found in Thomas Wilson's *State of England*, written in 1600, without indicating sources or methods of derivation. Wilson put the rent income of the 61 lords at £220,000 or £3,600 apiece.[19]

This compares with King's estimate for 1688 of the income of 160 lords of almost £450,000 or £2,800 apiece, figures revised by Lindert and Williamson to 200 lords with an average income of £6,060 or a total of slightly over £1.2 million. The relation of the average income in 1600 and 1688 is not unreasonable if the revised figures are accepted for 1688. The aggregate income of the lords according to these estimates would have been equal to about 0.6 percent of national product in 1600 but to 1.0 percent (King) or 2.2 percent (Lindert and Williamson) in 1688. The income of the 25 spiritual lords, whose number did not change, was put by Wilson at £22,500 and by King at £34,000, a reasonable relation. Caution is, of course, suggested about using Wilson's figures. Wilson's estimates for knights (500 with an average income of £1,000 to £2,000) and particularly that for esquires (16,000 with £500 to £1,000 apiece) appear to be greatly exaggerated even if the lower boundary for the average income is used.

More reliable though limited to a narrower group are the estimates of Stone that put the total gross income of the about 60 peers at £150,000 in 1559 and at £195,000 in 1602, equivalent to nearly 1 percent and 0.6 percent, respectively, of national product. Landed income is estimated at nine-tenths of the total, the remainder being ascribed to "fruits of office." Interest payments are put at £10,000 and £25,000, respectively, reducing net income of £140,000 and £170,000, the increase by one-eighth lagging well behind the increase in the price level (Stone, p. 762).

In the case of national wealth it is again necessary to start with King's estimates for 1688, which put it at nearly £300 million or 6.8 times his estimate of national income (King, pp. 32, 37, 39), though only 5.4 times the revised estimate of Lindert and Williamson. The still predominantly agricultural character of the English economy even at the end of the seventeenth century is reflected in the share of over one-half of agricultural land.

The figures for 1603, and still more those for 1565, must have been substantially lower, if only because of the smaller population, and of the lower level of prices, particularly for land, though the distribution should have been similar.[20] The stock of coined money, for example, has been put at only £3.5 million in 1603 compared to £11.5 million in 1688.[21] Land rents in 1600 were not much above two-fifths of the level of 1688 according to a contemporary estimate.[22] The value of agricultural land in 1600 may then have been on the order of £80 million. In that case total national wealth may have totaled about £130 million or about 4.0 times national product.[23]

Regional differences in wealth were substantial, apart even from higher levels in urban than in rural areas. In 1524–25 taxable wealth per square mile was below 10 sh (shillings) in the North of England and in Wales but above 30 sh in most of the counties south of a line stretching from the Wash to the Bristol Channel[24] and the relationships, if not the absolute values, should have been similar during Elizabeth's reign.[25] Differences in wealth per head were, of course, smaller. Another estimate referring to 1514 and 1535 assigns the first five places among 34 English counties to Middlesex (including London), Devon, Gloucester, Somerset, and Surrey, and the last five places to Stafford, Salop, Derby, Yorkshire, and Lancashire, all south and north, respectively, of the Wash–Bristol Channel line. Regional differences in wealth appear not to have changed substantially between the early fourteenth and sixteenth centuries (Schofield, Table 2) so that a substantial change during the rest of the sixteenth century is unlikely.

## 3     The monetary system

Elizabethan England like most premodern economies had a symmetallic monetary system in which both domestic gold and silver coins circulated and were legal tender but without a fixed ratio between the two metals. In the two decades before Elizabeth's accession England had experienced the most serious monetary upheaval in its history known as the Great Debasement.[26] During this period, and particularly between 1545 and 1551, the metallic content of gold coins had been reduced in several steps by one-fourth and that of silver coins by about four-fifths, leading to similar declines in their foreign exchange value. The operation yielded the crown a profit of about £1.2 million. While this represented only a small fraction of the period's national product – not more than about 2 percent – it constituted a substantial addition to current revenues, possibly more than one-half of them, an addition used to help finance foreign wars. Since most of the profits were made on silver coins, it was their holders, that is, in general the less well-off population, who suffered most of the loss, rather than the holders of gold coins, presumably mainly merchants and wealthier members of the population.

The first significant action taken by the new queen's government in the economic field, and arguably the most important one throughout Elizabeth's reign, was the recoinage of 1560–61, which has been called "a financial operation of unexampled magnitude" (Cunningham, p. 127) and was regarded, as attested by epitaph on the queen's tomb, as one of the three outstanding achievements of her reign next to the religious settlement and the maintenance of peace (Palliser, p. 139).

The operation was completed in less than one year ending in September 1561, using in addition to the main mint in the Tower of London about half a dozen temporary mints in the provinces.[27] Recoinage, limited to silver, provided nearly £800,000 of new coins, using mostly the metal of coins turned in, which had a face value of over £940,000 supplemented by £75,000 of silver bullion purchased in Antwerp.[28] As the costs of recoinage were substantial, the crown derived only a small profit from the operation.[29]

Silver coins were issued in denominations of 5 s (shillings), 2 s 6 d (pence), 1 s, 2 d, 1½ d, 1 d, ¾ d, and ½ d. They were minted – predominantly by hammering but in small amounts also by the newer milling technique – at the rate of 8 grains = 0.52 g of sterling silver per penny or 125 g per pound sterling. This restored the coins to the standard of the mid-1540s, though still leaving them one-fourth below that in force before the early 1520s, a standard that with only a very small reduction in 1601 remained unchanged, as for gold coins, until the twentieth century. The largest silver coin, the crown of 5 s issued only near the end of the queen's reign weighed about 30 g and had a diameter of fully 4 cm; the smallest, the halfpenny, was a diminutive piece of silver with a diameter of less than 1 cm, weighing only 0.25 g (Grueber, pp. 97–9 and plates XIX and XX; Feaveryear, pp. 435–9).

The gold circulation consisted of coins issued during Elizabeth's reign as well as of some older English coins and until their demonetization some foreign coins. Numerous types and denominations of gold coins were issued, most 980/1000 fine, but some only 917/1000 fine. The gold coins ranged from the sovereign with a value of 30 s, a weight of 15 g and a diameter of over 4 cm, which was minted only from 1584 on, to the half-crown (2 s 6 d) which weighed only ¼ g and had a diameter of less than 1.5 cm (Grueber, pp. 94–7 and plates XVIII and XIX; Feaveryear, pp. 436–8).

The smallest coin in circulation, the halfpenny, was still too large for many petty transactions as it was equal to nearly one hour's wage of a common laborer. As a result numerous types of tokens issued by cities or by private parties were in use about which little is known, but which in the aggregate can only have constituted a small fraction of the silver and gold coins in circulation. The gold coins, the smallest of which was equal to nearly a week's wages of a common laborer, were probably essentially limited to transactions among merchants or used for thesaurization.

The crown charged moderate fees for coining bullion brought to the mint, practicing in Knapp's terms hylolepsy, though it did not exchange coins for bullion, that is, did not have hylophantism. The charges for silver coins rose from 0.3 d per troy ounce in 1560 to 0.7 d from 1583 for seignorage and stayed at 1.2 d for expenses, a total of 2.5 and 3.2 percent, respectively. For gold coins the charges rose from 4.8 d per troy ounce to 10.9 d, or from 0.7 to 1.15 percent (Feaveryear, pp. 435–6). Under such a regime monetary policy was essentially limited to changes in the metallic content of the various coins minted.

The volume of coins in circulation immediately after the recoinage has been put at £1.45 million (Challis, cited Palliser, p. 136). Coinage during Elizabeth's reign is given as £5.4 million, predominantly silver (£4.6 million, including £0.8 million recoined). The sources of the silver minted are not well known. Most of it apparently came from Spanish America, partly as the result of naval or privateering operations.[30] Since the amount in circulation in 1603 has been estimated at only £3.50 million,[31] approximately £3.4 million appear to have been exported, used for plate or other nonmonetary purposes, or to have represented wear and tear of the coins in circulation – admittedly an improbably large amount. There is little doubt that a substantial part of the gold in circulation in 1561 left the country because the gold–silver ratio was somewhat higher than on the continent and by 1603 may have been as low as £0.15 million, notwithstanding a coinage of about £0.8 million. The share of gold in total circulation would then have fallen from about one-third in 1561 to only about 5 percent 40 years later, a possibly exaggerated decline, compared to a share of gold in total coinage during Elizabeth's reign of about one-fifth (excluding recoined silver).[32]

The estimates of total circulation of about £1.5 million in 1561 and of £3.5 million in 1603 both are equal to about one-tenth of national product. They thus imply an income velocity of about 10 with respect to total national product, but a substantially lower value, though not likely one below 5, with respect to monetized product at the end of Elizabeth's reign as well as in the mid-1560s. Since the volume of real national product can have expanded only slightly, the increase in money in circulation appears to have been only somewhat in excess of the rise in the price level. In other words in the quantity identity of $MV = PT$ between 1565 and 1603, $T$ changed only slightly while $M$ increased by over 50 percent and $V$ appears to have increased by about 40 percent in relation to total national product but somewhat less on the basis of monetized product. The inferred direction of $V$ is probably correct, though the size seems rather large.

## 4 Prices, wages, and interest rates

After commodity prices had approximately doubled between the mid-1520s and the 1550s, reflecting from the 1540s on primarily the debasement of the currency, they showed only minor fluctuations until the early 1570s. After a sharp rise in the mid-1570s they remained at a level about one-fourth higher until the mid-1590s. They then took another sharp upward turn under the influence of several very poor crops, reaching a peak at nearly three times the level of the 1560s in 1597. Though prices declined substantially from this peak, their level at the end of Elizabeth's reign (1599–1603) was still more than 80 percent higher than they had been at its start (1558–62), an annual rate of increase of 1.5 percent.[33] In a still predominantly agricultural economy annual price movements, mainly reflecting the size of the crops, were sometimes violent. Thus the price index increased by 36 percent in 1574, by 39 percent in 1587, and by 36 percent in 1597, probably somewhat overstating the increase in a more comprehensive unavailable measure such as the national product deflator. There were, however, also considerable differences in the trends in the prices of the various groups of commodities, which can be followed in Table 10-4 and 10-5 on a decadal or quinquennial basis. The main difference was that between agricultural prices (which between the 1560s and the 1600s increased by nearly 70 percent) and industrial prices (which advanced by only about 10 percent) there was a gap that has been interpreted as a reflection of the pressure of a rapidly growing population on a more slowly increasing volume of agricultural production. Differences were much smaller among agricultural prices. Between 1558–62 and 1598–1602 grain prices rose by 60 percent, livestock prices by 66 percent, and the prices of animal products by 77 percent. The increase in timber prices of 63 percent was of the same dimension.

Information on the movements of wages and rents are much poorer. Money wages appear to have increased by one-third in agriculture to somewhat over one-half for building craftsmen indicating a substantial decrease in real wages in the first case and a moderate one in the second case. All available evidence suggests a substantial increase in rents, but it is not firm or comprehensive enough to assert that, as seems probable, it was larger than the increase in prices (cf. Section 5).

There was no credit market that would make it possible to determine the levels of interest rates of different types and to follow their

Table 10-4. *Population, prices, wages, and exports in England,*
*1550–1609 (1550–1559 = 100)*

|  | 1550–59 | 1560–69 | 1570–79 | 1580–89 | 1590–99 | 1600–09 |
|---|---|---|---|---|---|---|
| Population[1] | 100 | 99 | 108 | 120 | 127 | 135 |
| Prices |  |  |  |  |  |  |
| Consumables[2] | 100 | 93 | 106 | 119 | 158 | 159 |
| Agricultural[3] | 100 | 104 | 116 | 132 | 167 | 171 |
| Industrial[4] | 100 | 117 | 120 | 124 | 128 | 138 |
| Wages |  |  |  |  |  |  |
| Money wages |  |  |  |  |  |  |
| Agricultural[5] | 100 | 111 | 129 | 127 | 137 | 137 |
| Building[6] | 100 | 127 | 127 | 154 | 157 | 155 |
| Real wages |  |  |  |  |  |  |
| Agricultural[7] | 100 | 112 | 117 | 97 | 83 | 85 |
| Building[8] | 100 | 122 | 125 | 112 | 92 | 90 |
| Cloth exports[9] | 100 | 87 | 91 | 99 | 102 | — |

[a] Building craftsmen.
*Sources:* [1] Wrigley and Schofield, p. 528; [2] Phelps-Brown and Hopkins, 1981, p. 29;
[3–5,7,8] Bowden, pp. 862, 865; [6] derived from Phelps-Brown and Hopkins, p. 29. The
figures for the first three decades refer to the years 1552, 1561–62, and 1565–69 and
1570–73, respectively; [9] Davis, p. 53; exports through London. The figures refer to the
averages of the years 1550–52, 1559–70, 1571–79, 1580–88, and 1589–94 plus 1598–
1600, respectively.

Table 10-5. *Agricultural and timber prices, 1553–1602*
*(1553–1557 = 100)*

|  | Grains (1) | Other arable crops (2) | Live- stock (3) | Animal products (4) | All agri- cultural products (5) | Timber (6) |
|---|---|---|---|---|---|---|
| 1553–57 | 100 | 100 | 100 | 100 | 100 | 100 |
| 1558–62 | 83 | 112 | 105 | 107 | 97 | 104 |
| 1563–67 | 92 | 111 | 107 | 119 | 100 | 106 |
| 1568–72 | 83 | 102 | 118 | 114 | 101 | 115 |
| 1573–77 | 100 | 116 | 135 | 129 | 117 | 123 |
| 1578–82 | 108 | 116 | 138 | 136 | 123 | 132 |
| 1583–87 | 119 | 131 | 134 | 141 | 129 | 148 |
| 1588–92 | 119 | 137 | 146 | 167 | 138 | 151 |
| 1593–97 | 179 | 180 | 163 | 178 | 175 | 173 |
| 1598–1602 | 149 | 157 | 174 | 189 | 164 | 169 |

*Source:* Bowden, pp. 848–49.

movements over the second half of the sixteenth century. One of the most important factors influencing interest rates, explicit or implicit, was the legislation against usury, a carryover from the Middle Ages.[34] In 1571 interest charges of not above 10 percent were legalized as non-usurious. One may be fairly certain that the actual effective rates were rarely below that level after or before that date. They were probably somewhat above the 10 percent level in most commercial transactions and far above it in the case of consumer credit.

## 5    Financial instruments and organizations

The financial system of Elizabethan England was characterized less by the volume of financial transactions, which was already substantial, than by its unorganized character evidenced by the sporadic nature of transactions, by their use for consumptive and often necessitous purposes rather than for facilitating production or distribution, and by the absence of specialized lenders.

The range of financial instruments was limited, though several forms of short-term debt were available under common or merchant law, including advance payments, open book credit, bills of exchange, bottomry loans,[35] recognizances, statutes, and mortgages. None of these instruments were transferable. Since commitments were legally limited to six months, periodic renewals were necessary for any longer-term loans. There were no standardized government obligations and only very few corporate securities.

Though many persons both in business and outside made loans more or less frequently, none specialized on lending money or on accepting deposits. There were thus no banks and no savings institutions, not even the charitable pawn-and-loan organizations found in some continental countries. Maritime insurance had been practiced for a long time, but here too there were no persons or organizations specializing in this activity, which was exercised more or less regularly, as a part of their main business, mainly by merchants, originally mostly foreigners but in the later sixteenth century increasingly Englishmen (cf. Martin, chapters 1–3).

## 6    Financing agriculture

In a country in which about two-thirds of the population depended for its livelihood on agriculture, which generated about three-fifths of national product and accounted for over four-fifths of national wealth, the sources and methods of financing agriculture played, of course, a decisive role in the process of national saving, investment, credit, and debt. The information available on these matters is unfortunately quite insufficient in comparison to their importance.

The development of agriculture in Elizabethan England was determined by an increase of its population by about one million, or fully one-third, of which about four-fifths lived in the countryside in the face of the country's self-sufficiency in food except in a few years of crop failures. Since it is unlikely that food consumption per head declined substantially – a tendency to decline as real wages fell being offset by an increase in the share of food in total expenditures in line with Engle's law – and since the increase in the area under cultivation appears to have been moderate (Ramsey, p. 45) there must have been a substantial increase in yields per acre that reflected improvements in some agricultural techniques.[36]

The demand for finance of agriculture as well as its forms and sources depended to a good extent on the distribution of ownership and the character of operation of agricultural enterprises because owners and particularly owner-operators were more likely to have demanded and obtained outside funds than tenants.

Of the approximately 18 million acres of cultivated land in England and Wales,[37] it may be roughly estimated that at the end of the sixteenth century, approximately 5 percent each were owned by the crown and by the church, about one-fifth by a small number of large secular owners – probably not more than a few hundred – and a full one-third by the county and parish gentry numbering nearly 20,000. This left about one-third of the cultivated area to be owned by freeholders, inheritable copyholders, and other smaller owners with less secure tenures.[38] The number of operating agricultural units has been estimated at about 250,000, apparently excluding the numerous subtenants. The average operating unit then would have had about 40 acres, allowing for subtenants, a figure in accord with the general impression that Elizabethan England was a country of medium-sized and small farms.[39]

The two-thirds of the cultivated land owned by the crown, the church, and the aristocracy was organized in several thousand manors, part of whose area was operated by the owners, while most of it was let to tenants under different forms of tenure. In a small group of 118 manors with 6,200 tenants, that is, slightly over 50 per manor, fully one-fifth were freeholders, nearly two-thirds customary, generally long-term, tenants and one-seventh, generally short-term, leaseholders.[40] About one-half of the land was still cultivated in common, while the other half was enclosed. The area enclosed appears to have increased only very slowly during Elizabeth's reign.[41] Mixed farming whose main products were barley followed by wheat, fodder crops, meat, and dairy products, prevailed in the eastern and southern counties of England and in western Wales, open pasture, chiefly for sheep, in the northwest, southwest, and the eastern part of Wales.[42]

A rough estimation of the number of agricultural units and their size and of that of manors around 1600 may then proceed as follows:[43]

1. Total agricultural area based on Gregory King's estimate for 1688: 18 million acres.
2. Number of agricultural units (including subtenants) based on a share of rural population of 60 percent or 4.5 million of which one-fourth landless laborers and an average agricultural household size of five persons (King, p. 31): 0.40 million.
3. Number of agricultural units in manors, assuming one-third of area to have been operated by freeholders and others outside of manors: 0.27 million.
4. Average size of agricultural units: 45 acres.
5. Number of manors of peerage[44] : 2,200.
6. Total number of manors, assumed to be proportional to share of peers in manorial lands, that is, one-fifth: 11,000.
7. Average size of manors: 1,310 acres.
8. Average number of tenants and subtenants per manor (3:6): 25.

In comparison to the information on agricultural lands and their ownership, operation, and production, the information on the use of credit in agriculture is minimal. The scattered evidence, which does not seem to have ever been studied systematically,[45] points, however, to a substantial though sporadic use of short-term credit, but to the practical absence of long-term credit. Short-term credit was, often in the form of advance payments by merchants to producers, usually needed to tie operators from one harvest to the next, was extended between villagers or between them and their landlord or the merchant who bought their produce, and often involved very high (implicit if not explicit) interest charges. Because the legal system did not acknowledge contracts for a period of more than six months, whatever effectively longer-term credit there was necessitated cumbersome and expensive rollover operations and was limited to landowners, excluding tenants. Many members of the aristocracy borrowed substantial sums, in part on the security in one form or another of their lands or rents, but most of the sums so raised were not used in their agricultural operations but for consumptive purposes, including the construction of often elaborate residences, which became common during Elizabeth's reign (cf., e.g., Palliser, p. 113). These are therefore discussed in Section 9 as consumer credits. The apparently very small volume of credit raised for agricultural investment is explained, apart from the lack of an organized credit market, by the small extent of agricultural improvement and the apparent stagnation in the number of livestock,[46] the main asset of agriculture other than land. Whatever capital investment was needed was apparently essentially supplied by the owner's or operator's saving (Tawney 1925, p. 43). Similarly the substantial amount of changes of hand of land appears to have been effected without more than the occasional use of credit. Quantification of the volume of strictly agricultural debt outstanding or of its change during Elizabeth's reign is precluded by the scarcity of relevant information.

## 7    Financing domestic handicrafts and trades

Elizabethan England had already a substantial sector of partly urban and partly rural handicrafts and trades evidenced by their estimated share in 1688 of as much as 27 percent in the number of families and of 31 percent in total personal income.[47] Of these about 4 percent with nearly one-fourth of the income were merchants, fully one-fourth with the same share in income shopkeepers and traders, and fully two-thirds with one-half of income were engaged in handicrafts, building, and mining. About one-half of them,[48] with a substantially higher share of their income, were independent operators. During Elizabeth's reign the shares of these groups were probably slightly lower.

Very little is known about the use of credit in this sector. Most transactions among merchants and a substantial part of those between artisans and traders are likely to have involved the extension of credit in the form of open book credit and of bills of exchange given the spread of credit as early as the later Middle Ages.[49] The great majority of credits were required for working capital rather than for fixed investments (Clarkson, pp. 98–9).

The total capital employed in domestic and foreign trade in 1600 has been put at £10 million (Scott, vol. I, p. 457), most of it undoubtedly in the former. The volume of credit contributing to this capital can have amounted to only a fraction of the total and probably exceeded the volume of credit used by artisans.

## 8　Financing foreign trade

Foreign trade played only a minor role in most sectors of the Elizabethan economy. Around 1600 exports had a value of £1.25 to £1.50 million,[50] or about 4 percent of national product, and imports must have been of about the same size. They were thus much smaller than a century later when the ratios were on the order of 10 percent.[51] Foreign trade was, however, of substantial importance as an outlet for English manufactured products and as a source of supply of them since exports and imports have been estimated to have accounted for about one-fourth of the total in both cases and in the case of the production of woolen textiles for as much as one-half (Davis, p.8). It is unlikely that the ratio of foreign trade to national product changed substantially during the second half of the sixteenth century.[52]

The number of overseas merchants has been estimated at 10,000 in 1688 with an income of £2.4 million, accounting with their families for about 0.7 percent of the population but for about 5 percent of national income.[53] Around 1600 the ratios were probably lower.

Exports were dominated by woolen cloths (about half in undyed and undressed state), which appear to have accounted for over four-fifths of the total, and for London, the chief port of origin, stayed close to 120,000 shortcloths a year from the 1560s to the turn of the century.[54] Tin and lead followed at great distance. The leading imports were wine and brandy; textiles, particularly linens and silks; and tropical foods, particularly sugar and pepper, which together accounted for over two-thirds of the total.[55]

During the Elizabethan period, particularly its first half, most of foreign trade was with continental Europe, much of it through Antwerp and Hamburg.[56]

In comparison to the volume and structure of foreign trade little is known about the methods of financing it. Imports were probably financed mainly by the foreign suppliers. The financing of exports was concentrated on that of woolen cloth, most of which were in the hands of members of the Merchants Adventurers[57] after the 1590s when the Hanseatic merchants who had previously participated in the trade were expelled. As a result the share of foreign merchants in cloth exports declined from about one-half in mid-sixteenth century to 3 percent early in the seventeenth century (Friis, p. 47) partly due to the higher rate of export duty for foreigners than for English merchants – 14 sh 6 d against 6 sh 8 d per cloth. Not all of the about 3,000 members[58] participated in the export of woolens, but for many of them, particularly the larger ones, it was their main activity.

Early in the seventeenth century (1606) 216 members of the Merchants Adventurers shared in the export of 94,000 cloths. The five largest exporters, averaging 2,200 cloths, accounted for about one-eighth of total exports and 26 others who exported over 1,000 cloths each for another one-third, leaving not much over one-half of total exports to the other 195 members who averaged about 270 cloths (Friis, p. 78). While the smaller exporters acted as individuals, most of the larger ones operated as small partnerships, often only for one or a few shipments. The chain of transactions involved was commonly financed by bills of exchange – at that time not yet transferable – between clothier and exporter and between exporter and his foreign client, in the first case on terms of 6 to 15 months (Friis, p. 25), or by bottomry loans. The bills apparently did not carry an explicit interest charge, which was included in the price (Ramsey, p. 90). The volume of credit involved in these two stages might therefore have been on the order of £2 million, or somewhat over 5 percent of national product. Most of the total was used in financing exports to the continent. The capital employed in trade with Russia, Africa, and India at the end of the sixteenth century has been estimated at only £0.25 million (Scott, vol. I, p. 457).

Outside funds were also raised by the joint-stock or regulated companies formed since the middle of the sixteenth century mainly to trade beyond the customary markets[59]: the Russia Company, incorporated in 1553, the Spanish Company (1577), the Northwest Company (1577), the Eastland Company (1579), the Levant Company (1581), and finally the largest of them, the East India Company (1600) (Coleman, p. 59; Scott, pp. 462ff). These companies were still very loosely organized, often collecting funds for individual voyages and distributing the proceeds after their completion. They were of modest size and had only a small number of shareholders. Six companies for which the information is available had a nominal capital of not much over £150,000 of which over two-fifths were accounted for by the East India Company (Scott, pp. 462ff).

## 9    Consumer financing

Loans to consumers, or more correctly loans to finance current consumption rather than investment, were pervasive throughout Elizabethan England, but as they were made sporadically, generally in small amounts and without an organized market or specialized lenders, very little is known about them except for those incurred by the aristocracy. They ranged from loans within families or among neighbors to accounts due to tradesmen, borrowings on pawns, and, where larger amounts were involved, borrowings by more formal instruments. How common borrowing was at least among the wealthier classes is indicated by the fact that in one county debts averaged nearly one-third of the value of widows' estates valued at more than £75 (Clarkson, p. 148). As most of these borrowings were necessitous, the explicit or implicit interest charges were usually very high, in part because interest rates of over 10 percent were illegal and loans involving them risky, apparently often in the range of 30 to 60 percent per year (Hudson, p. 32). Any quantification is out of the question except to say that the ratio of debt to income was certainly far below that of the aristocracy.

The only group of borrowers for which an estimate of debt, even if a rough one, can be ventured are the peers.[60] Around 1601 the debt of 13 of them – nearly one-fourth of their number – has been put at £150,000, or £11,500 per head. The average debt of the other 45 peers is likely to have been considerably lower. Putting it at £3,000, the amount assigned to the least indebted identified 13 peers, would yield a total debt of the group of close to £300,000. This amount would have been equal to 1.5 years of their income and to nearly one-tenth of their landed wealth, putting it at 18 times income from land. A similar figure is suggested by the group's estimated annual interest payments of £25,000 or one-eighth of their total gross income (Stone, pp. 762, 768). On this basis the peers' debt would have amounted to about 1 percent of national product and would have been approximately equal to that of the crown. The share of the peers in the debt of all sectors cannot be determined, but was certainly substantial. It is quite likely to have been well in excess of their share in national wealth, which seems to have been in the order of 4 percent.

Contrary to the mass of consumers peers appear to have paid only the legal rate of 10 percent on their debts (Stone, p. 530), partly because much of it was secured by mortgages and was often repaid out of the proceeds of land sales. Only near the end of the period a few men concentrated their business activities on money lending. Most of the loans seem to have been made by London merchants and by government officials as temporary investments of funds.

## 10    Financing the government

One of the important characteristics of the Elizabethan economy was the smallness of its public sector.[61] The current revenues of the queen never exceeded about 2 percent of national product. Even allowing for occasional forced loans, for extralegal charges by some officials,

Table 10-6. *Receipts of the Exchequer, 1580–1600*[a,b] *(1,000 pounds)*

| Average of | Total (1) | Crown lands (2) | Customs (3) | Subsidies (4) | Clergy (5) | 2 to 5 1 (6) |
|---|---|---|---|---|---|---|
| 1580–1582 | 237 | 60 | 70 | 51 | 22 | 0.86 |
| 1583–1585[c] | 250 | 59 | 83 | 44 | 24 | 0.84 |
| 1586–1588[d] | 268 | 58 | 79 | 49 | 30 | 0.81 |
| 1589–1591 | 341 | 68 | 98 | 83 | 30 | 0.82 |
| 1592–1594[e] | 339 | 68 | 109 | 75 | 30 | 0.83 |
| 1595–1597 | (330) | — | 109[f] | 72[g] | — | (0.84) |
| 1598–1600 | 382 | 61 | 102 | 126 | 32 | 0.84 |

[a] Fiscal years starting Michaelmas.
[b] Excludes receipts from loans.
[c] Two years 1583 and 1584 only.
[d] Year 1587 only.
[e] Year 1592 only.
[f] Dietz, p. 328.
[g] Dietz, pp. 389–97.
*Source of basic data:* Scott, pp. 518–21, 526.

and for not directly remunerated services by others such as justices of the peace and for taxes and other charges levied by municipal and local authorities – for all of which quantitative information is lacking – total revenues of the public sector are not likely to have reached 5 percent of national product. A contemporary's claim that England was the least heavily imposed – and also, it may be added, the least indebted European country (Palliser, p. 12) – thus seems to have been justified.

Net receipts of the crown averaged slightly more than £250,000 in 1560–62 (Scott, p. 513) – always fiscal years starting Michaelmas – which was the equal to about 2 percent of national product. They were still at the same level in the 1580s, as Table 10-6 shows, when the price level was about one-third higher. They jumped to £340,000 in the early 1590s and stayed close to that level to the end of the reign. At that time the price level was nearly twice as high as it had been 40 years earlier and the share of the queen's current revenue had declined to not much over 1 percent of national product, the result of the general failure to raise tax rates and possibly of declining administrative efficiency.

The two most important sources of current revenue within the queen's power were the income from crown lands and customs, while she depended on Parliament for two other important sources, the tenth and fifteenth assessed every 3 years on laity and clergy and the "subsidies," which were regarded as limited to meeting extraordinary military expenditures. These four sources provided fully four-fifths of total current revenues during the last two decades of the queen's reign, the only period for which detailed figures for most years are available. Within that period the share of the sources directly controlled by the queen in the four main sources declined from nearly two-thirds to one-half so that her finances became increasingly dependent on parliamentary politics.

The income from crown lands kept with only small fluctuations close to £60,000 throughout the queen's reign.[62] While the extent of the crown lands may have been slightly reduced – considerable sales having been partly offset by confiscation of land owned by rebels, for example, the Duke of Norfolk – it is evident that the crown failed to take advantage of the substantial increase in the level of rents that occurred during the period, probably more for political reasons than out of ignorance, or from the modest technological and administrative improvements taking place on at least part of the larger private manors. As a result the purchasing power of the revenue from the crown lands was almost cut in half and their share in national product declined even more sharply from about 0.5 to 0.2 percent.

The revenue from customs (including poundage and tunnage) had been sharply increased just before Elizabeth's accession, when they amounted to about £30,000 a year (Dietz, pp. 394ff), by the introduction of a new Book of Rates in 1558. Rates then remained unchanged until the 1590s, except for the introduction of duties on wine in 1573. As a result the values used in assessing customs duties in the early 1600s were estimated at only about two-fifths of current values (Dietz, p. 119). If an estimate of customs revenues of over £80,000 in the first year of Elizabeth's reign (Dietz, p. 17) is correct and typical for the 1560s, there was no increase until the late 1580s and the level of the 1590s of slightly over £100,000 per year was substantially lower in purchasing power and in relation to the value of foreign trade or of national product than it had been three decades earlier. It does not seem to be known how total customs revenues were divided between imports and exports and among individual commodities except for the duties on wines, which from 1580 on yielded nearly one-tenth of the total (Scott, pp. 518–21). The most important single component, the export duty of woollen cloth of $6\frac{2}{3}$ sh per shortcloth for native exporters and of $14\frac{1}{2}$ sh for foreigners and an export of about 100,000 cloths,[63] should have yielded at least £30,000 a year, or between two-fifths in the early years and nearly one-third of total customs revenues in the last years of the reign. In that case import duties of at most £70,000 around 1600 would have been equal to about 5 percent of the value of imports other than wine. Apart from the failure to adjust duties to increases in prices, the fact that most customs were farmed out after the late 1560s, except during the 1590s (Dietz, p. 324) leaving substantial profits to the customs farmers, seems to have been responsible for the unsatisfactory performance.

The current revenues granted by Parliament increased from about £50,000 a year in the 1560s (Scott, p. 526) to slightly over £70,000 in the 1580s, to somewhat over £100,000 in the early 1590s and to over £150,000 in 1598–1600, thus keeping approximately in line with national product at around 0.4 percent of it. Of the total balance one-third to one-fifth was furnished by the clergy as one-tenth of their income and first fruits and the rest by the laity. The tax on the laity was levied either as 20 percent of the assessed value of the income from land if it exceeded £1 or as 13.3 percent (⅔ per pound) on the value of movables if in excess of £3, whichever method yielded the higher assessment.[64] The low yield of the tax was due to the use of assessed values – often "ludicrously low" (Dowell, p. 150) it has been said – which were far below current values, were often arbitrary, and were not adjusted for changes in rents or prices, being kept, for example, a mere £5,000 for the peerage (Dietz, p. 384) whose rental income may have exceeded £150,000,[65] so that the effective rate of tax was about 3 percent of income.[66]

The most important nonrecurrent revenues were derived from the sales of crown lands. Since Henry VIII and Edward VI had already sold about seven-eighths of the lands they had taken from religious institutions, there was not much left for Elizabeth to dispose of. Nevertheless she raised slightly over £800,000 from crown land sales, about one-half in 1599 and 1601 when her financial situation was very tight (cf. Dietz, p. 298). In those years land sales yielded about as much as total current revenues, but for the preceding 40 years they were equal to less than 5 percent of current revenues. Another not negligible though not quantifiable source of noncurrent revenues were the queen's share in privateering expeditions, particularly Drake's of 1587, which is reported to have yielded her £150,000 (Cunningham, pp. 175–7), far larger than any other.

The regional distribution of the crown's revenue is not known. A substantial part of the total must have been collected in London as the city furnished most of the customs duties and a large part of the tax on goods. A contemporary estimate provides some indication of the distribution on what appears to be essentially the income from crown lands.[67] It indicates that of the revenue of the English counties (excluding the Duchy of Lancaster) nearly three-fifths came from those south of the Wash–Bristol Channel line. The revenue from Wales was equal to only 6 percent of that from England (now including the Duchy of Lancaster). On a per head basis revenues were 5½ sh for England and 3¼ sh for Wales, in line with the undoubtedly considerably lower level of wealth in Wales. As there are no estimates of the population of individual counties, differences in revenue per head cannot be calculated.

The size and structure of the expenditures of the crown, and hence of its finances, differ sharply between the first and the second half of Elizabeth's reign, the difference being the result of the heavy military expenditures after the start of the war with Spain in 1585. In the quarter-century before 1585, military expenditures totaled only about £1.0 million or £40,000 per year or not much over one-fifth of total expenditures. In the following two decades, in contrast, war expenditure exceeded £4.0 million or £210,000 per year and came to absorb over three-fourths of total expenditures.[68]

For the first half of the period an expenditure breakdown is available for only one year (1571–72) (Scott, p. 515). In that year – without a foreign war – military expenditures absorbed only £32,000 (including £15,000 for the border fortress of Berwick) or one-fourth of the total, reflecting the absence of a standing army. The largest civilian expenditures were for the queen's household (including privy purse and wardrobe), which required £50,000 or nearly two-fifths of the total. The only other civilian items exceeding 5 percent of total expenditures were annuities with £11,200 or 8.5 percent and posts with £7,000 or 5.3 percent.

How different the structure of expenditure during the last two decades of Elizabeth's reign was is evident from Table 10-7. For the 13 years of the period for which a detailed breakdown of expenditures is available, military expenditures absorbed four-fifths of the total, of which one-third for the "pacification" of Ireland, nearly another third for operations and subsidies in the Netherlands, and one-fourth for the maintenance of the navy. The changing geographical distribution of these expenditures reflects England's military problems during the later part of Elizabeth's reign. Of the civilian outlays about one-third was needed to cover the queen's household, a rather modest £22,000 a year, probably not more than five times that of some peers. All other civilian expenditures came to not much over £40,000 a year, not even

Table 10-7. *Government expenditures, 1583–1600 (%)*

|  | 1583 to 1586 (1) | 1592 to 1595 (2) | 1597 to 1600 (3) | Total (4) |
|---|---|---|---|---|
| I. Military expenditures | 70 | 83 | 80 | 79 |
| 1. Foreign | 24 | 43 | 14 | 24 |
| a. Low Countries | 24 | 43 | 71 | 23 |
| b. France | — | — | 3 | 1 |
| 2. Ireland | 24 | 12 | 39 | 28 |
| 3. England and Wales | 22 | 28 | 28 | 28 |
| a. Navy | 13 | 21 | 21 | 20 |
| b. Ordnance | 5 | 5 | 5 | 5 |
| c. Fortresses | 4 | 2 | 3 | 3 |
| II. Civilian expenditures | 30 | 17 | 20 | 20 |
| 1. Queen's household[a] | 9 | 6 | 7 | 7 |
| 2. Others | 21 | 11 | 13 | 14 |
| III. Total expenditures { percent | 100 | 100 | 100 | 100 |
| £1,000 per year | 190 | 315 | 419 | 310 |

[a] Mainly privy purse, wardrobe, cofferer of the household, treasurer of the chamber, jewels, and plate.
*Source of basic data:* Scott, pp. 522–25.

0.2 percent of national product, reflecting the small size of the crown personnel – put at only 1,200 (Palliser, p. 303) – who had to rely for part of their income on sources other than their low salaries, that is, bribes in one form or another.

Borrowing by the government was in Elizabethan England still an occasional, haphazard operation resorted to only in fiscal emergencies, for short periods, from a small number of lenders, often involving pressures of varying degree, without the creation of standardized securities, and often requiring specific pledges in contrast to the system developed during the eighteenth century that has been called a financial revolution[69] under which the government issued long-term securities in the form of transferable bonds sold to large numbers of investors solely on the government's full faith and credit.[70]

Elizabeth inherited a debt of about £200,000, which after some fluctuations had been repaid by 1574. During the next decade as part of a fiscal policy of frugality[71] Lord Treasurer Burghley managed to accumulate a surplus of as much as £300,000 by 1585 (Dietz, p. 48). The rising military expenditures of the two following decades first rapidly exhausted the surplus and then led to renewed borrowings – voluntary as well as forced, not covered here – which resulted in a debt of about £350,000 at the queen's death.[72] In view of the smallness of the sums involved – the crown's debt amounted to not much more than 1 percent of national product and its service can only rarely have required as much as one-tenth of its current revenues – the difficulties the treasury experienced in meeting its borrowing requirements testify to the narrowness of the country's capital market.

In 1559 the crown's debt totaled £227,000 of which £107,000 had been incurred in Antwerp and was due at the end of the year. About one-half of the domestic debt had been raised for needs of the royal household, the rest mostly for military purposes. By 1565 the debt had been reduced to £85,000, by 1571 to £60,000, of which one-half due in Antwerp, where Thomas Gresham acted as the crown's financial agent, and by 1574 to zero.[73] The foreign creditors were some of the period's leading financial houses, the domestic ones mostly London merchants. Less is known about the borrowings after 1585, which were all raised in London. The interest rates paid depended on both the state of the market and the crown's credit rating and for foreign loans varied between 10 and 18 percent (Clarkson, p. 186). The rates on borrowings in London appear to have been on approximately the same level. A loan of £15,000 in 1589, for example, carried an interest rate of 10 percent and was subscribed by over 100 persons, the average subscription of over £100 indicating that the buyers were generally wealthier members of the public. Borrowings in London were in the form of demand notes issued on printed forms that could be assigned, a privilege at that time not yet enjoyed by bills of exchange (Richards, pp. 6–7). It is difficult to be certain to what extent these borrowings were voluntary or the result of pressures of different kinds.

## 11    A national balance sheet for 1603

Notwithstanding its necessarily rough character, an estimate of the national balance sheet at the end of Elizabeth's reign provides a useful overview of the structure of wealth of the realm. The estimates, shown in Table 10-8, identify several important characteristics of that structure. The first is the small size of the financial superstructure, even though the financial interrelations ratio of about one-tenth involves a substantial margin of error. Such a ratio is well below the level found at the present time in even the least developed countries. Among financial assets the extremely low share of government securities of about 2 percent – 0.2 percent of national assets and 1 percent of na-

Table 10-8. *National balance sheet of England and Wales, 1603 and 1688*

| | Amounts (£ million) | | Distribution (%) | |
|---|---|---|---|---|
| | 1603 (1) | 1688 (2) | 1603 (3) | 1684 (4) |
| I. Land | 75 | 180 | 49.3 | 53.4 |
| 1. Agricultural | 72 | 175 | 47.3 | 51.9 |
| 2. Other | 3 | 5 | 2.0 | 1.5 |
| I. Reproducible tangible assets | 58 | 102 | 38.2 | 30.3 |
| 1. Structures | 15 | 25 | 9.9 | 7.4 |
| 2. Equipment 3. Inventories | } 20 | 33 | 13.2 | 9.8 |
| 4. Livestock | 8 | 16 | 5.3 | 4.7 |
| 5. Household goods | 15 | 28 | 9.9 | 8.3 |
| III. Tangible assets | 133 | 282 | 87.5 | 83.7 |
| IV. Gold and silver | 4 | 13 | 2.6 | 3.9 |
| V. Financial assets | 15 | 42 | 9.9 | 12.5 |
| 1. Claims against financial institutions | — | — | — | — |
| 2. Mortgages | — | 20 | — | 5.9 |
| 3. Trade credit | — | 15 | — | 4.5 |
| 4. Consumer credit | — | —[a] | — | —[a] |
| 5. Government securities | 0 | 3 | 0.2 | 0.9 |
| VI. National assets | 152 | 337 | 100.0 | 100.0 |

[a] Included in V.

*Sources:* Col. 1, Line I.1 – estimated at slightly over two-fifths of 1688 value on basis of movement of rents; line I.2 – estimated at one-fifth of Line II.1; lines II.1 to II.5 – estimated at about three-fifths of 1688 values in line with movement on national product. Line II.5 includes household goods of precious metals (£5 million in 1688 according to King, p. 34); line IV – based on estimate of coins in circulation (Challis); line V – Very rough estimate. The only component for which information is available is Line V.5 (£0.3 million); col. 2. – Goldsmith, 1985, p. 233, with small corrections, particularly slightly reducing estimate for land.

tional product – is remarkable. Although quantification is very difficult, a large proportion of all financial assets – probably over one-half – appears to have had the form of consumer credit – and most of the rest in that of trade credit for working capital, while only a small fraction financed capital investment. Absence of claims against financial institutions and hence of loans made by them should be noted. The second characteristic is the share of agricultural land of about one-half, not very high for an economy in an early stage of development.

Third, over one-fourth of reproducible assets, which represented less than two-fifths of total assets, were in the form of structures, predominantly one-family homes and attached shops. Livestock, an item somewhat less uncertain than some others, accounted for one-seventh of reproducible assets, and household goods about one-fourth, including substantial amounts of plate and other silver and gold articles, possibly as much as £2 million, which constituted an important component of the assets of the high-income groups other than their land and buildings.

The available data are not sufficient to construct a national balance sheet. There is no doubt, however, that tangible assets roughly estimated at about £130 million in Section 2 constituted most of it, probably slightly more than the 85 percent (excluding monetary metals) of total national assets, the ratio at which they have been put for 1688 (Goldsmith 1985, p. 232).

Of financial assets the order of magnitude is known only for the queen's debt of about £0.35 million and another, peers' debt, seems to have been of about the same magnitude. It is thus unlikely that all financial assets, mostly trade credit, moneylenders' credits and mortgages, could have been as high as £10 million, and they may have been not much in excess of £5 million, bringing national assets, including £3.5 million of monetary metals, to about £140 million, or about $4\frac{1}{4}$ times national product.

CHAPTER 11

# The financial system
# of the United Provinces
# at the Peace of Münster

The United Provinces in the seventeenth century are remarkable from an economic point of view for two reasons. The first is that a small country of hardly 2 million, or 2 percent of the population of Europe and 0.4 percent of that of the world (McEvedy and Jones, vol. 18, p. 342), should have become, even if only for a short period – essentially in the second and third quarter of the century – the center of the international economy, the owner of by far the largest and the most efficient of the world's high-sea fleets, the most important staple market for commodities and for precious metals, the initiator of many advances in commercial and financial as well as in agricultural and manufacturing techniques, and the possessor of the strongest navy and of an important colonial empire, though to speak of a Dutch "hegemony"[1] is an exaggeration. The second reason is that this episode constitutes the last case – Venice, Florence, Genova, Brugge, and Antwerp were earlier examples – of a single city being able to play such a role – Amsterdam with less than 200,000 inhabitants representing something like one-half of the economic power of the United Provinces (Barbour, p. 13, reiterated by Braudel, p. 145).

For the histories of financial systems and their relation to economic development possibly the most interesting and as yet unsolved problem is how the United Provinces managed to become the leading commercial and financial power of the seventeenth century with a monetary system and a system of public finance both of which have been characterized as "chaotic,"[2] though in some other features of its financial system the country was ahead of its contemporaries.

## 1 Population

With a population of about 1.8 million in 1650 on a territory of only 34,000 km$^2$ the United Provinces with slightly over 50 inhabitants per km$^2$ were, together with the Spanish Netherlands, the most densely

198

populated country of the time.[3] They were also, again with their southern neighbor, the most urbanized country. In 1675, about 40 percent of the population lived in 61 cities, one-fourth of them in Amsterdam (van der Woude, p. 135).

Population had grown rapidly, during the sixteenth and the first half of the seventeenth century at an average rate of slightly over 0.40 percent per year, partly as a result of immigration from the Spanish Netherlands beginning with the late sixteenth century.[4] Population growth then slowed rapidly, partly because of reduction in immigration, with the result that at the end of the eighteenth century it was only about one-fifth higher than in the mid-seventeenth century, and average growth of only 0.13 percent per year. The same trends are observed in the population of Amsterdam: from 14,000 in 1514 to 105,000 in 1622, nearly 200,000 in 1650, and 217,000 in 1795 with a share in total population rising from 1.5 percent in 1514 to about 10 percent in both 1650 and 1795 (de Vries 1974, p. 86; Braudel, p. 155). These movements reflect the character of economic development: rapid growth to the third quarter of the seventeenth century, stagnation during the eighteenth century.

There is no reliable information on birth and death rates before 1840 when they stood at 35 and 24 percent, respectively (Mitchell 1980, p. 116). They were undoubtedly considerably higher but closer together in the seventeenth century, and in the eighteenth century must have been practically equal.

Holland was always the most populous, politically dominating, and economically the most important province. Its share in the population of the seven provinces increased sharply from about one-fourth in 1514 to about two-fifths in 1622 and 1650 and to nearly one-half in 1680, but then declined to slightly below two-fifths in 1795 (for Holland, Faber et al., p. 60), a share it maintained until the present.[5] Of the other six provinces Friesland in 1650 accounted for about 8 percent of the country's population, Overijssel for about 3 percent, and Gelderland for fully 2 percent (Faber et al., pp. 65ff, 74, 93). Estimates for the remaining three provinces and the area along the southern frontier of the Republic directly administered by the States General are lacking. Zeeland was probably the most populous of them.

There are no comprehensive estimates of the industrial distribution of the population. In the first comprehensive enumeration of 1849, when the total population was 70 percent higher than two centuries earlier, agriculture accounted for over two-fifths of the labor force, manufacturing and services for about one-fifth each, and commerce and finance for one-sixteenth (Mitchell 1980, p. 67). In the mid-seventeenth century the share of agriculture should have been considerably higher as it has been put at about one-half as late as 1770 (Stuijvenberg, p. 108). In international comparison the shares of shipping and fishing were extraordinarily high.[6]

## 2    National product

The United Provinces are one of the few countries in which a contemporary estimate of national income and expenditure exists for a date as early as the late seventeenth century, though made by a foreigner who probably never visited the country. This is Gregory King's estimate for 1688 and for 1695 (King, pp. 49ff). Though King's estimate for England and Wales has been found to be of good quality – the most recent recalculation of national product is only one-fifth above King's figure (Lindert and Williamson, p. 393) – considerable more doubt exists about this estimate for the Netherlands, in particular because King did not indicate his sources nor, in contrast to his estimates for England and Wales, his methods of estimation. His estimate nevertheless remains of interest and value as it contains information not to be found in contemporary Dutch or in modern sources.[7]

King put the national income of the United Provinces in 1688 at £17.75 million, or at the current exchange rate at nearly f 190 million. He estimated that nearly one-fourth of the total represented rent of land and homes and fully three-fourths the income of "trade and business," thus apparently omitting the income of government employees, civil and military, and of some professions. He also estimated the main components of expenditure, putting private consumption at slightly over three-fifths of national income, expenditures on food accounting for somewhat over one-third, and those on clothing for one-sixth of the total, and government expenditures at fully one-fourth, leaving somewhat over one-tenth for capital formation.

On the basis of his estimate of 2.2 million inhabitants, King arrived at a per head national income of £7.9 per head or about f 85. If he derived his figures from aggregates rather than, what is less likely, on the basis of per head or per household estimates, the figure for per head national income would have to be increased to nearly f 100.

Very recently two estimates of the national product of the United Provinces at or close to the end of the seventeenth century have been published. The first puts the level of national product per head in the third quarter of the seventeenth century at twice Gregory King's estimate for 1688, that is, at f 168 or in 1700 prices at f 196, which for

Table 11-1. *The national product of the United Provinces, 1600–1913*

|  | Popu-lation (million) (1) | Current prices | | Constant prices | | | |
|---|---|---|---|---|---|---|---|
|  |  | Total (billion f) (2) | Per head (1,000 f) (3) | Total (4) | Per head 1913 = 100 (5) | 1970 $ per head (6) | Price level (7) |
| 1600 | 1.50 | 0.11 | 0.07 | 7.8 | 32.0 | 385 | 55 |
| 1650 | 1.80 | 0.20 | 0.11 | 11.7 | 40.0 | 480 | 66 |
| 1700 | 1.90 | 0.21 | 0.11 | 12.9 | 41.8 | 500 | 63 |
| 1780 | 2.03 | 0.25 | 0.12 | 12.3 | 37.5 | 450 | 78 |
| 1820 | 2.34 | 0.41 | 0.17 | 14.3 | 37.5 | 450 | 112 |
| 1870 | 3.61 | 1.02 | 0.28 | 40.6 | 69.4 | 831 | 99 |
| 1913 | 6.16 | 2.54 | 0.41 | 100.0 | 100.0 | 1,198 | 100 |

*Sources:* 1600 – col. 1, Maddison 1984, Table 7; col. 2, cols. 4 and 5, rough estimate; col. 6, 1700 value and col. 5; col. 7, based on movement of cost of living index in Leiden, (Posthumus 1939, p. 1010). 1650 – col. 1, based on 1600 and 1700 values; cols. 2, 4, and 6, as for 1600; col. 7, extrapolated on basis of Stuijvenberg and de Vrijer 1980, p. 8. 1700–1913 – cols. 1, 2, 4, and 7, Maddison 1984, Table 8.

a population of 1.9 million implies an aggregate national product of f 372 million (de Vries, 1984, pp. 163, 185). This is a judgmental estimate without any breakdown and for this one date only. The other estimate, which is obtained by retropolation from the first official estimates for the twentieth century, is much lower, namely, f 206 million for aggregate national product and hence to f 108 per head (Maddison 1984, Table 8). This estimate, which covers the period from 1700 to 1938, is summarized and roughly extended to 1650 and 1600 in Table 11-1. Resolving the difference between these two estimates will require considerable further study by specialists. For the time being the two estimates may be regarded as lower and upper boundaries with a figure on the order of f 150 for income per head and f 285 million for aggregate national product in 1700 as an acceptable compromise. It would be about 80 percent above King's estimate for England in 1688, but by nearly 40 percent only according to a recent revision of his estimate, the higher values for the United Provinces to be explained in part by the higher level of prices and wages[8] and in part by the higher real product per head. The figures of f 150 per head and of f 285 million for aggregate national product in 1700 and the rough extrapolations for 1650 and 1600 of f 150 and f 100 for product per head in current prices and of f 270 million and of f 150 million for aggregate national product are used as scalars for other magnitudes throughout this chapter.

By applying the time series for the real national product per head of the Netherlands to its value in 1970 dollars to similar figures for other countries, it is possible to compare the levels of real national product per head in 1700. This procedure leads to the suggestion that the real national product of the United Provinces of 1700 of about $500 (1970 dollars) was about one-third higher than the approximately $380 of Great Britain and probably also of France, and was nearly three times as high as the $170 of India (Maddison, 1984, Tables 7–9). Similarly the real per head national product of the United Provinces in 1700 of about $500 (1970 dollars) was about equal to that in 1950 of countries like Brazil, Ghana, Malaysia, Portugal, and Tunisia and about twice that of India (Summers et al., pp. 34ff). These figures, rough as they are, give some idea of the relative national product per head of the United Provinces in their golden age.

There are not sufficient data to estimate the distribution of national product by industries or by regions. The share of agriculture must still have been substantial, as over one-half of the active population seems to have been employed in agriculture. Even if average income in agriculture was one-third below the national average, a rather large difference in view of its progressive and relatively capital-intensive character, its share in national income would have been on the order of two-fifths.

There is little doubt that a substantial proportion – probably well over one-fourth – of aggregate national product was concentrated in the quadrangle between Amsterdam, Utrecht, Dordrecht, and The Hague, which encompassed less than 5 percent of the national territory, or that the majority of national product was urban, an exceptionally high share in the seventeenth century.

Gross as well as net capital formation during the first half of the seventeenth century must have been substantial, although there are no data to estimate directly its absolute size. The only component for which an estimate is possible is the cost of land reclamation. Between 1590 and 1664 about 109,000 hectares or 1,450 hectares per year are reported to have been reclaimed, reaching a peak of 1,760 hectares in 1615–39, at an average cost of something like f 300,000 a year.[9] This was equal to less than 0.2 percent of gross national product. The increase in the population by about 10,000 persons per year during the first half of the seventeenth century would have required the annual addition of at least 1,000 houses. There were also substantial outlays on dykes, canals, and roads. Among directly productive capital expenditures those on additions to the mercantile and fishing fleets were probably the largest ones.

An indirect estimate of gross capital expenditures can be derived from the Harrod formula. On the basis of an annual increase of population of nearly 0.4 percent from 1600 to 1650, an annual growth of real product per head of fully 0.4 percent per year as used in Table 11-1, and a ratio of reproducible investment to output as high as four because of the prevalence of very long lasting categories of expenditures, the rate of gross capital formation would be on the order of fully 3 percent and that of net capital formation considerably lower, say about 2 percent of national product. These figures should probably be regarded as maxima.

There is little doubt that the volume and rate of reproducible capital formation was lower during the second half of the seventeenth century. During the eighteenth century the rate was probably close to zero, but then there was a substantial volume of financial saving in the form of net foreign investment. If Dutch foreign assets in 1790 were worth f 500 to f 650 million (Kindleberger, p. 217), their annual average for the preceding full century would not have exceeded f 5 million, or about 2 percent of national product.[10] The ratio for the seventeenth century, even including direct investment, would have been considerably lower.

## 3    National wealth

Private urban wealth in the early 1630s should have been on the order of f 400 million on the basis of a figure of about f 90 million for the 30,000 Amsterdam households and as much as f 300 million for the about 125,000 households in other cities on the basis of the only slightly lower figures for Gouda and Leiden (cf. Table 11-3). An estimate is much more hazardous for the about 300,000 rural households. If their average wealth is assumed to have been equal to that in the smaller cities, it would have totaled over f 700 million; if on the other hand it had been only half as large, it would have been as low as f 350 million. Total private wealth would then have ranged between f 750 million and f 1,100 million. These figures would have to be increased only slightly as government property was small. A total of about f 1,000 million should give an indication of the order of magnitude involved.

Private wealth increased substantially during the seventeenth century. That of Amsterdam more than doubled between 1631 and 1675 (assessed wealth rose from f 65 million to f 158 million) (cf. Section

4), but the rate of increase for the United Provinces must have been considerably smaller as the share of Amsterdam in total population rose from about 7 percent to about 10 percent and as it is likely that the increase in wealth per head was more rapid in Amsterdam than in the rest of the country. The increase of total private wealth of the United Provinces between 1631 and 1676 is therefore not likely to have been much in excess of 50 percent, bringing it to about f 1,100 million to f 1,650 million, reflecting in part the sharp increase in land prices.[11] Such figures, particularly one near to their upper boundary, are not unreasonable as the assessed private wealth in 1787–88 has been reported at f 2,000 million (Baasch, p. 187), suggesting a market value of at least f 2,500 million as the level of wholesale prices rose by about one-half during the interval of fully a century, implying a stagnation of the value of real private wealth per head. On that basis the wealth–income ratio would have risen sharply from about 4.5 to 6.5 in 1631 to 5.25 to 8 in 1674 and to about 10 in 1787–88. Such an increase would have to be explained mainly by the decline in the level of interest rates as the degree of real capital intensity, if any, cannot have been substantial.

## 4    Size distribution of national wealth and income

While it is not possible to construct a size distribution of income or wealth for the United Provinces, data for some large cities permit the estimation of the degree of concentration for the urban population, which must have accounted for the majority of both aggregates.

In Amsterdam taxed wealth in 1631 was reported at f 63 million, but it is known that this represented a substantial understatement in the case of at least some of the large wealth holders (Dillen 1970, p. 311). The true value may have been close to f 90 million.[12] Only one out of eight households reported wealth above the taxable minimum of f 1,000, but the wealth of households below that limit should have been on the order of only one-tenth of the wealth of assessees. The concentration of wealth was very pronounced as is evident in Table 11-2. Assuming the degree of underreporting to have been the same at all levels, on the basis of assessed values the top decile of all wealth holders held about five-sixths of total wealth, the top percentile fully one-third, the top per mill, that is, the wealthiest 30 households, about one-ninth, and the household reporting the largest wealth (burgomaster Poppen who had come to Amsterdam from Holstein) 0.7 percent of the total. The Gini ratio was on the order of 0.85.

Wealth distribution in Amsterdam in 1631 was, however, somewhat

Table 11-2. *Size distribution of private wealth in Amsterdam, 1631*

| Size (1,000 f) | Number (1) | Assessed amount (million f) (2) | Number (%) (3) | Amount (%) (4) |
|---|---|---|---|---|
| I. Taxable assessed wealth | | | | |
| 1–20 | 3,097 | 13.8 | 76.3 | 22.0 |
| 20–50 | 584 | 18.9 | 14.4 | 30.0 |
| 50–100 | 281 | 14.6 | 6.9 | 23.2 |
| 100–200 | 74 | 9.4 | 1.8 | 14.9 |
| 200–400 | 23 | 5.7 | 0.6 | 9.1 |
| 500 | 1 | 0.5 | 0.0 | 0.8 |
| Total | 4,060 | 62.9 | 100.0 | 100.0 |
| II. Untaxed wealth | | | | |
| 0–1 | 25,940 | 6.5 | 86.5 | 9.4 |
| III. Total wealth | | | | |
| 0–500 | 30,000 | 69.4 | 100.0 | 100.0 |

*Sources:* Col. I.1 – Baasch, p. 187; col. I.2 – based on Dillen 1939, p. 966; col. II – average assumed at f 250 per household; col. III – based on population of 120,000 and average of four persons per household. (Average size in villages in North Holland in 1672–1748 was 3.7 members; deVries 1974, p. 114.)

though not much less pronounced than in Florence in 1427. The share of the top per mill of households of somewhat over one-tenth in Amsterdam compares with one of one-seventh in Florence, while that of the top percent was equal to fully two-fifths in both cities, the figures being in both cases based on assessed values (for Florence cf. Table 9-5).

There is little doubt that personal wealth was substantially less concentrated in the rest of the United Provinces. This is suggested by a comparison with the distribution of Gouda and Leiden, shown in Tables 11-3 and 11-4. While the top percentile of all households owned only about one-fifth of total wealth in Gouda and one-seventh in Leiden, its share in Amsterdam was well above two-fifths. At the other end the lowest nine-tenths of households appear to have accounted for only about one-fifth of the city's wealth in Amsterdam while their share in Gouda was in the order of one-third and in Leiden of one-fourth.

Between 1631 and 1674 the reported total of taxable wealth in Amsterdam rose sharply from f 64 million to f 158 million (Brugmans

Table 11-3. Distribution of assessed private wealth in four cities, 1623–31 (%)

| Size (1,000 f) | Number | | | | Wealth | | | |
|---|---|---|---|---|---|---|---|---|
| | Amsterdam 1631 (1) | Leiden 1623 (2) | The Hague 1627 (3) | Gouda 1625 (4) | Amsterdam 1631 (5) | Leiden 1623 (6) | The Hague 1627 (7) | Gouda 1625 (8) |
| 1. 1–10 | 62.7 | 69.6 | 52.3 | 79.6 | 13.6 | 23.2 | 9.6 | 39.5 |
| 2. 10–50 | 29.2 | 26.5 | 34.4 | | 38.8 | 47.4 | 30.4 | |
| 3. 50–100 | 5.7 | 3.1 | 8.8 | | 23.2 | 17.5 | 23.8 | |
| 4. 100 and more | 2.4 | 0.8 | 4.6 | 20.4 | 24.9 | 11.9 | 36.2 | 60.5 |
| 5. Total } percent | 100.0 | 100.0 | 100.0 | 100.0 | 100.0 | 100.0 | 100.0 | 100.0 |
| 6. } amounts | 4060 | 1829 | 960 | 1003 | 62.9 | 19.9 | 22.1 | 6.1 |
| 7. Households (1,000) | 30.0 | 11.0 | 4.5 | 3.6 | — | — | — | — |
| 8. Average } assessee | — | — | — | — | 15.5 | 14.3 | 22.9 | 10.0 |
| 9. Wealth[a] } household | — | — | — | — | 2.3 | 2.0 | 5.1 | 1.9 |

[a] In 1,000 f.

Sources: Rows 1–6 – Posthumus 1939, p. 966; Klein 1967, p. 47 (for Gouda). Rows 7–9 – Based on estimates of total population (Braudel, p. 155; Faber et al., p. 58; Klein 1967, p. 51) and assumptions of four persons per household and wealth below f 1000.

Table 11-4. *Distribution of private wealth in Gouda, 1625–1722*

| | 1625 (1) | 1638 (2) | 1653 (3) | 1675 (4) | 1702 (5) | 1722 (6) |
|---|---|---|---|---|---|---|
| **Wealth holders** | | | | | | |
| Number | | | | | | |
| Total[a] | 3,650 | 3,325 | 3,635 | 3,800 | 4,200 | 4,500 |
| Under f 1,000 | 2,647 | 2,626 | 2,911 | 3,149 | 3,748 | 4,123 |
| f 1,000–10,000 | 198 | 546 | 586 | 469 | 329 | 283 |
| f 10,000–30,000 | 176 | 133 | 104 | 129 | 100 | 64 |
| f 30,000 and over | 29 | 20 | 34 | 53 | 30 | 30 |
| Percent | | | | | | |
| Under f 1,000 | 72.5 | 79.0 | 80.1 | 82.9 | 89.1 | 91.6 |
| f 1,000–10,000 | 21.9 | 16.4 | 16.1 | 12.3 | 7.8 | 6.3 |
| f 10,000–30,000 | 4.8 | 4.0 | 2.9 | 3.4 | 2.4 | 1.4 |
| f 30,000 and over | 0.8 | 0.6 | 0.9 | 1.4 | 0.7 | 0.7 |
| **Wealth** | | | | | | |
| Amount (million f) | | | | | | |
| Total[b] | 6.78 | 5.29 | 5.58 | 7.37 | 5.51 | 4.72 |
| Under f 1,000 | 0.66 | 0.68 | 0.79 | 0.88 | 1.08 | 1.22 |
| f 1,000–10,000 | 2.42 | 1.74 | 1.77 | 1.45 | 0.99 | 0.80 |
| f 10,000–30,000 | 2.51 | 2.05 | 1.59 | 2.23 | 1.77 | 1.19 |
| f 30,000 and over | 1.19 | 0.82 | 1.38 | 2.81 | 1.67 | 1.51 |
| Percent | | | | | | |
| Under f 1,000 | 9.7 | 12.9 | 14.3 | 11.9 | 19.6 | 25.9 |
| f 1,000–10,000 | 35.7 | 32.9 | 32.0 | 19.7 | 18.0 | 16.9 |
| f 10,000–30,000 | 37.0 | 38.7 | 28.8 | 30.3 | 32.1 | 25.2 |
| f 30,000 and over | 17.6 | 15.5 | 25.0 | 38.1 | 30.3 | 32.0 |
| Per household (1,000 f) | 1.86 | 1.59 | 1.52 | 2.34 | 1.31 | 1.05 |

[a] Based on estimates of total population (Klein 1967, p. 51) of 14,600 in 1622 (used for 1625), 13,300 in 1632 (used for 1638) and 18,000 in 1720 (on basis of Klein's "less than 20,000"), using straight-line geometric interpolation between 1638 and 1722 and average size of household of four persons.
[b] Assuming wealth of households of less than f 1,000 assessed wealth to have risen from f 250 to f 300.
*Source:* Klein 1967, p. 47 for classes over f 1,000.

1944, p. 142), an annual increase of 0.9 percent per year, assuming the number of taxpayers to have grown by about two-thirds as did that of the population, in a period of stable prices. As the full record of the 1674 returns does not seem to have been published, it is uncertain whether the degree of concentration of wealth changed. Since the number of wealth owners of more than f 100,000 is reported to have increased from 100 to over 200, or from 0.33 percent to over

0.50 percent of the number of households, some increase in concentration is likely (Dillen 1970, p. 312).

Less detailed data are shown in Table 11-3 for four cities that together accounted for nearly one-third of the urban population of the United Provinces. The about 8,000 wealth tax assessees had an average assessed wealth of about f 14,000, which at market values was probably close to f 20,000. Since only about every sixth household was liable to tax as having taxable wealth of f 1,000 or more, average wealth per household was probably not much above f 3,000.

Average assessed wealth as well as its distribution showed considerable differences among the four cities. Average wealth was highest in The Hague, the country's political capital because of a high proportion of high officials, absentee landowners, and rentiers. It was followed by Amsterdam, the economic capital, and Leiden, then as the center of the linen industry the country's most important manufacturing city.

Concentration of assessed wealth, indicated by the Lorenz curve, was least pronounced in Gouda and most pronounced in The Hague and not much different in Amsterdam and Leiden. Similarly the proportion of holders of assessed wealth of f 100,000 or more was by far most pronounced in The Hague, followed by Amsterdam.

In the following half century the assessed wealth of the four cities, and presumably also its total private wealth, approximately doubled while wealth per head increased by only about one-third in a period of fairly stable prices. Development, however, differed sharply among the four cities. While wealth per household appears to have increased by one-third in Amsterdam, and not to have changed substantially in The Hague and in Gouda, it seems to have fallen by over one-fourth in Leiden whose main industries – linen and wool – were declining.

There were considerable differences in assessed wealth by occupation. In Leiden professionals were both in 1623 and in 1675 the wealthiest group, with median wealth about twice as high as the city median of somewhat over f 3,000 (the city average was about f 10,000). Assessees in the textile and building trades were in both years below the average, while differences among other trades were not large or constant, always measured by their median wealth. While for the city the share of assessees of more than f 20,000 was close to one-tenth in 1623 and in 1675, it was as high as one-fourth among professionals, and assessed wealth holders of more than f 20,000 were rare in most other groups except in the trade and transport group, numbering, for example, in the textile groups only 2 and 4 percent, respectively, of all assessees (Posthumus 1939, p. 971).

The only city for which data on taxable wealth and its distribution have been published for the entire seventeenth century is Gouda, which had a population of about 15,000, or something like 2 percent of the urban population (cf. Klein 1967). Gouda was an industrial rather than a commercial city, and it is impossible to say to what extent it was typical for the entire urban part of the United Provinces. It was, however, similar to the larger cities in that its economy and politics were dominated by a small group of regenten families, whose share in assessed wealth increased from 1625 to 1722 from 8 to 19 percent (Klein 1967, p. 51).

Since it may be estimated that the wealth of households below the exemption level of f 1,000 accounted for only a small proportion of total wealth, the data on taxable wealth provide a reasonably reliable picture of the movements of the wealth of the city and of its distribution over a century if it is taken into account that the absolute figures are probably considerably understated, that the types of assets taxed were apparently more limited from the 1630s on, and if it is assumed that the degree of understatement was about the same in the three classes of taxable wealth being distinguished.

Total assessed wealth was approximately the same in 1675 as half a century earlier, after a substantially lower level from the 1630s to the 1650s. However, its distribution showed a considerable increase in the top wealth group. From the 1690s on the absolute figures declined sharply for all three groups, probably in part reflecting changes in the scope of assets subject to tax at a rate of 0.5 percent until the 1653 benchmark and 1.0 percent thereafter, but the distribution among the three groups shows no clear changes.

Wealth was very concentrated throughout the century. The share of households with less than f 1,000 of assessed wealth, which can be only estimated roughly, who from 1625 to 1675 on the average apparently constituted about four-fifths of all households, was not much above one-eighth of total wealth if assessed values are accepted, and would probably be below one-tenth on the basis of market values. At the other extreme the top wealth holders increased their share from about one-sixth to nearly two-fifths on the basis of assessed values and on the basis of market values may by 1675 have accounted for nearly one-half of the city's wealth. Table 11-4 shows that between 1675 and 1722 there was a substantial reduction in the concentration of wealth in the households with wealth below f 1,000, increasing their share in the number of all households from 83 to 92 percent and doubling that in total wealth at assessment values from 12 to 26 percent. This reversion of trend may however reflect, at least in part, the effects of

Table 11-5. *Income distribution in Rotterdam and Leiden, 1674*

| Size of income (f) | Rotterdam | | Leiden | | Rotterdam | | Leiden | |
|---|---|---|---|---|---|---|---|---|
| | Number (1) | Amount (1,000 f) (2) | Number (3) | Amount (1,000 f) (4) | Number (%) (5) | Amount (%) (6) | Number (%) (7) | Amount (%) (8) |
| **I. Taxed Income** | | | | | | | | |
| 137 | — | — | 741 | 102 | — | — | 27.5 | 7.9 |
| 183 | 1,341 | 246 | — | — | 31.1 | 9.1 | — | — |
| 365 | 996 | 364 | 1,200 | 438 | 23.1 | 13.5 | 44.5 | 33.9 |
| 730 | 1,070 | 706 | 520 | 380 | 24.8 | 26.1 | 19.3 | 29.4 |
| 1,095 | 486 | 490 | 135 | 148 | 11.3 | 18.1 | 5.0 | 11.4 |
| 1,460 | 229 | 325 | 44 | 64 | 5.3 | 12.0 | 1.6 | 4.9 |
| 1,825 | 78 | 137 | 3 | 6 | 1.8 | 5.1 | 0.1 | 0.5 |
| 2,190 | 38 | 83 | 26 | 57 | 0.9 | 3.1 | 1.0 | 4.4 |
| 2,920 | 37 | 104 | 18 | 53 | 0.9 | 3.8 | 0.7 | 4.1 |
| 3,650 | 12 | 43 | 2 | 7 | 0.3 | 1.6 | 0.1 | 0.5 |
| 4,380 | 5 | 21 | 6 | 26 | 0.1 | 0.8 | 0.2 | 2.0 |
| 5,840 | 11 | 56 | 2 | 12 | 0.2 | 2.1 | 0.1 | 0.9 |
| >5,840 | 15 | 130 | — | — | 0.3 | 4.8 | — | — |
| Total | 4,318 | 2,705 | 2,697 | 1,293 | 100.0 | 100.00 | 100.0 | 100.0 |
| **II. Untaxed income** | | | | | | | | |
| 0–137 | 7,700 | 385 | 12,300 | 615 | 64.2 | 12.5 | 82.0 | 32.2 |
| **III. Total income** | | | | | | | | |
| All sizes | 12,000 | 3,090 | 15,000 | 1,908 | 100.0 | 100.0 | 100.0 | 100.0 |

*Sources*: Cols. I.1, and I.3 – Oldewelt, pp. 90–91; Cols. I.2 and I.4 – cols. 1 and 3 multiplied by size; Cols. II.2 and II.4 – based on total population (read off from deVries, 1974, p. 89) and assumptions of four persons per household and average income of f 500 for each untaxed household.

the change in the scope of assessed assets and shortcomings of estimation.[13,14]

Income size distributions are known for two of the large cities, of about 50,000 and 60,000 inhabitants, respectively, and summarized in Table 11-5. Income, as assessed for tax in 1674, was about equally concentrated at the top, though average income per household was about twice as high in Rotterdam as in Leiden. In both cities the top per mill of households received somewhat over 3 percent of total personal income and the top percent about 15 percent. However, the largest single income reported reached f 23,000 or about 0.8 percent of the city's total income in Rotterdam but was below f 6,000 or 0.3 percent of the city's total in Leiden. On the other end of the scale the bottom four-fifths of households may be estimated to have received about three-tenths of the city's total income in both cities. Thus the Lorenz curves were very similar for both cities for total as well as for the taxable population. These differences may reflect those between a rising commercial and a declining industrial city.

While the concentration of income in these two cities is probably somewhat higher than in the entire United Provinces, it may be compared to that in contemporary England and Wales. There the top per mill of households received nearly 6 percent of the country's total income and the top 1 percent about 14 percent of it (Lindert and Williamson, p. 393). Thus the share of the very top of the income pyramid, the top per mill, was about twice as large in England as in the two Dutch cities, while that of the top percentile was about the same in both cases. The share of the bottom four-fifths of the population, on the other hand, was somewhat higher in England and Wales and fully two-fifths against only about one-fourth in Rotterdam and Leiden. Hence the share of the 81st to 99th percentiles was considerably higher in the Dutch cities with about 55 percent than in England and Wales with not much over 40 percent. These differences are not unexpected as between an aristocratic and still predominantly agrarian and a bourgeois and predominantly urban society.

## 5    The monetary system

From the Union of Utrecht of 1579, which created the United Provinces, the monetary circulation[15] consisted of numerous types of gold, silver, and copper coins of varying weight and fineness issued by the central government and over a dozen provincial and municipal mints, as well as of coins issued in several foreign countries, particularly in the Southern Netherlands since there were for much of the period no legal obstacles to the import, export, or use of such coins. The situation, characterized as chaotic,[16] required the services of numerous money changers and involved continuous fluctuations in the relative values of the various coins and was at its worst early in the seventeenth century. It was only near its end that the issuance of silver 1- and 3-guilder (florin) pieces by the central government gradually led to the predominance of coins of the United Provinces among the money in circulation.

The major Dutch coins in circulation, issued by the central government and/or provinces and municipalities, were silver florins (or guilders) of a standard weight of 10.5 g and a fineness of 91 percent and its fractions, namely, schillings (f 0.15), double stuivers (f 0.10), stuivers (f 0.05), and groot (f 0.025), all of changing weight and silver content, as well as copper pennings and duits, 120 and 160 of which made one florin. In addition there were several types of daalders, worth about 2.5 florins, for example, the rijksdaalder, the leeuwendaalder of 28 g silver, and the kruisghsdaalder, so called by their motif, the latter two coined mainly for use in the Baltic, Levant, and Asiatic trade, and gold ducats of 3.5 g. Most of the many foreign coins in circulation were being or had been minted in the Spanish Netherlands, such as the karolus florins and coins with the image of Philip II, but they also included reals (pieces of eight) of 25 g of silver and gold doubloons. The domestic and foreign gold coins in circulation fluctuated in terms of silver. As the foreign silver coins were of lesser fineness than the domestic ones of the same face value, they tended to drive them out of circulation. From 1602 on the transferable claims against the Amsterdamsche Wisselbank due on demand denominated in banco-guilders provided a money of account of constant silver value.

In this situation there was little room for monetary policy and the United Provinces did not share the then common favorization by governments of the accumulation of stocks of precious metals. It is remarkable that this state of affairs does not seem to have seriously interfered with the development of the most sophisticated commercial and financial system in contemporary Europe. A possible, at least partial, explanation is that the country in fact had a two-currency system, one of book money of uniform metallic value for substantial commercial transactions, the banco florin, and another consisting of numerous coins of fluctuating value for the rest, particularly for wage payments and retail trade.

There is virtually no quantitative information on the volume of money in circulation or of changes in it. The output of Dutch mints has been estimated at about f 2.5 million per year, about evenly divided between gold and silver coins, for the period from 1586 to 1659, or a total of about f 185 million (Morineau 1974, p. 770). A considerable part of these issues was exported, possibly two-fifths to three-fifths of the total (Morineau 1974, p. 772). On the other hand, a substantial amount of money was in circulation when the United Provinces were formed, and there may have been a considerable net import balance of foreign coins though neither its size nor even its direction are known.[17] Any estimate of the amount of money in circulation in the United Provinces is therefore extremely hazardous. Only two of them have come to attention. A recent estimate suggests very tentatively an annual increase of f 0.5 to 1.0 million (Morineau 1974, p. 772), which implies for the mid-seventeenth century a total of f 30 million to f 60 million plus the money in circulation in 1579, and hence hardly more than f 50 million to f 100 million in 1650. This compares with Gregory King's estimate for the end of the seventeenth century of 6.9 million or f 90 million, of which f 70 million in gold and f 20 million in silver – a ratio contrasting with the near equality of issues by Dutch mints – plus f 15 in bars (King). If money in circulation had been close to f 100 million, it would have been equal to about half a year's national product, a reasonable relationship.

The absence of an upward trend in prices until the 1760s (Stuijvenberg and de Vrijer 1980), or in national product after the mid-seventeenth century, does not lead one to expect a substantial increase in transactions demand for money in circulation. Acceptance of a very tentatively advanced estimate of money in circulation near the end of the eighteenth century of f 150 million to f 200 million (Morineau 1974, p. 744), would suggest a substantial decrease in the income velocity of money, a development not incompatible with the economic stagnation and the increasingly rentier economy of the eighteenth century.

## 6    Financial instruments

The commonest and in the aggregate probably the largest financial instrument was trade credit, widely used in domestic and international commerce, but there is hardly any basis for estimating its volume. Information is equally deficient on three other important instruments: mortgages on agricultural land and on residential real estate and consumer credit. Bonds of private issuers, the United East India Company being the most important one, were of small size – on the order of f 10 million. Quantitative data are available only for two instruments, government obligations and shares.

There are no comprehensive statistics of the volume of government securities. Rough estimates, discussed in Section 11, put them at about f 200 million in the middle of the seventeenth century, rising to possibly f 250 million near its end. This would be approximately equal to or slightly above one year's national product, at that time a high ratio. The amount of tradeable government securities was, however, considerably smaller as a substantial though unknown proportion had the form of annuities.

The only two important issuers of corporate shares were the United East India and the West Indies companies with share capitals of about f 6 million and f 7 million, respectively. While the shares of the West Indies Company became almost worthless, those of the United East India Company were traded at well above their face value for most of their history (Dillen 1970, p. 126; Penso de la Vega, p. 23), and came to contribute an important part of the portfolio of many of the larger estates. Shortly after the initial offering, the shares were traded at 15 percent above par. Within a few years their price rose to 200 percent and in the 1640s was generally above 400 percent. This was not out of line with the dividends, which then averaged about 15 percent of par, indicating a yield of about 3.5 percent. At the highest price of 650, reached in the early 1670s, the equity in the company was valued at f 40 million, equal to about one-fifth of national product and near 5 percent of national wealth.

Some indication of the use of the different types of financial instruments among the rich is given by the few published statements of estates (Burke, pp. 113–14). They suggest that almost all wealthy Dutchmen had invested a substantial part of their estate in houses, land, and bonds. In 15 estates reported in the early eighteenth century, land constituted 6 percent (unweighted average), houses 12 percent, stocks, mostly of the United East India Company, 31 percent, and bonds, mostly Dutch government securities, 50 percent. There are not enough estates from the seventeenth century to permit a comparison, but they suggest lower shares of financial assets and higher shares of houses and land.

## 7     Financial institutions

The most important financial institution of the seventeenth century, and the only one about whose operations there is ample descriptive and quantitative information available, is the Amsterdamse Wisselbank organized in 1609 by the city of Amsterdam and patterned after the Venetian Banco di Rialto founded in 1587.[18] The bank had two main functions, primarily the establishment of a giro system based on accounts kept in guilders of constant silver content, and secondarily the purchase of coins and bullion for the country's mints or for resale. The extension of loans was limited to the city of Amsterdam, the province of Holland, and the United East India Company. In the 1680s the bank added loans on specie to its activities. The bank reached its largest size in the eighteenth century and lasted in much attenuated form until 1820.

Since all bills of exchange of over f 600 had to be made payable at the bank, most larger merchants and other entrepreneurs had to keep an account with the bank, as did many foreign merchants. The number of accounts increased from 730 in 1609 to about 2,000 in the 1660s and 1670, and to about 2,700 by the end of the century, and reached a temporary peak at about 2,900 in the 1720s.[19] At the level of 2,000 the number of account holders was equal to about 8 percent of that of households in Amsterdam, but was of course much higher in relation to that of the city's business community. No statistics have been found of the size distribution, of the local or of the industrial distribution of accounts.

The deposits bore no interest but could not be attached and were guaranteed by the city of Amsterdam. They increased from slightly below f 1.0 million in 1610 to an average of about f 7 million from 1640 to 1685. Average deposits per account rose from about f 1,300 in 1610 to about f 3,500 in the 1640–85 period. The volume of transfers in the books of the bank is not known, but appears to have been many times – possibly as many as 100 times – as large as deposits.[20] Overdrafts were prohibited and carried a penalty of 3 percent. The origin of the large depositors of the bank in 1620 is another evidence of the role of the immigrants from the Southern Netherlands in the financial life of Amsterdam. Of 119 such depositors 68 were southerners, 37 northerners, and 14 foreigners, including 7 Portuguese Jews (Dillen 1958, p. 95).

The bank had no capital, but the accumulated profits belonging to the city came by 1680 to represent over one-fifth of deposits and to equal the loans made to the city.

Most of the bank's assets (Table 11-6) consisted of its stock of coins and bullion, which generally was in excess of three-fourths of deposits. This stock represented a substantial but not dominating proportion of the total monetary stock of the Netherlands, possibly about one-tenth. Claims against the East India Company constituted a substantial proportion of assets only from 1619 to 1630, reaching a peak with f 1 million or about one-third of total assets in 1629.

Table 11-6. *Balance sheet of Amsterdamse Wisselbank,*
*1610–1700 (million f )*

| Jan 31 | Total assets or liabilities (1) | Cash (2) | Claims against | | Liabilities (5) | Reserve[a] (6) |
|---|---|---|---|---|---|---|
| | | | VOC (3) | City (4) | | |
| 1610 | 0.93 | 0.93 | — | — | 0.93 | — |
| 1620 | 2.09 | 1.86 | 0.10 | — | 1.94 | 0.15 |
| 1630 | 4.75 | 3.11 | 0.45 | 0.17 | 4.17 | 0.58 |
| 1640 | 9.25 | 5.82 | — | — | 8.08 | 1.17 |
| 1650 | 12.28 | 10.59 | 0.35 | 0.70 | 10.76 | 1.52 |
| 1660 | 9.17 | 6.85 | — | 1.83 | 7.60 | 1.57 |
| 1670 | 7.20 | 4.84 | — | 2.07 | 5.37 | 1.83 |
| 1680 | 10.13 | 6.16 | 1.61 | 2.07 | 7.95 | 2.18 |
| 1690 | 12.98 | 11.74 | — | 0.81 | 12.60 | 0.38 |
| 1700 | 16.88 | 13.37 | 0.50 | 2.38 | 16.28 | 1.60 |

[a] Accumulated profits and losses ascribable to the city of Amsterdam.
*Source:* Dillen 1964, pp. 382–4, 412–13.

There was no charge on transfers, the bank earning its expenses
and a modest profit, averaging about f 30,000 for the 1610–80 period, from its operations in coins and bullion and from interest on its
loans. The bank was administered by three commissaries appointed
by the city and a small staff housed since the middle of the century in
a few rooms in city hall.

From the middle of the seventeenth century on, when the quality
of the silver coins in general circulation deteriorated, the bank money
developed an agio that fluctuated, but usually was not in excess of 5
percent.

During the seventeenth and part of the eighteenth century the bank
was not only the most important financial institution in the Netherlands but to a substantial extent a clearing house for European international trade due to the role of the bill on Amsterdam. It was the
most important dealer in precious metals (Dillen 1926, passim). Smaller
banks operated on a similar pattern in Middleburg from 1616 on, in
Delft from 1621 on, and in Rotterdam beginning in 1635.

In Amsterdam, as well as in a few other cities, banks for small loans
(*bank van leening*) were set up early in the seventeenth century. They
were small institutions – the capital of the Amsterdam bank in 1616
was only f 1.2 million – whose main activities were the making of
small loans for consumption on the basis of pledges, but which also

made some loans to artisans to finance their business. These banks raised their funds, in addition to their capital, by the issuance of obligations at rates between 5 and 6¼ percent. There were numerous pawnbrokers and moneylenders of different size, but virtually nothing is known about their activities.

The existence of a substantial activity in property and particularly in maritime insurance for foreign as well as for Dutch vessels is attested by the organization as early as 1598 of a chamber of insurance, by the inclusion in the price courant of the Amsterdam exchange of maritime insurance rates, and by an estimate that in 1635 insurance premia registered with the chamber of insurance accounted to over f 4 million or about 2 percent of national product. Insurance was provided not by specialized institutions but during much of the sixteenth century by individual capitalists, generally only as part of their business activities, and was handled by brokers of whom there were about 100 in the early eighteenth century (Baasch, pp. 241–6; Barbour, pp. 33–35).

The Amsterdam exchange, installed since 1608 in its own large building, was until near the end of the seventeenth century a commercial rather than a financial institution.[21] The exchange was the single most important staple market not only for the United Provinces but for much of Europe. As early as 1639 as much as 360 types of commodities were traded and by 1685 the number had risen to 550 (Klompmaker 1966, p. 79), and the exchange's price list published since 1613 was one of the most important sources of information for the period's international trade. Transactions were handled by numerous sworn brokers, as early as 1612 360 of them (Verlinden, p. 333), and advanced methods of trading, such as futures and options, were developed, and speculation was at times very active. Trading in securities during the seventeenth century was limited to Dutch government securities and to the shares of the two large foreign trade companies. Even in the middle of the eighteenth century only 44 issues were quoted. In 1689 a tax on transactions of 0.25 to 0.50 percent was introduced.

## 8 Interest rates

The United Provinces had from the middle of the seventeenth century for about 100 years the lowest level of interest rates (Barbour, pp. 80ff; Homer, p. 177) in the world, with a declining tendency since the beginning of the seventeenth century. In the later half of the seventeenth century commercial credit was freely available at 3 to 4.5

percent, while the rates on government securities as well as for the obligations of the VOC (East India Company) fell during the century to about 3 to 4 percent and mortgages seem to have yielded about 5 percent. Small loans for consumption, of course, cost much more, but the rates charged by the Amsterdam loan bank declined from 16 percent in 1614 to 6 percent in the middle of the century. In the early eighteenth century short-term rates fell to 2 percent and long-term rates to below 3 percent. All these were far below comparable rates in England or France. The low level of interest rates during the first half of the eighteenth century is not astonishing as during that period the economy had stopped expanding. That of the seventeenth century apparently was due in part to a relatively high rate of saving and a low evaluation of risks.

## 9     Financing the private economy

The materials available for an analysis of the sources and methods of financing the various sectors of the private economy, let alone quantitative data, are insufficient for more than a few generalizations. No study devoted to the subject has been found, and it is virtually ignored in the publications dealing with the economic or even the financial history of the United Provinces in the seventeenth century.

It would be erroneous to conclude from the experience of the two large overseas trading companies that a large, let alone a dominating, proportion of the short- or long-term funds needed were provided by the issuance of securities and by borrowing. Internal financing was the rule except in foreign trade and in shipping. In the absence of institutional lenders all loans were among individuals, households, or business enterprises.

In agriculture the funds needed for the drainage of lakes and moors, the activity requiring the largest concentrated funds, were mostly provided by individual, generally urban, capitalists who then became proprietors of the land reclaimed. Debts among villagers and to outsiders appear to have been common but small in relation to their properties (de Vries 1974, pp. 222–4). There were no institutional sources of funds. The absence of data on agricultural debt is particularly unfortunate in view of the sharp rise in land prices.

There is no information about the methods of financing urban housing. Most of the funds were probably provided by the owner-occupiers or the landlords of rental housing. There was also a substantial amount of mortgages by small and large capitalists, but its size is unknown.

Most commercial and manufacturing enterprises were owned by individual proprietors or in the case of the larger ones by partnerships of family members or unrelated partners. Long-term funds were provided mainly by the owners, but a substantial part of short-term funds were supplied by trade credit.

Larger partnerships were common in shipping, where the number of co-owners went up to several dozen. To what extent these were supplemented by borrowing is unknown. Most individuals or partnerships owned only one ship, the average in the late eighteenth century being two boats (Kranenburg, pp. 59ff).

There were only two large organizations in a form approximating that of a modern corporation, the United East India Company (Verenigde East-Indische Compagnie) and the West India Company (West-Indische Compagnie).

By the middle of the seventeenth century the United East India Company had reached its definitive organizational form as the largest corporation of the age, had become the largest commercial enterprise in the country, if not the world, and had by military means acquired substantial territories in Indonesia, Ceylon, and the Cape. The company, however, never shed some of its early characteristics, such as its autocratic management, which left shareholders practically no say in its affairs, and the absence of any publicity of its finances, and never fully integrated the operations of its six chambers nor developed a system of accounts covering its activities in the Netherlands or in its possessions.[22]

The company, started in 1602 as the combination of partnerships, engaged in trade with the Spice Islands, operating in six cities (Amsterdam, Middelburg, Rotterdam, Delft, Hoorn, and Enkhuizen). It was created by an ordinance of the central government, which laid down its basic law and, most importantly, granted it a 21-year monopoly in the trade with all territories between the Cape and the Straits of Magellan. This privilege was renewed in 1623 and 1647 against substantial payments by the company.

The company had a two tiered management. The first of these was constituted by first 76 and later 60 governors (*bewindhebbers*), originally selected among the members of the partnerships that had been combined into the company, and later among holders of f 6,000 or more of stock, of whom there was only a couple of hundred. The second tier, which came increasingly to dominate the management of the company, were the 17 directors after whom the company often came to be referred to as the *Heren Zeventien*. Eight of them were delegated by the Amsterdam chamber, four by the Middelburg chamber, and five by the other four chambers. Although the Amsterdam chamber thus did not have an absolute majority in the management, in fact it always dominated it. Most of the governors and directors were members of the Regenten, a group of a few thousand individuals and families who in the seventeenth century dominated the economic and political life in the United Provinces.[23] The 17 directors, developing into full-time officers, received a relatively modest salary, f 3,000 in the Amsterdam chamber. The staff in the Netherlands remained very small, including a secretary and counsel and a few accountants and cashiers housed in half a dozen rooms of city hall. This is reflected in administrative expenses of less than f 70,000 a year, of which one-half was in Amsterdam, even at the end of the seventeenth century (Klerk de Reus, p. 59).

The offering of the company's stock in 1602, the only one ever, yielded f 6.25 million, of which 56 percent was subscribed by the Amsterdam chamber and 20 percent by the Middelburg chamber, the rest being divided among the four other chambers. This was at that time a very substantial sum, equal to about 3 percent of national product and to more than one-half of one percent of national wealth. The company's importance in the national economy is suggested by its share in the country's foreign trade in the later seventeenth century of about one-tenth (Brugmans 1948, p. 228). The dividends paid by the company, the profits made by governors and directors, and the repatriated savings of the company's staff in Indonesia are supposed to have made a substantial contribution to the saving of the United Provinces (Dillen 1970, p. 128).

The approximately 1,700 original subscribers represented about 0.5 percent of all households in the United Provinces. The proportion must, however, have been substantially higher in the cities, particularly in those in which a chamber was located. The 1,143 subscribers to the Amsterdam chamber, for example, were equal to about 4 percent of the households in the city, though the relevant proportion was lower as part of the subscribers did not live in Amsterdam. Similarly, the 88 persons subscribing f 10,000 or more to the Amsterdam chamber compared with 330 households with an assessed wealth of over f 50,000. Though merchants constituted most of the larger subscribers, the registers also showed many subscribers, particularly from the Northern Netherlands, who were members of the professions, government officials, or independent artisans and even some workmen and domestics.[24]

No regular cash dividends were paid during the first quarter century of the company's operations, though between 1610 and 1627 a total of 162.5 percent of the capital or slightly over f 10 million were distributed, partly in cash and partly in kind (spices), the latter awkward to realize for the shareholders who were not merchants. From there on substantial cash dividends were paid in most years at rates between 12.5 and 60 percent supplemented by a few dividends in kind and a few times, for example, in 1679–82 and 1696–98, in the form of the company's bonds rather than in cash. For the second quarter of the seventeenth century cash dividends averaged 14 percent per year, rising to 17 percent in the third and in the fourth quarter to 15 percent plus 5.5 percent in obligations.[25]

A large proportion of the shares of the company was subscribed by a small number of individuals. In the case of the Amsterdam and Middelburg chambers, which together accounted for about four-fifths of total subscriptions, the 1,387 subscribers averaged nearly f 3,600, a substantial amount as average annual income per household in the United Provinces was about f 250, but the 121 subscribers for f 10,000 or more, averaging a little over f 20,000, constituted one-half of the total, while the 522 small subscribers for less than f 1,000 probably provided less than 5 percent of the total. The largest subscription to the Amsterdam chamber, by the famous speculator Isaac le Maire, amounted to f 85,000 or 2.5 percent of the total, and the 10 largest subscriptions to f 435,000 or 12 percent of the total (Dillen 1958, p. 61).

The distribution of subscriptions reflected the large share of immigrants from the Southern Netherlands in the financial life of Amsterdam. Subscribers originating in the Southern Netherlands accounted for nearly two-fifths of the total, but their share in the large subscriptions of f 10,000 or more was slightly above one-half. Subscribers from the Northern Netherlands on the other hand contributed 55 percent of total capital but only two-fifths of large subscriptions. The difference is reflected in the average subscriptions, which for the immigrants with f 4,650 was almost twice as large as that of the natives with f 2,600, as well as in the number of subscribers – 785 from the north against 300 from the south. Foreign subscriptions provided less than 5 percent of the total, mostly by Germans (Dillen 1958, pp. 55, 60). As between the two chambers, that of Middelburg showed both a higher average contribution – about f 4,900 against f 3,300 – and a higher degree of concentration with a share of subscriptions of f 10,000 and more of 60 percent of the total against 45 percent in Amsterdam (Unger, pp. 8–9).

The balance sheets and income accounts of the VOC, which have only been collected very recently (de Korte, passim) are difficult to

Table 11-7. *Operations of VOC, 1600–1700 (million f)*

|  | Sales (1) | Expen-ditures (2) | Inventory change (3) | Result (4) | Divi-dends (5) | Retained income (6) |
|---|---|---|---|---|---|---|
| 1602–1650 | — | — | — | 52.2 | 51.7 | 0.5 |
| 1651–1660 | 84.2 | 73.5 | 0.7 | 11.4 | 10.3 | 1.1 |
| 1661–1670 | 92.3 | 83.3 | −1.4 | 7.5 | 9.5 | −2.0 |
| 1671–1680 | 91.3 | 79.7 | 2.0 | 13.6 | 13.6 | 0.0 |
| 1681–1690 | 104.5 | 100.3 | 2.1 | 16.3 | 15.1 | 1.2 |
| 1691–1700 | 127.4 | 110.1 | −7.2 | 10.0 | 13.2 | −3.2 |
| 1650–1700 | 499.7 | 446.9 | −3.9 | 58.8 | 61.7 | −2.9 |

*Source:* de Korte, p. 70.

interpret. For the first century of its operations the VOC accounts, summarized in Table 11-7, show profits of f 111 million, which were f 3 million below dividends paid out. As no capital was raised after the initial issue and borrowings were small, it is not evident how the increase in assets, particularly overseas, was financed.

During the second half of the seventeenth century net profits of f 59 million were shown on sales of f 500 million – approximately 3.5 percent of national product. Although sales increased at an annual average rate of 1 percent, profits showed no upward trend and the reported net profit margin decreased from 14 percent of sales in the 1650s to 8 percent in the 1690s. Gross profits on the merchandise sent home were, of course, much higher and averaged about 250 percent from 1640 to 1700 without substantial fluctuations (de Korte, pp. 60–61).

Assets in the United Provinces, mostly in Amsterdam, averaged about f 13 million, as shown in Table 11-8, not much over 1 percent of national wealth. They had predominantly the form of inventories of imported goods. Holdings of cash were relatively small.

No balance sheet seems to have been drawn up or survived for the company's overseas operations. The "capital in the Indies" has been reported as having increased from f 13 million in 1640 to f 32 million in 1700, but what these figures represent is not clear. They apparently refer to net expenditures, but are not derived from the value of total assets (de Korte, Appendix 8C). Total commercial assets have been estimated by an official of the company at about f 26 million near the end of the eighteenth century, while "capital" was reported as averaging f 28 million in the 1780s.

Table 11-8. *Balance sheet of VOC, 1638–1700 (million f)*

|  | 1638 | 1650 | 1660 | 1670 | 1680 | 1690 | 1700 |
|---|---|---|---|---|---|---|---|
| United Provinces |  |  |  |  |  |  |  |
| Total assets | — | 11.25 | 12.67 | 13.97 | 13.38 | 14.86 | 10.06 |
| Cash | 1.21 | 0.44 | 0.90 | 2.20 | 0.34 | 0.49 | 2.54 |
| Receivables | 1.94 | 0.57 | 0.77 | 1.75 | 1.28 | 0.48 | 0.81 |
| Inventories | 7.09 | 9.96 | 10.72 | 9.18 | 11.16 | 13.28 | 6.03 |
| Buildings | — | 0.28 | 0.28 | 0.83 | 0.59 | 0.61 | 0.67 |
| Payables | — | 0.55 | 0.22 | 0.38 | 0.21 | 0.71 | 0.72 |
| Debentures[a] | — | — | — | — | 2.03 | 1.04 | 0.00 |
| Obligations | — | — | — | — | — | — | 2.79 |
| Due chambers | 11.32 | 10.21 | 10.84 | 13.93 | 11.45 | 12.25 | 9.12 |
| Indies Capital | 12.62[b] | 16.35 | 15.95 | 25.36[c] | 18.33[d] | 25.33 | 31.85 |

[a] Mostly Anticipatiepenningen.
[b] 1640.
[c] 1669.
[d] 1681.
*Source:* de Korte, Appendices I-A, I-B, and 6-A.

The organization of the VOC was followed two decades later by that of a similar enterprise for trade with and colonization in the Americas and West Africa. The West India Company was capitalized at f 7 million, but it took about three years until the capital was fully subscribed in 1624. The Amsterdam chamber contributed 40 percent and the Middleburg chamber 13 percent, in both cases considerably less than in the case of the East India Company. The West India Company was by far the less successful of the two. It lost its colonies in Brazil and North America in the early 1660s to the Portuguese and the British, was in financial difficulties before the middle of the century, and was dissolved in 1675. A smaller successor company lasted until 1791.[26]

## 10   Foreign trade

The scarcity of relevant statistical information is also evident in the absence of comprehensive data on as important a subject as the volume of foreign trade and on its financing. One estimate puts total foreign trade in the middle of the seventeenth century at f 75 to 100 million (Wätjen, p. 330) or one-fifth to one-fourth of national product. A contemporary author estimated exports at £12 million (Petty, cited Baasch, p. 358), which would be well above one-half of national product, a very unlikely figure. There is no doubt, however, that the foreign trade of the United Provinces was more intensive, that is, higher in relation to population (Sombart, p. 957) or to national product, than in any other European country and that it was the backbone of the country's economy. The main imports were grains, which provided about one-half of the country's consumption (Braudel, p. 148); timber, essential for its shipbuilding industry, then the international leader; and spices and salt, most of which were reexported. The main exports, apart from the reexported items, were salt herring, a trade dominated by the Dutch, linen and woolen textiles, and ships. Little is known about the methods of financing foreign trade. Most imports apparently were paid for in cash, while a substantial part of exports required credit, particularly bills of exchange, provided in part by a number of large trading houses, mainly in Amsterdam, who also financed inventories of imported and for-export commodities.

In 1667–68 commodity imports of Amsterdam were valued at f 54 million, while exports amounted to f 29 million, a total of f 83 million (Morineau, in Aymard, p. 297). Since Amsterdam at that time accounted to fully one-half of the country's trade, the value for the United Provinces would have been on the order of f 150 million, or about three-fourths of national product. This, or a somewhat lower figure, seems to be the most likely value. If Amsterdam's trade was also representative of the value of imports and exports, these would have come to about f 100 million and fully f 50 million, respectively. An excess of commodity imports over exports is to be expected in view of the earnings of the United Provinces from shipping, other services, foreign investments, and the sale of ships.

The two largest categories of imports were textile raw materials and semifabricates and foodstuffs from Europe, each of which accounted for about one-fourth of the total. They were followed by spices with about one-eighth of the total. Textiles accounted for over one-third of exports and (reexport) spices for fully one-eighth.

One of the relevant series available concerns the shipping (export and import) tax, which provides information on the share of the various ports in foreign trade. Table 11-9 shows that during the second half of the seventeenth century Amsterdam was by far the most important port of origin and destination, accounting for fully one-half of the total of the United Provinces. Rotterdam was a far-behind second with less than one-tenth, followed by the two Zeeland ports (Middelburg and Vlissingen) with together another one-tenth.

The series also, and possibly more importantly, provides a measure of the movements in the value of foreign trade. It then indicates an

Table 11-9. *Local distribution of shipping tax, 1625–1700* (%)

| | 1625 (1) | 1650 (2) | 1674 (3) | 1700 (4) |
|---|---|---|---|---|
| Amsterdam | 46.9 | 65.1 | 64.2 | 66.3 |
| Arnhem | 3.5 | 2.3 | 1.7 | 0.4 |
| Rotterdam | 10.2 | 8.3 | 10.3 | 12.0 |
| Dordrecht | 9.5 ⎱ | | 2.4 | 1.5 |
| Nijmegen | 7.5 ⎰ | (5.3) | 1.8 | 2.5 |
| s'Hertogenbosch | (2.5) ⎰ | | 2.4 | 1.1 |
| Enkhuizen | 5.7 | 5.5 | 2.3 | 1.2 |
| Zwolle | 0.3 | 0.4 | 1.2 | 2.6 |
| Middelburg | 6.1 | 6.7 | 8.1 ⎱ | (11.0)[b] |
| Vlissingen | 5.3 | 4.7 | 2.5 ⎰ | |
| Harlingen | 1.2 | 1.3 | 2.8 | 1.1 |
| Groningen | 1.6 | 0.5 | 0.3 | 0.3 |
| 12 ports | 100.0 | 100.0 | 100.0 | 100.0 |
| Republic (%) | 118[a] | 124 | 113[a] | — |
| Republic (million f) | (1.30)[b] | 2.36 | (1.30)[b] | (2.50)[b] |

[a] Based on totals for 1626 and for 1671, nearest year available.
[b] Estimates.
*Source:* This table is based on Becht's figures in his Table III (A). Those for Amsterdam have recently been corrected by Westermann (B), with the following result:

| | A | B |
|---|---|---|
| 1625 | 565 | 659 |
| 1650 | 1241 | 1241 |
| 1674 | 736 | 980 |
| 1700 | 1579 | 1212 |

Westermann's corrections for the years following 1650 eliminate the effects of changes in tariff to produce a series reflecting change in the value of goods exported or imported. The corrections therefore should not greatly affect the distribution of receipts among stations except possibly in 1625. If Westermann's correction is accepted, the share of Amsterdam in 1625 would be increased from 43 percent of the total for the Republic to 50 percent, bringing it closer to that of 1650 of 53 percent.

increase by about 50 percent between 1624–26 and 1646–50, a period of stable wholesale prices; stability during the following decade; a decline during the next 20 years; a peak in 1681–85; and another decline to the early eighteenth century. As a result the value of trade in 1701–05 was nearly one-fifth higher than in 1624–26, while the wholesale price index was 5 percent lower suggesting an increase in the volume of exports plus imports by about one-fourth, or at an annual rate of 0.3 percent, that is, only marginally above the increase in population.[27] This is a relevant finding for a country as dependent on foreign trade as the United Provinces.

## 11     Financing the government

The complex and almost chaotic state of government finance in the
seventeenth century with its often overlapping functions and revenues and expenditures of the central government, the provinces, and
the municipalities, is reflected in the scarcity of statistical data and
even of systematic descriptions.[28]

The only comprehensive estimate, a contemporary one, possibly on
the high side, put total government revenues in 1688 at £4.73 million
(King, p. 51), that is, at about f 50 million or one-fourth of national
product. That was for seventeenth century Europe a high ratio – the
ratio for Great Britain at the end of the century was about 3 percent[29]
– and accords with the general impression that the United Provinces
were a high-tax country and its revenues perhaps larger in relation to
national product than in any other European state of the time. About
one-half of total revenues were received by the central government,
for example, about f 20 million in 1653 (Ballhausen, p. 137), which
needed them mainly to cover its military expenditures for the numerous wars fought during the century. Most of the central government's
revenues had the form of contributions by the provinces on the basis
of quotas fixed early in the seventeenth century. Under the arrangement Holland contributed 58 percent of the total, Friesland 12 percent, and Zeeland 9 percent leaving only a little over 20 percent for
the other provinces (Sickenga, p. 107). The provinces in turn recovered their payments from the municipalities. Taxes on imports
and exports whose yield was moderate – on the average only about
f 2 million (cf. Table 11-7), or 5 percent of all government revenues
– were collected only by the central government, but the very numerous other taxes, mostly excises, predominantly on foodstuffs, were
levied at all levels of government and on terms and at rates varying
among provinces and municipalities. The province of Holland, for
example, collected about 40 different excises,[30] often through tax
farmers. But there were also substantial direct taxes, particularly a
tax, transmitted to the central government, of 20 percent on the rental
value of land and of 12.5 percent on that of buildings (Dillen 1970, p.
272), which in the middle of the century is reported to have yielded
about f 2.5 million (Ballhausen, p. 136) or about 5 percent of total
government revenues. Another direct tax was a 0.5 or 1.0 percent
levy on taxable wealth, which was assessed at irregular intervals. An
idea of its yield is given by the f 2 million collected in 1673 in the
province of Holland on a 1 percent basis.[31]

An indication of the level and trend of municipal revenues is provided by those of Amsterdam, which rose from f 0.7 million in 1601–05 to f 2.4 million in 1651–55, and to f 3.5 million in 1701–05 (Koenen, pp. 121ff), probably more rapidly than those of all municipalities in the country.

There are no data that permit an analysis of the incidence of the tax system as a whole, but it would appear to have been regressive, particularly because of the predominance of excises on articles of mass consumption and of the absence of a graduated tax on commercial profits and on the income from financial assets. The heavy burden of indirect taxes was also one of the factors in the internationally high level of commodity prices and hence of wages in the United Provinces.

The available data do not permit calculating the balance between revenues and expenditures of the different levels of government. The substantial increase in public debt suggests, however, that in the aggregate deficits prevailed, though probably by not by much more than about f 1 million per year, or one-half of one percent of national product.

The United Provinces financed most of the expenditures of its long war with Spain before the armistice of 1612 by internal borrowing and so accumulated a large debt. By the middle of the century, as well as in the late 1660s, the debt of the province of Holland has been put at about f 130 million, which near the end of the century increased to about f 170 million (Dillen 1970, p. 283). No information exists about the aggregate debt of all governmental units, but since it has been asserted that the debt of the province of Holland was "far larger than that of the Union and the other provinces" (Dillen 1970, p. 283), this aggregate should have been on the order of f 200 million by the middle and of f 250 million by the end of the century. This figure is identical with Gregory King's estimate of £25 million for 1695 (King, p. 53). A substantial part of the total had the form of annuities, but most of it consisted of long-term obligations, both widely held.[32]

At f 200 million, the total government debt was equal to approximately one year's national product, a high ratio for the time – that in Great Britain was on the order of less than one-fourth[33] – and in the absence of institutional holdings must have been in the hands of individual investors and have constituted a substantial proportion of their total assets. If total individuals' wealth is put roughly at f 1,000 million (cf. Section 2), the proportion would be about one-fifth.

As the interest rate that the governmental issuers had to pay declined substantially during the century – from over 10 percent to 3 to 4 percent (cf. Section 6) – interest payments declined, possibly from f 15 million to less than f 10 million, or somewhat less than 5 percent of national product and nearly one-fifth of government revenues. Even then the interest burden was still considerably higher than in Great Britain, where it was below 2 percent of national product, though its share in government revenues was about the same.[34]

## CHAPTER 12

# Similarities and differences

The purpose of this chapter is to permit a comparison of the main characteristics of the 10 cases presented by giving at least an idea of their similarities and differences[1] without being able to do justice to their individualities or to explain the reasons for them. This goal is attempted by providing a very condensed description of the main characteristics of the economic infrastructure of each country covered – the population, urbanization, and size and distribution of income and wealth – and of its financial structure – monetary system, financial instruments and organizations, interest rates, and methods of financing the main sectors, particularly the government. These descriptions are necessarily so condensed that an appreciation of the significance of these features and of the limitations of the underlying evidence requires consultation of the relevant chapters. Thus most statements should be read as being prefaced by such expressions as "apparently," "probably," or "approximately." An attempt to go beyond these descriptions has been made on only a few points. The time for an explanation of the reasons of the observed differences or for a synthesis of the financial history of the world before the eighteenth century does not yet seem to have come, if only because of the limitations of the available data, particularly if they are to be expressed in quantitative terms, the approach attempted throughout the study.

Information, particularly in quantitative form, is unfortunately scarcer on the specific financial aspects of the economy, with the exception of the monetary system, interest rates, and government revenues, expenditures, and debt, than on the economy's infrastructure of population and income, although some of those aspects such as urbanization and the size distribution of income and wealth have considerable influence on financial structure. In the case of financial instruments and organizations whatever information is available is generally impressionistic and nonquantitative.

To facilitate comparisons each chapter discusses as far as possible

229

the same topics and in the same order. Considerable differences, however, remain – due mainly to the literature available and to the importance of the topic for a given case – in the detail in which these topics are covered and in the extent to which the information could be presented in quantitative terms. For similar reasons the quality of the various chapters varies, even in the author's eyes; those on Athens, Rome, Mughal India, Florence, Elizabethan England, and the United Provinces are less deficient than those on the Abbasid caliphate, the Ottoman Empire, and Tokugawa Japan.

An attempt has been made to present each chapter in a form to be readable as an independent brief case study. For this reason the publications cited are shown separately for each chapter at the end of the volume rather than being submerged in a long consolidated bibliography.

The term *premodern financial system* as used in this study is to be understood in a rather narrow sense. It is meant simply to describe the total of all financial organizations in existence, which include the usually predominating small one-man operations, even when financial operations were sporadic and ancillary to other economic activities. The term does not imply a regular or close relationship among financial organizations even of the same type, though some such relationships generally existed, or between organizations of different types or the existence of markets for financial instruments. Many, and usually most, financial transactions were of a local character, though in all of the cases included in this study there existed connections between financial organizations in different parts of the territory and even with those in foreign countries.

In making comparisons among the 10 cases, it is necessary always to keep in mind the wide range in the dates to which the facts and figures refer – extending from the fifth century B.C. to the seventeenth century A.D., even disregarding the ancient Near East – the wide geographic distances – from western Europe to East Asia – and the differences in size – from about 300,000 people for Periclean Athens and 400,000 for the Florentine Republic to over 50 million for the Roman Empire and over 100 million for Mughal India via the United Provinces with 2 million, Elizabethan England with less than 5 million, Tokugawa Japan with about 20 million, and the Abbasid caliphate and the Ottoman Empire with about 25 million – as well as the differences in the level of their economic development, which cannot be measured accurately but which on the basis of rough estimates of real national product per head is likely to have varied in a ratio of one to at least three. These differences by themselves explain part of the observed differences and similarities in financial structure among the 10 cases.

Among the 10 premodern financial systems described two groups may be distinguished. The one, and more numerous, group of countries possessed only a fairly rudimentary system. Financial instruments were essentially limited to metallic coins (missing in the ancient Near East), necessitous consumer loans, mostly from landlords to tenants, and short-term trade credit. Transactions were sporadic and there was no market for any instrument. Financial organizations were limited to money changers, pawnbrokers, and moneylenders, for whom financial transactions often were ancillary to their other economic activities. This group includes Mesopotamia, Periclean Athens, the Augustan Roman Empire, the early Abbasid caliphate, the Ottoman Empire of the mid-sixteenth century, Mughal India under Akbar, early Tokugawa Japan, and probably also Elizabethan England. In the second group of countries – Florence of the fifteenth century and the United Provinces in the mid-seventeenth century – the financial system was considerably more developed and larger in relation to the nonfinancial economy. In this group financial instruments were more numerous and varied, including many types of trade credit, mortgages, and, though on a small scale, government and corporate securities. Financial organizations were more specialized and independent and included deposit banks.

Population growth was in most cases low by modern standards with both high birth and death rates. The highest rates of growth were shown by Athens in the half-century before 430 B.C. with possibly as much as 1 percent per year, in part reflecting immigration; by Elizabethan England with 0.7 percent; by the United Provinces in the first half of the seventeenth century with 0.5 percent, partly as a result of immigration; and by early Tokugawa Japan with about 0.3 percent. In the other cases the rate of growth appears to have been close to or below 0.2 percent per year.

More important from the point of view of financial development is the level of urbanization and of changes in it because use of credit is higher in cities and financial institutions are concentrated in them. Here differences were very considerable and in part explained by the size of the territory. Urbanization was higher in states like Periclean Athens with over one-half and in the Florentine Republic in the early fifteenth century with about one-third than in large empires like Rome, the caliphate, the Ottoman Empire, and Mughal India. In the Augustan Roman Empire the urbanization ratio was about one-tenth, in the Abbasid caliphate around 800 A.D. slightly lower, in the Ottoman Empire in the mid-sixteenth century somewhat over 5 percent, in Mughal India around 1600 A.D. close to one-sixth, and in early Tokugawa Japan around one-tenth, all below the ratio of Mesopotamia in the third to the first millennium B.C., which seems to have been on the order of one-fifth. In Elizabethan England the ratio was close to one-fifth. It was much higher in the United Provinces, which had less than one-half the population of England, with about two-fifths in the mid-seventeenth century. The differences in the share of the capital city were equally pronounced. Athens accounted for about one-half of the population of Attica, by far the highest share. In the other cases the ratios ranged from about 15 percent in the Florentine Republic and 10 percent in the United Provinces to 5 percent in Elizabethan England and to about 2 percent in the Roman Empire, the Abbasid caliphate, and the Ottoman Empire, and to probably only about 1 percent in Tokugawa Japan, and to about 0.5 percent in Mughal India.

An attempt has been made to estimate in each case aggregate and per head national product. Given the nature of the available data, such estimates can at best indicate the order of magnitudes involved, and their limitations will be evident from the description of their derivation in Chapters 3 to 11. The estimates put national product per head per year at nearly 100 drachmas per head for Periclean Athens, somewhat less than HS 400 for Augustan Rome, 250 dirhams for the Abbasid caliphate around A.D. 800, less than 100 akche for the Ottoman Empire in mid-sixteenth century, 6 rupees for Mughal India around A.D. 1600, 1 ryo for Japan early in the seventeenth century, 10 florins for the Florentine Republic in A.D. 1427, £7 for England around A.D. 1600, and somewhat over 100 florins for the United Provinces in the mid-seventeenth century. Of the estimates those for Athens, Rome, the Florentine Republic, England, and the United Provinces are better founded than those for the other cases.

These figures are useful for comparison with other important economic magnitudes such as money in circulation, foreign trade, government receipts, and expenditures, and the relevant ratios permit comparisons among cases. In the absence of sufficient information on prices and hence the purchasing power of the various currencies, the estimates, however, do not permit comparisons of the level of real national product per head. Almost the only comparison that can be made is that of the gold equivalent of the national product per head because the gold price is known in all cases. This comparison, however, is also of limited value as the price of gold in terms of other commodities is not known and cannot be assumed to have been the same, or even similar, in the different cases. In terms of gold annual national product per head appears to have been close to 1 oz in Athens, Rome, the Abbasid caliphate, and the Florentine Republic, to only 0.25 oz in Mughal India, but to 2 oz in Elizabethan England, and to 3.5 oz in the United Provinces. These differences reflect to a substantial degree differences in the purchasing power of gold rather than those in real product per head.

The available data do not permit to estimate directly the rate of growth of national product per head. They are sufficient, however, to assert that the rate was very low – not above 0.2 percent per year – for periods of several decades in all cases, except possibly for the United Provinces in the first half of the seventeenth century where it appears to have been close to 0.5 percent. Such low rates imply very low rates of gross and net capital formation, as the capital–output ratios are not likely to have changed rapidly, and very low rates of saving.

National balance sheets, which provide the most useful aggregative picture of financial structure, can unfortunately not yet be constructed for most premodern countries, partly because of the impossibility of even roughly estimating the volume of financial assets. There is, however, little doubt that the financial interrelations ratio (financial: tangible assets) was very low – probably generally not in excess of 0.10 – and thus much lower than it has been in developed countries since the late nineteenth century, where ratios between 0.50 and 1.50 are common.[2] Florence – and probably also some other Italian cities – was an exception as the ratio appears to have been over 0.40. The United Provinces may have been another.

Even the structure of national wealth can be approximated in only too few cases and with too large margins of uncertainty to permit comparisons. The available fragments suffice, however, to suggest that the bulk of total wealth consisted, except in city states, of agricultural land; that among structures the share of dwellings was relatively low; and that the share of precious metals in the form of coins or ornaments was relatively high.

The size distribution of income and wealth is of substantial importance for a country's financial structure because in most premodern societies the ownership of financial assets (other than coins) and the use of financial instruments was limited to the upper income and wealth groups. Comprehensive estimates such as the Gini ratio or the Lorenz curve are unavailable, but in most cases it is possible to estimate the order of magnitude of the share of the very top of the income or wealth pyramid or to indicate the relation between the income of the small top income group to the average family income or to the wage of an unskilled laborer. One difficulty in comparing such estimates among cases is the need to base the comparison in feudal societies on the net income, excluding the cost of maintaining retainers.

In Periclean Athens the wealth of the top percent of families has been estimated at about one-fifth of total private wealth and that of the top 5 percent at well over two-fifths, while that of the lowest two-thirds of the population seems to have been on the order of only one-eighth of the total.

In Augustan Rome the 600 senators out of about 15 million families had a total income, it is estimated, of about 0.5 percent of all personal income, their average income being equal to that of over 100 families or to about 200 times the annual income of a laborer. The emperor's income appears to have amounted to about 0.1 percent of all personal incomes. The top 3 percent of income recipients may have accounted for nearly one-fourth of all personal income with an average income equal to that of eight average families.

In the city of Florence in 1427 the wealthiest 1 percent of households held over one-fourth of total declared wealth and the top one-tenth about two-thirds, leaving only 3 percent for the poorest half. Income concentration though considerably less pronounced was high too.

In England in 1688 to 200 temporal lords out of fully 1 million families are credited with over 2 percent of personal income, or on the average with about 150 average family incomes. The share of the top 1 percent of families exceeded one-eighth of total personal income. Concentration of income was probably only slightly less pronounced in Elizabethan England.

In Amsterdam the top 100 families out of 30,000 appear to have accounted in 1631 for nearly one-fourth of total assessed private wealth and the top 1 percent for well over two-fifths. Concentration of wealth, and still more of income, was considerably lower but still pronounced in smaller cities and in the United Provinces as a whole.

Data are even scarcer for the feudal monarchies, but as far as inferences for them are permitted, concentration was more pronounced than in the preceding five cases.

No estimate is possible for the Abbasid caliphate, though an indication of the inequality of incomes is given by the estimates that the income of a chief minister was up to that of 1,600 laborers and that of a bourgeois family equal to that of 12 to 18 laborers.

In the Ottoman Empire the top 1.5 percent of income recipients appear to have accounted for about one-third of total agricultural income, and probably about the same share of total personal income on a gross but for considerably less on a net basis.

In Mughal India under Akbar 1,700 nobles and the emperor out of over 20 million families received about one-sixth of total personal income before and over 5 percent after maintenance of their retainers. Their average net income was equal to that of about 800 laborers.

Concentration of income and wealth was also very pronounced in Tokugawa Japan, as the shogun owned about one-fourth of the land and about 200 daimyos out of about 5 million families received a large part of the income of the rest of the population. Their net income, however, was considerably smaller as a substantial proportion was required, particularly in the case of the daimyos, for the maintenance of their retainers (samurai).

In view of the nature of the data comparisons among countries are hazardous and are possible only for the very top of the income or wealth pyramid, say for what may be called the chiliadic and myriadic ratios, that is, the share of the top one-thousandth or ten-thousandth of all families in personal income or in private wealth. With due reservations the figures shown in Table 12-1 should give at least an idea of the differences in the seven cases for which the figures can be roughly estimated.

Even allowing for a substantial margin of uncertainty in the estimates, the differences were large. Concentration apparently was higher in the feudal monarchies, higher in city states than in large countries, and of course higher for wealth than for income. It is also evident

Table 12-1. *Comparison of personal wealth and income*

|  | Top (%) | |
| --- | --- | --- |
|  | 1/10,000 | 1/1,000 |
| Income | | |
| Augustan Rome, A.D. 14 | 1.0 | 4.0 |
| Ottoman Empire, ca. 1550 | — | 15.0[a] |
| Mughal India, ca. 1600 | 5.0[a] | — |
| England, 1688 | 2.0 | 6.0 |
| Wealth | | |
| Attica, 430 B.C. | — | 20.0 |
| Florence, 1427 | — | 15.0[b] |
| Amsterdam, 1631 | 2.0[b] | 10.0[b] |

[a] Net, i.e., after maintenance of retainers.
[b] Assessed values, hence probably understated.

that the degree of concentration at the top of the income and wealth pyramid was much higher in all cases than in modern mid-twentieth century countries. (The myriadic income ratio after tax in the late 1970s was about 0.1 percent in India and in England and 0.25 percent in the United States.)

Because the use of credit is generally more important in foreign trade than in the rest of the economy, the share of foreign trade in national product is an important determinant of the size of a country's financial superstructure. It is therefore unfortunate that the value of foreign trade can only be very roughly estimated for premodern periods and often is even beyond such estimates. The available material is, however, sufficient to confirm that as in modern times the share of foreign trade was negatively related to the size of the country. Thus the share of exports plus imports may be put at nearly two-fifths of national product for Periclean Athens and probably was also high for the Florentine Republic, although relevant figures are missing. In the United Provinces in mid-sixteenth century the share has been estimated at one-fifth to one-fourth of national product. In contrast, the share was undoubtedly very small for the large countries. It was probably below 2 percent in the Roman Empire and is likely to have been even lower for the caliphate and the Ottoman Empire and well below 1 percent for Mughal India around 1600 A.D. as well as in Tokugawa Japan where it was held to an extremely small size by government policy. Elizabethan England with a share of close to one-tenth occupied an intermediate position.

In all cases other than in Mesopotamia money in circulation had the form of metallic coins – gold, silver, copper, or bronze – minted by various governmental authorities, and also served as means of thesaurization. The mints in most cases issued coins, usually at a substantial seignorage for metal offered to them, but did not redeem coins at fixed rates. The rates of exchange among coins of different metals varied over time and were determined by the market. For this reason as well as for the varying weight – in the absence of milled edges – and fineness of coins, money changers were needed and important. Paper money existed in only one case (Tokugawa Japan) and was there of only little importance. So were transfers of deposits in banks in the few cases where they developed, except in the United Provinces.

In Mesopotamia silver, though not in coins but by weight, predominated as means of payment and standard of value and by the seventh century B.C. in the form of bars had become the sole money. Gold was treated as a commodity whose silver price varied.

Athens' currency was the first example of monometallism, consisting exclusively of silver coins of different denominations that because of their purity and standard weight came to be used throughout a large part of the Greek world in addition to local currencies.

The Roman Empire had after the Augustan reform a symmetallic system in which gold and silver coins, the first issued only by the imperial mints, both had legal tender. Though the mints did not exchange the two types of coins at fixed rates, a rate implying a 12 to 1 ratio was decreed and apparently accepted until the second century A.D., although the precious metal content of silver coins was reduced more than that of gold coins. Small change was provided by copper or bronze coins, which were not legal tender, but were issued by many territorial units. The imperial mints stood ready to deliver a fixed amount of coins against bullion tendered at a substantial seignorage, but not bullion against coins.

In the Abbasid caliphate and in the Ottoman Empire gold and silver coins issued by the government's mints as well as some foreign gold and silver coins and many types of copper coins circulated at exchange rates determined by the market. In both cases the precious metal content of the coins, particularly silver coins, was repeatedly reduced after the early eighth and mid-sixteenth centuries, respectively.

In Mughal India the silver rupee was the standard coin and the unit in which accounts were kept, supplemented by fractional silver coins down to ½₀ rupee. Gold coins of larger or smaller size were apparently used mainly for thesaurization. Small change was provided mainly by copper coins and by cowrie shells. The different types of coins were exchanged at varying rates determined by the market, but during the reign of Akbar there were customary relations between gold, silver, and copper coins, implying ratios between the three metals of about 1 to 10 and 1 to 80. The government's mints stood ready to issue coins of the three metals, charging a substantial seignorage.

In early Tokugawa Japan gold coins minted by the government were the basis of the monetary system. Silver, which predominated in western Japan, was used by weight at rates determined by the market. This difference between the two parts of the country required an extensive system of money changers and interregional money transfers. The metal content of the coins was reduced several times and substantially from the late seventeenth century on. Paper money was issued in relatively small amounts by local feudatories (*hansatsu*) in the later Tokugawa period.

In the Florentine Republic gold coins minted by the government – the florin, which became an international currency – silver coins, and copper coins circulated simultaneously at rates determined by the market.

In Elizabethan England gold coins and silver coins, down to halfpenny pieces, were issued by the queen's mints. Both metals were legal tender, but no fixed ratio was established between them. In the absence of governmental coins of smaller denominations, numerous types of tokens issued by municipalities or private parties were in use. The crown charged moderate fees for coining bullion brought to the mint, but did not exchange coins for bullion. The metal content of the coins remained unchanged after the recoinage in 1560–61 of the silver coins with lower metal content, which followed the "Great Debasement" of the preceding decades.

In the United Provinces a multitude of domestically minted and foreign coins circulated at rates determined by the market until the end of the seventeenth century when the silver coins minted by the central government became dominant. The banco guilder of fixed silver content evidenced by entries in the books of the Wisselbank of Amsterdam constituted a supplementary money for commercial use.

In these situations monetary policy was essentially limited to the change – in practice always a reduction – in the precious metal content of the coins.

There are unfortunately hardly any data on the volume of minting of coins or of money in circulation, which would permit the calculation of its velocity on the basis of estimates of total let alone of monetized national product. The few very rough estimates that can be made point to large differences among the cases.

In Athens the money supply appears to have been on the order of one year's national product; in the Roman Empire, in Mughal India, in the Florentine Republic, and in the United Provinces to somewhat less than one-half year's product, but in Elizabethan England – possibly the least conjectural figure – to not much more than one-month's product. These figures are unfortunately of limited value in determining the most relevant magnitude, the velocity of circulation in relation to monetized product, as the numerator includes nonmonetized product and the denominator coins thesaurized rather than circulating, both factors of considerable but varying importance in premodern countries, which offset each other to a greater or smaller extent. In general the share of nonmonetized product should have been larger than that of thesaurized coins and hence the velocity of coins in circulation to monetized product somewhat lower than that obtained from the comparison of total national product and total money supply.

The information of the specific characteristics of financial structure – the types of financial instruments in use, the financial organizations in existence, and the sources and methods of financing the various sectors of the economy – is very scarce for premodern societies, particularly outside of Europe, and it is only very rarely susceptible to quantification, which would permit relating it to other relevant economic magnitudes such as national product. Government finances and interest rates are an exception but only in a few cases. One is therefore mostly limited to inferences from scattered materials, which often are not sufficient for more than a broad comparison of the situation in different countries and at different times.

All premodern countries covered in this study had a few financial instruments – coins (except Mesopotamia), trade credit among merchants and small loans to consumers against pawns, and loans in money or in kind between landlords and tenants – but generally no economic units specializing in financial activities, except possibly some money changers and pawnbrokers; and the volume of financial transactions was usually small. At the time at which their financial structure is described in most of the cases, the types of financial instruments had become more numerous, and in most of them some types of financial transactions had become the main activities of some units, particularly moneychanging and pawnbroking, and in some of them – particularly Athens, Rome, Florence, and the United Provinces – banks had appeared. In all of them, however, an important if not dominating part of short- and long-term lending and of maritime insurance were still occasional or secondary activities of merchants, officials, landowners, or other citizens. In only one case – the United Provinces – did a substantial market for financial instruments exist.

Negative statements can be made with more confidence. In most premodern situations, except in Western Europe since the thirteenth century, there were no government or private securities, no paper money (except in Japan), and no deposit banks or insurance organizations.

It is fairly clear, and very important, that such investment as there was, was almost exclusively financed internally, except in long-distance trade.

The importance of financial transactions within the economy undoubtedly varied considerably, though the data are insufficient to measure by how much. It was, however, certainly much smaller in the empires – Rome, the caliphate, the Ottoman Empire, and Mughal India, and probably also Tokugawa Japan – than in Athens, Florence, the United Provinces, and probably also Elizabethan England.

Similarly, although some modern short-term instruments such as bills of exchange, letters of credit, and bottomry loans were known in some premodern systems and book credit among merchants was common, long-term instruments such as rural and urban mortgages, government or corporate bonds, insurance and pension claims, and corporate stocks were absent in most premodern systems, partly reflecting the limitations of property rights. Moreover whatever financial instruments there were, were of much smaller size in comparison to national product, partly because of the generally much lower degree of monetization of the economy, with the possible exception of small and necessitous consumption loans. This reflected the much lower share of capital formation and the much lower share of external financing in it.

While the main differences in the structure of premodern and contemporary financial systems are thus fairly clear, even though they cannot be quantified, it is much more difficult to be certain about the differences among premodern systems, particularly in quantitative terms, or to rank them with respect to their degree of development, which certainly was not unilineal over time.

As credit in foreign transactions was limited in premodern periods to short-term transactions, differences between the value of exports and imports had to be settled in coin, because of the amounts involved generally in gold. Thus the Roman Empire had regularly a passive balance in foreign trade, which may have been as high as one-half of one percent of the national product a year. The situation was similar in the Abbasid caliphate and in the Ottoman Empire, though the balance was probably smaller in relation to national product. On the other hand Mughal India undoubtedly had a positive balance, though it was small in relation to national product. In Periclean Athens a large passive balance in foreign trade was offset by the contributions of the other members of the Delian league. Elizabethan England and the United Provinces probably generally had small negative or positive balances, respectively, but their size is unknown. That of early Tokugawa Japan should have been very small.

In Mesopotamia loans in barley or silver – by weight as there were no coins – attested since the third millennium, were made mainly by temples, royal treasuries, landowners, and merchants. Those by landlords and temples were made mostly to peasants and for short periods, those by treasuries and merchants to traders, particularly for foreign operations. Some loans became transferable, but bills of exchange or other standardized forms of credit did not develop. There were no banks, no insurance and facilities, and no securities. The entire financial system thus remained rudimentary and very small.

The financial system of Athens was considerably more developed in size and variety beginning with the second half of the fifth century A.D., though even then most domestic transactions were settled in domestic or foreign coins, requiring the services of many money changers. There were only a few bankers of small size. The loans they and others made were mainly for consumption or for the religious and political obligations of richer citizens. Mortgages were rare, but there were substantial debts of tenants to landlords. Credit was much more important in foreign trade, where bottomry loans, which combined credit and maritime insurance, made by individuals or groups were common. There was no government borrowing.

The financial structure of the early Roman Empire was generally similar to that of Athens and not more developed than that of some of the Hellenistic monarchies. Regional differences appear to have been substantial, the eastern provinces (except Egypt) generally being monetized to a higher degree and financially more developed than the western provinces (except Italy). The four most important financial instruments were trade credit (including bottomry loans in overseas trade), personal loans either in small amounts to consumers or in larger amounts for the financing of political expenditures, advances of landlords to their tenants, and mortgage loans on land. Short-term loans were made mostly by professional moneylenders and bankers who often also were money changers and handled interlocal money transfers, but mortgages were made mostly by private individuals. Tax farming was an important financial activity exercised by groups of individuals. However, financial transactions remained sporadic, and there was no market for any financial instrument. There was no government debt.

The financial structure of the Abbasid caliphate reflected in its western provinces that of the Byzantine Empire and in its eastern provinces that of the Sassanid kingdom. The most common financial instrument, apart from consumer loans, particularly advances from landlords to tenants, was trade credit, which seems to have been common in wholesale and retail trade, often in the form of participation in the profit to circumvent the strict Koranic prohibition of interest. For that reason long-term loans were rare. Nonnegotiable letters of credit in various forms were used for the interlocal transfer of funds, issued by some of the ubiquitous money changers as well as by merchants. There were no banks or insurance organizations or government securities.

The situation was similar in the Ottoman Empire of the sixteenth century whose financial structure was not more developed than the Abbasid caliphate, which occupied a similar territory, had been seven centuries earlier, partly because of the limitations imposed by the prohibition of interest. The extension of credit remained essentially an activity ancillary to commodity trading and the property administration of wealthy individuals, landlords, and religious foundations.

In Mughal India around 1600 A.D., as in the subcontinent through the nineteenth century, the most common and probably most important financial instrument were the short-term loans made to the peasantry for consumptive purposes by the ubiquitous moneylenders who also acted as money changers, or by the wealthier peasants, landlords, and tax collectors. In cities loans to nobles were an important outlet of funds of moneylenders and merchants. Some of the larger moneylenders also accepted interest-bearing deposits. Trade credit among merchants was common, often in the form of hundis, similar to bills of exchange, which were also used for the interlocal transfer of funds. In the seventeenth century bottomry loans were added. Long-term loans were rare, partly because the land was legally the property of the emperor. There was no long-term government debt.

The financial structure of Japan at the beginning of the Tokugawa period was still rudimentary but developed rapidly during the seventeenth century. To the money changers, which were important because western Japan was on a silver standard but eastern Japan on a gold standard, and the local money-lenders were added numerous bankers, mainly in Osaka, who advanced funds to the nobles. The use of trade credit became more common and employed a number of new credit instruments, including transferable bills of exchange and rice delivery orders. Long-term loans remained rare and there were no government or private securities.

The financial structure of the Florentine Republic in the mid-fifteenth century was characterized by the existence, beyond the usual money changers and pawnbrokers, of numerous banks, the most important one being the Medici bank with half a dozen foreign branches, which accepted deposits and made loans to business, individuals, and governments, and by a large public debt, largely the result of compulsory contributions, titles which were transferable and actively traded. Trade book credit was common in domestic trade and bills of exchange in foreign trade. Long-term credit was rarer and there were no private securities.

In Elizabethan England short-term trade credit and consumer loans were still the most important forms of financial instruments, supplemented by bottomry loans and marine insurance in foreign trade. Credit was predominantly furnished by merchants, officials, landlords, and wealthy individuals sporadically and as a part of their economic activities rather than by specialized lenders. Members of the aristocracy were the most important large borrowers. Short-term instruments had different forms, including bills of exchange, but were not transferable. Long-term credits had to be in the form of renewals every six months. There were no banks or saving institutions. The government debt was very small and there were only a few corporate securities.

The United Provinces in the mid-seventeenth century had the most developed premodern financial system, and Amsterdam was the financial center of Europe. Various forms of short-term credit among merchants were common in domestic and foreign trade, including transferable bills of exchange. So were consumer credit and rural and urban mortgages. There was a large public debt and a substantial volume of corporate securities, mainly of foreign trading companies, which were traded for immediate or future delivery. There was also an active market in maritime insurance. The most important financial institution, besides the usual numerous money changers and small moneylenders, was the Amsterdamsche Wisselbank whose transferable deposits provided a sort of supplementary currency in use among domestic and foreign merchants. A few municipal loan banks provided credit to artisans and consumers.

There is hardly any information on possibly the most important characteristic of financial structure in premodern financial systems, the methods of financing the various sectors of the private economy, both their consumption and their investment, and the information is certainly not sufficient to trace variations in form, terms, and size among the different cases in detail. All that can be said is that outside of long-distance and particularly of overseas trade external financing was the exception rather than the rule. There were a few major exceptions to this statement. One, and probably the most common one, was the necessitous borrowing of peasants in cases of crop failures, other calamities, or for traditional obligations, mainly from landlords, local moneylenders, or tax collectors, usually at usurious rates, often leading to loss of property or in antiquity or outside Western Europe even to servitude or enslavement. Another were the borrowings, usually by members of the upper classes, for consumption or political purposes in excess of their income. In all these cases, with the exception of seed loans to peasants, the loans were nonproductive. The extension of short-term credit in various forms by sellers to buyers financed part of trade and some activities of artisans and hence served to carry part of the economy's inventories. Although quantitative data are lacking, the proportion of inventories thus financed probably increased over time and was generally higher in long-distance than in local trade. The volume of private investment was relatively low in relation to national product, particularly in equipment. There is little doubt that only a very small proportion of these expenditures was externally financed, except in the case of irrigation works, rather than by the investor himself and his family, or through compulsory labor services or by cooperative arrangements among neighbors. The volume of productive external financing outside of trade remained thus very small. This was partly the consequence of the absence of specialized lenders for such purposes and of markets for any type of financial instrument that could be used in long-term external financing. External financing of private capital formation other than of commodity inventories on a substantial scale had to await the creation of financial intermediaries such as commercial, investment, savings, and mortgage banks and of corporations and the popularization and standardization of instruments such as rural and urban mortgages and of corporate bonds and stocks, that is, in most now developed countries until the early nineteenth century, developments which in turn were called for by rapid urbanization, by the growth of the railroads with their demands for large amounts of external long-term funds and by the large-scale financing of military expenditures through the issuance of long-term government bonds, and the creation of markets, first local or regional and later national and international, for the resulting instruments. It is only since then, and often only since the twentieth century, that this process can be followed in quantitative terms.

Interest rates are one of the most important characteristics of a financial system. Effective rates are, however, difficult to ascertain for premodern systems because there were only few standardized rates and the transactions often involved costs not included in the quoted rates, partly because interest prohibitions or legal maximum rates led to the use of subterfuges. On the other hand rates were in many cases customary and valid for protracted periods. Although more quantitative information is available on interest rates than on most other aspects of the financial system, it is still very patchy, particularly for the two most common forms of credit, trade and consumer credit.

The level of interest rates in Mesopotamia to the end of the second millennium was very high, ranging from 20 to 50 percent per year even among traders and was even higher for consumer credit.

In Periclean Athens even well-secured business loans cost 12 percent per year; lesser-quality loans, 18 percent; and unsecured consumer loans, 36 percent or more.

In Augustan Rome the level of interest rates was lower, indeed probably the lowest in antiquity and in Europe until the sixteenth century. The rates on prime loans, particularly those secured by land, ranged from 4 to 6 percent in the western provinces, from 8 to 9 percent in the eastern provinces, and were around 12 percent in Egypt – compared to an empirewide legal limit of 12 percent – the strong regional differences indicating the absence of a national market. Consumer loans were much more expensive, rates of up to 48 percent per year being common.

Since the Koran was interpreted as forbidding every type of interest, various kinds of circumventions were developed, among businessmen in the form of profit sharing. Information on effective rates is therefore lacking for the Abbasid caliphate as well as for the Ottoman Empire. In the latter short-term business loans seem to have cost 10 to 15 percent per year. Rates on consumer loans were undoubtedly much higher.

In Mughal India the usual bazaar rate appears to have been on the order of 1 percent a month, and the rate on an important financial instrument, the hundi, similar to a bill of exchange, on the order of 18 percent per year; but consumer credits to peasants, handicraftsmen, and nobles were much more expensive.

In Tokugawa Japan 12 to 20 percent per year were charged on commercial loans, but there were additional charges and rates on consumer loans were much higher. No interest was paid on deposits.

In fifteenth-century Florence, where the canonic prohibition of interest was widely disregarded with or without ecclesiastic or governmental sanction, rates on commercial credit ranged from 12 to 15 percent. Those on consumer credit were much higher as lenders were allowed 20 to 25 percent and effective rates were higher. The commune offered 5 percent on its long-term largely forced debt, but paid it only intermittently and the effective yield based on the market price of the obligations; the rates of short-term borrowings were substantially higher. Banks paid 6 to 8 percent on deposits.

In Elizabethan England commercial loans and loans on land seem to have been made at rates somewhat above the legal maximum of 10 percent, with much higher rates for unsecured consumer loans. The crown paid 10 to 18 percent on its small foreign borrowings.

The United Provinces had from the mid-seventeenth century on the lowest level of interest rates known up to that time (except in Genoa). Business loans cost 3 to 4.5 percent, governments could borrow at 3 to 4 percent, and mortgages were available at 5 percent.

In most cases effective interest rates were lowest for mortgages, highest for unsecured consumer loans, and at an intermediate level for business loans. For each of the three types of loans rates were generally higher in the Orient than in the Occident. Determinants of the differences among cases are difficult to find, though the arbitrariness of the government and the effectiveness of the legal system appear to have been positively or negatively related to the level of rates.

Foreign lending or borrowing except to a limited extent in connection with foreign trade was nonexisting or of minimal importance in Athens, the Roman Empire, the Abbasid caliphate, the Ottoman Empire, Mughal India, and Tokugawa Japan. Some Florentine bankers had foreign branches and foreign deposits and loans, but they were relatively less important than in some other Italian cities. In Elizabethan England the crown borrowed abroad – in Antwerp – but on a rather small scale. Foreign lending was more important in the United Provinces, which for over a century were the chief center of international finance, though their role as issuer of foreign loans developed on a substantial scale only in the eighteenth century. Although quantification is difficult, there is no doubt that foreign financing in premodern systems was considerably smaller in relation to domestic financing or to national product than it became in many countries beginning with the early nineteenth century.

The role of foreigners in financial activities varied greatly as did that of national minorities in large empires. It was probably largest in Athens, where a large proportion of economic activities were in the hands of metics, mostly from other parts of the Greek world, who not possessing citizenship were excluded from political activities. It was also important, but by no means dominant, in Elizabethan England in the person of some Italians, Netherlanders, and Germans. It was small in comparison in Florence, the United Provinces unless the immigrants from the Spanish Netherlands were regarded as foreigners, and particularly in Tokugawa Japan. Among the empire's foreigners, in the early period mostly Italians, were of some importance in the Ottoman Empire. In the other empires a substantial part of financial activities were in the hands of some national minorities, for example, Greeks, Levantines, and Jews in the Roman Empire, of Greeks, Armenians, and Jews in the caliphate, or of certain castes as in Mughal India.

The ratio of government revenues or expenditures to national product is an important characteristic of financial structure. It is unfortunately difficult to measure if the numerator is understood, as it should be, as the total of resources unavailable for private consumption and investment. In premodern systems there is at best information on the revenues and/or expenditures of the central government, thus omitting those of local governments, those of the feudatories, and the expenditures required by private citizens for certain religious, cultural, or military purposes (leiturgies). Similarly, in the numerous cases where taxes were farmed, the amounts collected from taxpayers exceed those received by the governments. The reported ratios of central government receipts and expenditures are therefore minima and are, and sometimes substantially, below the more appropriate ratios based on the broader concept, which can only be approximated.

From the point of view of government finance the nine cases, as well as numerous others, can be arranged in two groups. In the first group, which may be called feudal, taxes were levied not only by the central government, and to a much smaller extent by local governments, but also and generally in considerably larger amounts by feudatories in return for their own military services and for the maintenance of troops. In the second group the governments collected all taxes, either directly or through tax farmers. Of the nine cases, the caliphate, the Ottoman Empire, Mughal India, and Tokugawa Japan belong to the first group; Athens, Rome, the Florentine Republic, Elizabethan England, and the United Provinces to the second.

Government finances in Periclean Athens were characterized by the fact that about one-half of total revenues were contributed by its allies, the members of the Delian league. As a result, the revenues raised in Attica amounted to only about one-tenth of its national product. Over one-third of expenditures were military, mostly for the navy; over one-fourth each for public works and for welfare and religious or political activities, leaving less than one-tenth for officials' salaries. Substantial additional expenditures for the navy and for festivals were imposed on wealthy citizens. The most important sources of internal revenue were customs duties, taxes on slaves and metics and state properties, particularly the silver mines of Laureion.

The revenues of the Augustan empire did not exceed 5 percent of national product, including those of local governments and the profits of tax farmers. The three main sources of revenue of the central government were the provincial tributes, mostly from Gaul and Egypt, with nearly one-third collected mainly from agricultural land; customs duties with about one-fourth; and public lands with about one-sixth. The armed forces accounted for about three-fifths of imperial expenditures, about one-eighth each being required by the free food distributions to the population of Rome and one-tenth by the civil service.

The expenditures of the Florentine Republic in the early fifteenth century, which considerably exceeded current revenues, were close to one-third of national product. About one-half of the total were military, largely the pay of expensive mercenaries, while civilian administration required about one-fifth and the service of the public debt one-third. Taxes, mainly sales taxes, provided only a good one-third of the total, equal to about one-tenth of national product. The difference was covered by borrowing, largely in the form of forced loans from citizens.

In Elizabethan England the queen's current revenues were never much above 1 percent of national product. Even including the revenues of local governments and the exactions of officials, they can hardly have exceeded 2 percent. Of the queen's revenues around 1600 about one-sixth was provided by crown lands, one-third by parliamentary grants, less than one-tenth by the clergy, and fully one-fourth by customs duties. About four-fifths of expenditures were military after 1585, though only one-fifth earlier. Civilian expenditures were small, in the last two decades of the sixteenth century only one-fifth of the total, or about 0.2 percent of national product.

Total government expenditures in the United Provinces have been put at about one-fourth of national product, possibly an overestimate. About one-half of the total was made by the central government, mostly for the armed forces, and were furnished to them by the provinces and to those partly by municipalities. The bulk of the taxes were indirect in the form of numerous sales taxes, mostly on articles of mass consumption.

Quantitative data are much scarcer for the feudal-type governments. There is no doubt, however, that in all four cases a tax on land or its products in cash or kind was the most important single source of revenue; and regional differences in the effective rate of taxation were large. Notwithstanding the roughness of the few available data, it also appears that the share of taxes and other exactions in the crops was high – for the country as a whole probably between one-fourth and one-half – though somewhat less in relation to national product as the effective burden on nonagricultural incomes was much lower.

Most of the financial markets of premodern countries were not developed enough to permit regular borrowings by the government, particularly on long-term. The only exception among the ten cases are the United Provinces whose debt by the middle of the seventeenth century was equal to about one year's national product. (The partly short-term debt of the English crown around 1600 amounted to only 1 percent of national product.) Most of the debt of the Florentine

Republic, which in 1427 came to over 1.5 years' national product at face value but only about half as much at market value, represented forced loans. It is, however, known that a number of governments in the premodern period borrowed on long term, particularly city governments in the form of annuities, or on short term with many extensions and ultimate repudiation, for example, the English crown in the fourteenth century and the Spanish monarchy in the seventeenth century.

A comparison of government finance in the ten cases, which may be regarded as representative of many others, permits only four conclusions. One of them is that in all cases military expenditures were the most important single category and generally accounted for between one-third and two-thirds of the total. This suggests that the burden of taxation was strongly influenced by the country's military posture, its military organization and the level and methods of payment of its armed forces. Notwithstanding this similarity in the structure of government expenditures, their ratio of national product shows (second conclusion) great differences ranging from a few percent in Augustan Rome and Elizabethan England to between one-fourth and one-third in the Abbasid caliphate, the Ottoman Empire, Mughal India, and Tokugawa Japan, suggesting that a feudal organization of the economy tends to put a heavy burden on the peasantry. The structure of revenues showed similar differences. In the feudal states the bulk of the revenues was provided by the tax on land levied in kind or cash. In the city states – Athens and Florence – but also in the Roman Empire, in Elizabethan England, and in the United Provinces the share of the land tax was considerably smaller, while indirect taxes, particularly customs revenues and excises, became important sources of revenue.

Of the ten cases covered in this study there are only three – the Florentine Republic, Elizabethan England, and the United Provinces, although separated by up to fully two centuries – whose financial systems can be regarded as connected in the sense that financial instruments and organizations developed in one of them influenced those used in one of the others. This refers to sophisticated instruments and institutions such as letters of credit, bills of exchange, bottomry loans, maritime insurance, mortgages, annuities, government securities, various forms of business partnerships, and deposit banks (often based on Roman law) rather than to advances of landlords to tenants, small consumer loans, undocumented trade credit among merchants, and the activities of money changers, which are found in virtually all but primitive nonmonetized economies. These instruments and institutions developed first, after the dissolution of the Roman Empire, in some cities of central and northern Italy, particularly in Lucca, Siena, Florence, Genoa, and Venice, beginning in the twelfth century, and the development was fairly completed by the fifteenth century. From there these first components of what may be called a financial system spread to large parts of western and southern Europe, particularly its cities. A second financial center developed in the Low Countries between the fourteenth and the seventeenth centuries, particularly first in Brugge and then in Antwerp and in Amsterdam (which from the sixteenth century on became more important in international trade and finance than Italy) and some cities in South Germany, particularly Augsburg, occupying an intermediate position at least during the fifteenth and sixteenth centuries. The only important additions to financial instruments and organizations until the eighteenth century after the level reached in Italy in the fifteenth century were corporations with their bonds and stocks, mostly active in overseas trade, and securities exchanges, both still operating on a small scale.

In the other seven cases whatever financial instruments and organizations developed must be regarded as at least partly autochthonous. Thus the financial system of Athens, the other Greek cities, and the Hellenistic monarchies and the eastern provinces of the Roman Empire, which succeeded them, do not appear to have been strongly influenced by what existed in the ancient Near East. The influence of the Hellenistic systems on Roman Italy may have been more important, and the example of Italy on the western provinces certainly was, partly a result of the spread of Roman law and administration throughout the empire.

The financial system of the caliphate appears to have been mainly derivative, given the practical absence of one in Arabia, primarily from that found in its western provinces, which had belonged to the Byzantine Empire, and hence from that of the Roman Empire. If anything, however, the system was less advanced than that of the Roman Empire. Development appears to have been slow and uneven as the system of the Ottoman Empire was basically similar to that of the caliphate and showed only a limited influence of its contacts with Mediterranean Europe. Such independence appears to have been even more pronounced in the case of Mughal India, at least before the eighteenth century, for example, the development of the hundi similar to the transferable bill of exchange in the west, as well as in Tokugawa Japan, Chinese influences having ceased considerably earlier.

When premodern financial systems, that is, those operating in Europe before about 1700 and in much of the rest of the world before the twentieth century, are compared with contemporary systems, the qualitative and quantitative differences are evident. The number of different types of financial instruments and of financial institutions was much smaller in premodern systems. Many, if not most, of the most important institutions of contemporary systems were missing, or scarcely represented, in premodern systems, for example, central banks, commercial banks, savings institutions, investment banks, mortgage banks, and life insurance and pension organizations, and the few organizations existing in all premodern systems – in most cases only money changers, small moneylenders, and pawnbrokers – with some exceptions were limited to one office and in most cases were also or even predominantly engaged in nonfinancial activities. Similarly, some of the most important modern financial instruments, particularly paper money, checks, nonagricultural mortgages and government and corporate securities were missing in most cases. Lending in premodern systems was still predominantly a sporadic nonspecialized activity exercised by merchants, landlords, tax collectors, and wealthier individuals. Loans were made mainly for consumptive purposes at high rates of interest, the main exception being loans among merchants to finance long-distance trade, and were overwhelmingly made for short periods.

Although the various chapters describe the financial structure of the country at one point of time, or during a relatively short period, this must not give the impression that changes over time were absent or even of only minor importance quantitatively or qualitatively, or that the situation at a time selected to reflect the country at or near the point of its greatest economic, political, and military influence also represented its financial structure at the latter's most developed stage. On the contrary in many if not in most cases the financial structure continued to develop in the use of additional financial instruments and the rise of new financial organization, particularly banks, though the country stagnated or even declined economically, politically, and militarily. This was definitely the case in Athens after the age of Pericles, in the caliphate after the early eighth century, in the Ottoman Empire after the sixteenth century, in Mughal India after Akbar, and in the United Provinces from the late seventeenth century on. The contrast was less pronounced in the Roman Empire, in Florence after the fifteenth century, and in Tokugawa Japan until the late eighteenth century, and was absent in England after the age of Elizabeth. A description and a possible explanation of this divergence of financial development on the one hand and of economic, political, and military absolute or relative strength on the other after the peak of the latter – a phenomenon also observable in other countries and at other times – is beyond the scope of this study as it would require investigating the financial and economic history of the ten cases, and possibly those of other countries, over several centuries. The problem, however, remains one of the most interesting ones in financial history, and as far as can be seen one not yet posed or answered.

# Notes

## Chapter 2

1. Meissner 1920, p. 187. This estimate appears to be on the high side. A map in Diakonov (1959) suggests an area of not much over 10,000 km², which is also the present-day productive area (McEvedy and Jones, p. 149).
2. McEvedy and Jones, p. 150. The figures for Mesopotamia may be on the low side.
3. At least two dozen cities, other than the half dozen large ones, have been identified (e.g., *Cambridge Ancient Economic History*, vol. II, p. 1, map facing p. 192, and Oppenheim 1964, map p. 47). Their population may easily have totaled 100,000 in addition to a nearly equally large number in the few largest cities. Considerably higher estimates can be found, for example, over 100,000 for Lagash and 200,000 for Ur (Kramer, p. 89).
4. Harris, p. 333. The number of slaves has been characterized as not very high (Westermann, p. 75). On the other hand it cannot have been negligible as slave merchants are attested (Leemans, 1968, pp. 182–183), records of many sales of slaves have survived (e.g., Harris, pp. 342–3) and the share of slaves in the population of Lagash has been put at about one-fourth (Diakonov, 1959, p. 37).
5. Based on data in Schneider, pp. 114–15; for Sumerian measures compare Kramer, p. 107.
6. Estates of nobles and priests, not to speak of those of temples and kings, extended to "hundreds of acres" (Kramer, p. 76). The estimates on the average size of plots found in the literature differ greatly. Meissner put the size, presumably for grain land, in the eighteenth century B.C. at 6.5 hectars, but less later on (1920, p. 180). The average of 652 lots in Lagash was 3¼ hectars (Foster, p. 239), that of 18 fields in Akkad in the twenty-third century B.C. 3½ hectars (Limet, pp. 33–4), and that of 173 fields sold in Sippar (Harris, p. 210) nearly 2 hectars (5.3 gan). Schneider, on the other hand, asserted that 0.70 hectars (2 gan) sufficed for a small family and that the size of the fields allocated to artisans ranged from 0.35 to 2.10 hectars (p. 35). According to Falkenstein (p. 802), finally, subsistence plots measured about 0.35 hectar. (For comparison: In India

253

food-grain area per cultivator in 1971 averaged about 2 hectars). It is difficult for an outsider to choose among these estimates of Sumerologists, but figures on the order of 3 has seem reasonable.

7. Lehmann, pp. 58, 68; Oppenheim 1964, pp. 86–7. Gold, copper and tin were used to a lesser extent as means of payment but not as units of account.

8. Heichelheim, pp. 212, 214. In foreign trade silver bars of much larger size were also used, bars of 5 to 30 minas (300 to 1,800 shekels) having been found (Garelli, p. 266).

9. The main sources of this paragraph are Bogaert, Chapter III, and Lehmann.

10. The main sources for interest rates are, again, Bogaert and Lehmann.

11. The most common rate among about 100 loans among Assyrian traders in Cappadocia early in the second millennium was 30 percent. Rates charged by the Assyrians to natives were higher, averaging about 50 percent (Garelli, p. 259).

12. Considerably more importance and sophistication is ascribed to financial affairs by Heichelheim, vol. I, pp. 133–6.


## Chapter 3

1. This view is now prevalent among classicists and economic historians (e.g., Bolkestein, Bücher, Finley, and Flacelière) in contrast to an earlier tendency to regard the economy of ancient Greece as closer to that of modern countries and even to qualify it as capitalistic (e.g., Beloch, Glotz, Meyer). One description of daily life in Athens speaks of "malodorous narrow streets, poorly designed, unlit houses of mediocre quality and without architectural beauty" (Flacelière, p. 330), and it has been asserted that for most of the population barley gruel and a bread described by modern standards as fit only for consumption by pigs (Jasny, p. 244) and lentils together with olive oil and wine constituted the bulk of the diet.

2. The figures on population are taken from the most recent detailed estimate (Gomme 1963), which also discusses earlier estimates. The first serious estimate made early in the nineteenth century (Böckh 1817) arrived at a much higher total of 500,000 inhabitants for Attica, of which 180,000 were in Athens and Peiraios, and allocated the impossibly high proportion of nearly three-fourths to slaves (Böckh 1886, pp. 52, 97). A later estimate in the standard work on the demography of Greece put the population of Attica for 431 B.C. at only 235,000, about equally divided between Athens and the rest of the country and allocated about 100,000 each to citizens and slaves and about 25,000 to metics (Beloch 1886, pp. 100–01).

3. Based on a total population of Greece (modern boundaries) of nearly 3 million (McEvedy and Jones, p. 113). The share would be lower if ac-

count were taken of the Greek population in western Asia Minor and in southern Italy.

4. This ratio assumes that one-half of citizens, most of the metics, one-half of industrial and agricultural slaves, and almost all domestic slaves lived in the city.

5. Gomme characterizes his estimates for citizens and metics as minima and that for slaves as a maximum (pp. 27–8).

6. In the most detailed study of the slave population of Attica, published slightly before Gomme's, the number of slaves before the Peloponnesian War was put at 73,000 or 97,000 as approximate maxima (Sargent, p. 126). Of these, using the higher total (which is much closer to Gomme's figure of 115,000), 29,500 were allocated to household slaves, 11,000 to agriculture, 17,500 to mining and 29,000 to other industries, and 850 to the state, leaving 9,500 children under nine years.

7. Based for the top three classes on estimates by Cavaignac (1923, p. 58). Two other estimates put the share of the thetes at about one-third of all free households (Francotte, p. 160) or of all males over 18 years (Meyer, cited Sargent, p. 62).

8. This is the estimated number of males 18–59 years old.

9. Swoboda cited *Der Kleine Pauly*, vol. 3, p. 253, and Schulthess in Pauly-Wissowa, vol. XI, part 1, p. 823.

10. Compare, for example, Böckh 1886, p. 149; Facelière, p. 162; Guiraud, p. 183; Mauri, p. 76; Spaventa, p. 113. Glotz asserts that the data show "uniformly a daily wage rate of one drachma" (1913b, p. 267). The only dissenting voices are Beloch's estimate of 3 obols equal to ½ drachma for the lowest paid workers (1913b, p. 427) and Gardner's of one-half to one drachma (p. 19).

11. Böckh, pp. 148ff; Glotz 1913b, p. 427. Characteristic of the small differences in labor incomes is the fact that an army commander (*strategos*) received only four times and an officer (*lochagos*) only twice the pay of a common soldier (Büchsenschütz, p. 355), a range radically narrower than that found in the Roman or in medieval armies (Goldsmith 1984, pp. 276, 284).

12. As the value of private buildings has been put below at only 1,500 talents, annual depreciation allowances would have been well below 50 talents. Indirect taxes can hardly have exceeded 100 talents (Section 10).

13. Clark (1951, p. 566) implies a national income, conceptually slightly below gross national product, of 6,000 talents without explaining the basis of his estimate.

14. Similar and even higher ratios are found in contemporary poor countries. In India, for example, the share of cereals in total household expenditures in 1973–74 was found in a national sample survey to amount to two-fifths (Fertilizer Association of India, *Fertilizer Statistics* 44, 110, 1980–81).

15. This is considerably below two other unexplained estimates of 360 drach-

mas (Gardner, p. 19) and probably less so for another of 400 drachmas for 400 B.C. (Böckh 1886, p. 141) because prices before the war were substantially lower. Glotz's estimate of the "minimum for an adequately nourished man" of 120 drachmas (1913b, p. 210) suggests about 100 drachmas per head.

16. If the estimate from the income side is regarded as approximately correct, consumer expenditures would have had to be on the order of 4,500 talents or 85 drachmas per head or nearly five times the expenditures on grain, an unacceptably high ratio. On the other hand the estimate from the expenditure side implies a national product per head of about 80 drachmas. Such a figure requires a very low number of work days and a very low ratio of income recipients or a daily wage or equivalent below the generally accepted value of one drachma.

17. A rule derived from the national accounts of Western countries in the nineteenth and twentieth centuries puts the average gross national product per head at 200 times the daily wage of an unskilled worker (Bairoch, p. 777). On that basis the national product per head in Attica before the Peloponnesian War would have amounted to 200 drachmas compared to the estimate just derived of between 75 and 115 drachmas. The main reasons for the difference are, first, that in Athens average income per head was about the same as the daily wage of an unskilled worker while the ratio implied in the formula is considerably higher, probably on the order of 1½; second, that the average work year has been assumed to be 250 days instead of about 300 days; and third, that the ratio of income recipients to population has been put at less than two-fifths instead of about 45 percent, partly because of the low labor force participation rate of women.

18. Only three attempts to estimate the purchasing power of the drachma in Athens around 400 B.C. have been found. The first puts it at two International Units (IU), that is, $2 of U.S. prices of 1927–34 (Clark 1951, p. 551; 1957 p. 663). The value should have been slightly higher in 431 B.C. because prices were somewhat lower, say 2½ IU. On that basis a per head national product of Attica before the Peloponnesian War of about 100 drachmas would have been equal to about 250 IU. This value compares with the following estimates by the same author shifted from averages per occupied person to those per head of the population; England and Wales 1688, 210 IU; 1801–10, 205 IU; United States 1820, about 200 IU; France 1830, 115 IU; Germany 1854, 130 IU; Russia, 1913, 105 IU; Greece 1913, about 180 IU; India 1867–68 about 50 IU; Japan 1887, nearly 40 IU; Brazil 1928, 60 IU. (These figures do not appear in Clark 1957.) It is obvious that a purchasing power for the drachma of 431 B.C. of 2½ IU leads to an improbably high level of national product per head, though there is no way of saying how large the overstatement is.

Two other estimates made by classicists assert that the purchasing power of the drachma compared to contemporary, that is, early twentieth century, situations was at least three or even four times as high as its metal value (Beloch 1885, p. 428; Glotz 1965, p. 306). Such ratios put the purchasing power of the drachma around 430 B.C. at one or 1⅓ g of gold, that is, then at about $0.70 or $0.90. On that basis national product per head in late-fifth-century Athens would have been about $60 or $80, compared with an average in 1913 of about $400 in the United States, but one of $70 in the United States in 1820, of $140 in Italy in 1931, and of $70 in Greece in 1913 (Clark). The assumption of a purchasing power of the drachma of three, let alone four, times its metal value thus appears to be exaggerated.

19. Glotz suggested that prices doubled between 480 and 404 B.C. (1965, p. 237), but most of the increase probably occurred during the Peloponnesian War and it may be assumed that some of the wartime inflation was reversed in the following decade.

20. A radically lower figure of only about 2,000 talents is proposed by Beloch (1885, p. 243) on the basis of the capitalization at 8 percent of estimated net income of 150 talents and a crop worth about 300 talents. This implies an average price of only about 15 drachmas per plethron, which is much below what little is known about land prices (cf. Section 7).

21. The number of dwellings should have been on the order of 20,000 on the basis of a total population of Attica of nearly 320,000 (Gomme, p. 26) and the share of Athens of about one-half, of which fully one-half were slaves (Beloch 1886, pp. 100–01). The average price is difficult to estimate. If that of a "modest dwelling" of 300 drachmas (Cavaignac 1908, p. 95) is accepted as a minimum, an average for all dwellings of about 750 drachmas seems reasonable. A combination of these two rough estimates yields a value for the stock of dwellings in the order of 1,500 talents.

22. On the character of houses and furniture see, for example, Büchsenschütz, pp. 80–82; Hermann, pp. 143–71.

23. Böck's estimate of 6,000 talents is far too high as it is based on 360,000 slaves compared to recent estimates of not much over 100,000. On the other hand, his average price of 100 drachmas is far too low, all recent estimates being close to 200 drachmas.

24. The different estimates are discussed in Thomsen (pp. 49 ff), who does not propose one of his own.

25. Andréades' estimate of 10,000 to 12,000 talents (p. 346) refers to 378 B.C. He suggests that before the Peloponnesian War the amount of wealth "must have been decidedly, even incomparably, greater." Cavaignac qualifies his estimate of private wealth for 427 (1908, p. 83) by saying that the yield of 200 talents suggests the idea of a total capital of 20,000 talents. To obtain figures for tangible assets, all figures would have to be reduced by about 2,000 talents for slaves.

26. An estimate of an average fortune of adult male citizens of 1,000 to 1,200 drachmas in 398 B.C. (Thomsen, p. 96) implies a total private wealth of

8,750 to 10,500 talents if also applicable to metics, and to the population of 431 B.C. Per head wealth may well have been higher in 431 B.C. than in 378 B.C.

27. Andréades comes to a total of 8,000 talents on the basis of estimates of Francotte and Zimmern, while two other authors (Schmidt and Zengele) put the figure at slightly above 6,000 talents (Andréades, p. 234). Of the 8,000 talents, 1,100 talents are attributed to the Parthenon and the Propylaia; 1,200 talents to statues, of which 1,000 talents for the gold and ivory statue of Athena; 3,000 talents to mostly civilian construction, particularly the long walls and harbor works; and 2,700 talents are left to other temples and monuments. More recently considerably lower figures have been proposed for the Parthenon and the Propylaia, namely, about 700 talents based on detailed calculations for the Parthenon, and a slightly lower figure of 850 talents for the statue of Athena. An estimate of 2,000 to 2,500 talents probably refers only to temples (Burford, cited Bodei-Giglioni, p. 47). Assuming a similar difference for the other items the lower boundary of Andréades' range, that is, 6,000 talents appears to be more in line with the more recent estimates.

28. This is one of the few precise and generally accepted figures, see, for example, Meritt et al., p. 338.

29. Probably the nearest parallels will be found in some European territories in the twelfth to fourteenth century, particularly in France, but no relevant quantitative estimates appear to have been made.

30. A total of private wealth, excluding slaves, of nearly 12,000 talents can also be reached by another approach, namely,

| | | |
|---|---|---|
| 1. | Declared wealth of citizens subject to eisphora | 6,000 talents |
| 2. | Wealth of metics above exemption level (assumed at one-fifth of 1) | 1,200 talents |
| 3. | Wealth of citizens and metics below exemption level assumed at 1,000 drachmas and average of 2,000 drachmas. | 5,000 talents |
| 4. | Underdeclaration (25 percent of 1 + 2) | 1,800 talents |
| 5. | Total | 14,000 talents |
| 6. | Slaves | 2,000 talents |
| 7. | Total, less slaves | 12,000 talents |

In this estimate the margin of error is largest in item 3 because the exemption level, and hence the number of exempt households, is unknown. If the limit had been as high as 2,500 drachmas (St. Croix and Jones, cited Gera, p. 64) most households would have been exempt. Using what seems more reasonable, an average wealth of exempt households of 1,000 drachmas − Socrates who was exempt put the value of his house and furnishings at 500 drachmas (Gera, p. 64) − the aggregate exempt private wealth would probably still have exceeded 5,000 talents close to the value used above.

31. Approximately the proportion for 425 and 323 B.C. (Gomme 1963, p. 26).
32. Estimated on the basis of Cavaignac's data for 378 B.C. (1923, p. 61).
33. Cavaignac's own estimates, however, show no change in wealth distribution between 428 and 378 B.C. (1923, pp. 58, 61).
34. For reproductions, compare Seltman 1952, p. 22.
35. The exception was the emergency issue of gold and bronze coins during the late part of the Peloponnesian War, the former coined from the gold of the chryselephantine statue of Athena on the Acropolis.
36. The main sources for the operation of the Laureion mines are Ardaillon (1897), Wilsdorf (1952), and Lauffer (1979). A popular, sometimes panegyric description is provided by Calhoun, Part IV.
37. Aeschylus, *The Persians,* p. 238 (the Athenians) have a treasure in their soil, a fountain of silver.
38. Although the silver produced by the mines of Laureion, which started to operate on a substantial scale around 480 B.C. and probably reached their highest output in the 430s, played a crucial role in financing Athens's grain imports, its military expenditures, and its political position and provided the basis for its currency; and though hundreds of pages have been published on the techniques of production and the conditions of the workers, not a single estimate, contemporary or modern, has been found of the economically most important fact, the volume of output of the mines. So resort must be had to circuitous approaches.

The most promising approach starts from the cost of production. On the basis of an average daily wage and of an allowance for operating profits and for the rent payable to the state, which together may be put as between one-fourth and one-half of wages, disregarding depreciation and depletion and allocating about nine-tenths of the value of output to silver, the remainder consisting of lead, the value of daily output per worker would have been on the order of 1¼ drachmas, representing somewhat over 5 g of silver. This compares with ⅗ drachmas, or 2½ g of silver, for the largest silver mine of antiquity situated in southeastern Spain near New Carthage (Carthagena), which is reported to have produced 25,000 drachmas per day with 40,000 workers (Saglio in Daremberg-Saglio 1873, p. 410). It is difficult to evaluate the reasonableness of such a great difference in productivity as the richness of the ore in the two mines is not known. Assuming a working year of 300 days, thus excluding only holidays, the annual value of output per man would then be about 375 drachmas or 1.5 kg of silver.

The main difficulty in estimating the output of the Laureion mines is the wide range of the estimates of the labor force, which extend for the fifth century from 10,000 to 30,000 (Lauffer, p. 142) and is put in the most recent estimate at 25,000 (Lauffer, p. 162). These estimates imply that between nearly one-tenth and over one-fifth of the total labor force of Attica worked in Laureion, a relation not considered by the various estimators. A figure between 15,000 and 20,000 appears to be the most reasonable one. The total annual silver output of Laureion would then have been between 5.6 million and 7.5 million drachmas, or 930 to 1,250 talents on the basis of a working year of 300 days, or to 22.5 to 30 tons of silver a year. The Laureion mines would thus have been of about the same size as those of New Carthage (30 tons) and as one of the largest silver mines of medieval Europe (Annaberg in Saxony), which is reported to have produced in the sixteenth century 20 tons per year (Sombart, p. 517) or about one-third of the total production of Europe (*Palgrave's Dictionary of Political Economy*, 1926, vol. III, p. 399). This level was decisively surpassed only with the discovery of the Potosi lode and the introduction of the quicksilver process, leading to their annual silver output of over 300 tons in 1545–60 (Sombart, p. 517).

39. Some authors accept Thucydides' statement of a maximum size of about 10,000 talents (e.g., Böckh 1886, p. 9; French, p. 103; cf. Andréades, p. 321), but the investigators of the tribute lists of the Delian confederacy assert that it did not exceed about 6,000 talents in minted silver, the level prevailing from 448 to 432 B.C. (Merrit et al., p. 338).

40. It has been claimed that an "infinitely larger quantity of uncoined treasure [i.e., larger than the 6,000 talents of coined money] was sterilized in the temple [of Athena] . . ." (Finley 1973, p. 174) without specification of what "infinitely" may mean arithmetically. It is also remarkable that the Athenians would have left this "infinite" treasure untouched in their desperate straits late during the Peloponnesian War when they melted down the gold of the statues on the Acropolis.

41. The estimate of an annual rate of wear of 2 percent per year implying a half-life of only 35 years is difficult to accept (Patterson, p. 220).

42. The main source is still Billeter published in 1898. Most of the available data refer to the fourth century B.C. but are probably also applicable to the late fifth century B.C. Compare also Böckh 1886, pp. 156ff.

43. Fine asserts that before the Peloponnesian War there is, with one exception, "no reference to mortgage or the sale of land" (p. 196).

44. A recent detailed treatment of Athenian banks is provided by Bogaert (1968) and a shorter one by Musti, pp. 108–22. Among older discussions compare Hasebroek 1920 and Heichelheim 1964.

45. Hasebroek 1928, p. 89. The view that Athenian banking was still in a primitive stage even in the fourth century B.C. may be regarded as now the prevailing one, held for example by Bogaert (1966), Bolkestein, Finley, Hasebroek (1928), and Michell in contrast to older authors, particularly Glotz and Heichelheim.

46. Based on estimates of tillable land of nearly 70,000 hectars (Jardé, p. 49) of which about one-tenth has been estimated to have been owned by non-profit organizations (Andreiev 1967, p. 72) but was mostly operated by small-scale tenants, and a number of landowners of about 22,000 to 32,000 which in turn is derived from an estimate that between one-half and three-fifths of all citizens owned some land (Finley 1952 p. 58), and a number

of 43,000 male citizens 18 to 59 years old (Gomme, p. 26). Another estimate is 4 to 5 hectars as typical for a property (Jameson, p. 131). One estimate put the average price of plots in Attica at about 2,700 drachmas, which it may be assumed is somewhat above the value of the on the average smaller plots not changing hands.

47. This figure is compatible with Böckh's estimate of 50 drachmas per plethron of grain land if it includes the more valuable land devoted to other cultures.

48. The value of the olive crop per hectar has been estimated at ten times that of the grain crop (Cavaignac 1923 p. 59).

49. Wallon's estimate was 800,000 to 1 million medimni (pp. 269, 277).

50. Glotz estimated the cost of grain imports at between 500 and 700 talents (1965, p. 313).

51. In the fourth century B.C. when the volume of imports was in the order of only 800,000 medimni because the population was much smaller than it had been before the Peloponnesian War, about one-half of total imports came from the Black Sea region while the other half was divided among several suppliers in Greece, for example, Boeotia and Euboia and overseas, primarily Sicily and Egypt (Beloch 1923, p. 412).

52. Cavaignac felt that the value of trade was "certainly far higher than 2,000 talents in more prosperous periods" (1951, p. 78). He even put it at 3,000 to 4,000 talents, or nearly equal to total national income (1923, p. 59), both most unlikely figures.

53. For lists of imports and exports without indication of quantities and values, compare Glotz, p. 312; Knorringa, pp. 74–6; Speck, passim.

54. Based on a slave population of slightly over 100,000 and a death rate of 4 percent.

55. The smallness of exports of manufactures has been stressed by Finley 1973, pp. 134ff.

56. On bottomry loans see Bogaert 1968, pp. 373–74 and Calhoun, 1929–30, passim.

57. As asserted by Hasebroek (p. 5).

58. Bogaert 1968, p. 373; the range has been put at 2,000 to 5,000 drachmas (Hasebroek, p. 99).

59. This section is based on Böckh 1886, still the most detailed, and as far as description goes generally accepted, treatment and on Adréades; all estimates of revenues and expenditures are taken from, or based on, Andréades unless otherwise indicated.

60. This is the sum of ordinary military expenditures of well over 300 talents and of about 30 talents expenditures on fortifications, an average of Andréades' estimate of 1,000 talents of expenditures on fortification under Pericles.

61. Andréades put public works expenditures for 420 B.C. at 50 talents (p. 265), but from the history of the buildings on the Acropolis and other monuments, it is known that they were much higher before the war.

62. Bolkestein (p. 153) for the period 447 to 438 B.C.

63. This figure apparently includes miscellaneous foreign income, such as that of the gold mines of Thasos, as the tribute proper has been put on the basis of the tribute lists at 388 talents for 433 B.C. (Meritt et al., p. 334).

64. Andréades, p. 280; elsewhere it is said that internal taxes "can hardly have surpassed 400–500 t." or "averaged 400–500 t." (pp. 266, 355).

65. Böckh's (1886) estimate is only 30 to 40 talents in Themistocles' time (p. 379).

66. The share of government properties in the total value of grain land has been estimated at fully 5 percent (Böckh, p. 574).

67. The higher figures of 30 to 40 talents usually cited (e.g., Francotte, p. 14), which lead to the estimates of the trade turnover of 1,800 to 2,000 talents, refer to the turn of the century when the rates were 2 percent rather than the 1 percent rate levied before the war (Heichelheim, p. 184). The value of imports and exports is likely to have been higher before than after the war, possibly substantially so as asserted by Cavaignac (1951, p. 78).

68. Based on Andréades (p. 280). It is based on 24,000 metics, far above Gomme's estimate of 9,500 male metics 18 to 50 years old (p. 26), which implies a revenue of only 20 talents.

69. Bücher's estimate, apparently accepted by Andréades (p. 283). A yield of 38 talents implies at an average slave price of 200 drachmas and about 57,000 transactions, most of which are attributed to the import and export of slaves accompanying visitors and only 4,000 to the net import of slaves for use in Attica, equal to about 3.5 percent of the total number of slaves in Attica (Gomme, p. 26). The estimate has been rejected as much too high by Beloch (1923, p. 432).

70. Since Athens is reported by Thucydides to have had at the beginning of the Peloponnesian War about 300 triremes (Brillant, p. 456) the annual cost of maintaining them would have been on the order of 200 talents at a rate of even only 4,000 drachmas. It is therefore likely that in peace time not all the triremes in the Athenian navy were in operation. During the Archidamian War, that is, in the 420s B.C. the number of trierarchs has been put at 400 (Davies XXIX) suggesting that in any one year not more than about 200 citizens were burdened with this leiturgy.

71. For a detailed description of the methods of financial administration, compare Böckh 1886, pp. 187–253.

72. Heichelheim (p. 142), referring to Greece in general but also applicable to Athens.

### Chapter 4

1. This section is based on, and occasionally repeats, Goldsmith (1984), but omits the footnotes that in that article provide references to sources and explanations of some of the statements.

2. For a provincial city in Italy (Pompeii), expenditures on a modest scale

have been put at about HS 2 per day (Breglia, pp. 47, 53) or somewhat over HS 700 per year. The average for the empire was certainly substantially lower as nine-tenths of the population lived in the country, and it is likely that costs of living were lower in the provinces – considerably so in Egypt, which accounted for about one-eighth of the population of the empire – than in Italy. This estimate is therefore not irreconcilable with the one of about HS 350 for the empire, though it suggests a somewhat higher figure for the latter.

3. Goldsmith, 1984, footnote 56. I am now inclined to think that a ratio of one-half may be too high, though not by much.

4. This is argued by Hopkins, for example, p. 112.

5. The characterization of "stability" seems apposite in the economic field, though in other areas the near-century after Augustus' death has been characterized by the empire's greatest historian as "rich in calamities, cruel in its wars, rent by uprisings and harsh even in peace," [(Tacitus, *Historiae*, vol. I, p. 2) "opimum casibus, atrox proeliis, discors seditionibus, ipsa etiam pace saevum")].

6. Of 697 aurei minted under Augustus found in hoards, 85 percent weighed between 7.70 and 7.90 g for an average of 7.85 g (Bolin 1958, p. 183). For a table of weight and fineness of aurei and denarii, see West, pp. 17–26.

7. These are terms coined by Knapp (pp. 71, 73) but despite their usefulness rarely used. For absence of hylolepsy compare Nicolet, p. 1232.

8. It is not fully understood how this maintenance of parity among the different types of coins worked.

9. See article "Agio" in Pauly and Wissowa, Supplement IV; Kahrstedt 1958, p. 209.

10. Bolin 1958, p. 322; assuming his figures refer to the Roman pound of 325 g.

11. Minting of gold coins ceased early in the third century A.D. (Segré, p. 375).

12. The problem of the price ratio of gold and silver is discussed by Kleiman.

13. Several hundred cities have been identified as issuers (Pekary, p. 103).

14. West and Johnson, pp. 1–2. The main coins circulating in Egypt were copper oboloi and silver drachmas (equal to about one denarius, though they had a smaller and decreasing silver content) and tetradrachmas. Coins of larger value were apparently not needed.

15. Quiring, p. 138; for a detailed discussion of location of gold mines and mining techniques; compare Quiring, pp. 107ff, and Healy, Chapters IV and VI, and for mine administration Healy, Chapter V.

16. The number of these slaves has been put at 150,000 (Patterson, p. 225), so that the total work force must have been in excess of 200,000, or about 1 percent of the total and 4 percent of the nonagricultural labor force.

17. It is difficult to reconcile the high proportion ("greater part") of Republican denarii in hoards of the late first century A.D. (Bolin, 1958, p. 53) with the short life – a half-life of 35 years – by Patterson (p. 218).

18. Hopkins, p. 109; the estimate is qualified to such an extent that it is not clear what figure the author regards as the most likely one.
19. Patterson (p. 218) puts wear and tear at 2 percent per year.
20. Another basis for an approximation to the stock of silver coins is provided by the estimate that output of sliver may have risen to about 150 tons a year, equal to HS 150 million late in the first century B.C. (Healy, p. 198, after Patterson). This figure must substantially exceed the volume minted because of nonmonetary uses. On the basis of a half-life of 35 years (Patterson, p. 218), the stock would be as high as HS 5 billion in A.D. 14 if coinage had averaged HS 100 million for the preceding century, but less in proportion to the extent that the average was below HS 100 million a year.
21. Quiring, p. 138, who characterized the estimate as "very difficult to make and tentative."
22. Regling, p. 481, "Caesar's massive issue of gold coins."
23. LoCascio, p. 82, Augustus' Egyptian booty has been put at HS 1 billion (Frank 1933, p. 146), much of which was probably in gold.
24. Regling et al. p. 105, "gold was the main circulating medium for large payments," and his characterization of the Roman monetary system as a gold standard. Even stronger Bahrfeldt ("since 46 B.C. gold coins maintained at all times their dominating position among Roman coins," p. 30) contrasting with the assertion that denarii were predominant in hoards until the second century A.D. (Bolin 1958, p. 60).

   About two-thirds of the value of the hoards unearthed in Pompeii consisted of gold coins and about one-third of silver coins, while subsidiary coins accounted for only about 2 percent of the total. The distribution, however, differed greatly among large and small hoards. In the 25 hoards, containing over HS 1,000 each with an average of fully HS 2,600 and a maximum of nearly HS 9,500, gold coins accounted for three-fourths of the total value and silver coins for one-fourth. In the 59 small hoards, which averaged about HS 250 and accounted for less than one-fifth of the value of the 84 hoards gold coins represented hardly 35 percent of the total, silver coins about 55 percent, and subsidiary coins about 10 percent. (Derived from data on individual hoards in Breglia, Tables A and B). There is, of course, no possibility of assessing to what degree this total, which is equal to not much more than 1 : 100,000 of the total monetary stock of the empire and probably only about 1-in-200 of of all families in Pompeii, is representative. Since the hoards come from an urban area, one would expect the share of gold coins to be lower for the entire empire. On the other hand, since the largest of the 84 hoards was below HS 10,000 the holdings of wealthy citizens and of businessmen, which presumably consisted mainly of gold coins, are underrepresented.
25. Pekary, pp. 102–03. On *tesserae* compare Lafaye in Daremberg and Saglio, vol. 5, p. 125 after Rostovtsev.
26. The only estimate of money in circulation that has been found, published about 150 years ago, which put the stock of gold and silver coins at the

time of Augustus' death at £358 million (Jacob, vol. I, p. 225), equivalent on the basis of gold content to about HS 32 billion, can be rejected as much too high. It would be equal to about 1.5 times total national product and approximately three times monetized product and implies a velocity of circulation of approximately two-thirds for total and about one-third for monetized production.

27. An entirely different approach starts from the statement, based on archeological evidence, that the inhabitants of Pompeii carried between HS 2 and HS 20 with them (Breglia, pp. 47, 53). Assuming these figures applied to heads of households, they imply a total of about HS 30 million and HS 300 million for the empire. This figure, probably mostly representing subsidiary coins, is so small that it can be ignored in estimating the total stock of money. In addition households kept coins in their home. In Pompeii 84 such hoards contained an average of HS 950 in coins. Multiplied by the number of households in the empire of about 15 million, an estimate of HS 14 billion is obtained. This is certainly too high as the average of the coins held by the rural population and outside of Italy must have been much smaller. The figure would be of the same order of magnitude as that indicated by the other estimates if the average for the empire were half as large as that for Pompeii, which is not an unreasonable relation. Assuming the Pompeian figure to be applicable to the urban population for which it implies an income velocity of circulation of about three, and the virtual absence of cash among slaves, it would put the average holdings for the remaining three-fourths of the population of about HS 50 per family, equal to about two weeks' expenditures, which does not seem to be on the high side.

28. A positive role for monetary policy is claimed by LoCascio, but it refers mainly to the period after the first century A.D. and to reductions in the metallic content of silver coins.

29. For the view that the volume of minting was determined by fiscal and particularly military needs, compare Crawford, p. 48.

30. On these loans (*fenus nauticum*), compare Rougé, part III, chapter III, and for the law, Daremberg and Saglio, vol. IV, pp. 1, 13–17.

31. Herzog 1919; Herzog 1937, pp. 1422ff lists 145 *tesserae* including 35 issued in Augustus' reign with name of nummularius and date.

32. While bills of exchange were unknown in the Roman Empire, there were several forms of order of payment (Oehler, p. 708).

33. The main source is still Billeter, published in 1898; compare also article *"Fenus"* in Pauly and Wissowa vol. VI, pp. 2, 2187ff.

34. For three very small loans identified in Pompeii the monthly rate of interest averaged 3.7 percent (Breglia, p. 52).

35. Plinius early in the second century A.D. reported to the Emperor Trajan a 9 percent rate on private loans in Asia Minor (Finley, p. 118).

36. Finley, p. 117, ". . . one can easily count the known examples of borrowing on property for purposes of purchase or improvement. The mortgage was a disaster."

37. A standard work on agriculture in Roman Italy does not even mention agricultural debt except for Plinius' problems with the rent arrears of some of his tenants (White, pp. 407–08).

38. Statements about increasing trade are common. The only quantitative evidence offered – the number of shipwrecks – (Hopkins, p. 106) however, shows a small decline for the first two centuries A.D. compared to the preceding two centuries, which witnessed a sharp increase compared to the level of the fourth and third centuries B.C.

39. The most informative study on Mediterranean trade is Rougé.

40. This is suggested by the discussion by Crawford and by Hopkins, p. 104.

41. For lists of import and export products compare, for example, Cagnat, pp. 110–11, Frank, 1940, pp. 285ff, Miller, pp. 203ff; Spreck, passim; and Warmington, passim.

42. For India compare Warmington, pp. 71–2; for finds in Germany compare Bolin, 1926.

43. *Historia Naturalis*, vol. XII, p. 84, a figure often quoted, but called "dubious" by Finley, p. 132.

44. Miller seems to be alone in suggesting that there may not have been a negative balance in the empire's eastern trade if allowance is made for invisible items, mainly shipping (pp. 221–2, 241).

45. For India, Mitchell (p. 386) for imports; rough estimate of national product based on 1860 figure (Goldsmith, 1983a p. 5); for Japan for imports Mitchell, p. 387, for national product Goldsmith, 1983a, p. 38 (Ohkawa's estimate).

46. No comprehensive study of the finances of the early empire has been published since Marquardt and Hirschfeld and there is no summary comparable to that of Chapter XIII of Jones (1966) for the late empire. A combination of de Laet and Neesen covers most of the revenues, but nothing comparable is available for expenditures. An adequate treatment is difficult because of the "incredible scarcity of evidence about the Roman tax system," (Hirschfeld, p. 99), a comment that also applies to non-military expenditures. This state of affairs is due not to the absence of relevant contemporary documents since statements of revenues and expenditures (*rationes imperii*) were complied under Augustus (Jones 1950, p. 24), but to their not having been preserved.

47. On the administration of revenue, compare particularly Marquardt, Hirschfeld, and Neesen.

48. Rostovtsev's monograph published in 1902 is still the main authority.

49. The first estimate is derived from MacMullen's estimate of HS 270 million for the army (1985, fn 4) plus HS 5 million for the navy and HS 75 million for separation payments (Frank, pp. 4, 7) and the assumption that the costs of the army accounted for 58 percent of total expenditures (Frank, pp. 4, 7). The second estimate is based on Hopkins' estimate of HS 15 per head (p. 120) and a population of 55 million. Both figures are well above Frank's older estimate (p. 7) of HS 475 million. On the other hand they are somewhat below another estimate, without breakdown or justi-

fication, of at most HS 1 billion (Pekary, p. 105). An estimate of HS 4 billion for the mid-first century A.D. which is accepted by a classicist (Bernardi, pp. 19, 22) and even regarded as possibly on the low side, can be rejected out of hand as it would be equal to about one-fifth of total national product.

50. Goldsmith, 1984, p. 283. Compare the comparison in terms of kilograms of wheat per head by Hopkins (p. 120) – a less appropriate comparison because of the great differences in the relative prices of wheat.

51. The *tributum* was described as "the backbone of the finance" of the empire (Dessau, 1902, p. 149), as the main levy on the provinces (Ziegler et al. vol. 5, 1952, probably following Marquardt, vol. V, p. 234). On the other hand Rostovtsev (p. 409) called the customs duties "the most important part of the government's revenues" and de Laet (p. 448) regarded them as comparable to or even larger than *tributa* and *stipendia* and asserted that "many other scholars" shared Rostovtsev's opinion. None of these opinions, of course, are based on estimates of the size of the different revenues and astonishingly do not mention the revenues from government lands.

Only two estimates of the value of *tributum* have been found. Gibbon estimated it as "seldom less than £15–20 million" for all provinces (vol. I, p. 154) which, on the basis of the gold equivalent of the two currencies corresponded to HS 1,350 to HS 1,800 million. Cavaignac's estimate of 25,000 talents (1923, p. 158) is equal to HS 600 million. Both estimates, and particularly Gibbon's, are much higher than can be accommodated in the better founded estimate of total expenditures.

52. Compare particularly Neesen, a large part of whose recent study is devoted to *tributum;* for a summary compare Ziegler et al., vol. 5, pp. 952–4.

53. On the land tax in Egypt compare Neesen, pp. 86ff.

54. Portoria have been described in detail by de Laet and earlier by Cagnat.

55. de Laet lists about 150 customs stations on which information has been found, but their total number probably was considerably higher.

56. Cagnat, p. 232; nothing seems to be known about details or revenue.

57. Compare Cagnat, pp. 175–226, who estimated that about one-half of the wealth of Roman citizens was subject to the tax. It may be supposed that the emperor, who was often left a substantial part of large estates, was not subject to the tax.

58. Figures as high as HS 100,000 (Cagnat, p. 226) have been mentioned, but other estimates are much lower, (Pauly and Wissowa, vol. VIII, p. 2473).

59. Public auctions apparently had a much broader scope than in modern times, including many transactions handled by brokers so that their volume could be described as "immense" (Mommsen, pp. 92, 98). This explains that the tax was so resented by the public that Tiberius felt compelled to reduce it from 1.0 to 0.5 percent and Caracalla abolished it (Pauly and Wissowa, vol. III, pp. 2 1928). Auctioneers fees in general

amounted to 1 percent and a similar fee had to be paid to the crier (*praeco*) (Mommsen, pp. 92, 98). Some authors have regarded the tax as applicable to all sales (Gibbon, vol. I, p. 166; Rougé, p. 442).

60. On *aurum coronarium* compare Daremberg and Saglio, vol. I, pp. 578–9; Speck, p. 599, asserts that the amounts were "important," though this should apply only after Augustus' reign.

61. Frank, p. 7; Hopkins' apparently independent estimate (p. 125) of HS 67 million does not include separation payments for praetorians and urban cohorts, which should bring the total close to HS 80 million. The HS 170 million of his own money with which Augustus started the fund (Frank, p. 9) would have financed its expenditures for little more than two years and thus cannot greatly affect any estimates of the sums paid by the *aerarium*.

62. If both Frank's estimates for expenditures and revenues (pp. 4–7) were accepted, there would have been a surplus of HS 50 million a year or one-eighth of revenues, which is unlikely. If total expenditures are assumed to have been equal to revenues, other not specifically estimated expenditures would have totaled about HS 60 billion or fully one-eighth of aggregate expenditures.

63. For the location of legions compare McEvedy, p. 77.

64. These transfers have been stressed by Hopkins, pp. 101–103.

65. The exception is Tiberius who is reported to have accumulated over the 23 years of his reign between HS 2,700 million and HS 3,300 million (Cavaignac 1923, p. 158; Speck, p. 603), which would be equivalent to about one-fifth of total revenues, an unlikely high ratio. This accumulation was rapidly dissipated under his successor Caligula.

66. Frank (p. 6) suggested that Augustus increased the *tributum* of these two provinces before his death.

67. If Ulpian's statement that the *tributum* equaled military expenditures (Hopkins, p. 117), which referred to the late second century, was also applicable to Augustan Rome and was more than an indication of broad orders of magnitude, it would imply a *tributum* of between HS 270 and 370 million or about 45 percent of total expenditures if military expenditures did not include separation payments, and of about HS 80 million more, or between 55 and 60 percent if they did. These are improbably high figures and ratios.

68. de Laet (p. 448) declared over 30 years ago categorically that "it is entirely impossible to evaluate even approximately the revenues which the fiscus derived from the portorium," but then asserted that "customs duties have constituted a very important part of the revenues of the fiscus . . . comparable or even higher than tributa and stipendia of the various provinces; certainly much larger than the total of all other vectigalia (indirect taxes)." How did he know without making rough estimates of the amounts involved?

69. Frank, p. 7; refers to yield under Tiberius.

70. Marquardt (p. 268) asserted that receipts from inheritance tax were "very

substantial," and Hirschfeld (p. 97) called the tax "one of the remunerative sources of revenue."

71. The estate multiplier has been estimated at around 30 for France and Italy around 1900 (Gini, pp. 120–22) and at about 40 for the United States in 1922 (Lampmann, p. 54). Even the French and Italian values are too high for the Roman Empire with its shorter length of life.

72. The legal minimum to be left to a son was one-fourth of the estate, (Gibbon, vol. I, p. 167), a proportion that apparently applied to the total of all persons who qualified as close relatives, that is, parents, grandparents, children, grandchildren, and siblings (Cagnat in Daremberg and Saglio, vol. V, pp. 826–27).

73. Duncan-Jones, p. 12. The numerous individual slave prices cited by Westerman (Pauly and Wissowa, Suppl. VI, pp. 1010–14) vary so much that no average can be based on them.

74. The yield of the tax has been called "considerable" (Daremberg and Saglio, vol. I, part 1, p. 580).

75. Rents from public lands have been called "one of the important regular sources of imperial revenue" (Neesen, p. 152; at the same time deploring the dearth of information on their types, level, and development). On imperial properties compare Hirschfeld, who calls them "the largest landed properties assembled in one hand in older or modern times," (p. 574) – probably unaware of the situation in Mughal India – and lists many individual properties (pp. 544ff), and according to whom the largest imperial domains were in Africa and most of them were rented, sometimes in large units that were subleased. Compare also His.

76. Based on a consumption of between 35 and 40 modii of wheat per head and a ratio of seed to consumption of one-third (Hopkins, p. 118) and a price of HS 3 per modius.

77. This qualification rules out a comparison with city states such as Athens (Chapter 3) or Florence (Chapter 9) or some others for which data on the structure of government revenues and expenditures are available.

78. Liebenam, p. 164; his study, now over 80 years old, is the only detailed treatment of the subject. For a shorter discussion compare Frank, Chapter IV, and Abbott and Johnson, Chapter X.

79. For payments for municipal offices compare Duncan-Jones, pp. 147ff.

80. Liebenam (pp. 68–173) describes more than a dozen types of expenditures.

## Chapter 5

1. The material for the study of the economic or financial history of medieval Islam is much scarcer than that for classical antiquity. As a result "there is no general study of economic life in Islamic countries" (Sourdel 1968, p. 646), "the economic history of the Middle East in the 7th to 9th centuries will never be fully and precisely known" (Lapidus, p. 177), and "there does not exist any financial history of the Muslim world" (*Encyclo-*

*paedia of Islam*, p. 1147). Another difficulty is the acceptance of figures reported by Arab authors without sometimes sufficient scepticism. Thus we read – probably an extreme example – that "in Baghdad under Harun-al-Rashid . . . every year the public treasury received . . . 750 tons of coined gold or 1½ bill. dinars" (Lombard 1971, p. 118), without the author's realizing that this quantity would have been equal to the gold production of the entire Old World for the period from A.D. 501 to 900 (Quiring, p. 197), and that the value would have amounted to over one-half of the annual national product of the caliphate. Lombard may have obtained the figure by misinterpreting an equally fantastic one of Hammer (p. 41), where it is given as "7500 Centner," that is, 375 tons.

The difficulties are increased by the substantial regional differences among the provinces of an empire stretching in early Abbasid times from the Indus to North Africa, the failure in many cases of exact identification of date and location of the scarce data that have survived, and the disagreements among modern authors on many important points of interpretation. A description of the economic structure and still more of the financial system of the caliphate at the beginning of the ninth century A.D. can therefore be given only in general terms, can only rarely be supported by quantitative data and cannot answer several important questions.

2. While no point of time can be regarded as fully representative of as long a period as medieval Islam or even the Abbasid caliphate, the choice of the first years of the ninth century A.D. needs little justification. While at that date Spain and the western part of North Africa had become independent, in fact the reign of Harun-al-Rashid is generally regarded as the cultural and political and probably also the economic zenith of the caliphate. Indeed the period from al-Mansur to al-Mamun, that is, the years 754 to 833, have been called the "belle époque" of the caliphate and "the golden age of Islamic civilization" (Sourdel 1968, p. 69), and there is no doubt about a rapid decline in many fields after the middle of the ninth century, evidenced by a substantial inflation and the formation of independent dynasties in an increasing part of the original area of the caliphate, which by the eleventh century had been virtually reduced to Mesopotamia.

3. Wiet, p. 63. In the same vein the Abbasid caliphate has been called "the Indian summer of the Hellenistic and Persian civilizations" (Løkkegaard, p. 92)

4. It should be kept in mind that the chapter tries to describe the situation around A.D. 800. Many features of the caliphate changed substantially after the middle of the ninth century A.D. when the empire began to disintegrate and one province after the other became in fact independent politically and financially, the price level rose and the economic situation deteriorated. The only fields in which the ninth and tenth centuries A.D. showed progress were banking and foreign trade. Similarly, the situation in the first and one-half century after the conquest, essentially the period

of the Umayyad caliphate, was in some respects different from that prevailing in the early ninth century A.D., in particular in a more rapid increase in population, agricultural production, and urbanization and in a much greater influence of the Arab element in government and army.

5. While the three estimates for the total population of the caliphate (using the midpoints of Issawi's range) are very similar, differences for individual provinces are large for several cases and remain substantial even for the three broad areas into which they can be combined, ranging from 7 to 10 million for the eastern region, from 10 to 14 million for the central region, and from 4.5 to 9 million for the western region. In general Issawi's and McEvedy and Jones's estimates are closer to each other than to Russell's. Preference has generally been given to McEvedy and Jones' estimates because they are the most recent ones and seem to have been derived by comparable methods. The exceptions are Iraq, where McEvedy and Jones' estimate appears to be too low and for Arabia where it seems to be too high.

6. Population from Table 5-1; areas from McEvedy and Jones (total) and Table 5-2 (cultivated).

7. In the case of Syria the number of Arabs has been put at less than 200,000 (Ashtor 1969, p. 236 citing Lammens) or well below one-tenth of the total population. In view of the proximity of Syria to Arabia the ratio should have been considerably lower for most other parts of the caliphate particularly in Egypt, North Africa, and the eastern provinces. For Churasan their number has been estimated at not much over 200,000 (Wellhausen, p. 307), which may have been as much as one-tenth of the population, but the proportion apparently was much less for all Iran (Cahen 1975, pp. 306–07).

8. In Egypt the majority of the population in the ninth century A.D. still adhered to the Coptic faith (Cahen 1970a, p. 115). In Iran conversion did not become universal until the tenth century (Cahen 1975, p. 306).

9. McEvedy and Jones, passim. The increase there indicated would seem to be too low if there was a "heavy growth of the rural population," (Watson 1974, p. 17).

10. For Baghdad, Kennedy (p. 88), but only 200,000 to 300,000 in other estimates (Grünebaum 1966, p. 138; Lapidus, p. 61). For Basra, Kufa, and Wasit (Lombard 1971, p. 27, "certainly number hundreds of thousands of inhabitants") who puts Samarkand at 500,000 (p. 132) and Baghdad at nearly 2 million (p. 121), certainly an exaggeration. No estimate of total urban population has been found.

11. Cahen 1970a, pp. 99–100; the exceptions were the sugar plantations in southern Iraq.

12. It has been asserted that any but the poorest urban households had one or two slaves (Cahen 1970b, p. 515).

13. "There is no major overall treatment of slavery in Islam" (Müller, p. 78).

14. Cahen's estimate for Baghdad is 300 to 400 dirhams per year when the poverty limit entitling a person to aid was 200 dirhams (1961, p. 49).

15. The wage, in terms of bread, has been estimated to have declined between the eighth and eleventh century by nearly two-thirds, recovering in the twelfth century to one-half of the level of four centuries earlier (Ashtor 1969, p. 465).
16. Ashtor 1969, pp. 66, 71. Incomes as high as 1.5 to 3 million dirhams are reported for viziers and 600,000 to 750,000 dirhams for the provincial administrators (Sourdel 1968, p. 460).
17. Ashtor 1969, p. 62. The relations were similar though at a higher nominal level in thirteenth century Egypt, namely, 4 to 6 dinars per month for a household of the small bourgeoisie, 10 to 20 dinars for one of the middle, and 30 and more dinars for one of the upper bourgeoisie compared to 1.5 to 2.5 dinars per month earned by a workman or a domestic servant (Ashtor 1959, pp. 274–5).
18. No discussion of the monetary system of the caliphate has been found that meets even modest requirements of economists. This section therefore has had to be based on the generally brief passages devoted to the subject in the standard literature of the economy and the administration of the caliphate, on Lombard's paper, and the relevant articles in the *Encyclopaedia of Islam*, such as *dhahab* (gold), *djabadh* (money changer), dinar, dirham, and fals, and Ehrenkreutz's article (1977a).
19. Udovitch, s.v. *fals*, in *Encyclopaedia of Islam*, vol. 2.
20. Reports on the dinar–dirham ratios differ, partly because not exactly dated or located; compare, for example, Ashtor 1969, p. 40; Ehrenkreutz 1977a, p. 95; Grierson, p. 259.
21. Based on daily wage of one dirham and a price of bread of one dirham for 2 kg.
22. Ehrenkreutz 1970, p. 40; Udovitch 1979; Fischel, pp. 341ff; *Encyclopaedia of Islam*, 1st ed., s.v. *djabadh*.
23. The need to handle gold and silver coins on the base of weight rather than of tale is indicated by the fact that 127 dinars issued between 698 and 955 A.D. weighed between 3.25 and 4.67 g, the range being equal to about one-third of the standard weight of 4.25 g, and the average of 4.13 g, while the weight of 302 dirhams ranged from 1.97 to 4.53 g, a range of nearly nine-tenths of the standard weight of 2.97 g, and the average of 2.87 g. For the 46 dinars issued by the first five Abbasid caliphs between A.D. 754 and 805, the range was smaller, but still substantial, namely, 15 percent of the standard weight for dinars and 37 percent for dirhams (based on Lane-Poole, p. 84). While some of these differences reflect wear and tear, particularly for the silver coins, it is evident that differences in weight at issue were not negligible even in the best of times.
24. Lombard 1971, p. 107. Systematic looting of Pharaonic tombs has been regarded as another source of gold for the caliph's mints. On gold movements compare particularly, though without any quantitative data, Lombard 1947.
25. Compare, for example, "The Muslim empire was well provided with gold," followed immediately that its volume "can hardly be ascertained," (Eh-

renkreutz, *Encyclopaedia of Islam,* vol. II, p. 214); and even "one then [early tenth century] was swimming in gold," Kremer 1887, p. 10) and "abundance, down to the smallest cities, of gold and silver coins," (Lombard 1971, p. 111, citing Ibn Khordadbeh), statements that may be meant to apply to the eleventh and later centuries, "the great period of Muslim gold" (Duplessy, p. 119). On the other hand compare statements about shortages of coins such as Cahen 1970a, p. 86; and Ashtor 1971, p. 31, and Cahen 1970b, p. 526, for silver.

26. The most recent and best brief treatment is Udovitch 1979. Compare also Bogaert, pp. 161–3 and Fischel, pp. 341ff.
27. Udovitch 1979, p. 266; these rates seem astonishingly moderate.
28. Cahen, 1961; *Encyclopaedia of Islam,* 1st ed., vol. 1, s.v. *wakf.*
29. Based mainly on Udovitch 1979. Compare also Grasshoff and Cahen 1970a, pp. 139–41.
30. Compare *Encyclopaedia of Islam,* 1st ed. vol. 3, s.v. *riba* (Schacht).
31. To what transactions the rates reported for tenth century A.D. Iraq of 10 to 15 percent (Ashtor 1978, pp. 193, 207) refer, how common they were, and how they circumvented the Koranic prohibition of interest is not clear.
32. Ehrenkreutz 1972, p. 100. An idea of the extent of the land held by the caliph is given by the report that in the second half of the seventh century such land in the *sawad* (central Mesopotamia) yielded 100 million dirhams in taxes (Dennett, p. 31), probably an exaggerated figure as it would have constituted about 5 percent of national product.
33. The most detailed treatment is Watson 1981, and more briefly Watson 1974 and 1979. Watson goes as far as calling developments an "agricultural revolution." If his views become accepted, many earlier assessments will have to be revised.
34. For an exception, the financing of the textile industry in Egypt, the most important of the caliphate, compare Frantz-Murphy.
35. The situation in Cairo in a somewhat later period where barter is supposed to have accounted for 90 percent of transactions and only 10 percent were settled in gold (Gottschalk, p. 177) is not likely to be representative.
36. Compare particularly Lombard 1971, Ch. VIII, and Cahen 1970a, pp. 127ff and the maps of trade routes in Brice, p. 7; Lombard 1971, pp. 165, 175, 198–200; Roolvink, pp. 16–17; and Sourdel 1968, pp. 320–1.
37. Duplessy, pp. 119–20; here again most of the coins are from the tenth century or later.
38. For Mediterranean trade compare Ashtor 1970, p. 188.
39. No aspect of the economy of the caliphate has been studied as much and has produced such a plethora of articles, beginning with the report of de Saucy, one of the scholars who accompanied Napoleon's Egyptian expedition, as its revenue system. Nevertheless a comprehensive authoritative treatment is still missing. This section is based on the two most detailed modern monographs (Dennett and Løkkegaard), the relevant passages

in less specialized works, for example, Becker vol. I; Kremer, Chapter VII; and a number of articles in *Encyclopaedia of Islam*, such as *bayt-al-mal, dariba, djizya, karadj, ushr,* and *zakat,* mostly by Cahen. Many features of the revenue system, particularly its quantitative aspects, are still unknown or in dispute.

40. A somewhat more detailed schedule for a district in Iran in the ninth century shows considerably higher rates, for example, for wheat 3.5 to 15 dirhams per djarib for land of different quality, but similar relationships among products (Lambton, p. 35).

41. Even though referring to the sixteenth century a calculation of the tax burden in two districts in Egypt is of interest (Hansen, pp. 478–83). In a district in Lower Egypt the tax per taxable feddan (0.64 hectar) was 108 paras while in a district in Upper Egypt it was 324 paras. However, because of higher yields in Upper Egypt, though the difference in the share of the tax in the peasants' income was equally large, namely, below 20 or even 15 percent in Upper Egypt compared to 48 percent in Lower Egypt, the amount of wheat left to the farmer and his family was not too different in both locations, namely, 0.6 to 0.8 kg of wheat per day per consumer unit in Lower Egypt and almost 0.6 kg in Upper Egypt. This emphasizes the great regional differences, which may be assumed to have been larger within the caliphate than within Egypt.

42. In an Egyptian Coptic village in A.D. 704–05 a group of about 50 households paid, in addition to small amounts of wheat, on the average about 4 solidi (derived from Morimoto, pp. 140–41) equal to about 4.5 dinars and at a rate of 15 dirhams per dinar nearly 70 dirhams, about two-thirds for land tax and one-third for poll tax. Although the average income of these households is not known, the two taxes together are likely to have absorbed a considerable proportion of it. Dennett asserts, without citing figures, that the poll tax was equal to and frequently higher than the land tax paid in money (p. 107).

43. Compare *Encyclopaedia of Islam,* 1st ed. vol III, s.v. *ushr* (Grohmann) and *zakat* (Schacht).

44. In the first century after the conquest, Arab warriors received substantial pensions (cf. s.v. *ata, Encyclopaedia of Islam,* 729, 130; and Ehrenkreutz 1977, p. 488) since at that time they had not been given agricultural land. These pensions seem to have been abolished under the Abbasid caliphate.

45. Compare Waines, p. 286. The provincial totals for one or more of the estimates are reprinted in Hammer, pp. 39–41; Hussaini, pp. 199–203; Kremer, vol. I, pp. 356–79; and Slane, pp. 179–80. None of the authors discusses the statistical problems raised by the figures in the form found in the Arabic manuscripts and reprinted in literal translation.

46. This is the predominant opinion among Islamists; compare, for example, Becker, vol. I, p. 110; Dennett, p. 31; Grünebaum 1966, p. 140; Hussaini, p. 198; Kremer, p. 263; Mez, p. 108; Sourdel 1959, p. 586.

47. In A.D. 730 of a revenue of Egypt of 4 million dinars, 2.7 million, or two-thirds, were transferred to Damascus, the capital of the Umayyad caliphate (Becker, vol. I, p. 110). Whether this ratio was applicable to the other provinces and to the Abbasid caliphate half a century later it is impossible to say.

48. Of the several versions of the list, which differ only slightly in total, but substantially for a few provinces, that printed in Kremer, vol. I, pp. 356–9, has been used. The figures for Isphahan and Homs, which are not included there, have been taken from el-Ali, pp. 310ff. The figures given in dinars are translated into dirhams at rate of 15 : 1 used by Kremer.

49. The revenue districts shown in the original (for their boundaries cf. Roolvink, p. 7) have been combined into regions to correspond as closely as possible to the areas of the states of today, which are the only units for which estimates have been made (population) or are available (cultivated area).

50. This ratio is implied in the figures reported by Hussaini, p. 198, for total revenues and those received in cash.

51. In the early tenth century one of the Iranian provinces (Fars) has been called the by far most heavily taxed one (Mez, p. 123), without indication of evidence.

52. Its cash revenue amounted to 90 million dirhams (Kremer, p. 356).

53. Here are three characterizations of the burden of taxation in Egypt: the fiscal regime was *impitoyable* (Ashtor 1969, p. 73); the country was "drained without mercy by the government" (Becker, p. 155); and Egypt was "a colony of exploitation, where the fiscal regime was particularly oppressive" (Cahen 1970b, p. 184).

54. The court's expenditures under the caliph al-Mamun (A.D. 813–833) have been reported at 2.2 million dinars per year (Kremer, vol. I, p. 280), equal at the rate of 15:1 to 33 million dirhams or about 8 percent of the cash income of the central treasury.

## Chapter 6

1. The *devshirme* is described in all histories of the Ottoman Empire, for example, Gibb and Bowen, vol. I, pp. 180ff; Itzkowitz, pp. 49ff; and Ménage. The number of conscripts has been put at an annual average of about 1,000 (Ménage, p. 212). Much higher figures going up to 10,000 per year are very unlikely (Ménage, p. 212).

2. The estimates of area and total population (28 million for the end of the sixteenth century) are based on McEvedy and Jones, pp. 133ff.

3. For 1520–35 the population of the European provinces and of Anatolia has been put at about 6 million each on the basis of contemporary censuses (Barkan 1958, p. 25), very close to McEvedy and Jones' estimates.

4. Barkan, 1958, p. 20. Another estimate for the second half of the sixteenth century allocates nearly three-fifths of the population of Istanbul

to Muslims, nearly one-third to Christians, and about one-tenth to Jews (Matran, 1962, p. 45). The share of non-Muslims in most trades and professions was probably considerably higher.

5. Based on estimates for 1500 and 1600 in McEvedy and Jones. Barkan puts the increase between 1520 and 1600 at "at least 40 percent" (1958, p. 24) or fully 0.4 percent per year. If one accepts this rate of growth and starts from a total population of about 26 million in 1550, the figures for 1520 and 1600 would be approximately 23 and 32 million.

6. For example, Jorga, vol. 2, p. 220. This figure cannot be reconciled with the average of 55 akches per year or 0.15 akche per day reported by Hammer-Purgstall for the 1520s (1827, vol. 3, p. 181) or of 275 akches per year, that is, 0.75 akche per day for 1588.

7. Based on 60 akches per gold piece, the average for 1550 and 1570 (Matran 1962, table 2, following p. 244).

8. Based on the silver content of the two coins.

9. Based on McEvedy and Jones' estimates.

10. Compare Section 6. In the 1660 budget the revenues of the crown lands destined for high officials and wives of the sultan are given as 49 million akches (Hammer 1827ff, vol. 3, p. 181).

11. This is suggested by Braudel's statement of a "modicité déconcertante des prix par rapport á l'Europe occidentale" (vol. 3, p. 407).

12. Inalcik 1969, pp. 108–09; 1973, p. 162 for Bursa. Since people leaving no or a negligible estate are probably not included in the statistics, the figures slightly overstate the concentration of wealth; for Edirne using Barkan's data (1958, p. 124).

13. Basic data from Tischendorf, pp. 62ff. On the characteristics of fiefs compare Deny.

14. No comprehensive description of the monetary system of the Ottoman Empire has been found. Compare, however, Gibb and Bowen, vol. II, pp. 49ff, and Matran 1962, pp. 233ff. The recent article by Gerber covers only some of the problems and deals mainly with the seventeenth and eighteenth centuries.

15. A sharp increase in the amounts of credit among individuals between the fifteenth and sixteenth centuries has been reported for Bursa (Gerber, p. 317).

16. Such rates are quoted by Gerber, p. 320.

17. There is nothing to be compared, for example, with the *Cambridge Economic History of India*, the specialized journals dealing with India's economic history, or the monographs of Moreland and Habib. Similarly the Ottoman Empire is much more sparsely covered in the two editions of the *Encyclopaedia of Islam* than the caliphate or Mughal India. (The Turkish edition of the *Encyclopaedia*, which apparently is less deficient in this respect, was not accessible to me.) This difference in the availability of information may be reflected in the allocation of space in Braudel's text: about 15 pages to the Ottoman Empire compared to about 25 pages to Mughal India and 80 pages to the United Provinces.

18. The studies of Shaw on Ottoman Egypt and of Gerber on Bursa indicate the possibilities.
19. Compare "credit facilities remained at a primitive state" (Inalcik 1969, p. 138) and the prevalence of cash transactions and poor development of credit and "a certain archaism in exchange transactions" even in the eighteenth century (Braudel, vol. 3, p. 407).
20. Matran 1979 pp. 177–8, stresses the lack of information on quantities, prices, methods of trade, and participants.
21. On the organization of financial administration compare Hammer-Purgstall 1828.
22. The use of the budget for 1660, apparently the earliest one that has survived (Hammer-Purgstall 1815, vol. 2, 170ff) is hazardous even for structural relations and still more for absolute amounts, in part because the then price level was much higher – probably at least three times as high – than a century earlier and because the practice of tax farming had become much more common.
23. Hammer-Purgstall 1828, vol. 2, p. 182. This figure is suspiciously low as revenues in 1518 have been estimated at 3.1 million ducats excluding Egypt and Iraq (Morawitz, p. 8), which suggests a total of close to 4 million ducats for the area of 1564.
24. In 1660 the head tax on non-Muslims yielded 112 million akches or nearly one-fifth of total revenue. If this ratio also applied a century earlier, the yield would have been 34 million akches, or three-tenths of the 1660 yield. As the tax was apparently in terms of gold coins such a relation – 3.3 to 1 – is compatible with the depreciation of the akche in terms of gold coins during that century (cf. Matran 1962, Table 2).
25. In the budget for 1660 (Hammer-Purgstall 1815, vol. 2, pp. 172ff) – a year without major campaigns – military expenditures accounted for over two-thirds of the total, most of the rest being absorbed by the court (*serai*). The items clearly not belonging to either of these two categories accounted for only about one-tenth of total expenditures. Whether or how the distribution in the mid-sixteenth century was different is not known.
26. The supposedly wild fluctuations in the government's revenues and expenditures in the century after Suleiman's death are shown in the table on page 278, reported by a Turkish author of the seventeenth century (cited Hammer-Purgstall 1815, vol. 2, pp. 182–3).
27. This section is based on Shaw 1962 and 1968.

## Chapter 7

1. This is the most recent estimate (Habib 1982, p. 166). It is compatible with another recent estimate of 130 million for the subcontinent (McEvedy and Jones, p. 185) since the empire contained about four-fifths of the total. It is somewhat lower than an older estimate of 125 million (Davis, p. 24), and somewhat higher than the upper range of over 95 million of another recent estimate (Desai 1978, pp. 72–3) but equal to a revision of

| Year | Revenues | Expenditures (million akches) | Deficit |
|------|----------|-------------------------------|---------|
| 1564 | 183 | 190 | 7 |
| 1591 | 193 | 360 | 167 |
| 1597 | 300 | 900 | 600 |
| 1640 | 362 | 550 | 188 |
| 1650 | 533 | 687 | 144 |
| 1669 | 181 | 591 | 410 |

In evaluating these figures, supposedly based on official accounts, the depreciation of the akche must be taken into account, which fell from about 70 to the gold coin in 1570 to 220 in 1590, and recovered to 150 in 1641 and 225 in 1669 while food prices in Istanbul approximately tripled over the century. If the figures are to be believed, revenues in terms of gold or in commodities in 1669 were two-thirds below those of a century earlier, while expenditures were unchanged. For a number of other estimates of doubtful reliability compare Jorga, vol. 3, p. 230. It is astonishing that no turcologist seems to have analyzed the in part very strange figures, at least in Western languages, or to have compared them to fragmentary other relevant figures on government revenues and expenditures.

that estimate to 108 million (Moosvi 1973, p. 194). On the other hand, Moreland's estimate of 100 million for the subcontinent (1920, p. 21) published over 60 years ago, which corresponds to one of about 75 million for Mughal India may now be disregarded. (For a listing of various estimates of population cf. Visaria, p. 466.) It is not clear to what extent this estimate includes the tribal population, which has been put at 10 percent of the total labor force (Maddison 1971, p. 33; no absolute figures given). Because practically nothing is known about it and as their role in the economy, not to speak in the financial system, was negligible, the tribal population is generally disregarded throughout this chapter.

2. The estimates for world population (545 million), for China (150 million), Europe (100 million), France (16 million), and Muscovy (15 million), are taken from McEvedy and Jones (pp. 342, 171, 18, 59, 79, respectively).

3. Based on map in Schwartzberg, p. 45.

4. Based on share of Lahore, Delhi, and Agra provinces in number of villages and land tax assessments and area around 1600 (Tables 7-1 and 7-2).

5. Blochmann, p. 528, and Moreland 1920, p. 65, on basis of biographies in the *Ain-i-Akbari*.

6. Derived from estimates for 1500, 1600, and 1700 (McEvedy and Jones, p. 185).

7. The birth rate was still as high as 4.9 percent in 1881–91 (Davis, p. 69).

8. This was the value for 1872–81 (Davis, p. 62) when sanitary conditions had already considerably improved.

9. The average household size in 1971 was 5.6 persons, with practically no difference between rural and urban households (U.S. Bureau of Commerce, 1979, p. 594). In a small sample of households in Chittagong in 1849, the only one found for the nineteenth century, the average was 5.0 persons, but the difference between rural and urban households was large, namely, 6.2 compared to 4.4 (Gujral, p. 4).

10. These figures adopt the usual definition of the labor force, which excludes females engaged only in domestic activities. In the Republic of India in 1971 the labor force participation rate for males was 62 percent, for females 36 percent, and for the entire population 49 percent (International Labor Office, 1983, p. 23).

11. Habib 1982, p. 170. This is lower than Maddison's (1971) estimate of 18 percent of the labor force (p. 33) unless it is assumed that labor force participation was lower in urban than in rural areas.

12. Habib 1982, p. 171. On the basis of these estimates the share of cities of over 100,000 inhabitants in total urban population would have been between 22 and 25 percent, which compares with one of 26 percent in 1901 in the territory of the Republic of India (Tata Services 1980, p. 41).

13. The figure refers to the late seventeenth century (Habib 1963, p. 4) but is not likely to have been substantially different around 1600 A.D.

14. There is no information on the distribution of the 470,000 villages among settlements of different size compared to the average of about 180 persons or about 35 families. An idea of the character of the distribution may perhaps be obtained from that of villages in modern India where the average village had 760 inhabitants and 135 families. In 1961 in four states, which accounted for fully one-fourth of the rural population of the Republic (West Bengal, Maharashtra, Gujerat, and Madras), the census reported that slightly over two-fifths of the villages had less than 500 inhabitants, one-fourth between 500 and 1000 inhabitants, one-fifth between 1,000 and 2,000 inhabitants, and one-eighth more than 2,000 inhabitants. Only one-eighth of the total rural population lived in the smallest villages, one-fifth in villages with 500 to 1,000 inhabitants, fully one-fourth each in those with between 1,000 and 2,000 and over one-third in those with over 2,000 inhabitants. For Mughal India the distribution must, of course, be shifted toward the smaller villages. At that time most of the villages – probably more than two-thirds of them – had a population of less than 200 and only about one-eighth had one of more than 500 and villages of over 1,000 inhabitants must have been rare if the distribution curve was similar to that of modern India. Again, if modern India can be used as a source of information regional differences in the average size and the size distribution of villages must have been substantial – in 1961 average size ranged among the larger states from under 300 to over 1800.

15. On the basis of an estimate that the "menial castes," who may be assumed

to have been landless, accounted for between one-fifth and one-fourth of the rural population (Habib 1982, p. 249).

16. The problem of the peasants' flight from the land is discussed in all studies of the agriculture of Mughal India; compare for example, Habib 1963, p. 328.

17. Even the most recent and most detailed study of the Indian economy during the sixteenth to eighteenth centuries, Chapters VI to X of volume 1 of the *Cambridge Economic History of India* (CEHI) (Raychaudhuri and Habib) published in 1982 does not discuss national product directly nor does it provide an estimate, except by implication when it is asserted that the realized income of the government has been "estimated at something between a third and a half of the gross national product" (Raychaudhuri 1982, p. 178), implying a national product of R 200 million to R 300 million since government revenue was on the order of R 100 million, the result of the author's mistaking the gross product of agriculture for total national product.

18. For a listing of the assessment figures by provinces for about a dozen dates between 1595–96 and the mid-eighteenth century, compare Siddiqui, pp. 164–71.

19. For two groups of 78,000 and 75,000 villages the amounts collected amounted to 84 and 78 percent, respectively, of the amounts assessed (Habib 1963, p. 273).

20. The ratio was 3.4 percent for the 12 old provinces, which accounted for about five-sixths of the total assessment (Antonova, p. 107). There were, however, about 130 parganas in which over 5 percent of the land was tax exempt, the ratio going up to 17 percent. Not astonishingly the parganas with a high ratio of tax-exempt land generally had Muslim zamindars (Moosvi 1978, pp. 282, 287–8).

21. Moosvi 1978, p. 364. The ratio of 16 percent may be a misprint as the average for the four provinces for which estimates are shown is 10 percent.

22. Assuming that about three-fifths of the male, but only one-fifth of the female, urban population were in the labor force since in medieval oriental cities wage work by women was rare.

23. All authors seem to accept the figures of *Ain-i-Akbari*, (Blochmann, vol. I, p. 225).

24. The approximately 200,000 cavalrymen alone (Habib 1969), who with their families represented about 6 percent of the urban population, would have had an income of about R 25 million.

25. Based on Maddison's allocation of 3 percent of total income to tribal population (1971, p. 33).

26. The distribution among the three groups is similar from that of Maddison (1971), which does not show any absolute figures and the derivation of which is not explained in detail, if his after-tax distribution is shifted to a before-tax basis, namely, 12 percent for court and nobles (including

zamindars), 28 percent for urban, 57 percent for rural, and 3 percent for tribal population.

27. The only recent estimate of national product, and it is an implicit one, contained in a footnote and characterized as "nothing definite" was published in 1980 (Moosvi 1980, p. 329). It expressed national product as a multiple of the net land revenue, putting the ratio at between 18 and 26 percent thereof, without giving an absolute figure for net land revenue. These ratios were obtained by assuming that "(a) agriculture accounted for 80 percent of GNP; (b) the land revenue amounted to between a third and a half of the total agricultural product; (c) the actual share of the land revenue collected by the Emperor [and the nobles] was 6/10 . . .; (d) taxes other than revenue accounted for 10 percent of the net estimated revenue (*jama*), i.e., were equal to 1/9 of the net land revenue . . ." As the *jama*, that is, the amount assessed rather than the actually collected revenue is generally accepted as having amounted to below R 130 million in 1595–56, the implied gross national product for that year is between R 500 million and R 720 million. The midpoint of this range of about R 610 million is fairly close to the estimate derived here on the basis of a more detailed approach and the use of somewhat different assumptions.

28. The Taj Mahal is reported to have cost R 92 million (Moreland 1923, p. 196). This would have been somewhat over one-tenth of a year's national product and still about one-half of one percent of national product if spread evenly over the Taj's construction period of fully two decades.

29. Moreland 1920, p. 52; similarly Smith (p. 394), putting the increase in the price level between 1600 and 1900 at 500 to 600 percent. The cost of living index increased between 1860 and 1900 or 1912 by 57 or 93 percent, respectively (Goldsmith 1983, p. 56).

30. The conclusion that real product per head in 1600 was about equal to that of the mid-nineteenth century and was only by about one-fourth below that of the mid-twentieth century is not incompatible with statements that "India's per capita income in 1750 was probably similar to that in 1950 . . ." (Maddison 1971, p. 18), that "India was almost certainly not richer than she is now and probably she was a little poorer," (Moreland 1920, p. 274), and with two statements of the probably most knowledgeable economic historian of Mughal India, namely, that "it would hardly be possible to consider agricultural output as being lower in 1600 than in 1900," and that output per head of the urban population "could invite comparison with the early decades of this century," (Habib 1969, pp. 35, 61), particularly if it is taken into account that a much larger proportion of the urban labor force was engaged in unproductive service activities in Mughal India than in modern India and the relative prices of some important components of national product such as transportation, communication, and energy were much lower from the late nineteenth century on than in the seventeenth century. At most one may admit a small decrease in real output per head in 1860 compared to 1600, particularly

of food grains, but the difference, if any, must have been small. The conclusion, however, is not compatible with the assertions of some Indian economic historians, usually not quantified, that the standard of living in Mughal India was much higher than that in modern India, one of which goes as far as to claim that "for peons Jahangir's India was a paradise" and the weaver in the time of Jahangir "compared to his modern representative lived in luxury" (Narain, pp. 25–26). More specifically it is incompatible with an estimate that real wages in mid-nineteenth century were nearly 50 percent below the 1600 level for unskilled and by 70 percent below it for skilled workers (Mukherjee, p. 54). Although the movements of real wages, supposedly of urban workers, cannot be without further evidence equated to those of real national product per head, a decrease of real wages by 50 to 70 percent cannot be reconciled with equality or something near it in national product per head unless there had been a sharp increase in the ratio of average rural to urban earnings for which there is no evidence. (Assume that in 1600 aggregate rural income had been three times that of urban wage earners and average real wages had declined by 60 percent between 1600 and 1850. Then if real income per head of the country had not changed, average real rural income per head would have had to have risen by one-fifth and the ratio of rural to urban average incomes would have been three times as high in 1850 as in 1600 – hardly credible.) Alternatively, if the movement of real wages is assumed to represent that of real national product per head, the latter in India in 1600 would have been about $450 in 1970 prices, that is, 2.5 times that in contemporary England and 1.5 times that of Great Britain, France, and the United States in 1800, and about equal to that in Tunisia, Iraq, Malaysia, Portugal, or Turkey in 1950. This is most unlikely. On the question of the standard of living contemporary evidence is relevant. Here two contemporary quotations for many: "The condition of the common people in India is very miserable" and "the nobles live in indescribable luxury and extravagance," (de Laet, pp. 88, 90). It is difficult to believe that the many foreign visitors, from different countries and in diverse occupations, some of whom had lived for many years in the country and had excellent contacts, who came to similar conclusions – such as Bernier and de Laet – all were biased, maybe even because they were capitalists and racists as some Indian and Marxist historians seem to imply. It is less farfetched to believe that the situation actually was more or less as they reported it. It was then rather prescient of de Laet writing around 1630, or only a quarter of a century after Akbar's death, to conclude that the Mughal Empire was not "stable enough even now to endure for long" (p. 241) even if one does not share his explanation that this was due to the poor personal qualities of Akbar's successors (p. 246).

The satisfactory comparison of real national product per head in Akbar's time and from the late nineteenth century on or between Mughal

India and contemporary Western or undeveloped countries requires much better and more comprehensive price indices than are now available. Although there is a plethora of information on prices on wages in the 1590s in the *Ain*, at least for Agra, data for the seventeenth to nineteenth centuries are scarce and in part contradictory and have not yet been comprehensively collected or analyzed. At the moment the margin of uncertainty is much greater for an appropriate deflator than for the estimates of national product in current prices.

31. Maddison (1983 p. 28) puts the rate of growth of real per capita income from 1820 to 1870 at zero.

32. The estimates of this table are compatible with those of Maddison, whose derivation is not explained, namely, that it is conceivable that the per capita product was comparable with that of Elizabethan England, that by mid-eighteenth century "per capita product [was] perhaps two-thirds of that in England and France" and that in 1750 it was "probably similar to that in 1950, that is, about $150 at 1965 prices," that is, about $185 at 1970 prices (1971, p. 18).

33. An alternative calculation starting from Clark's estimates of national product in International Units (in 1925–34 dollars) for 1913 rather than from the estimates for 1950 of Summers, Kravis, and Heston in 1970 dollars leads to a similar conclusion, namely, that around 1700 the per head national product of Mughal India was at about the level of the leading European countries and that of the United States, though the results are slightly more favorable to India.

| | | International units | | |
|------|-------|------------------|--------|-----------------|
| Year | India | Great Britain | France | United States |
| 1913 | 80 | 432 | 274 | 511 |
| 1857 | 63 | 238 | 139 | 201 |
| 1800 | 56 | 113 | 82 | 109 |
| 1700 | 70 | 81 | 64 | 78 |
| 1600 | 63 | 54 | — | — |

*Source:* 1913 based on Clark, pp. 46, 63, 80, 124; Indian value shifted from 1925–29 to 1925–34 basis in line with movement of national product deflator (Goldsmith 1983, p. 69).

34. The number of mansabdars is given as 1571 in Moosvi 1980, p. 340, but the addition of the 27 groups shown separately yields a total of 1671.

35. In the 1660s some merchants in Surat are supposed to have had fortunes of R 5 million to R 8 million (Habib 1969, p. 72), which suggests incomes

of over R 0.5 million, equal to that of the top nobles. Fortunes of this size are unlikely under Akbar, as those of the 1660s probably were derived from a foreign trade much larger than it had been around 1600.

36. Similar comparisons cannot be made for another group whose income is known to be far above the average, the zamindars. While their total net income has been put at about R 20 million or about 3 percent of the total, their number is not known. The only indication of their density that has been found – 70 per pargana in 7 parganas in Bengal in the late eighteenth century (Cohn, p. 96) – would lead to an estimate of a total number of about 200,000 or not much over two villages per zamindar. This is likely to be much too high a figure for the entire empire during Akbar's reign as it would imply an average net income of only about R 100 per zamindar equal to only six times the average income of a peasant household.

37. Lindert and Williamson, p. 393. In the absence of income tax the share was the same on a net and a gross basis.

38. Derived from Government of India 1977–78, p. 448; 1979, p. 365; International Monetary Fund 1983, p. 275.

39. Phelps-Brown and Hopkins, p. 11, on basis of a work year of 300 days.

40. U.S. Bureau of Commerce 1983, pp. 133, 265; *U.N. Demographic Yearbook*, 1983, 744 for number of households.

41. U.S. Bureau of Commerce 1982–83, p. 256, and information from Internal Revenue Service.

42. The main sources are Habib 1960 and 1982 (Chapter XII of Raychaudhuri and Habib); Blochmann, p. 31.

43. Most of the coins existed in several types. As a result there were in circulation during Akbar's reign at one time or another nearly 50 types of gold coins, 125 types of silver coins, and well over 200 types of copper coins (Jain, p. 13).

44. For accounting purposes the dam was divided into 25 jetals, but no coins of this denomination were minted.

45. The average of a range of 2,300 to 4,480 cowries per rupee (Jain, p. 11), which is close to an estimate of 3,200 cowries per rupee as a standard (Sircar, p. 282). Two other estimates give ranges of 4,000 to 4,800 and 4,800 to 5,200 cowries per rupee (Mukherjee, p. 38), although Tavernier in the 1630s reported a range of 2,300 to 4,500.

46. Moreland 1920, p. 240. At Akbar's death his treasure is supposed to have contained R 98 million of gold coins in heavy special issues plus uncoined gold of possibly about equal value (de Laet, p. 107), together equal to as much as one-third of a year's national product.

47. Blochmann (p. 21) lists 26 gold coins of different denominations and shapes, down to one of 1/32 of a mohur and hence weighing only about one-third of a gram.

48. Compare the listing of the gold coins in Akbar's and Jahangir's treasure (de Laet, pp. 107, 109).

49. Hasan 1979, p. 101; it is not clear from the chart nor explained in the

text what the basis of the index of currency in circulation is, nor whether it is limited to silver coins.

50. A parallelism between silver production in Peru and the minting of Indian silver coins has been asserted (Hasan 1969, 1970) and denied (Prakash and Krishnamurty).

51. The price level has been estimated to have about doubled between 1595 and 1660 (Habib 1982, pp. 375–6). The information of price movements during the seventeenth century is insufficient for a confident statement about the size and rhythm of the undoubtedly substantial rise.

52. The figures about the coins in the emperor's treasure have some relevance to the size of the stock of precious metals in Mughal India. At Akbar's death his treasure is reported (de Laet, pp. 107–108; figures still used by Aziz, p. 29, in 1972) to have contained R 98 million in gold coins, all in large-size special issues, and R 100 million in silver, obviously a rounded and therefore suspect figure, apparently in standard rupee coins. The total (excluding uncoined gold) would have represented about 8 years of the emperor's gross or about 40 years of his net income. It is, therefore, likely that either the reported amounts are exaggerated and/or that part, if not most, of the treasure represented not the emperor's current saving but was the result of booty, of the escheat of the estates of nobles and others, and of more or less voluntary gifts. Therefore, neither item can be used as a basis of an estimate of the coins in circulation, but provides a minimum for the amounts of the hoards of both metals, which must have been several times as large as the emperor's holdings of about 120 tons of gold and 1,100 tons of silver. In 1835 India's gold stock has been estimated at about 440 tons (Prakash, p. 286). Around 1600 the absolute amount must have been smaller but probably not very much so. At, say, 300 tons it would have been worth R 250 million or nearly two-fifths of a year's national product. (In 1860 a gold stock of about 650 tons or R 585 million was equal to nearly 10 percent of national product. A substantial decrease in the ratio between 1600 and 1860 is not unreasonable.)

In the case of silver the 1,100 tons left by Akbar compared with a silver equivalent of about 2,750 tons of the coin supposedly in circulation and a total stock of India in 1835 of about 4,200 tons (Prakash, p. 286). These figures suggest that the estimates of both Akbar's treasure and of silver coins in circulation may be substantially exaggerated.

53. This is the most commonly quoted rate – it was used by the East India Company as late as 1651 – but rates between 24 and 33 pence are found in contemporary reports (Mukherjee, pp. 29–30).

54. On *hundis* compare Habib 1963, p. 70; 1982, pp. 362–3; Jain, p. 14; Raychaudhuri 1982, pp. 346–7. Habib's article on *hundis* in *Proceedings of the Indian Historical Congress 1972* was not accessible.

55. Jain, p. 11, citing Tavernier. Since the average village had less than 50 families and most of them had only a few dozen, moneylending must often have been combined with other activities.

56. The main source on financial establishments are Habib 1960, 1964, and Jain, pp. 11ff.
57. "It is likely that the peasant indebtedness in Mughal India was more widespread than has hitherto been supposed" (Habib 1963, p. 43).
58. Raychaudhuri 1982, Chapter XI, for detailed description of commodities traded and trade routes.
59. "Long-distance trade . . . was backed by an exceptionally well-developed system of finance and credit" (Habib 1963, p. 69).
60. Thus "exchange accounted for a relatively small proportion of economic activity" – and this includes local market activities – but nevertheless "exchange of foods, found at virtually every level and sphere of economic life, was impressive in its magnitude and complexity" (Raychaudhuri, 1982, p. 325).
61. Chaudhuri 1963, p. 25, assuming imports of commodities from India to have been equal to the company's export of bullion and merchandise to India.
62. For detailed descriptions, particularly of the land tax administration, compare primarily Moreland (1929), Habib (1963 and 1982, Chapter IX), and Siddiqui. Shorter discussions can be found in practically every study of the economic history of the Mughal Empire. A good part of the *Ain-i-Akbari* is a detailed instruction manual for revenue officers rather than a description of actual practices. The subject is so complex, and some of its features are so far from known in quantitative terms, that only a summary of its main aspects can be presented here.
63. de Laet (p. 113), who asserts that the nobles "very rarely" provided the number of troops they were supposed to keep.
64. On the zamindars' activities compare Habib, 1963, Chapter V; 1982, 244ff; Hasan; Moosvi 1978; Moreland 1929, Chapter IV.4; Siddiqui, Chapter II.
65. The number of the troops maintained by the zamindars was reported in the *Ain* as 4.4 million footsoldiers and 0.3 million cavalrymen, probably scheduled strength well above actual numbers. That these figures cannot have referred to full-time soldiers is evident from the fact that on the basis of a monthly pay of R 2.5 for footsoldiers – 60 percent above the wage of a common laborer – and of R 25 for cavalrymen, as estimated by Moosvi (1978, p. 363), their annual pay would have amounted to about R 220 million, or more than twice the total land tax revenue, about nine times zamindars' total gross income, and about one-third of gross national product. The fact that their supposed number was equal to about one-fourth of the heads of agricultural households is another evidence for their short-term service. These men obviously served and were paid for only a small part of the year – certainly less than one month – and were recruited from the ranks of the peasants and constituted a rural gendarmerie (the translation by the German term *Landwehr* by Blochmann is suggestive) rather than a body of trained fighting men. Their military value must have been very low.

66. The figures for assessed land are incompatible with those for total area in Table 7-1 for two small provinces, Awadh and Kandesh. In the case of Awadh the assessed area estimated on the basis of the ratio of measured to unmeasured villages reported for the mid-seventeenth century of 71,000 km$^2$ is slightly in excess of the total area of 69,000, while it would be expected to be somewhat below the total area. The difference is, however, small enough to be explained by the application of the average area of the 34,000 measured villages to the 19,000 unmeasured ones. In Kandesh the estimated assessed area of 47,000 km$^2$ is, however, so far in excess of the total area of 20,000 km$^2$, which is fairly accurately known that the difference cannot well be explained by the application of the average assessed area of the reasonable value of 7.5 km$^2$ of the 2,832 measured to the 3,507 unmeasured villages. The difference must therefore remain unresolved. (A change in the boundaries of the province between 1595 and the mid-seventeenth century is a possibility.) Fortunately it is so small in comparison to the totals for the empire that it cannot significantly affect any of the conclusions.

67. Compare Habib 1963, pp. 243ff, for other rural revenues. On customs and transit duties Moreland 1920, pp. 43ff.

68. On escheat compare Sarkar, pp. 44–57.

69. On the basis of 5,000 ladies average daily expenditures per head would have been R 6, as suggested somewhat overestimated, equal to the wages of 120 common laborers. Harem ladies of the highest rank are reported by Abul Fazl, who should have known, to have had an expense allowance of from R 1,028 to 1,610 per month, that is, about R 12,300 to R 19,300 per year, the wages of about 8,200 to 12,900 common laborers "not counting the presents, which his Majesty most generously bestows" (Blochmann, p. 44).

## Chapter 8

1. In contrast to the other chapters in this one only a minority of the relevant sources could be used as most of the numerous books and particularly articles that deal entirely or in part with all or with aspects of the financial system of the Tokugawa period, and in particular with the first half of the seventeenth century, that have been published during the last two to three decades are available only in Japanese and have as yet not been assimilated into publications in Western languages. A review of recent publications on Japanese economic history (Yonekawa) lists 151 items of which about two dozen deal, entirely or in part, with the Tokugawa period, but they are all in Japanese.

2. The closing sentences of an article published over two decades ago by the scholar who has probably dealt with these problems more intensively than any other in Western languages seem still valid: "Unfortunately, insufficient statistical material is now available on prices, incomes and the way in which incomes were spent to make possible a quantitative analysis of

these effects in the seventeenth century. Neither is it possible to assess quantitatively the relation of the credit system and money market to such factors as the price of rice, government financial policy, foreign trade or increasing indebtedness of the han," (Crawcour, 1961 pp. 359–60). If not for a specialist, how much less for an amateur! Unfortunately, the estimates of different specialists about different crucial magnitudes and their interpretation also continue to vary greatly.

3. The necessary evidence and references will be presented in the sections dealing with the different subjects.

4. The degree and progress of monetization during the first half of the seventeenth century appears to be still in dispute among the specialists.

5. These are the estimates of Rozman (p. 285) and McEvedy and Jones, particularly p. 181. An estimate of Hayami of 12.3 million (cited Hanley and Yamamura 1977, p. 44) is improbably low as it would imply an increase by about 16 million or nearly 0.7 percent per year between 1600 and 1721 when the first census was taken by the Tokugawa government compared to a rate of 0.16 percent between 1721 and 1872. Another estimate of 18 million for 1573–91 (Yoshida, cited Ishii, p. 4) implies a figure of about 20 million for 1600. It is difficult to understand three other estimates (cited Yamamura 1981, p. 336) of annual growth rates between 1600 and 1750 of 0.78, 0.96, and 1.34 percent since they imply for 1600 population totals of only 7.4, 4.2, and 3.2 million, respectively, starting from a generally accepted figure of about 30 million in 1750.

6. In the 1880s the share of the cultivated land was 12 percent (Bank of Japan, p. 18).

7. As late as 1878, 81 percent of the gainfully occupied population was allocated to agriculture and forestry in Ohkawa's estimate (Bank of Japan, p. 56).

8. Four estimates are 5 to 6 percent (Fuji Bank, p. 21); 6 to 7 percent (Hirschmeier and Yui, p. 14); 5 to 8 percent (Nakamura, p. 273); and 7 to 10 percent (Hanley and Yamamura 1977, p. 45), an average of nearly 7 percent.

9. On the economic situation of the samurai compare Yamamura 1974.

10. The growing role of the merchants is one of the economic features of the Tokugawa regime covered in detail in the literature in Western languages, compare, for example, Crawcour; Hirschmeier and Yui; Hauser; Honjo; Sheldon; and Toyoda.

11. Based on Rozman's estimate (p. 78) of 7 million families for Japan.

12. Rozman (p. 46), similarly McClain (p. 1) "Japan's urban growth between 1580 and 1700 constituted one of the most extraordinary periods of urban development in world history."

13. On *sankin-kotai* compare Tsukahira.

14. For population of a number of individual cities compare Smith 1969, p. 67; for Kanazawa, McClain, p. 73.

15. Data for 1898 are based on Bank of Japan, p. 14.

16. The only relevant information that has come to attention is that in 1633

a daimyo with a revenue of 100,000 kokus had to mobilize, if required, nearly 3,000 warriors (Sansome 1815–67, p. 26), or one for about each 35 koku of revenue. Since the average remuneration of a warrior, which had also to sustain his family, can hardly have been less than 10 koku a year, the remuneration of 3,000 men would have required about 30,000 koku or nearly one-third of the daimyo's gross income.

17. Norman's estimate (p. 13) is 28 or 29 million koku, without specifying the date or whether this figure included the rice equivalent of other grains.

18. It has sometimes been asserted that actual yields were somewhat above assessed yields. This, if true, need not have substantially affected the size distribution measured by assessed yields.

19. Sansome, p. 4. It is assumed that these holdings explain the difference between 8.5 million koku ascribed to Tokugawa family and the 6.4 million koku of Ieuasu's direct holdings.

20. Iwahashi (pp. 239, 274) for wholesale prices.

21. In analogy to other premodern societies, for example, Rome, Chapter 4.

22. Hanley and Yamamura (p. 70) assert that the growth rate for 1645–1873 was "undoubtedly" higher than 0.12 percent.

23. On Tokugawa coinage cf. for example, Fuji Bank, pp. 4–5; Sakudo, 1956; Shinjo, pp. 5–7; Toyoda, ch. 4.

24. Two exceptions that have been encountered are a figure of 1.5 ryos per year for agricultural day laborers around 1640 (Smith 1959, pp. 121–22), which may not include their food and probably is lower than either wages of urban workers or the earnings of farmers; and a government edict of 1657 fixing wages in Edo at 3 momme, equal to 0.05 ryo per day excluding meals worth 1.2 momme. That would be equivalent for a working year of 250 days to 12.5 ryo, a rather astonishingly high figure though certainly above the country average.

25. This section is based essentially on Crawcour 1961; compare also Hirschmeier and Hui, Chapter 1.

26. On pawnbrokers compare, for example, Sheldon, p. 70 and Toyoda, p. 85.

27. Though overall estimates are impossible, some idea of the orders of magnitude involved may be obtained from the loans made by one of the Big Ten bankers near the end of the seventeenth century of about 0.1 million ryo. If this is regarded as representative of the Big Ten and it is assumed that loans constituted as little as one-half of total assets and liberal allowance is made for the assets of the smaller bankers, the unduplicated total for all banks could hardly have exceeded 3 million ryo, then possibly 5 percent of national product, though a higher ratio of monetized national product. The ratio would, of course, have been considerably lower in the early Tokugawa period.

28. The most detailed description of agricultural improvements in 1550–1650 (Yamamura 1981) says little about the methods of financing.

29. On land tax, Smith 1968, and Totman, Chapter VI. The shogun's lands were concentrated in southeast Honshu (Totman, p. 71).

30. On kandaka compare, for example, Nagahara, pp. 58–9, and Wakita, passim.
31. The kandaka system has been called "one of the most remarkable land tax systems in history," (Hall 1981, p. 222).
32. In the later Tokugawa period cost of residence in Edo and elaborate processions to and from Edo has been estimated at about one-half of daimyo's income and hence "ruinous" (Tsukahira, pp. 97, 103).

## Chapter 9

1. This chapter, as any description of the financial system of fifteenth century Florence, could not have been written without four studies published during the past two decades: de Roover's *The Rise and Decline of the Medici Bank, 1397–1494* of 1963, Molho's *Florentine Public Finances in the Early Renaissance, 1400–1433* of 1971, Herlihy and Klapisch-Zuber's *Les Toscans et leurs Familles* of 1978, and Goldthwaite's *The Building of Florence* of 1980. The numerous references to these studies will indicate how much this chapter has had to rely on them.
2. The *catasto* of 1427 – apparently strongly influenced by Venetian practice – represented an administrative rather than a substantive reform of the property levy. It substituted a detailed property inventory, well-defined methods of valuation, and a uniform flat rate of tax of 0.5 percent for the previous lump-sum assessments (*stime*) by tax officials, whose arbitrariness and inequality had been the subject of many complaints and were retained for only very small fortunes. In the words of Macchiavelli "the law rather than men decided on the levy's distribution" ("avendola pertanto a distribuire la legge e non gli uomini"; p. 202). Nevertheless, the size distribution of the top wealth holders as well as the distribution among the four sections (*quartieri*) of the city are very similar in the levies of 1409 under the old and in that of 1427 under the new system (based on data of 600 individual top wealth holders shown in Martines, pp. 353ff). Evidence that before 1427 the assessments were judgmental rather than statistical is the fact that most of them were in round florins as shown in the list of the 150 highest taxpayers in each of the four *quartieri* in 1409 (Martines, pp. 353ff). Thus in the S. Croce quarter of the 150 highest assessments all but 31 were in round florins – from f 4 to f 199. Notwithstanding these features the *catasto* was abolished after less than two decades of operation.
3. Based on population of 7 million in 1400 (McEvedy and Jones, p. 107).
4. Lopez and Miskimin, p. 419; Hoshino, cited in Goldthwaite 1980, p. 61; and Brucker 1983b, p. 606.
5. The capital of the Peruzzi has been put at about f 105,000 in 1310 (Lopez and Miskimin, p. 1424) and that of the Bardi was probably somewhat larger (Sapori 1926, p. 74) compared to that of the Medici bank of f 40,000 in 1427 (Table 9-6). The Medici bank had 60 employees in 1469 compared to 95 in 1336 of the Peruzzi.

6. The minimum additions to the population of Florence reported in the *catasto* are about 1,100 monks and nuns and about 500 transients (Herlihy and Klapisch-Zuber, pp. 60, 142, 157) bringing the total to 39,000. Even an unusually small undercount would raise the actual population to over 40,000. For the Republic as a whole the undercount has been estimated at one-tenth (Conti, cited in Herlihy and Klapisch-Zuber, p. 162) bringing its total population to 290,000. This is likely to be on the low side since the population of the countryside not covered by the *catasto* has been estimated at 20,000 to 25,000 or 9 to 12 percent of the population outside Florence enumerated in the *catasto* (Herlihy and Klapisch-Zuber, p. 140) and there were 10,000 to 11,000 ecclesiastics who are likely to have escaped inclusion in the *catasto* (Herlihy and Klapisch-Zuber, p. 160). Thus estimates of 40,000 people for Florence and of 300,000 for the Republic should be considered as minimal, though not substantially below the most likely accurate figures. The considerably higher estimates of Pardi (p. 731) of 62,000 as the "effective population" of Florence in 1427, published nearly 70 years ago, which assumes that 25,000 poor, who did not pay taxes, were omitted from the *catasto*, apparently have not been accepted by any later estimator.

7. For a detailed discussion of these questions compare Herlihy and Klapisch-Zuber, Chapters XI, XV, and XVI.

8. The rather complicated details of the levy are described in varying detail in Canestrini, de Roover 1963, Herlihy and Klapisch-Zuber, and Molho 1971. The Latin text of the law is reprinted in Karmin.

9. For level of wages compare Goldthwaite 1980, pp. 436–8.

10. The salaries of the middle-level government officials specified in the commune's budget for 1401 were, of course, higher (Molho 1971, pp. 200ff); thus notaries were paid f 48 to f 72 per year and the first cashier of the finance department as well as accountants f 72. On the other hand retirement pay for civil servants (Molho 1971, p. 208) was low, ranging from f 6 to f 24 a year indicating that at least the upper boundary was regarded as sufficient to provide a minimum of existence for a family. The low level of domestics' salaries of about f 15 per year (Herlihy and Klapisch-Zuber, p. 258) reflects the fact that their housing and food were provided to their employees.

11. In Pistoia annual wages averaged f 9 to f 12 a year in 1417–24 (Herlihy 1967, p. 150), which would be only about one-third of the wages of unskilled workers in Florence. On the other hand the f 10 for a servant girl were of the order of two-thirds of the Florentine level.

12. For England and Wales in 1688 the share of wages in national product may be estimated at about 30 percent (derived from Lindert and Williamson's revisions of Gregory King's estimates, p. 393).

13. Most authorities agree on the poverty and low standard of living in the Florentine countryside in the fifteenth century, summarized in a chapter entitled "Un mondo di povere cose" in a detailed description (Mazzi and Ravaggi, p. 199). The consumption of the poorest but very numerous

class, the *mezzadri* (tenants on half rents), was well below f 25 per family and probably on the order of only f 2 to f 3 per person. This may be inferred from the share of families with consumption of below f 25, which ranged from 63 to 92 percent in these small samples for various dates in the fifteenth century (Kotelnikova, p. 99).

14. Wages and wheat prices were not substantially different around 1480 from what they were in the 1420s (Goldthwaite 1980, pp. 318–19).

15. Herlihy and Klapisch-Zuber, p. 243, assuming that most of the total wealth of the inhabitants of the countryside but only a minority of the real estate owned by city dwellers was attributable to agriculture.

16. It has been estimated that in 1409 about one-eighth of the land in the *distritto* was owned by citizens of Florence (Herlihy and Klapisch-Zuber, p. 246) and the ratio was probably higher in the *contado* nearer to Florence. In S. Gimigniano in 1419 Florentine residents owned 17 of 395 properties, which accounted for 12 percent of the total crop (Fiumi 1965). An indication of absentee ownership in the Republic is given by the fact that in a sample of 16,000 agriculturalists (Herlihy and Klapisch-Zuber, p. 288) 55 percent were tenants. Residents of Florence probably constituted a substantial proportion of the landlords.

17. A contemporary radical put the share of ecclesiastical property at one-fifth to one-fourth (cited Molho 1971, p. 57), which would be equal to one-fourth to one-third of the property of laics. This estimate, which probably refers to real property only, may be regarded as an upper limit. In S. Gimigniano and in Prato the share of church property has been estimated at over one-fourth of the total (Fiumi, cited Herlihy and Klapisch-Zuber, p. 244) or over one-third of the real property of laics.

18. Livestock was included in real property, apparently at low value (Herlihy and Klapisch-Zuber, p. 57).

19. A house valued at f 1,200 and household goods of f 800 in a total estate of slightly over f 7,000 in 1425 (Simone Strozzi, Goldthwaite 1968, p. 40) was, of course, atypical except for possibly a few dozens of families, not only as to its absolute value, but also in the ratio of content to structure value. Upper-middle-class residences such as that of the humanist Matteo Palmieri seem to have had a value of a few hundred florins (Molho 1971, p. 95). The painter Benozzo Gozzoli rented a house, supposedly a middle-class habitation, for f 13 a year (Goldthwaite 1980, p. 307) suggesting a value of f 100 to f 150. The value of working men's houses was very small, certainly well below f 100 and probably as low as f 50 as indicated by rents generally between f 2.5 and f 5 in a sample with a median of about f 5 (Goldthwaite 1980, p. 343).

20. Gregory King estimated the value of "money, plate, jewels and household goods" in England and Wales in 1688 at £ 28 million (Barnett, p. 32), equal to £5 per head or 60 percent of national product per head (Lindert and Williamson, p. 393). Deducting coins valued at £17.3 million (Barnett, p. 34), the other items come to about £17 million or £3 per head or nearly one-third of national product. Applied to the Florentine Republic

these figures correspond on the basis of the price of gold to about f 5 per head, or f 1.5 million for the Republic, or on the national product basis to f 1.0 million.

21. In England and Wales in 1688 inventories have been estimated at fully one-tenth of national wealth and about one-third of national product. The ratios to national product were somewhat higher in France in 1815, Germany in 1850, and Japan in 1885, but lower in relation to national wealth (Goldsmith 1985, Tables A5, A6, A7, and A13).

22. Compare advice of a Florentine citizen to his family to overstate debt in *catasto* (Herlihy and Klapisch-Zuber, p. 259).

23. Herlihy and Klapisch-Zuber, p. 250. It has been argued (communication from Professor Goldthwaite) that concentration was considerably less because of the omission of assets of many poor from the *catasto* and that it declined after 1427 because of the fall in the price of Monte credits.

24. The largest Florentine fortune in the mid-fifteenth century, and also one of the largest in Europe (Brucker 1983, p. 87), that of Cosimo de' Medici, may have been as large as f 300,000 – about one-tenth of the Republic's national product and over one percent of its total wealth – as he left about f 230,000 at his death in 1464, which was considerably smaller than what it had been at its peak. (Fryde, p. 457).

25. Such distinctions might well appear if *catasto* data were available for each of the 16 gonfalonieri and for the more numerous parishes (cf. list in Herlihy and Klapisch-Zuber, p. 123).

26. About two decades earlier – in 1409 – the distribution of the annual net wealth of the top 150 wealth holders in each quarter (derived from the data on individuals assessed in Martines, pp. 353ff) was about the same (S. Croce 24 against 20 percent; S. Giovanni 35 against 34 percent; Santa Maria Novella 20 against 21 percent; and S. Spirito 21 against 25 percent) notwithstanding the different methods of assessment in the two years.

27. Herlihy and Klapisch-Zuber, p. 299. The figures are of limited value because nearly one-half of taxpayers were not identified as to occupation.

28. The value of slaves was not included in the *catasto* (Herlihy and Klapisch-Zuber, p. 60), but the amounts involved were apparently not large enough to affect substantially the amount, the structure, or the size distribution of wealth. Although no estimate of the number of slaves – mostly female – has been found, it seems not to have been above a few hundred (suggested by Herlihy and Klapisch-Zuber, pp. 142, 339), practically all owned by the top wealth holders (Origo, p. 327). The average slave price has been estimated at f 65 to f 75 for the first half of the fifteenth century by one source (Origo, p. 337), but at only f 40 by another (Ashtor, p. 502), equal to 1.5 to 2.5 years' wage of an unskilled worker. In either case their aggregate value would be very small – not above f 25,000 or hardly 0.1 percent of total wealth. The assertions of Origo (pp. 321, 323) that "every noble or prosperous merchant had at least two or three" and that slaves "came to form a sufficiently large proportion of the population to affect the Tuscan stock" suggest much higher figures, but the author does not

offer an estimate of their number. To constitute even one percent of the wealth of the city, the number of slaves would have had to exceed 2,000 or 100 percent of the entire female population. Any figure of this order would have to include former slaves and their free descendants.

29. For a detailed description of the monetary system, not including an estimate of the volume of money in circulation in the fourteenth century, which essentially still applies to the first half of the fifteenth century, compare de la Roncière 1974, p. 504ff.

30. Florence had in Knapp's terminology (pp. 77–78) hylolepsy, that is, the government stood ready to return a fixed number of gold or silver coins for a pound of each monetary metal after deduction of seignorage, small (about 0.5 percent) for florins but substantial for silver coins (Bernocchi, vol. III, pp. 39–40), but did not practice hylophantism, that is, did not redeem gold or silver coins for fixed quantities of metal.

31. This practice may have been copied from the Islamic world where sealed bags of coins were known early (G.C. Miles in *Encyclopaedia of Islam*, vol. II, p. 305).

32. Money changers were taxed at a rate of 2.5 percent of their transactions.

33. The two contemporary estimates that have been found unfortunately lead to very different results. The first (Goldthwaite 1980, p. 316) puts coin in circulation at f 150,000. Even if this figure refers, as is likely, only to the city of Florence, it could hardly lead to an estimate for the Republic of over f 250,000, which implies the extremely high (indeed impossible) value of about 12 for the income velocity of circulation. The second estimate, made by a banker in his memoirs (Giovanni Ruccellai, cited Molho 1971, p. 5) asserts that around 1420 "merchants held about f 2 million in money and commodities," that is, inventories. As the ratio between the two components is not known and the estimate again probably refers to the city of Florence only, it is not clear what money stock for the Republic it implies. If one assumes that the share of Florence was in excess of that in personal income, that is, was on the order of two-thirds, and that inventories were on the order of f 1.5 million (cf Section 3), the money stock of the Republic would have been about f 1.5 million, implying a very low income velocity of about approximately two per year.

34. Mint statistics, which have been preserved for about half of the years between 1345 and 1451 (Day, p. 26), indicate a total coinage of f 4.27 million of gold and of 32.3 ton of silver or about f 0.84 million for the 51 and 41 years, respectively, for which they are reported. If it is assumed that the years in which the value of coinage was reported are representative for the period as a whole, total for the 1345 to 1451 period would be about f 9.0 million of gold and f 2.2 million of silver. Neither of these sets of figures can be regarded as a measure of the money stock in the mid-1400s – indeed they are certainly much too high, particularly for gold coin – because the stock of 1350, when the florin was at the height of its role as an international currency, is unknown, as are the losses through wear and tear, the amounts of foreign coins in circulation, and, most importantly, the net balance with the rest of the world.

35. The third approach starts from the difference between the *catasto* values for financial assets excluding claims against the Monte and of deductions, presumably mainly debts, of f 1.15 (Table 9-3), which might be on the order of f 2 to f 3 million if account is taken of the understatement of the claims of probably not less than one-third and the overstatement of debts. This difference corresponds conceptually to the value of the capitalized true business profits less the holdings of coins. It would easily accommodate an estimate of coins of f 1.0 to f 1.5 million.

36. A final, admittedly hazardous, approach is the use of estimates of the value of money in circulation per head in other countries and at other dates in terms of gold or of the relation of the stock of money to national product or national wealth. The rough estimates of King for the end of the seventeenth century put coins in circulation per head at £ 2.10 for England and Wales, at £ 1.15 for France, £ 3.50 for Holland, and £ 1.20 for Europe (Barnett, p. 34). On the basis of gold content these figures correspond to approximately f 1.85, f 1.00, f 3.10, and f 1.05 per head, and on the basis of 300,000 inhabitants of the Republic to f 0.56, f 0.30, f 0.93, and f 0.32 million, implying income velocities of circulation of about 5.4, 10.0, 3.2, and 9.4.

37. In estimating the effective volume of the money stock, consideration should be given to the use of Monte credits in making payments, the extent of which is unknown.

38. The relative modernity of fifteenth century Florentine banking has been particularly championed by Melis (1966–67, p. 105; "in the second half of the 14th century there became solidly established banks with truly modern characteristics and functions").

39. That the share was high is suggested by the fact that of f 437,000 lent in 1430–32 to one of the organizations of the commune by 11 banking houses, 35 percent were supplied by Cosimo de' Medici and his son Lorenzo. The Pazzi were second with 14 percent, followed by the Strozzi and the della Luna with 8 percent each and by seven others with 5 percent each (Molho 1971, p. 181).

40. The operations have been classified in detail by de Roover 1963 (cf., e.g., Chapter VI).

41. de Roover 1963, p. 121, Luzzatto, p. 390. Homer, gives for "Italy" a range of rates of short-term commercial loans from 5 to 15 percent (p. 110; for his sources cf. p. 602).

42. With the present information, reflected in Table 9-8, it is not possible to construct a satisfactory comprehensive picture of the finances of the Florentine Republic. In particular the figures indicate a deficit, which would have had to be filled essentially by short-term borrowing for which no data exist, of a size difficult to reconcile with other information. There is no doubt, however, that the financial situation of the Republic became critical in the late 1420s.

43. In the early fifteenth century a platoon of three mercenaries was paid between f 12 and f 15 per month, that is, between f 4 and f 5 per man (Molho 1971, p. 46) or approximately the same as a skilled workman

(Goldthwaite 1980, p. 437). If it is assumed that all of the Republic's military expenditures of f 450,000 to f 600,000 in years of hostilities (Molho 1971, p. 61) went for mercenaries' pay, a ratio which cannot be far from the truth, and that they went to pay between 12,000 and 19,000 men (Molho 1971, pp. 13–14), the average annual pay would have been between f 30 and f 40 per mercenary, that is, between six and eight months' wages of a skilled workman, which suggests that they served for only part of the year. The condottieri themselves received between f 30,000 and over f 100,000 per year (Molho 1971, p. 17), well above the income of any citizen – and several times the profit of the Medici bank (Table 9-8) – and on the order of fully 1 to 3 percent of the entire personal income in the Republic.

44. By chance the revenues of the Florentine Republic in the early fifteenth century can be compared with those of the Venetian Republic. Around 1420 the revenue of the Venetian Republic (including *terra firma*) were put in Doge Mocenigo's testament (Braudel, pp. 97–8; Kretschmayr, vol. II, pp. 317–19) at 1.62 million ducats for a population of 1.5 million or about 1.1 ducats per head, equivalent to nearly f 0.7 per head. In contrast the annual revenues of the Florentine Republic per head during the first three decades of the fifteenth century were close to f 3. Even if income per head should have been somewhat lower in the Venetian Republic, it is evident that fiscal pressure was much heavier in the Florentine Republic, nearly one-third of national product against probably not more than one-tenth in the Venetian Republic, in part probably because of the income the latter derived from its colonial empire.

45. Military expenditures of the United Kingdom during the 1794–1815 period, one of the longest periods of substantial hostilities before World War I, averaged about 15 percent of the country's gross national product (Mitchell and Deane, pp. 366, 391, 396). Braudel (p. 263) concluded that in pre-industrial societies government expenditures ranged between 5 and 10 percent of national product – one-fifth to two-fifths of the Florentine ratio – and characterizes the Venetian ratio of 14 to 16 percent at the end of the sixteenth century as "une pression fiscale énorme pour l'époque" (p. 264).

46. Among the evidence of the relative, and probably also the absolute, impoverishment of the countryside is the reduction of its share in government revenue from about one-fourth around 1330 to 10 to 15 percent in the 1430s (Molho 1971, p. 45). To what extent a reported decline in the assessed value of property in the Florentine countryside between 1404 and 1427 by about 50 percent (Becker) reflects real impoverishment or changes in methods of assessment is not clear.

47. For example from 1427 through 1431 33 *prestanze* were levied, (Becker 1965, p. 465) implying assessments of 16.5 percent of wealth, and hence well over 100 percent of property income, though collections were somewhat smaller, in 1423–24 about four-fifths of assessments (Molho 1971, p. 87) though they rose above 90 percent for a few years after the introduction of the *catasto* (Herlihy and Klapisch-Zuber, p. 43).

48. These figures are derived from reported figures for 15 years of the period (Molho 1971, p. 62) and interprolations for the remaining 12 years.

49. Canestrini (p. 151), for city of Florence. About one-half of families were assessed small amounts and one-fourth paid only a very small head tax on adult males.

50. It has been asserted that from the late fourteenth century on the Monte was "the central financial institution of the Republic" (Marks, p. 131) and the "Monte and its management became the single most important economic determinant of public policy" (Becker 1968, p. 161).

51. Cipolla, p. 87; other authors give somewhat different figures, for example, Molho 1971, pp. 71–73.

52. In general claims against the Monte were assessed at 50 percent of their face value, but some issues at 60 or 70 percent (cf. Herlihy and Klapisch-Zuber, p. 645), which seems to be higher than the market price which appears to have been only slightly above one-third from 1380 to 1430 (Becker 1965, p. 455), a level recognized in the second *catasto*.

53. Few foreign creditors were in the position of Pope Eugene IV who, when payments on his large and high-yielding substantial holdings in the Monte acquired in 1432 from the estate of his predecessor Martin V became irregular, was able in 1447 to force full service by measures his Holiness took against Florentine citizens in Rome, including the Florentine ambassador, and their property (Kirschner, pp. 344ff).

54. Becker 1968, p. 158, "by the 1350s virtually every Florentine active in public affairs was a large shareholder in the Monte" and by 1427 the amounts held must have been substantially larger.

## Chapter 10

1. In contrast to the situation in most other chapters, the problem in this one is the plethora of relevant literature. There are literally hundreds of books and articles that deal, in their entirety or in part, with the subjects discussed in this chapter. No one but a specialist in Tudor economic history could have absorbed them. The best that can be hoped for is that no important relevant quantitative information has been missed. In general attention has been limited to publications of the last half-century. The main single source used is the most recent, most detailed, and fortunately numerate study by Palliser, particularly Chapters 2 to 10.

2. The title of Dickson's well-known study published in 1967.

3. This section is mainly based on Wrigley and Schofield, particularly p. 528. As a result of this recent study, more is known, or supposed to be known, about the demography of Elizabethan England than about that of any other country before at least the eighteenth century.

4. Gregg, p. 203. The map refers to 1701, but the situation should have been similar a century earlier.

5. Palliser, pp. 217–18. In 1665, according to the hearth tax returns, 60 provincial towns had an average population of 6,000 to 7,000 (Everitt, p. 479), or a total of about 400,000. The figure for 1600 should not have

been much smaller, equal to over 10 percent of the country's population or including London to close to 20 percent.

6. In 1568 the number of foreigners in London was put at nearly 7,000, or possibly 5 percent of the population, mostly Netherlanders. Their share of about one-third of the population of Norwich of nearly 20,000 was undoubtedly unusually high even for substantial cities (Palliser, p. 57).

7. If the total of groups I, II, and IV is assigned to the rural population, their shares in households and in income would be 63 and 49 percent, respectively, to which part of group III would have to be added.

8. The ratios are medians derived from data for Chester, Coventry, Leicester, Northampton, Norwich, Worcester, and York (Clarkson, pp. 88–89).

9. A recent estimate puts the increase in per head real national product at slightly above 0.3 percent per year for the periods 1700 to 1740 and 1740 to 1780 (Cole, p. 64). It is unlikely that the rate would have been as high in the sixteenth or in the seventeenth century.

10. Based on £36 per pound troy (Craig, p. 414).

11. The estimate of £32 million in 1603 is closer to the upper than to the lower boundary of Lindert's wide range of £19 million to £38 million, but only 11 percent above its midpoint.

12. Pollard and Crossley, p. 155. This ratio is derived from King's total of £43.5 million. If the revised estimate of the total of £54.4 million is accepted, the share of agriculture would be 65 percent if it is assumed that the total difference between Lindert and Williamson's estimate and King's figure is attributable to agriculture and 44 percent if none of it is allocated to agriculture, two very unlikely extreme values.

13. A value in the order of three-fifths is somewhat above the average ratio for low-income countries as late as 1960 of 51 percent, but about equal to that of some important countries such as Bangladesh and Tanzania (World Bank, p. 138).

14. Lindert and Williamson's revision (p. 393) of King's estimates.

15. Using the share of 44 percent for nonagricultural incomes (Pollard and Crossley, p. 155).

16. This is the ratio derived from King's estimate (p. 31), including the stock of money, plate, and household goods, but apparently not including private buildings.

17. Since this table is based on average incomes for different occupational groups, it is not a strict ranking of individual incomes and therefore understates the degree of concentration.

18. Robert Cecil near the end of his life (died 1612) is estimated to have had a recurrent annual income of at least £25,000 (Stone 1961, p. 103), equal to nearly 0.1 percent of total personal income in England and Wales, to over eight times the average income of temporal lords around 1600, as estimated by Stone, and still over four times their level in 1688, as estimated by Lindert and Williamson, and to about 6 percent of government revenue (cf. Section 6).

19. Wilson 1925, p. 30. This compares with an estimate of an average lay

peers' rental income, which represented nearly 90 percent their total income, of £1,680 in 1559 (Stone, cited Palliser, pp. 96, 102). The difference, however, should not be interpreted by itself as indicating a more
than doubling of average income during the interval that almost spans
Elizabeth's reign. Using Stone's estimate (p. 760), the share of lay peers'
rental income of £112,000 in national product in 1559 would have been
0.8 percent, which is slightly higher than the 0.65 percent ratio implied
for 1600 in Wilson's guess but almost double Stone's estimate of £140,000
for 1602, or 0.41 percent of national product.

20. It seems inadvisable to use the ratios of wealth in 1600 and 1688 ascribed
to Davenant and King of one-fifth and three-fifths (Lipson, vol. III, p.
209) as the absolute values cited are unbelievably low and in the case of
King are far below those in Barnett, p. 32.

21. For 1603 Challis, for 1688 King.

22. Davenant's estimate, cited Sombart, vol. II, p. 1051. The price of arable
land in Norfolk and Sussex is estimated to have increased at a rate of 2.1
percent per year between the 1550s and the 1640s, and that of pasture
and meadows at rates of 0.8 and 1.3 percent, respectively (Coleman, p.
39). If these rates are applicable to the seventeenth century, they imply
rises of about 520, 100, and 210 percent, respectively, for the 1600–88
period.

23. An indication of the distribution of the moveable wealth in smaller towns
is provided by the tax assessments in 16 towns in 1524–25 (Cornwall, p.
63). They show that the 5.5 percent of households out of a total of nearly
2,300 assessed at £20 and more – apparently well below true values –
accounted for about two-fifths of the total assessed value of goods, though
the ratio varied from zero to somewhat over one-half. The 30 percent of
households assessed at from £3 to £20 owned slightly over two-fifths of
total assessed value. In contrast the nearly two-thirds of households assessed at £1 and £2 – apparently fairly arbitrary values – owned hardly
one-fifth of the total, their share ranging from 11 to 29 percent. It is not
likely that the distribution was much different half a century later, suggesting a Gini ratio of not more than one-half if the ratio of true to assessed value was not correlated to the level of the latter. Concentration
was, however, considerably more pronounced because most of the households were not assessed – in York, not included in the 16 towns, in 1546
about four in five (Palliser, p. 101). Adjusting for this omission it would
be the top 1 percent of assessees who held over one-third and the top 7
percent who held nearly four-fifths of total assessed goods – not including real estate – and the Gini ratio might have been as high as three-
fourths.

24. Compare chart in Palliser, p. 100 based on J. Sheail.

25. Schofield (p. 499) claims that there was no significant change in the regional distribution of wealth in the later sixteenth century.

26. The literature on the Great Debasement is vast; the most recent treatment is Gould.

27. On the recoinage compare, for example, Craig, pp. 119–22, Cunningham, pp. 127–37, and Feaveryear, pp. 76–87.
28. This is Craig's figure; Feaveryear implies an amount of less than £50,000.
29. Craig (p. 122) gives £14,000; Feaveryear (p. 84), £40,000.
30. Craig, pp. 414–15. The amount of silver captured from Spain has been put at £1.25 million (Craig, p. 127).
31. Challis, cited Palliser, p. 136; this amount is in line with Spooner and Challis' estimate that in normal times circulation would not be lower than the mint output of the preceding 30 years (Palliser, p. 135).
32. If Palliser's estimate that in 1603 silver circulation was 4.5 times as high as that in 1526 while gold circulation in 1603 had fallen to one-fourth that of 1526 is accepted (p. 136), and that total circulation in 1603 was £3.50 million and in 1526 was close to the level of 1544 of £1.23 million (Challis' estimates), then silver in circulation would have increased from somewhat over £0.70 million in 1526 to about £3.30 million in 1603 while gold circulation would have declined from about £0.50 million to about £0.15 million, or from about two-fifths to only one-seventh of total circulation.
33. This description of price movements follows Phelps-Brown and Hopkins' index of the price of consumables (p. 29) and Bowden (pp. 818ff) of agricultural prices.
34. The outstanding treatment is R.H. Tawney's long Introduction to Thomas Wilson's *A Discourse upon Usury* of 1572.
35. Compare article *bottomry* in Walford, vol. I.
36. This is one of the most controversial subjects in English agrarian history of the period – together with that of enclosures – opinions ranging from a virtual denial of technical progress in agriculture (e.g., Clarkson, pp. 13–14) to asserting the advent of an "agricultural revolution" (Kerridge). For a nonspecialist a position between the two extremes appears the most prudent one to take. Compare the summary in Palliser (pp. 193–201).
37. Gregory King put arable land at 11 million acres and pasture and meadows at 10 million acres in 1688 (p. 35), figures that should have been only slightly smaller in the second half of the sixteenth century. His figure is practically identical in the case of the crop area with an estimate of 11.1 million acres in 1827 (Mulhall, p. 13, citing Porter).
38. Based on Clarkson (pp. 62 ff) for areas; Lindert and Williamson (p. 393) for numbers. King's estimate for the number of agricultural units is considerably higher – about 310,000 (p. 30) – assuming as in the text that the aristocratic owners operated part of their holdings, the demesne, themselves directly or through an employee. On subtenants compare Palliser, p. 175.
39. The commonest size of tenant farms has been put at 30 to 50 acres (Coleman, p. 66) or 30 to 60 acres (Palliser, p. 173). It is not clear whether subtenants' farms are included in these figures.
40. Tawney, p. 25, proportionately distributing the 7 percent of "uncertain" holders. It is not clear whether the figures include subtenants.

41. According to the most recent estimate (Wordie, p. 502) about 45 percent of total surface area was already enclosed in 1558 and only 2 percent were added in the following half-century. For regional differences compare map in Palliser, p. 166.

42. Compare maps in Palliser (pp. 163–64 and 168–69) and description in Clarkson (pp. 45 ff), Palliser (pp. 163ff) and in more detail in Thirsk.

43. There are two main problems with these estimates. The first is the small number of tenants (including subtenants) per manor of 25 which is only half that in Tawney's small sample of 50, which may even not include subtenants. The second is the implication that only about every second of the estimated number of peers, baronets, knights, esquires, and gentlemen owned at least one manor, though it is known that many of them owned more than one. Since the estimate of total agricultural units, and even that of agricultural units in manors, cannot be too far off, it is difficult to see how a much larger number of manors can be accommodated. The numbers of manors would have been considerably higher – and their average size and number of tenants considerably and even improbably smaller – if the average of 330 manors per county (Palliser, p. 87, citing Tawney) were representative of all 50 counties in England and Wales even if the count was exhaustive for the 10 sample counties. The information now available appears to be insufficient to resolve these difficulties.

44. Although the number of manors owned by the peerage declined from about 3,400 in 1558 to 2,200 in 1602 (Stone, p. 764), their size distribution does not seem to have changed substantially. Both in 1535 (1,118 manors) and around 1600 (345 manors) the top percentile of manors accounted for 5 and 4 percent, respectively, of their aggregate value, the first decile for about 30 percent and the second decile for nearly 20 percent, leaving one-half for the remaining four-fifths of the manors covered. Among those, however, the share of the third to fifth deciles rose from fully three-fifths to over three-fourths, indicating a slight increase in concentration (derived from Stone, p. 763).

45. Tawney's study of over 600 pages of *The Agrarian Problem of the 16th century* of 1912 does not contain, by the evidence of its index, a single reference to topics such as credit, debt, or mortgages. References to credit are extremely scarce even in more recent treatments of Elizabethan agriculture such as Clarkson, Coleman, Palliser, and Thirsk. Stone has an entire 40-page chapter (IX) in *The Crisis of the Aristocracy 1558–1641*, but it deals almost exclusively with the debt of the peerage for consumptive purposes. So does Tawney's section "Needy gentlemen" (1925, pp. 31–42).

46. King (p. 32) put the value of livestock in 1688 at £25 million or 14 percent of that of agricultural land or somewhat below one-half of national income (Lindert and Williamson, p. 393). On that basis its value around 1600 would have been about £15 million.

47. These are Lindert and Williamson's estimates (p. 393), which are far above

King's of 100,000 families with income of £420 million or 7 percent of all families and 10 percent of total personal income. If Lindert and Williamson's estimates are correct, they imply that the majority of persons engaged in handicrafts and in commerce lived in rural areas since their alleged share in the population of over one-fourth is well above the total urban population of not more than one-fifth, even if small towns are included (cf. Section 1).

48. Based on share of urban wage earners (Clarkson, p. 47).
49. Postan, passim, for example, "ubiquity and variety of medieval credit" (p. 255).
50. This estimate is based on the value of London exports other than short-cloths in 1598 to 1603 of slightly over £40,000 a year (Davis, p. 53), a share of cloths in total London exports of seven-eighths (p. 52), and a share of London in total English exports of about 70 percent.
51. Based on average values of exports of £6.4 million and imports of £5.8 million in 1699 to 1701 (Davis, p. 56) and a gross national product of about £60 million, slightly above the £54 million of 1688 (Lindert and Williamson, p. 393).
52. Davis (p. 11) assumes a "modest rising tendency" of exports.
53. Lindert and Williamson (p. 393) accept King's estimates (p. 31) of the number and income of overseas merchants. However, because Lindert and Williamson's estimates of the number and income of all persons in commerce and industry are much higher than King's, the share of overseas merchants is much lower in Lindert and Williamson's estimates (2.5 and 12.3 percent) than in King's (9.1 and 36.4 percent).
54. Davis (p. 53), allowing for understatement of official statistics by one-ninth.
55. These are the ratios for London imports in 1621 (Davis, p. 55).
56. Even as late as 1621 when trade with the Levant was considerably larger than in the second half of the sixteenth century, over three-fifths of London imports came from continental Europe north of the Alps and Pyrenees. (Davis, p. 55).
57. On the organization and operations of the Merchant Adventurers, compare Friis (Chapters I and II), Lingelbach, and Palliser (pp. 281ff), and particularly for their activities in Antwerp, de Smedt.
58. Around 1617 members numbered about 3,500, who have been estimated to have constituted over one-half of all wealthy traders in the chief commercial cities. (Lingelbach, p. 20).
59. The main source for the activities of these companies is still Scott's three-volume study published in 1910–12. Compare also Clarkson, pp. 140ff. For a list of individual companies compare Scott, vol. III, pp. 462ff.
60. The source is Stone, Chapter IX.
61. There is no comprehensive study of the public finance of Elizabethan England more recent than Dietz's, now over half a century old, which specialists do not regard as always reliable and which while providing

many individual quantitative data lacks aggregative statistics or time series.

62. Revenues were £66,000 in 1559 (Dietz, p. 296).
63. Dietz (p. 383) for tax rates; Fisher (1940, p. 96) for cloth exports.
64. For methods of assessment and collection compare Dowell, pp. 151ff.
65. Stone's estimate is £140,000; for Wilson's estimate of £220,000 compare footnote 19.
66. The relation between the yields from the tax on rents and that on goods does not seem to be known. A solitary report for Gloucestershire for which less than one-third of the total was attributable to the tax on rent (Dowell, p. 156) cannot be regarded as representative, partly because Gloucestershire included Bristol, the second largest city in England.
67. Wilson, pp. 26–27. The figures are difficult to evaluate because it is not clear exactly what types of revenues are covered – the total of £124,000 apparently referring to a year shortly before 1600 is equal to about one-third of the crown's current revenues – and how the figures were obtained though the mostly unrounded amounts suggest a documentary source.
68. War expenditures from Scott, p. 527.
69. The title of P.G.M. Dickson's book.
70. No study devoted to the public debt during Elizabeth's reign has been found. The story has therefore been pieced together from occasional information in the standard sources for the economic history of the period.
71. "The Frugal Years," that is, 1572–1585, the title of Chapter II of Dietz.
72. This is the figure cited by Palliser, p. 109; Craig, p. 220 and Sombart, p. 1098, give £400,000.
73. These are the only three dates for which the information is given in Scott, pp. 510–11.
74. Goldsmith, 1985, p. 232.


## Chapter 11

1. Cf. Wallerstein; cf. critical review by Mokyr, *Journal of European Economic History*, 12, 671–3, 1983.
2. For the monetary system compare, for example, Klein 1970, p. 181; for public finance, Baasch, p. 180.
3. Densities have been estimated at 24 for the British Isles, 31 for Germany, 37 for Italy, and 38 for France (McEvedy and Jones, *passim*).
4. On the basis of a population of 0.95 million in 1500 (Maddison 1982, p. 180).
5. For 1830 Mitchell 1980, p. 74; for 1982 *Statistical Abstract* 1983, p. 33.
6. Shipping and allied trades, including shipbuilding and possibly fishing and overseas trade, have been estimated to have employed 25,000 men

in the mid-seventeenth century (Baasch, p. 160), which would have represented over one-fourth of the labor force.

7. The sharp critique of some of King's estimates for France by Leroy-Ladurie (*Annales*, 1968), suggests caution. However, King's estimate has been regarded as acceptable by a modern Dutch economic historian of the seventeenth century (Klein 1977, p. 81).

8. King estimated prices in the United Provinces to be 20 to 30 percent above those in England. The daily wage of a building laborer around 1700 was f 1.05 (deVries 1982, p. 42) compared to one of 13 d or f 0.55 in England (Phelps-Brown and Hopkins, p. 11). Contemporary observers regarded real income per head in the United Provinces as considerably higher than in any other European country without being able to quantify the difference.

9. deVries 1974, p. 194, using the estimated cost per hectar of f 200 for a 18,000-hectar polder (p. 195).

10. The estimates of some Dutch economists are, however, much higher, for example, f 1.25 billion (Klein 1970, p. 41), and nearly f 1.5 billion (Stuijvenberg, p. 107). In that case the average annual net foreign investment in the eighteenth century would have been as high as 5 to 6 percent of national product, though again considerably lower in the seventeenth century.

11. An index of agricultural rents rose between the second and the third quarter of the seventeenth century by 75 percent (deVries 1974, p. 189), and one of agricultural land prices approximately tripled between 1600 and 1650, though by 1675 it had fallen back to twice the 1600 level (Stuijvenberg, p. 220).

12. The amounts reported for the wealth tax apparently did not include gold, silver, and stocks of merchandise. These, however, are unlikely to have constituted more than a few percent of the total.

13. Even if the average wealth of the households below f 1,000 had declined from the assumed f 250 to f 200, their share in total wealth would still have increased from about one-eighth to nearly one-fifth of the total.

14. Posthumus estimated the number of households not assessed for the wealth tax, whom he calls the "propertyless" ones, at less than twice that of the assessees in The Hague, in Amsterdam at nearly four times, and in Leiden at five to six times (1939, p. 966). These ratios are difficult to reconcile with the ratio of the number of all households to that of assessees on the basis of the estimates of total population (e.g., Braudel, p. 155) and an assumed average size of household of four persons, namely: Amsterdam, 4,060 assessees and about 30,000 households; Leiden, 1,830 assessees and about 12,500 households; The Hague, 960 assessees and about 5,000 households. Posthumus' ratios, in contrast, imply approximately the following numbers of households: Amsterdam, 11,000; Leiden, 8,800; The Hague 2,700. Alternatively Posthumus' implied figures for the total number of households presuppose about six persons per household in

Amsterdam, about four persons in Leiden, and about seven and one-half persons in The Hague.

15. The literature on the monetary system of the United Provinces is scarce compared with that devoted to other subjects. Use has been made here mainly of Dillen, 1970; Gelder; Klein 1977; Klompmaker, 1980; Kuyk and Gelder; and Morineau, 1974.

16. Klein 1970, p. 181; "coins in common circulation in indescribable confusion" Houtte, p. 213.

17. The more than f 10 million of precious metal captured in 1628 with the Spanish silver fleet (Barbour, p. 50), must have constituted a substantial addition to the monetary stock of the United Provinces.

18. The main sources of information are several publications by Dillen, for example, 1925, 1934, 1964, and 1970; also Barbour, Ch. II and, much older, Mees, Chs. II, III, and V.

19. Read off from chart following p. 392 in Dillen 1964.

20. Of total turnover, similar as an indicator of business activity to present-day clearings, part reflected financial transactions, but most probably originated in domestic and foreign commerce.

21. All economic histories of the period contain some description of the activities of the exchange. For studies devoted to the exchange compare Grossman and Penso de la Vega. Price lists for 1624–26 are reprinted in Ackerle.

22. Most economic histories of the United Provinces in the seventeenth century include a more or less detailed description of the activities of the company. The most exhaustive of them is still Klerk de Reus', now nearly a century old. No comprehensive modern analysis based on the company's records has been found. In addition use has been made particularly of Barbour, Dillen (1970, chapter 6), and Steensgaard.

23. Compare the definition in the standard Dutch encyclopedia of the regents as a "close caste among whose family members the important and profitable posts were distributed" (*Grote Winkler-Prins*, vol. 16, p. 204, 1966). On the regent class compare Geyl, pt. 2, pp. 190ff.

24. Compare descriptions in list of subscribers in Dillen 1958, pp. 106ff.

25. A list of all dividend payments between 1610 and 1782 is provided in Appendix VI of Klerk de Reus.

26. On the West India Company compare Dillen 1970, chapter 7; Laspeyres, pp. 56ff; and Menkman.

27. For values of trade compare Westerman, p. 10; for prices Stuijvenberg and de Vijver 1982, p. 707.

28. There is no comprehensive study of government finance in the seventeenth and eighteenth centuries meeting modern standards, as there was none more than a century ago (Laspeyres, p. 217), and the recent assertion that "the finances of the Dutch Republic remain only imperfectly known" (Parker, p. 592), may well be regarded as an understatement. Still more astonishingly, the general political and economic histories of

the period, such as the two editions of *Allgemeene geschiedenis der Nederlanden* almost ignore the subject. So one has to make do with Koenen (1855), Sickenga (1864), and de Vrankrijker (1969), and the relevant fairly short sections in Baasch (1927) and in Dillen (1970). The book by Oldewelt was not accessible to me.

29. Based on government revenues of about £4 million in 1689–93 (Mitchell and Deane, p. 386) and gross national product of about £75 million, roughly increasing estimate of £55 for England and Wales (Lindert and Williamson, p. 393).

30. For a list of excises compare Vrankrijker, p. 51.

31. Dillen 1970, p. 277. In 1672 to 1677, a period of heavy military expenditures, the receipts from the flat wealth and income tax in Holland yielded f 65 million, partly as forced loans (p. 276).

32. One estimate puts the number of annuitants at over 65,000 or over one-tenth of householders (Kindleberger, p. 70).

33. Based on a debt of £17 million in 1698 (Mitchell and Deane, p. 401) and a gross national product of £75 million.

34. Based on debt charges averaging £1.3 million for 1697–99 (Mitchell and Deane, p. 389).

## Chapter 12

1. Specific references are omitted as they are given in Chapters 2 to 11.

2. R.W. Goldsmith, *Comparative National Balance Sheets*, Chicago, Chicago University Press, 1985. Table 19.

# Bibliography*

### Chapter 2

Bogaert, R., *Les origines antiques de la banque de dépôt*, Leyden, Sijthoff, 1966.

Bromberg, B., "The origin of banking: Religious finance in Babylonia," *Journal of Economic History*, 2, 1942.

Bury, J.B. et al., eds., *Cambridge Ancient Economic History*, Cambridge, University Press, 1923ff.

Curtis, J.B., and Hallo, W.W., "Money and Merchants in Ur III," *Hebrew Union College Annual*, 30, 1959.

Diakonov, I.M., *Obtschestvennii gosudastvennii stroi drevnego abypetchia shumer*, Moscow, Isdatelstvo Vostotchnoi Literaturi, 1959.

*Structure of Society and State in Early Dynastic Sumer*, Los Angeles, Undena Publications, 1974.

Ebert, M., ed. *Reallexikon der Vorgeschichte*, Berlin, de Gruyter, 1924ff.

Falkenstein A., "La cité-temple sumérienne," *Cahiers d'Histoire Mondiale*, I, 1953–54.

Foster, B., "A new look at the Sumerian temple state," *Journal of the Economic and Social History of the Orient*, 24, 1981.

Garelli, P., *Les Assyriens en Cappadoce*, Paris, Adrien Maisonneuve, 1963.

Harmatta, J., and Komorczy, G., *Wirtschaft und Gesellschaft im alten Vorderasien*, Budapest, Akademia Kiadó, 1976.

Harris, R., *Ancient Sippar*, Istanbul, Nederland, Hist-Archeol Instituut, 1975.

Heichelheim, F.M., *An Ancient Economic History*, Vol. I., Leyden, Sijthoff, 1958.

Helck, H.W., *Wirtschaftgeschichte der Alten Ägyptem im 3 und 2 Jahstausend vor Chr*, Leiden, Brill, 1975.

Klengel, H., *Handel and Händler im Alten Orient*, Wien, Hermann Böhlau, 1979.

Kramer, S.N., *The Sumerians*, Chicago, University of Chicago Press, 1963.

Kraus, F.R., "Le rôle des temples depuis la 3$^e$ dynastie d'Ur jusqu'á la 1$^e$ dynastie de Babylone," *Cahiers d'Histoire Mondiale*, I, 1953–54.

Laum, B., "Banken, I Alter Orient," in Pauly-Wissowa, *Reallexikon der Classichen Altertumswissenschaft, Supplement IV*, Stuttgart, J.B. Metzler, 1924.

---

*The bibliography is limited with few exceptions to publications cited in text and notes.

Leemans, W.F., *Old Babylonian Letters and Economic History*, Leyden, Brill, 1968.
*The Old Babylonian Merchant*, Leyden, Brill, 1950.
Lehmann, E., *Capital, Credit and the Banking System: A Historical Approach*, Tel Aviv, Foerder Institute, 1980.
Limet, H., "Les métaux précieux à l'époque d'Agade, (2370–2250 av. J. Ch)," *Journal of the Economic and Social History of the Orient*, 15, 1973.
McEvedy, C., *The Penguin Atlas of Ancient History*, London, Penguin Books, n.d.
McEvedy, C., and Jones, R., *Atlas of World Population History*, Harmondsworth, Penguin Books, 1978.
Meissner, B., *Babylonien und Assyrien*, Heidelberg, Carl Winter, 1920, 1925.
*Warenpreise in Babylonien*, Berlin, Akademie der Wissenschaften, 1936.
Oppenheim, A.L., *Ancient Mesopotamia*, Chicago, Chicago University Press, 1964.
"Trade in the ancient Near East," Fifth International Congress of Economic History, Moscow, Nauka, 1970.
Powell, M.A., "Texts from the time of Lagalzagesi," *Hebrew Union College Annual*, 49, 1978.
Schneider, A., *Die Anfänge der Kulturwirtschaft: Die Sumerische Tempelstadt*, Essen, Baedeker, 1920.
Westermann, W.L., "Slavery," *Encyclopedia of Social Sciences*, Vol. XIV, 1934.

## Chapter 3

Aeschylus, *The Persians*, ed., H.W. Smith, London, Heinemann, 1930.
Andréades, A.M., *A History of Greek Public Finance*, Cambridge, Harvard University Press, 1933.
Andreiev, V.M., "Atticheskoie obshestvennie semlevlademie, VIII–III bb. do n.c.," *Vestnik Drevnei Istorii*, 2, 1967.
"Some aspects of agrarian conditions in Attica in the 5th to 3rd centuries B.C.," *Eirene*, 12, 1974.
Ardaillon, E., *Les Mines de Laurion*, Paris, Thorin, 1897.
Bairoch, P, "Estimations du revenu national dans les sociétés occidentales préindustrielles et au dix neuvième siècle," *Revue d'Economie Politique*, XXVIII, 1977.
Beloch, J., "Das Volksvermögen von Attika," *Hermes*, 20, 1885.
*Die Bevölkerung der Griechisch-römischen Welt*, Leipzig, Duncker und Humblot, 1886.
*Griechische Geschichte*, Berlin, de Gruyter, 1923.
Billeter, G., *Der Zinsfuss im Griechisch-Römischen Altertum bis auf Justinian*, Leipzig, Teubner, 1898.
Böckh, A., *Die Staatshaushaltung der Athener*, 1st ed., Berlin, Real-schulbuchhandlung, 1817.
*Die Staatshaushaltung der Athener*, 3rd ed., rev. by M. Frankel, Berlin, Georg Reimer, 1886.

Bodei-Giglioni, G., *Lavori pubblici e occupazione nell'antiquita classica*, Paris, Patron, 1974.

Bogaert, R., *Banques et banquiers dans les cités Grécques*, Leyden, Sijthoff, 1968.

*Les origines antiques de la banque de dépôt*, Leyden, Sijthoff, 1966.

Bolkestein, H., *Economic Life in Greece's Golden Age*, Leyden, Brill, 1958.

Brilliant, M., "Trierarchia," in Daremberg et Saglio, Vol. V., 442ff. *Dictionnaire des Antiquités Grécques et Romaines*, Paris, Hachette,

Bücher, K., *Beiträge zur Wirtschaftsgeschichte*, Tübingen, Laupp, 1922.

Bury, J.B., et. al., eds., "Athens, 471–401 B.C.," in *The Cambridge Economic History, Vol. V.*, Cambridge, Cambridge University Press, 1927.

Calhoun, G.M., *The Business Life of Ancient Athens*, Chicago, University of Chicago Press, 1926.

Cavaignac, E., *Population et capital dans le monde mediterranéen antique*, Strasbourg, Librairie Istra, 1923.

*L'économie grécque*, Paris, Plon, 1951.

Clark, C., *The Conditions of Economic Progress*, London, Macmillan, 1951.

Daremberg E., and Saglio C., *Dictionnaire des Antiquités Grécques et Romaines*, Paris, Hachette, 1873ff.

Davies, J.K., *Athenian Propertied Families*, Oxford, Oxford University Press, 1971.

Fine, A., "Horoi, Studies in mortgage, real security and land tenure in ancient Athens" in *Hesperia*, Princeton, Institute for Advanced Study, Supplement IX, 1951.

Finley, M.I., *Studies in Land and Credit in Ancient Athens*, New Brunswick, N.J., Rutgers University Press, 1952.

"Land, debt and the man of property in classical Athens," *Political Science Quarterly*, 68, 1953.

*The Ancient Economy*, Berkeley, University of California Press, 1973.

Flacelière, R., *La vie quotidienne en Grèce ar siècle de Périclès*, Paris, Hachette, 1960.

Francotte, H., *L'industrie dans la Grèce ancienne*, Liège, Vaillant, 1900–01.

French, A., *The Growth of the Athenian Economy*, London, Routledge and Kegan Paul, 1964.

Gardner, P., *A History of Ancient Coinage 700–300 B.C.*, Oxford, Clarendon Press, 1918.

Gera, G., *L'imposizione progressiva nell'antica Athene*, Roma, Giorgio Bretschneider, 1975.

Glotz, G., *Ancient Greece at Work*, New York, Barnes & Noble, 1965.

"Les prix a Dèlos," *Journal des Savants*, 98, 1913a.

"Les salaires a Dèlos," *Journal des Savants*, 98, 1913b.

Goldsmith, R.W., *The Financial Development of India, 1860–1977*, New Haven, Yale University Press, 1983.

"An estimate of the size and structure of the national product of the early Roman Empire," *The Review of Income and Wealth* 30, 1984.

*Comparative National Balance Sheets*, Chicago, University of Chicago Press, 1985.

310    **Bibliography**

Gomme, A.W., *The Population of Athens in the Fifth and Fourth Centuries*, Chicago, Argonaut, 1963.

Guiraud, P., *La main d'oeuvre industrielle dans l'ancienne Grèce*, Paris, Felix Alean, 1902.

Hasebroek, J., *Staat und Handel im alten Griechenland*, Tübingen, Mohr, 1928. "Zum griechischen Bankwesen der klassischen Zeit," in *Hermes*, 55, 1920.

Heichelheim, F.M., *An Ancient Economic History*, Vol. II, Leyden, Sijthoff, 1964.

Hermann, K.F., *Lehrbuch der Griechischen Staatsaltertümer*, Freiburg, Mohr, 1889.

Jameson, M.H., "Agriculture and slavery in classical Athens," *Classical Journal*, 73, 1927–28.

Jardé, A., *Les Céreales dans l'Antiquité Grécque*, Paris, deBoccard, 1925.

Jasny, N., "The daily bread of the ancient Greeks and Romans," *Osiris*, 9, 1950.

Knorringa, K., *Emporos*, Amsterdam, Paris, 1926.

Lauffer, S., *Die Bergwerkssklaven von Laureion*, 2nd ed., Wiesbaden, Franz Steiner, 1979.

Mauri, A., *I cittadini lavoratori dell Attica nei secoli V e IV A.C.*, Milano, Hoepli, 1895.

McEvedy, C., and Jones, R., *Atlas of World Population History*, New York, Penguin Books, 1978.

Meritt, B.S., Wade-Gery, H.T., and McGregor, M.F., *The Athenian Tribute Lists*, vol. III, Princeton, Princeton University Press, 1950.

Meyer, E., *Forschungen zur Alten Geshichte*, Halle, Max Niemeyer, 1899.

Michell, H., *The Economics of Ancient Greece*, New York, Macmillan, 1940.

Musti, D,. *L'Economia in Grecia*, Milan, Laterza, 1981.

Patterson, C.C., "Silver stocks and losses in ancient and medieval times," *Economic History Journal*, XXV, 1972.

Robinson, E.S.G., "The Athenian currency decree and the coinage of Athens," *Hesperia*, Supplement, VIII, 1949.

Saglio, C. "Argent," in Daremberg and Saglio *Dictionnaire des Antiquités Grécques et Romaines*, Paris, Hachette, 1873ff.

Sargent, R.L., *The Size of the Slave Population at Athens during the 5th and 4th Centuries* B.C., Urbana, University of Illinois, 1925.

Seltman, C.T., *Greek Coins*, London, Methuen, 1933.
   *A Book of Greek Coins*, London, Penguin, 1952.

Sombart, W., *Der Moderne Kapitalismus*, München, Duncker and Humblot, 1928.

Spaventa, L., *I Prezzi in Grecia e a Roma*, Rome, Cuggiani, 1934.

Speck, E., *Handelsgeschichte der Altertums*, Vol. 2, *Die Griechen*, Leipzig, Friedrich Brandstetter, 1901.

Starr, C.G., *Athenian Coinage 480–449* B.C., Oxford, Clarendon Press, 1970.

Thomsen, R., *Eisphora: A Study of Direct Taxation in Ancient Athens*, Copenhagen, Gyldendal, 1964.

Wallon, H., *Histoire de l'esclavage dans l'antiquité*, Paris, Hachette, 1879.

Weil, R., "Das Münzmonopol Athens im ersten Attischen Seebund," *Zeitschrift für Numismatik*, 25, 1906.

Wilsdorf, H., *Bergleute und Hüttenmänner im Altertum bis zum Ausgang der Römischen Republik*, Berlin, Akademie Verlag, 1952.

Ziegler K., and Sontheimer, W., *Der Kleine Pauly*, Stuttgart, Druckenmüller, 1964.


## Chapter 4

Abbott, F.F., and Johnson, A.C., *Municipal Administration in the Roman Empire*, Princeton, Princeton University Press, 1926.

Bahrfeldt, M., *Römische Goldmünzprägungen*, Halle, Riechmann, 1923.

Beloch, J., *Die Bevölkerung der griechisch-römischen Welt*, Leipzig, Duncker and Humblot, 1886, (anastatic reprint, 1968, Rome, L'Erma).

Bernardi, A., "The economic problems of the Roman Empire at the time of its decline," in Cipolla, C., ed., *The Economic Decline of Empires*, London, Methuen, 1970.

Bernhart, M., *Handbuch zur Münzkunde der Römischen Kaiserzeit*, 2 vols., Halle, Reichmann, 1926.

Billeter, G., *Geschichte des Zinsfusses im griechisch-römischen Altertum bisauf Justinian*, Leipzig, Teubner, 1899.

Bodei-Giglioni, G., *Lavori pubblici e occupazione nell'antichità classica*, Bologna, Petron, 1979.

Bogaert, R., s.v., "Geld, VI," in *Reallexikon für Antike und Christentum*, vol. 9., Stuttgart, Anton Hiersemann.

Bolin, S., *Finden av romerska mint i det fria Germania*, Lund, Svenska Central-trykeriet, 1926.

*State and Currency in the Roman Empire to 300* A.D., Stockholm, Almquist and Wicksell, 1958.

Breglia, L., "Circolazione monetaria ed aspetti di vita economica a Pompeii," in *Pompeiana*, Naples, Macchetti, 1950.

Burns, A.R., *Money and Monetary Policy in Ancient Times*, London, Kegan Paul, 1927.

Cagnat, M.R., *Etude historique sur les impôts indirects chez les Romains*, Paris, Imprimerie Nationale, 1882.

Cavaignac, E., *Population et capital dans le monde méditerranéen antique*, Strasbourg, Istra, 1923.

"Les métaux précieux; Les mînes d'Espagne au IIᵉ siècle av. J.C.," *Annales*, 8, 1953.

Clark, C., *The Conditions of Economic Progress*, 3rd. ed., Cambridge, Cambridge University Press, 1957.

Crawford, M., "Money and Exchange in the Roman World," *Journal of Roman Studies*, 60, 40–48, 1970.

Daremberg, C., and Saglio, E., *Dictionnaire des Antiquités Grécques et Romaines*, Paris, Hachette, 1873ff.

de Laet, S.J., *Portorium*, Brugge, De Tempel, 1949.

Dessau, H., "Finanzen des alten Roms," in *Handwörterbuch der Staatswissenschaften*, 2ᵈ ed., vol. 2, Jena, Fischer, 1898ff.

Duncan-Jones, R., *The Economy of the Roman Empire – Quantitative Studies*, Cambridge, Cambridge University Press, 1982.

312    Bibliography

Finley, M.I., *The Ancient Economy*, Berkeley, University of California Press, 1973.

Frank, T., *An Economic Survey of Ancient Rome*, Baltimore, The Johns Hopkins Press, 1933–40.

Gibbon, E., *The History of the Decline and Fall of the Roman Empire*, London, Strahan and Cadell, 1776ff.

Gini, C., *L'ammontare e la composizione della ricchezza delle nazioni*, 2nd. ed., Torino, UTET, 1962.

Goldsmith, R.W., *The Financial Development of India, 1860–1977*, New Haven, Yale University Press, 1983a.

*The Financial Development of Japan, 1868–1977*, New Haven, Yale University Press, 1983b.

"An estimate of the size and structure of the national product of the early Roman Empire," *Studies in Income and Wealth*, 1984.

*Comparative National Balance Sheets*, Chicago, Chicago University Press, 1985.

*Handwörterbuch der Staatswissenschaften*, 2nd. ed., Jena, Fischer, 1898ff.

Healy, J.F., *Mining and Metallurgy in the Greek and Roman World*, London, Thames and Hudson, 1978.

Heichelheim, F., *An Ancient Economic History*, Leyden, Sijthoff, 1958–70.

Herzog, R., *Aus der Geschichte der Bankwesens in Altertum: Tesserae Nummulariae*, Giessen, Alfred Töpelmann, 1919.

"Nummularius," in Pauly A.F., and Wissowa, G., eds., *Realencyclopädie der klassichen Altertunswissenschaft*, Stuttgart, Druckenmüller, vol. XVII, part 2, 1937.

Hirschfeld, O., *Die Kaiserlichen Verwaltungsbeamten bis auf Diokletian*, 2nd ed., Berlin, Weidmannsche Buchhandlung, 1905.

His, R., *Die Domänen der römischen Kaiserzeit*, Leipzig, Veit, 1896.

Homer, S., *A History of Interest Rates*, New Brunswick, Rutgers University Press, 1963.

Hopkins, K., "Taxes and trade in the Roman Empire (200 B.C.–A.D. 400)," *Journal of Roman Studies*, 70, 1980.

International Bank for Reconstruction and Development, *World Development Report*, Washington, D.C., 1983.

Jacob, W., *An Historical Inquiry into the Production and Consumption of Precious Metals*, London, John Murray, 1831.

Jones, A.C. "Roman Egypt" in Frank, T., *An Economic Survey of Ancient Rome*, Vol. II, Baltimore, The Johns Hopkins Press, 1934.

Jones, A.H.M., *The Later Roman Empire, 284–602*, Oxford, Blackwell, 1953.

*The Decline of the Ancient World*, London, Longmans, 1966.

Kahrstedt, U., "Uber die Bevölkerung Rom's," in L. Friedlaender, *Darstellungen aus der Sittengeschichte Rom's*, Vol. 4, 9th and 10th eds., Leipzig, S. Hirzel, 1921ff.

*Kulturgeschichte der Römischen Kaiserseit*, 2d. ed., Bern, Francke, 1958.

King, G., *Two Tracts*, Baltimore, The Johns Hopkins Press, 1936.

Kleiman, E., *Gold and silver in the second century* A.D. – *A Talmudic evidence*, Jerusalem, unpublished memorandum, n.d. (ca. 1975).

Knapp, G.F., *Staatliche Theorie der Geldes*, Leipzig, Duncker and Humblot, 1905.

Lampmann, R., *The Share of Top Wealth-holders in National Wealth, 1922–56*, Princeton, Princeton University Press, 1962.

Laum, B., "Banken," in Pauly A.F., and Wissowa, G., eds., *Realencyclopädie der klassichen Altertunswissenschaft*, Stuttgart, Druckenmüller, Suppl. IV., 1924.

Liebenam, W., *Städteverwaltung im Römischen Kaiserreiche*, Leipzig, Duncker and Humblot, 1900.

LoCascio, E., "State and coinage in the late Republic and early Empire," *Journal of Roman Studies*, LXXI, 76–86, 1981.

MacMullen, R., *Roman Social Relations 50 B.C. to A.D. 284*, New Haven, Yale University Press, 1974.

"The Roman Emperors' army costs," *Latomus*, 44, 1985.

Marquardt, J., *Römische Staatsverwaltung*, 2nd. ed., Leipzig, Hirzel, 1884.

Mattingly, H., and Sydenham, E.A., *The Roman Imperial Coinage*, 2 vols. Cambridge, The University Press, 1923.

McEvedy, C., *The Penguin Atlas of Ancient History*, London, Penguin Books, n.d.

Mickwitz, G., *Geld un Wirtschaft im Römischen Reich des 4ten Jahrhunderts n. Chr.*, Helsingfors, Centraltryckeri, 1932.

Miller, J.I., *The Spice Trade of the Roman Empire, 29 B.C. to A.D. 641*, Oxford, Clarendon Press, 1969.

Mitchell, B.R., *International Historical Statistics, Africa and Asia*, New York, New York University Press, 1982.

Mitchell, B.R., and Deane, Ph., *Abstract of British Historical Statistics*, Cambridge, Cambridge University Press, 1962.

Mommsen, Th., "Die pompeiansichen Quittungstafeln des L. Caecilius Jucundus," *Hermes*, 12, 1877.

Neesen, L., *Untersuchungen zu den Direkten Staatsausgeben der Römischen Kaiserzeit*, Bonn, Rudolf Habelt, 1980.

Nicolet, C., "Les variations des prix, et la theorie quantitative de la monnaie, à Rome de Ciceron à Pline l'Ancien," *Annales*, 26, 1971.

Oehler, "Argentarius," in Pauly, A.F., and Wissowa, G., eds., *Realencyclopädie der klassichen Altertunswissenschaft*, Stuttgart, Druckenmüller, vol. II, part 1, 1895.

Oertel, F., "The economic unification of the Mediterranean region: Industry, trade, and commerce," *Cambridge Ancient History*, X, 1934.

Oliva, A., *La politica granaria di Roma antica dal 265 A.C. al 410 D.C.*, Piacenza, Federazione Italiana dei Consorzi Agrari, 1930.

Patterson, C.C., "Silver stocks and losses in ancient and medieval times," *The Economic History Review*, XXV, 205–220, 1972.

Pauly, A.F., and Wissowa, G., eds., *Realencyclopädie der klassichen Altertunswissenschaft*, Stuttgart, Druckenmüller, 1893ff.

Pekary, Th., *Die Wirtschaft der griechisch-römischen Antike*, Wiesbaden, Franz Steiner, 1979.

Plinius, C. Secundus, *Naturalis Historiae Libri XXXVII*, Stuttgart, Teubner, 1967.

Preisigke, F., *Girowesen im griechischen Agypten*, Strassburg, Schlesier and Schweikhardt, 1910.

Quiring, H., *Geschichte der Goldes*, Stuttgart, Enke, 1948.

Regling, K., "Münzwesen," in Pauly, A.F., and Wissowa, G., eds., *Realencyclopädie der klassichen Altertunswissenschaft*, Stuttgart, Druckenmüller, vol. XVI, vol. 1, 1933.

Regling, K., et. al., *Handwörterbuch der Münzkunde*, Berlin, de Gruyter, 1930.

Rostovtsev, M. *Geschichte der Staatspacht in der Römischen Kaiserzeit bis Diocletian*, Leipzig, Dieterischsche Verlagsbuchhandlung, 1902.

Rougé, J., *Recherches sur l'organisation du commerce maritime en Mediterranée sous l'empire Romain*, Paris, S.D.V.P.E.N., 1968.

Segré, A., *Metrologia e circolazione monetaria degli antichi*, Bologna, Zanichelli, 1928.

Speck, E., *Handelsgeschichte des Altertums*, vol. 3, part 2, Leipzig, Brandstetter, 1906.

Sydenham, E.A. "The Roman monetary system," *Numismatic Chronicle*, 4th series, vol. 19, 1918–19.

Tacitus, P.C., *Historiae*, London, Putnam Sons, 1925.

Warmington, E.H., *The Commerce Between the Roman Empire and India*, Cambridge, The University Press, 1928.

Weber, M., *Die Römische Agrargeschichte*, Stuttgart, Enke, 1891.

West, L.C., *Gold and Silver Coin Standards in the Roman Empire*, New York, American Numismatic Society, 1941.

West, L.C., and Johnson, A.C., *Currency in Roman and Byzantine Egypt*, Princeton, Princeton University Press, 1941.

Westermann, W.L., "Slavery-Ancient," in *Encyclopaedia of Social Sciences*, vol. XIV, New York, Macmillan, 1934.

White K.D., *Roman Farming*, London, Thames and Hudson, 1970

Ziegler, K., Sontheimer, W., and Gärtner, H., *Der Kleine Pauly*, 5 vols., München, Alfred Druckenmüller, 1964–1975.

## Chapter 5

el-Ali, S.A., "A new version of Ibn-Mutarrif's list of revenues in the early times of Harun-al-Rashid," *JESHO (Journal of the Economic and Social History of the Orient)*, 14, 1971.

Ashtor, E., "Quelques indications sur les revenus dans l'orient musulman au haut moyen âge," *JESHO*, 1959.

*Histoire des prix et des salaires dans l'Orient Medieval*, Paris, SEVPEN, 1969.

*A Social and Economic History of the Near East in the Middle Ages*, London, Collins, 1976.

*The Medieval Near East, London Social and Economic History Collected Studies*, London Varionrum Reprints, 1978.

Becker, C.H., *Islamstudien*, vol. 1, Leipzig, Quelle and Meyer, 1924.

Beg, M.A.J., "A contribution to the economic history of the caliphate: A study of the cost of living and the economic status of artisans in Abbasid Iraq." *The Islamic Quarterly*, XVI, 1972.

Bogaert, R., *Les origines antiques de la Banque de dépôts*, Leyden, Sijthoff, 1966.

Brice, W.C., *An Historical Atlas of Islam*, Leyden, Brill, 1981.

Cahen, C., "Reflexions sur le wakf ancien," *Studia Islamica*, XIV, 1961.

*L'Islam des origines au début de l'empire Ottoman*, Paris, Bordaz, 1970a.

"Economy, society, institutions," in P.M. Holt et al., eds., *The Cambridge History of Islam*, Vol 2, Cambridge University Press, 1970b.

"Tribes, cities and social organization," in R.N. Frye, ed., *The Cambridge History of Iran*, vol. 4, Cambridge, Cambridge University Press, 1975.

Center for Medieval and Renaissance Studies, University of California, Los Angeles, *The Dawn of Modern Banking*, New Haven, Yale University Press, 1979.

Dennett, D.C. Jr., *Conversion and the Poll Tax in Early Islam*, Cambridge, MA, Harvard University Press, 1950.

Duplessy, J., "La circulation des monnaies arabes en Europe du VIIIᵉ au XIIIᵉ siecle," *Revue Numismatique*, 5, 18, 1956.

Ehrenkreutz, A.S., "Money" *Handbuch der Orientalistik*, VI, 61, 1977a.

"Another orientalist's remarks concerning the Pirenne thesis," *JESHO*, 15, 1972.

"Numismatics Re-monetized," in L.L. Orlin, ed., *Michigan Oriental Studies in Honor of George G. Cameron*, Ann Arbor, University of Michigan, 1976.

"Numismatic-statistical reflection on the annual gold coinage production of the Tulunid mint in Egypt" *JESHO*, 20, 1977b.

*Encyclopaedia of Islam*, E.J. Brill; London, Luzac; 1st ed., 1913ff, 2d ed., 1960ff.

Fischel, W., "The origin of banking in Medieval Islam: A contribution to the economic history of the Jews of Baghdad," *Journal of the Royal Asiatic Society*, 1933.

Food and Agriculture Organization of the United Nations, *FAO Production Yearbook*, 16, 1962.

Forand, P.G., "The status of the land and inhabitants of the Sawad during the first two centuries of Islam," *JESHO*, 14, 1971.

Frantz-Murphy, G., "A new interpretation of the economic history of medieval Egypt: The role of the textile industry 567–1171," *JESHO*, 24, 1981.

Frye, R.N., ed., *The Cambridge History of Iran*, vol. 4, Cambridge, Cambridge University Press, 1975.

Gibb, H.A.R., and Kramers, J.H., *Shorter Encyclopaedia of Islam*, Leyden, Brill, 1965.

Gottschalk, H.L., "Die Kultur der Araber," in *Die Kultur des Islam*, Frankfurt, Athenaion, 1971.

Grasshoff, R., *Das Wechselrecht der Araber*, Berlin, Liebmann, 1899.

Grierson, P., "The monetary reform of Abd-al-Malik," *JESHO*, 3, 1960.

Grünebaum, G.E. von, *Der Islam in seiner klassischen Epoche 622–1258*, Zürich, Artemis, 1966.

Hammer, J.v., *Über die Länderverwaltung unter dem Chalifate*, Berlin, Akademie der Wissenschaften, 1835.

316    Bibliography

Hansen, B., "An economic model for Ottoman Egypt: The economies of collective tax responsibility," in A.L. Udovitch ed., *The Islamic Middle East, 700–1900*, Princeton, Princeton University Press, 1981.

Hinz, W., "Lebensmittelpreise im mittelalterlichen vorderen Orient," *Die Welt des Orients*, II, 1954.

Holt, P.M., et al., eds. *The Cambridge History of Islam*, vol. 2, Cambridge, University Press, 1970.

Hussaini, S.A.Q., *Arab Administration*, Madras, Abdur Rahman, 1949.

Issawi, Ch., "The area and population of the Arab Empire: An essay in speculation," in A.L. Udovitch, ed., *The Islamic Middle East, 700–1900*, Princeton, Princeton University Press, 1981.

Jones, W.R., "Pious endowments in medieval Christianity and Islam." *Diogenes*, 109, 1980.

Kennedy, H., *The Early Abbasid Caliphate*, London, Croome Helm, 1981.

Kremer, A. von, *Culturgeschicte des Orients unter den Chalifen*, Wien, Wilhelm Braumüller, 1875.

*Uber das Einnahmebudget des Abbasiden Reiches vom Jahre 300 H. (918–919)*, Wien, Carl Gerold's Sohn, 1887.

Labib, S.Y., "Capitalism in medieval Islam," *Journal of Economic History*, XXIX, 1969.

Lambton, A.K.L., *Landlord and Peasant in Persia*, Oxford, Oxford University Press, 1953.

Lane-Poole, S., "The Arabian historians on Muhammadan numismatics," *Numismatic Chronicle*, 4, 1883–84.

Lapidus, I.M., "Arab settlement and economic development of Iraq and Iran in the age of the Umayyad and Early Abbasid caliphs," in A.L. Udovitch, *The Islamic Middle East, 700–1900*, Princeton, Princeton University Press, 1981.

Lewis, B., et. al., *Wirtschaftsgeschichte des Vorderen Orients in Islamischer Zeit*, Teil 1 (*Handbuch der Orientalistik*, 1, Abt. Bd. 6,6), Leyden, Brill, 1977.

Lombard, M., "Les bases monétaires d'une suprematie economique: Or Musulman du VIIᵉ au XIᵉ siècle," *Annales*, 2, 1947.

*L'Islam dans sa première grandeur (VIIIᵉ–XIᵉ siècle)*, Paris, Flammarion, 1971.

Løkkegaard, F., *Islamic Taxation in the Classic Period*, Philadelphia, Porcupine Press, 1978 (reprint) (orig. Copenhagen, Brauner og Kroch, 1952).

Lotz, W., "Staatsfinanzen in den ersten Jahrhunderten des Khalifenreichs," in München, *Sitzungsberichte der Bayrischen Akademie der Wissenschaften*, Philosophisch-Historische Klasse, 1937.

McEvedy, C., and Jones, R., *Atlas of World Population History*, Middlesex, Penguin Books, 1978.

Mez, A., *The Renaissance of Islam*, London, Luzac, 1937.

Miles, G.C., "Numismatics," in *Cambridge History of Iran*, vol. 4, Cambridge, University Press, 1975.

Morimoto, K., "Land tenure in Egypt during the early Islamic period," *Orient*, XI, 1975.

Mottahedeh, R., "The Abbasid Caliphate in Iran," in *The Cambridge History of Iran*, vol. 4, 1975.

Müller, H. "Sklaven," in Lewis, B., et al., *Wirtschaftsgeschichte des Vorderen Orients in Islamischer Zeit*, Teil 1, Leyden, Brill, 1977.

Quiring, H., *Geschichte des Goldes*, Stuttgart, Enke, 1948.

Rodinson, M. "De l'archéologie à la sociologie historique," *Syria*, 38, 1961.

*Islam et capitalisme*, Paris, Editions du Seuil, 1966.

Roolvink, R., *Historical Atlas of the Muslim People*, Amsterdam, Djambatan, 1957.

Russell, J.C., "Late ancient and medieval populations," *Transactions of the American Philosophical Society*, 48, 1958.

Shimizu, N., "Les finances publiques de l'état abbaside," *Der Islam*, 42, 1965.

Slane, M.G., de, "Notices sur Codama et ses écrits," *Journal Asiatique*, 1862.

Sourdel, D., *Le vizirat Abbaside, de 749 à 936.*, Damascus, Institut Français, 1959.

Sourdel, D., and Sourdel, J., *La civilisation de l'Islam classique*, Paris, Arthaud, 1968.

Udovitch, A., *Partnership and Profit in Medieval Islam*, Princeton, Princeton University Press, 1970.

*The Islamic Middle East, 700–1900: Studies in Economic and Social History*, Princeton, Darwin Press, 1981.

"Bankers without banks: Commerce, banking and society in the Islamic world of the middle ages," in Center for Medieval and Renaissance Studies, University of California, Los Angeles, *The Dawn of Modern Banking*, New Haven, Yale University Press, 1979.

Waines, D., "The 3rd century internal crisis of the Abbasids," *JESHO*, XX, 1977.

Watson, A.M., "The Arab agricultural revolution and its diffusion, 700–1100," *Journal of Economic History*, 34, 1974.

"A medieval green revolution: New crops and farming techniques in the early Islamic world," in A.L. Udovitch, ed., *The Islamic Middle East, 700–1900*, Princeton, Princeton University Press, 1981.

*Agricultural Innovation in the Early Islamic World*, Cambridge, Cambridge University Press, 1984.

Wellhausen, J., *Das Arabische Reich und sein Sturz*, Berlin, Reimer, 1902.

Wiet, G., "L'empire neo-byzantin des Omeiyyades et l'empire neo-sassanide des Abassides," *Cahiers d'Histoire Mondiale*, I, 1953–54.

## Chapter 6

Barkan, O.L., "Quelques observations sur l'organisation économique et sociale des villes Ottomanes des XVI<sup>e</sup> et XVII<sup>e</sup> siècles," in *Receuils de la Société Jean Bodin*, VII, Bruxelles, Editions de la librairie encyclopedique, 1955.

"Essai sur les données statistiques des registres de recensement dans l'Empire

318     **Bibliography**

Ottoman aux XVᵉ et XVIᵉ siècle," *Journal of the Economic History of the Orient*, 1, 1958.

"Les mouvements des prix en Turquie entre 1490 et 1655," in *Mèlanges Braudel, Histoire Economique*, Paris, 1973.

Braudel, F., *Civilisation matérielle, économie et capitalisme, XVᵉ–XVIIIᵉ Siècle*, Paris, Armand Colin, 1979.

Deny, J., "Timar" in *Encyclopaedia of Islam*, 1st ed., vol. 4, 767ff.

Gerber, H., "The monetary system of the Ottoman Empire," *Journal of the Economic and Social History of the Orient*, XXV, 198.

Gibb, H.A.R., and Bowen, H., *Islamic Society in the 18th Century*, London, Oxford University Press, 1957.

Goldsmith, R.W., "An estimate of the size and structure of the national product of the early Roman Empire," *Review of Income and Wealth*, 30, 3, 1984.

Hammer-Purgstall, J. von, *Des Osmanischen Reichs Staatsverfassung und Staatsverwaltung*, Wien, Camesianische Buchhandlung, 1815.

*Geschichte des Osmanischen Reiches*, Pest, Hartleben, 1827ff.

Hansen, B., "An economic model for Ottoman Egypt: The economies of collective tax responsibility," in A.L. Udovitch, ed., *The Islamic Middle East*, Princeton, Princeton University Press, 1981.

Inalcik, H., "The capital formation in the Ottoman Empire, *Journal of Economic History*, XXIX, 1969.

*The Ottoman Empire: The Classical Age 1300–1600*, New York, Praeger, 1973.

*The Ottoman Empire: Conquest, organization and economy*, London, Variorum Reprints, 1978.

Itzkowitz, N., *Ottoman Empire and Islamic Tradition*, Chicago, Chicago University Press, 1972.

Jorga, N., *Geschichte des Osmanischen Reiches*, Gotha, Friedrich Andreas Perthes, 1909.

Matran, R., *Istanbul dans le seconde moitiédu XVIIᵉ siècle*, Paris, Adrien Maisonneuve, 1962.

*La vie quotidienne à Constantinople au temps de Soliman le Magnifique et ses successeurs (XVIᵉ et XVIIᵉ siècles)*, Paris, Hachette, 1965.

"L'empire Ottoman et le commerce asiatique aux 16ᵉ et a7ᵉ siècles," in D.S. Richards, ed., *Islam and the Trade of Asia*, Oxford, Bruno Cassirer, 1979.

McEvedy, C., *The Penguin Atlas of Medieval History*, Harmondsworth, Penguin Books, 1972.

McEvedy, C., and Jones, R., *Atlas of World Population History*, Harmondsworth, Penguin Books, 1978.

Menage, V.L. "Devshirme" in *Encyclopaedia of Islam*, 2d. ed., IV, 1964.

Morawitz, Ch. *Les finances de la Turquie*, Paris, Guillaumin, 1902.

Raymond, A., "La population du Caire et de l'Egypte à l'époque Ottomane et sous Muhammad Ali," in *Memorial Omer Lutfi Barkan*, Paris, Adrien Maisonneuve, 1980.

Richards, O.S., ed., *Islam and the Trade of Asia*, Oxford, Bruno Cassirer, 1970.

Shaw, S.J., *The Financial and Administrative Organization of Ottoman Egypt 1517–1798*, Princeton, Princeton University Press, 1962.

*The Budget of Ottoman Egypt 1005–1006, (1596–1597),* The Hague, Mouton, 1968.

Tischendorf, P.A. von, *Das Lehnswesen in den Moslemischen Staaten imbesonderen im Osmanischen Reiche,* Leipzig, Giesecke and Devrient, 1872.

Udovitch, A.L., ed., *The Islamic Middle East; Studies in Economic and Social History,* Princeton, Darwin Press, 1981.


## Chapter 7

Antonova, K.A., *Ocherki obshchestvennykh otnosheniy i politicheskogo stroia Mogolskoi Indii vremeyi Akbara (1556–1605 gg),* Moscow, Adademia Nauk, 1972.

Aziz, A., *The Imperial Treasury of the Indian Mughals,* Delhi, Idarah-i-Adabiyat, 1972.

Bernier, F., *Travels in the Mogul Empire A.D. 1656–1680,* A. Constable and V.A. Smith, eds., London, Humphrey Mitford, 1916.

Blochmann, H., *The Ain-i-Akbari by Abul Fazl'Allami,* vol. 1, Calcutta, Asiatic Society of Bengal, 1873.

Chandra, S., "Standard of living, 1," in Raychaudhuri T., and Habib, I., eds., *The Cambridge Economic History of India,* vol. 1 Cambridge, Cambridge University Press, 1982–83.

Chaudhuri, K.N., "European trade with India," in Raychaudhuri, T., and Habib, I., eds., *The Cambridge Economic History of India,* Cambridge, Cambridge University Press, 1982–83.

"The East India Co. and the export of treasure in the early 17th century," *Economic History Review,* II, 16, 1963–64.

Chaudhuri, U.D.R., "Income distribution and economic development in India since 1950–51," *Indian Economic Journal,* 25, 1977.

Clark, C., *The Conditions of Economic Progress,* London, Macmillan, 1951.

Cohn, B.S., "Structural changes in rural society," in Frykenberg, R.E., ed., *Land Control and Social Structure in Indian History,* Madison, University of Wisconsin Press, 1969.

Council of Economic Advisers, *Economic Report of the President,* annual.

Craigie, R., Presidential Address, *Journal of the Royal Statistical Society,* London, 1902.

Dasgupta, A., "Indian merchants and the trade in the Indian Ocean," in Raychaudhuri, T., and Habib, I., eds., *The Cambridge Economic History of India,* Cambridge, Cambridge University Press, 1982–83.

Davis, K., *The Population of India and Pakistan,* Princeton, Princeton University Press, 1951.

de Laet, J., *The Empire of the Great Mogol,* Delhi, Idarah-i-Adabiyat, 1928.

Desai, A.V., "Population and standards of living in Akbar's time," *Indian Economic and Social History Review,* IX, 1972.

"Population and standards of living in Akbar's time – a second look," *Indian Economic and Social Review* XV, 1978.

Frykenberg, R.E., ed., *Land Control and Social Structure in Indian History,* Madison, University of Wisconsin Press, 1969.

320　Bibliography

Ganguli, B.N., ed., *Readings in Indian Economic History*, London, Asia Publishing House, 1964.

Goldsmith, R.W., *The Financial Development of India, 1860–1977*. New Haven, Yale University Press, 1983.

"An estimate of the size and structure of the national product of the early Roman Empire," *Review of Income and Wealth*, 1984.

*Comparative National Balance Sheets*, Chicago, Chicago University Press, 1985.

*Brasil 1850–1984*, Rio de Janeiro, Banco Bamerindus do Brasil and Editora Harper and Row do Brasil, 1986.

Government of India, *Statistical Abstract*, Delhi, annual.

Grover, B.R., "Nature of land rights in Mughal India," *Indian Economic and Social History Review* 1, 1963–64.

Gujral, S.S., "New evidence in Indian 19th century family budgetary studies," *Indian Economic Journal*, 27, 1979.

Habib, I., "The currency system of the Mughal Empire (1556–1707)," *Medieval India quarterly*, IV, 1960.

*Agrarian System of Mughal India*, Bombay, Asian Publishing House, 1963.

"Usury in medieval India," *Comparative Studies in Society and History*, VI, 1964.

"Banking in Mughal India," in *Contributions to Indian Economic History*, Raychaudhuri, T., ed., Calcutta, Mukhopadyay, 1960.

"Potentialities of capitalistic development in the economy of Mughal India," *Journal of Economic History*, 29, 1969.

"Agrarian relations and land revenue, 1," in Raychaudhuri, T., and Habib, I., eds., *The Cambridge Economic History of India*, Cambridge, Cambridge University Press, 1982–83.

"Monetary system and prices," in Raychaudhuri, T., and Habib, I., eds., *The Cambridge Economic History of India*, Cambridge, Cambridge University Press, 1982–83.

"Population," in Raychaudhuri, T., and Habib, I., eds., *The Cambridge Economic History of India*, Cambridge, Cambridge University Press, 1982–83.

"The systems of agricultural production, 1," in Raychaudhuri, T., and Habib, I., eds., *The Cambridge Economic History of India*, Cambridge, Cambridge University Press, 1982–83.

*Atlas of Mughal History*, Delhi, Oxford University Press, 1982.

Hambly, G.R.C., "Towns and cities, 1," in Raychaudhuri, T., and Habib, I., eds., *The Cambridge Economic History of India*, Cambridge, Cambridge University Press, 1982–83.

Hasan, A., "The silver currency output of the Mughal Empire and prices in India during the 16th and 17th centuries," *Indian Economic and Social History Review*, VI, VII, 1969–1970.

Hasan, S.M., "Zamindars under the Mughals," in Frykenberg, R.E., ed., *Land Control and Social Structure in Indian History*, Madison, University of Wisconsin Press, 1969.

Heston, A., "Official yields per acre in India, 1886–1947: Some questions of interpretation," *IESHR*, X, 1973.

Hodivala, S.H., *Historical Studies in Mughal Numismatics*, Bombay, Numismatic Society of India, 1976.

Homer, S., *A History of Interest Rates*, New Brunswick, Rutgers University Press, 1963.

International Labor Office, *Yearbook of Labor Statistics*, Geneva, annual.

International Monetary Fund, *International Financial Statistics Yearbook*, Washington, D.C., annual.

Jain, L.C., *Indigenous Banking in India*, London, Macmillan, 1929.

Jarrett, H.S., *The Ain-I-Akbari of Abul Fazl-I-Allami*, vols. II and III, Calcutta, Asiatic Society of Bengal, 1891, 1894.

Kravis, I.B., Heston, A., and Summers, R., "New Insights into the structure of the world economy," *Review of Income and Wealth* 27, 1981.

Kumar, D., and Megnad, D., *Cambridge Economic History of India*, vol. II, Cambridge, Cambridge University Press, 1983.

Lebergott, S., *The Americans*, New York, Norton, 1984.

Leonhard, K., "The 'Great Firms' theory of the decline of the Mughal Empire," *Comparative Studies in Society and History*, 21, 1979.

Lindert, P.A., and Williamson, J.G., "Revising England's social tables, 1688–1812," *Explorations in Economic History*, 19, 1982.

Maddison, A., *Class Structure and Economic Growth: India and Pakistan since the Mughal*, London, Allen and Unwin, 1971.

"A comparison of the levels of GDP per capita in developed and developing countries, 1700–1980," *Journal of Economic History*, XLIII, 1983.

McEvedy, C., and Jones, R., *Atlas of World Population History*, Harmondsworth, Penguin Books, 1978.

Mitchell, B.R., and Deane, P., *Abstract of British Historical Statistics*, Cambridge, University Press, 1962.

Moosvi, S., "Production, consumption and population in Akbar's time," *IJESR*, X, 1973.

"Suyurghal statistics in the Ain-i-Akbari—an analysis," *Indian Historical Review* II, 1976.

"The zamindars' share in the peasant surplus in the Mughal empire—Evidence of the Ain-i-Akbari statistics," *IESHR*, XV, 1978.

"Share of the nobility in the revenues of Akbar's empire," *IESHR*, XVII, 1980.

Moreland, W.H., *India at the Death of Akbar*, London, Macmillan, 1920.

*From Akbar to Aurangzeb, a Study in Indian Economic History*, London, Macmillan, 1923.

*The Agrarian Systems of Modern India*, Cambridge, Cambridge University Press, 1929.

Mukherjee, R., *The Economic History of India, 1600–1800*, London, Longmans, Green, 1940.

Narain, B., *Indian Economic Life Past and Present*, Lahore, Uttar Chand Kapur, 1929.

Parghad, A.D., *Some Aspects of Indian Foreign Trade 1757–1893*, London, King and Son, 1932.

## 322    Bibliography

Phelps-Brown, H. and Hopkins, S., *A Perspective of Wages and Prices*, London, Methuen, 1981.

Prakash, O., and Krishnamurty, J., "A critique," *IESHR*, VII, 1970.

Quiring, H., *Geschiche der Goldes*, Stuttgart, Enke, 1948.

Raychaudhuri, T., ed., *Contributions to Indian Economic History*, Calcutta, Muklopadyay, 1960.

"Inland Trade," in Raychaudhuri, T., and Habib, I., eds., *The Cambridge Economic History of India*, Cambridge, Cambridge University Press, 1982–83.

"The state and the economy," in Raychaudhuri, T., and Habib, I., eds., *The Cambridge Economic History of India*, Cambridge, Cambridge University Press, 1982–83.

"Non-agricultural production, 1," in Raychaudhuri, T., and Habib, I., eds., *The Cambridge Economic History of India*, Cambridge, Cambridge University Press, 1982–83.

Raychaudhuri, T., and Habib, I., *The Cambridge Economic History of India, vol. I: c. 1200–c. 1750*, Cambridge, Cambridge University Press, 1982–83.

Sarkar, J., *Mughal Administration*, Patna, Patna University, 1920, 1925.

Schwartzberg, J.E., ed. *A Historical Atlas of South Asia*, Chicago, University of Chicago Press, 1978.

Siddiqui, N.A., *Land Revenue Administration under the Mughals (1700–1750)*, New York, Asia Publishing House, 1970.

Sircar, D.C., *Studies in Indian Coins*, Delhi, Motilal Banersidas, 1968.

Smith, V.A., *Akbar The Great Mogul, 1542–1605*, Oxford, Clarendon Press, 1919.

Summers, R., Kravis, I.B., and Heston, A., "International comparison of real product and its composition: 1950–77," *Review of Income and Wealth*, 26, 1980.

Tata Services, *Statistical Outline of India*, Delhi, annually.

Tavernier, J.B., *Travels in India*, London, Macmillan, 1889.

Thomas, E., *The Revenue Resources of the Mughal Empire in India from* A.D. *1593 to 1707*, London, Trübner, 1879.

United Nations, *Demographic Yearbook*, New York, annual.

U.S. Bureau of Commerce, *Statistical Abstract of the United States*, annual.

Visaria, L., and P., "Population (1757–1947), in *Cambridge Economic History of India*, Raychaudhuri, T. and Habib, I. eds., II, Cambridge, Cambridge University Press, 1982–83.


## Chapter 8

Andréades, A., *Les finances de l'empire Japonais et leur évolution (1869–1931)*, Paris, Felix Alcan, 1932.

Bairoch, P., "Estimations du revenu national dans les sociétés occidentales preindustrelles et au dix neuvième siècle", *Revue d'Economie Politique*, XXVIII, 1977.

Bank of Japan, *Hundred Year Statistics of the Japanese Economy*, Tokyo, 1966.

Crawcour, E.S., "The development of the credit system in 17th century Japan," *Journal of Economic History*, XXI, 1961.

Fuji Bank, *Banking in Modern Japan*, Tokyo, 1967.

Glass, D.V., ed. *Population in History, Historical Population Studies*, London, Edward Arnold, 1965.

Hall, J.W., "The castle town and Japan's modern urbanization," in Hall, I.W., and Jansen, M.B., eds., *Studies in the Institutional History of Early Modern Japan*, Princeton, Princeton University Press, 1968.

Hall, J.W., and Jansen, M.B., eds., *Studies in the Institutional History of Early Modern Japan*, Princeton, Princeton University Press, 1968.

Hall, J.W., Keiji, N., and Yamamura, K., eds., *Japan before Tokugawa*, Princeton, Princeton University Press, 1981.

Hanley, S., and Yamamura, K., *Economic and Demographic Change in Preindustrial Japan, 1600–1868*, Princeton, Princeton University Press, 1977.

"A quiet transformation in Tokugawa economic history," *Journal of Asian Studies*, 30, 1971.

"Population trends and economic growth in preindustrial Japan," in Glass, D.V., ed., *Historical Population Studies*, London, Edward Arnold, 1965.

Hauser, W.B., *Economic Institutional Change in Tokugawa, Japan. Osaka and the Kinai Cotton Trade*, Cambridge, Cambridge University Press, 1974.

Hirschmeier, J., and Yui, T., *The Development of Japanese Business 1600–1973*, Cambridge, Cambridge University Press, 1975.

Honjo, E., *The Social and Economic History of Japan*, New York, Russell and Russell, 1965.

International Monetary Fund, *International Financial Statistics*, Washington D.C., monthly.

Ishii, R., *Population Pressure and Economic Life in Japan*, London, King, 1937.

Iwahashi, M., *Kinsei Nihon bukkashi no kenkyu*, in *Studies in Modern Japanese Price History*, Tokyo, Ohasa Shinsei Sha, 1981.

McClain, J.L., *Kanazawa: A Seventeenth-century Japanese Castle Town*, New Haven, Yale University Press, 1982.

McEvedy, C., and Jones, R., *An Atlas of World Population History*, Harmondsworth, Penguin Books, 1978.

Nagahara, K., "The Sengaka daimyo and the Kandaka system," in Hall, J.W., et al., eds., *Japan before Tokugawa*, Princeton, Princeton University Press, 1981.

Nakamura, J.I., "Human capital accumulation in premodern rural Japan," *Journal of Economic History*, XLI, 1981.

Nakamura, J., and Minamoto, N., "Social structure and population change: A comparative study of Tokugawa Japan and Ch'ing China," *Economic Development and Cultural Change*, Chicago, University of Chicago Press, 1982.

Norman, E.H., *Japan's Emergence*, New York, International Institute of Pacific Relations, 1940.

Ohkawa, K., and Shinohara, M., *Pattern of Japanese Economic Development: A Quantitative Appraisal*, New Haven, Yale University Press, 1979.

## 324    Bibliography

Ohkura, T., and Shimbo, H., "Tokugawa monetary policy in the 18th and 19th centuries," *Exploration in Economic History*, XV, 1978.

Rathgen, K., *Japans Volkswirtschaft und Staatshaushalt*, Leipzig, Duncker and Humblot, 1891.

Richards, J.F., *Precious Metals in Later Medieval and Early Modern World*, Durham, NC, Carolina Academy Press, 1983.

Rozman, G., *Urban Networks in Ch'ing China and Tokugawa Japan*, Princeton, Princeton University Press, 1973.

Sakudo, Y., "Currency in Japanese feudal society," *Osaka Economic Papers*, 4, 1955.

"Monetary system in feudal Japan," *Osaka Economic Papers*, 5, 1956.

*Kinsei hoken shakai no kahei kinyu kozo [Monetary and Financial Structure of Modern Feudal Society]*, Tokyo, Hanawa Shobo, 1971.

Sansome, G., *A History of Japan, 1334–1615, 1615–1867*, Stanford, Stanford University Press, 1961, 1963.

Sheldon, Ch.D., *The Rise of the Merchant Class in Tokugawa Japan*, New York, Augustin, 1972.

Shimbo, H., *Kinsei no bukka to keizei hatten [Prices and Economic Development in Modern History]*, Tokyo, Toyokeizai, 1978.

Shinjo, H. *History of the Yen*, Tokyo, Kinokuniya, 1962.

Smith, N.S., ed. *Materials on Japanese Social and Economic History, I*, London, King, 1937.

Smith, T.C., *The Agrarian Origins of Modern Japan*, Stanford, Stanford University Press, 1959.

"The Japanese village in the 17th century," in Hall and Jansen, *Studies in the Institutional History of Early Modern Japan*, Princeton, Princeton University Press, 1981.

"Farm family by-employments in preindustrial Japan," *Journal of Economic History*, 29, 1969.

"The land tax in the Tokugawa period," in Hall and Jansen, *Studies in the Institutional History of Early Modern Japan*, Princeton, Princeton University Press, 1968.

Taeuber, I., *The Population of Japan*, Princeton, Princeton University Press, 1958.

Totman, C., *Politics in the Tokugawa Bakufu 1600–1843*, Cambridge, Harvard University Press, 1967.

Toyoda, T., *A History of Pre-Meiji Commerce in Japan*, Tokyo, Kokusai Bunka Shinkokai, 1969.

Tsukahira, T.G., *Federal Control in Tokugawa Japan: The Sankin-kotai System*, Cambridge, Cambridge University Press, 1966.

Wakita, O., "The kokudaka system: A device for unification," *Journal of Japanese Studies*, 1, 1975.

Yamamura, K., *A Study of Samurai Income and Entrepreneurship*, Cambridge, Harvard University Press, 1974.

"Returns on unification: Economic growth in Japan 1550–1650," in J. W.

Hall, et. al., *Japan before Tokugawa*, Princeton, Princeton University Press, 1981.

Yamamura, K. and, Kamiki, T., "Silver mines and Sung Coins: A monetary history of medieval and modern Japan," in J. F. Richards, ed., *Precious metals in Later Medieval and Early Modern World*, Durham, NC, Carolina University Press, 1983.

Yonekawa, S., "Recent writings on Japanese economic and social history," *The Economic History Review*, XXXVIII, 1985.


## Chapter 9

Ashtor, E., *Histoire des prix et des salaires dans l'Orient mediéval*, Paris, SEVPEN, 1969.

Barbadoro, B., *Le finanze della republica fiorentina*. Firenze, Olschki, 1929.

Barnett, G., *Two tracts*, Baltimore, Johns Hopkins University Press, 1936.

Becker, M., "Problemi della finanza pubblica fiorentina della seconda metá del Trecento e dei principi del Quattrocento," *Archivio Storico Italiano*, XXIII, 1965.

*Florence in Transition*, Baltimore, Johns Hopkins University Press, 1968.

Bernocchi, M., *Le monete della Repubblica Fiorentina*, Firenze, Olschki, 1976.

Braudel, F., *Le temps du Monde*, Paris, Armand Colin, 1979.

Brown, J.C., *In the Shadow of Florence*, Oxford, Oxford University Press, 1982.

Brucker, G., *The Civic World of Early Renaissance Florence*, Philadelphia, Pennsylvania University Press, 1977.

*Renaissance Florence*, Berkeley, University of California Press 1983a.

"Tales of two cities: Florence and Venice in the Renaissance," *American Historical Review*, 88, 1983b.

Canestrini, G., *La scienza e l'arte di stato*, Firenze, Le Monnier, 1862.

Cipolla, C.M., *The Monetary Policy of 14th Century Florence*, Berkeley, University of California Press, 1982.

Cohn, S., Jr., *The Laboring classes in Renaissance Florence*, New York, Academic Press, 1980.

Conti, E., *I catasti agrari della Repubblica Fiorentina*, Rome, Istituto Storico Italiano per il Medio Evo, 1966.

Davidsohn, R., *Geschichte von Florenz*, Berlin, Mittler, 1896–1927.

Day, J., "The great bullion famine of the fifteenth century," *Past and Present*, 79, 1978.

de la Roncière, Ch., "Indirect taxes or 'gabelles' at Florence in the 14th century," in Rubinstein, N., ed., *Florentine Studies*, Evanston, Northwestern University Press, 1968.

Pauvres et pauvreté à Florence au 14ᵉ siècle," in Mollat, M., ed., *Études sur l'histoire de la pauvreté (Moyen âge – 16ᵉ siècle)*, Paris, Sorbonne, 1974.

*Florence, centre économique regional au XIVᵉ siècle*, Aix en Provence, s.o.d.e.b., n.d.

de Roover, R., *The Rise and Decline of the Medici Bank, 1397–1494*, Cambridge, Harvard University Press, 1963.

"Labor conditions in Florence around 1400" in Rubinstein, N., ed., *Florentine Studies*, Evanston, Northwestern University Press, 1968.

Edler, F., "Early examples of marine insurance," *Journal of Economic History*, V, 1945.

Fiumi, E., "Fioratura e decadenza dell'economia focrentina," *Archivio Storico Italiano*, 116–177, 1958–59.

"Stato di popolazione e distribuzioni della ricchezza in Prato secondo il catasto del 1428," *Archivio Storico Italiano*, 1965.

Fryde, E., "Lorenzo de Medici's finances and their influence on his patronage of art," in *Studi in memoria di Federigo Melis*, vol. 3, Naples, Giannia, 1978.

Goldsmith, R.W., "An estimate of the size and structure of the national product of the early Roman empire," *Review of Income and Wealth*, 40, 1984.

*Comparative National Balance Sheets*, Chicago, Chicago University Press, 1985.

Goldthwaite, R.A., *Private Wealth in Renaissance Florence*, Princeton, Princeton University Press, 1968.

*The Building of Renaissance Florence*, Baltimore, Johns Hopkins University Press, 1980.

Herlihy, D., *Medieval and Renaissance Pistoia*, New Haven, Yale University Press, 1967.

"Family and property in Renaissance Florence," in Miskimin, H.A., et al., eds., *The Medieval City*, New Haven, Yale University Press, 1977.

Herlihy, D., and Klapisch-Zuber, C., *Les Toscans et leurs familles; une étude du catasto florentin de 1427*. Paris, Presses de la Fondation Nationale des Sciences Politiques, 1978.

Homer, S., *A History of Interest Rates*, New Brunswick, Rutgers University Press, 1963.

Hoshino, H., *L'arte della lana a Firenze nel basso medievo*, Firenze, Olschki, 1980.

Karmin, O., *La legge del catasto Fiorentino del 1427*, Firenze, Bernardo Seeberg, 1906.

Kirshner, J., "Papa Eugenio IV e il Monte Comune," in *Archivio Storico Italiano*, 127, 1969.

Kirshner, J., and Molho, A., "The dowry fund and the marriage market in early Quattrocento Florence," *Journal of Modern History*, 50, 1978.

Knapp, G.T., *Die Staatliche Theorie des Geldes*, Leipzig, Duncker and Humblot, 1905.

Kotelnikova, L.A., "Condizione economica dei mezzadri toscani nel secolo XV," in *Atti della Sesta Settimana di Studio*, Instituto Internazional di Studi, Florence, Olschki, 1978.

Kretschmayr, H., *Geschichte von Venedig*, Gotha, Perthes, 1905–34.

Lindert, P.A., and Williamson, J.G., "Revising England's social tables, 1688–1812," *Explorations in Economic History*, 19, 1982.

Lopez, R, and Miskimin, H., "The economic depression of the Renaissance," *Economic History Review*, 14, 1961–62.

Luzzatto, G., *Breve storia economica dell'Italia medievale*, Torino, Einaudi, 1958.

Macchiavelli, N., *Storie Fiorentine*, Carli, P., ed., Firenze, Sanzoni, 1927.

Marks, L.F., "The financial oligarchy in Florence under Lorenzo," in Jacob, E.F., ed., *Italian Renaissance Studies*, London, Faber and Faber, 1960.

Martines, L., *The Social World of the Florentine Humanists*, Princeton, Princeton University Press, 1963.

Mazzi, M.S., and Raveggi, S., *Gli uomini e le cose nelle campagne Fiorentine del Quattrocento*, Florence, Olschki, 1983.

McEvedy, C., and Jones, R., *Atlas of World Population History*, London, Penguin Books, 1978.

Melis, F., *Documenti per la storia economica dei secoli XIII–XVI*, Florence, Olschki, 1972.

*Tracce di una storia economica di Firenze e della Toscana in generale del 1252 al 1550*, Firenze, Universitá degli Studi, 1966–67.

Miskimin, H.A., *The Economics of Early Renaissance Europe, 1300-1460*, Cambridge, Cambridge University Press, 1976.

ed., *The Medieval City*, New Haven, Yale University Press, 1977.

Mitchell, B. R., and Deane, Ph. *Abstract of British Historical Statistics*, Cambridge, Cambridge University Press, 1962.

Molho, A., "The Florentine tassa dei traffichi of 1451, *Studies in the Renaissance*, XXVII, 1970.

*Florentine Public Finances in the Early Renaissance, 1400–1433*, Cambridge, Harvard University Press, 1971.

Mollet, M., *Histoire de la pauvreté (Moyen age–16ᵉ siècle)*, Paris, Sorbonne, 1974.

Origo, I., "The domestic enemy: The Eastern slaves in Tuscany in the 14th and 15th centuries," *Spectrum*, XXX, 1955.

Pardi, G., "Disegno della storia demografica di Firenze," *Archivio Storico Italiano*, LXXIV, 1916.

Renard, G., *Historie du travail à Florence*, Paris, Editions d'Art et de Litterature, 1914.

Rubinstein, N., *Florentine Studies*, Evanston, Northwestern University Press, 1968.

Sapori, A., *La crisi delle compagnie mercantili dei Bardi e dei Peruzzi*, Firenze, Olschki, 1926.

"I beni del commercio internazionale nel Medioevo," *Archivio Storico Italiano*, 113, 1955.

*Studi di storia economica secoli xiii–xiv–xv*, Florence, Sanzoni, 1955–67.

## Chapter 10

Barnett, G.E., *Two Tracts by Gregory King*, Baltimore, Johns Hopkins University Press, 1936.

Bowden, P.J., "Agrarian prices, farm profits and rents," in Thirsk, J., ed., *The Agrarian History of England and Wales*, vol. IV, Cambridge, Cambridge University Press, 1967.

Central Statistical Office, *Annual Abstract of Statistics*, London, H.M. Stationery Office.

Challis, C.E., *The Tudor Coinage*, Manchester, University of Manchester Press, 1978.

"The debasement of the coinage, 1542–1551," in *Economic History Review*, XX, 1967.

Clarkson, L.A., *The Pre-industrial Economy of England, 1500–1750*, London, Batsford, 1971.

Cole, W.A. "Factors in Demand, 1700–1800," in Floud, R., and McCloskey, D., eds., *The Economic History of Britain since 1700*, Cambridge, Cambridge University Press, 1981.

Coleman, D.C., *The Economy of England 1450–1750*, London, Oxford University Press, 1977.

Cornwall, J., "English country towns in the fifteen-twenties," *Economic History Review*, 15, 1962–63.

Craig, J., *The Mint*, Cambridge, University Press, 1953.

Cunningham, W., *The Growth of English Industry and Commerce in Modern Times*, Cambridge, Cambridge University Press, 1925.

Davis, R., *English Overseas Trade, 1500–1700*, London, Macmillan, 1973.

Dickson, P.G., *The Financial Revolution in England*, London, Macmillan, 1967.

Dietz, F.C., *English Public Finance, 1558–1641*, New York, Century, 1932.

de Smedt, O., *De Engelse natie te Antwerpen in de 16° eeuw (1496–1582)*, Antwerp, de Sikkel, 1950, 1954.

Dowell, S., *History of Taxation and Taxes in England*, London, Longmans, 1888.

Everitt, A., "The marketing of agricultural produce," in Thirsk, J., ed., *The Agrarian History of England, 1500–1640*, Cambridge, Cambridge University Press, 1967.

Feaveryear, A.E., *The Pound Sterling*, 2nd. ed., Oxford, Clarendon Press, 1963.

Fisher, F.J., "Commercial trends and policy in 16th century England," *Economic History Review*, 10, 1940.

   ed., *Essays in the Economic and Social History of Tudor and Stuart England*, Cambridge, Cambridge University Press, 1961.

Friis, A., *Alderman Cockayne's Project and the Cloth Trade*, Copenhagen, Levin and Munksgaard, 1927.

Goldsmith, R.W., *Comparative National Balance Sheets*, Chicago, The Chicago University Press, 1985.

Gould, J.D., *The Great Debasement: Currency and the Economy in Mid-Tudor England*, Oxford, Clarendon Press, 1970.

Gregg, P., *Black Death to Industrial Revolution*, London, Harrap, 1976.

Grueber, H.A., *Handbook of Coins of Great Britain in the British Museum*, London, Trustees of the British Museum, 1899.

Hudson, K., *Pawnbroking*, London, The Bodley Head, 1982.

Kerridge, E., *The Agricultural Revolution*, London, Allen and Unwin, 1967.

King, G., "Natural and political observations," in G.E. Barnett, *Two Tracts by Gregory King*, Baltimore, Johns Hopkins University Press, 1936.

Lindert, P.H., *Some Economic Consequences of English Population Growth 1541–1913*, Davis, University of California, Agricultural History Center, Working Paper Series, No. 14, 1983.

Lindert, P.H., and Williamson, J., "Revising England's social tables 1688–1812," *Explorations in Economic History*, 19, 1982.

Lingelbach, W.C., *The Internal Organization of the Merchant Adventurers of England*, Ph.D. Thesis, University of Pennsylvania, 1903.

Lipson, E., *The Economic History of England*, 6th ed. London, Adam and Charles Black, 1956.

Martin, F., *The History of Lloyd's and of Marine Insurance in Great Britain*, London, Macmillan, 1876.

Miskimin, H., "Population growth and the price revolution in England," *Journal of European Economic History*, 4, 1975.

Mulhall, G.M., *Dictionary of Statistics*, 4th ed., London, Routledge and Sons, 1899.

Outhwaite, R.B., *Inflation in Tudor and Early Stuart England*, London, Macmillan, 1969.

Palliser, D.M., *The Era of Elizabeth*, London, Longmans, 1983.

Phelps-Brown, H. and Hopkins, S.V., *A Perspective of Wages and Prices*, London, Methuen, 1981.

Pollard, S., and Crossley, D.W., *The Wealth of Britain, 1085–1966*, London, Batsford, 1968.

Postan, N. "Credit in medieval trade," *Economic History Review*, I, 1942.

Ramsey, P.H., *The Price Revolution in 16th Century England*, London, Methuen, 1971.

Richards, R.D., *The Early History of English Banking*, London, King and Son, 1929.

Schofield, R.S., "The geographical distribution of wealth in England: 1334–1649," Economic History Review, XVIII, 1965.

Scott, W.R., *The Constitution and Finance of English, Scottish and Irish Joint Stock Companies, 1558–1720*, Cambridge, Cambridge University Press, 1910–1912.

Sombart, W., *Der Moderne Kapitalismus*, Munich, Duncker and Humblot, 1928.

Stone, L., *The Crisis of the Aristocracy, 1558–1641*, Oxford, Clarendon Press, 1965.

Tawney, R.H., *The Agrarian Problem in the 16th Century*, London, Longmans, 1912.

ed., Thomas Wilson, *A Discourse Upon Usury*, London, G. Ball, 1925.

Thirsk, J., ed., *The Agrarian History of England and Wales*, vol. IV, 1500–1640, Cambridge, Cambridge University Press, 1967.

Unwin, G., "The Merchants Adventurers' Company in the reign of Elizabeth," in Tawney, R.H., ed., *Studies in Economic History: The Collected Papers of George Unwin*, London, Macmillan, 1927.

Walford, C., *The Insurance Cyclopaedia*, London, Leyton, 1871ff.

Wilson, Th., *A Discourse Upon Usury*, London, Ball, 1925.

"The state of England," ed. by F. J. Fisher, in *Camden Miscellany*, XVI, 1926, London of the Society.

Wordie, J.R., "The chronology of English enclosures, 1500–1914," *Economic History Review*, XXXVI, 1983.

World Bank, *World Development Report 1981*, Washington, D.C., 1981.
Wrigley, E.A., and Schofield, R.S., *The Population History of England, 1541–1871*, Cambridge, MA, Harvard University Press, 1981.
Youngs, J., *Sixteenth century England*, Harmondsworth, Penguin Books, 1984.


## Chapter 11

Ackerle, H.W., "Amsterdamer Börsenprislisten, 1624–1626," *Economisch-Historisch Jaarboek*, 13, 1927.
Aymard, M., ed. *Dutch Capitalism and World Capitalism*, Cambridge, Cambridge University Press, 1982.
Baasch, E., *Holländische Wirtschaftsgeschichte*, Jena, Gustav Fischer, 1927.
Ballhausen, C., *Der erste Englisch-Holländische Seekrieg 1652–1654 sowie der Schwedisch-Holländische Seekrieg 1658–1659*. Haag, Martinus Nijhoff, 1923.
Barbour, V., *Capitalism in Amsterdam in the Seventeenth Century*, Ann Arbor, University of Michigan Press, 1963.
Becht, H.E., *Statistische gegevens betreffende den handelsomzet van der Republic der Vereenigde Nederlanden geducende de 17ᵉ eeuw, (1579–1715)*, s'Gravenhage, Boucher, 1908.
Braudel, F., *Le temps du monde*, Paris, Armand Colin, 1979.
Brugmans, T.J., *Opkomst en bloei van Amsterdam*, Amsterdam, Meulenhoff, 1944.
"De Oost-Indischhe Compagnie en de welvaart in de Republiec," *Tijdschrift voor Geschiedenis*, 61, 1948.
Burke, P., *Venice and Amsterdam*, London, Temple Smith, 1974.
Cipolla, C.M., ed. *The Fontana Economic History of Europe 1500–1730*, Glasgow, Collins/Fontana, 1974.
Dillen, J.G., van, "Amsterdam marché mondial des métaux précieux aux XVIIᵉ et au XVIIIᵉ siècle," *Revue Historique*, 152, 1926.
   *Bronner tot de geschiedenis der Wisselbanken (Amsterdam, Middelburg, Delft, Rotterdam)*, s'Gravenhage, Martinus Nijhoff, 1925.
   *History of the Principal Public Banks*, The Hague, Martinus Nijhoff, 1934.
   *Het oudste andeelhouderregister van de Kamer Amsterdam der Oost-Indische Compagnie*, s'Gravenhage, Martinus Nijhoff, 1958.
   "Bloeitijd der Amsterdamsche Wisselbank 1687–1781," in *Mensen en Achtergronden*, Groningen, Wolters, 1964a.
   "Oprichting en functie der Amsterdamsche Wisselbank in de zeventiends eeuw 1609–1686", in *Mensen en Achtergronden*, Groningen, Wolters, 1964b.
   *Mensen en Achtergronden*, Groningen, Wolters, 1964c.
   *Van rijkhdom en regenten*, s'Gravenhage, Martinus Nijhoff, 1970.
Elias, J.E., *De vroedschap van Amsterdam 1578–1795*, Amsterdam, Israel, 1903–05.
Faber, J.A. et. al., "Population changes and economic developments in the Netherlands: a historical survey," *A.A.G. Bijdragen* 12, Wageningen, 1965.
Fanfani, A., *Città mercanti, dottrine nell'economica Europea del IV al XVIII secolo*, Milano, Giuffré, 1964.

Gelder, H.E., van, *Munthervorming tijdens de Republiek, 1659–1694*, Amsterdam, van Kampen en Zoon, 1949.

Geyl, P., *The Netherlands in the 17th Century*, London, Ernest Benn, 1961, 1964.

Glamann, K., *Dutch-Asiatic Trade, 1620–1740*, Copenhagen, Danish Science Press, 1958.

Grossmann, J., *Die Amsterdamer Börse vor 200 Jahren*, The Hague, Martinus Nijhoff, 1876.

Homer, S., *A History of Interest Rates*, New Brunswick, Rutgers University Press, 1963.

Houtte, J.A., van, *Economische en sociale geschiedenis van de Lage Landen*, Zeist, de Haan, 1964.

Kindleberger, C.P., *A Financial History of Western Europe*, London, Allen and Unwin, 1984.

King, G., *Two Tracts*, Baltimore, Johns Hopkins University Press, 1938.

Klein, P.W., "De heffing van de 100ᵉ amd 200ᵉ penning van het vermogen te Gouda, 1599–1722," *Economisch-historisch Jaarboek*, 31, 1967.

"Stagnation economique et emploi du capital dans la Hollande des XVIIIᵉ et XIXᵉ siècles," *Revue du Nord*, LXII, 1970.

"De Zeventiende eeuw (1585–1700), J.H. van Stuivenberg, *De economische Geschiedenis van Nederland, 1977*.

Klerk de Reus, G.C., *Geschichtlicher Überblick der administrativen, rechtlichen und finanziellen Entwicklung der Niederländisch-Ostindischen Compagnie*, Batavia, Bataviaasch genootschap voor Runsten en wetenschappen, Verhandelingen, 47, 3, ca. 1894.

Klompmaker, H., *De handel in de gouden eeuw*, Bussum, van Dishoek, 1966.

"Handel, geld en bankwezen in de Nordelijke Nederlander 1580–1650," in *Allgemene Geschildenis der Nederlanden*, Haarlem Fibula-van Dishoek, 1980.

Koenen, H.J., *Voorlezingen oven de geschiedenis der finantien ver Amsterdam*, Amsterdam, Binger en Zonen, 1855.

de Korte, J.P., *De jaarlikse financiele verantwoording in de VOC*, Leiden, Martinus Nijhoff, 1984.

Kranenburg, H.A.H., *De Zeevischerij van Holland in de tijd de Republiek*, Amsterdam, H.J. Paris, 1947.

Kuyk, J., van, and Gelder, H.E., van, *De penningen en het geld van den tachtigjaringen oorlog*, s'Gravenhage, Martinus Nijhoff, 1948.

Laspeyres, E., *Geschichte der volkswirtschaftlichen Anschauungen der Niederländer und ihre Litteratur zur Zeit der Republik*, Leipzig, Hirzel, 1863.

Leroy-Ladurie, E., "Les comptes fantastiques de Gregory King," in *Annales* 1968. (Reprinted in *Le Territoire de l'historien*, Paris, Gallimard, 1973).

Lindert, P.H., and Williamson, J.G., "Revising England's social tables 1688–1812," *Explorations in Economic History*, 19, 1982.

McEvedy, C., and Jones, R., *Atlas of World Population History*, Harmondsworth, Penguin Books, 1978.

Maddison, A., *Phases of Capitalist Development*, Oxford, Oxford University Press, 1982.

Dutch income in and from Indonesia 1700–1938, Mimeograph, 1984.

Mees, W.C., *Proeve eener geschiedenis van het bankwezen in Nederland gedurende de tijd der republik*, Rotterdam, Messchert, 1838.

Menkman, W.R., *De West-Indische Compagnie*, Amsterdam, van Kampen, 1947.

Mitchell, B.R., *European Historical Statistics, 1950–1975*, New York, Facts on File, 1980.

Mitchell, R.R., and Deane, P., *Abstract of British Historical Statistics*, Cambridge, University Press, 1962.

Mokyr, J., Review of M. Aymard, ed., "Dutch capitalism and world capitalism," *Journal of European Economic History*, 12, 1983.

Morineau, M., "Quelques remarques sur l'abondance monétaire aux Provinces Unies," *Annales*, 29, 1974.

"Hommage aux historiens hollandais et contribution à l'histoire economique des Provinces Unies," in Aymard, N., ed., *Dutch Capitalism and World Capitalism*, Cambridge, Cambridge University Press, 1982.

Oldewelt, W.F.H., "De beroepsstructuur van de bevolking der Hollandse stemmehebben de steden . . ." in *Economisch Historisch Jaarboek*, XXIV, 1950.

Parker, G., "The emergence of modern finance in Europe, 1500–1730," in Cipolla, C.M., ed., *The Fontana Economic History of Europe*, vol. 2, Glasgow, Collins/Fontana, 1974.

Penso de la Vega, J., *Confusion de confusiones*, s'Gravenhage, Martinus Nijhoff, 1939.

Phelps-Brown, E., and Hopkins, S., *A Perspective on Wages and Prices*, London, Methuen, 1981.

Posthumus, N.W., *De geschiedenis van de Leidsche lakenindustrie*, s'Gravenhage, Martinus Nijhoff, 1939.

*Inquiry into the History of Prices in Holland*, Leyden, Brill, 1946, 1984.

Price, J.L., *Culture and Society in the Dutch Republic during the 17th Century*, London, Batsford, 1974.

Sickenga, F.N. *Geschiedenis der nederlandschen belastingen sedert* 1810, Utrecht, F.L. Beijers, 1883.

Sombart, W., *Der moderne Kapitalismus*, München, Duncker and Humblot, 1928.

*Statistical Yearbook of the Netherlands*, The Hague, Central Bureau voor Statistiek.

Steensgard, N., "The Dutch East India Company as an institutional innovation," in Aymard, M., ed., *Dutch Capitalism and World Capitalism*, Cambridge, Cambridge University Press, 1982.

Stuijvenberg, J.H., van, "De economie in de Nordelijke Nederlanden 1770–1970," in *Allgemene Geschiedenis der Nederlanden*, part 1, 1981.

Stuijvenberg, J.H., van, and de Vrijer, J.E.J., Prices, Population and National Income in the Netherlands 1620–1978, Amsterdam, Research Memorandum 8101, 1980.

"Prices, Population and National Income in the Netherlands 1620–1978," *Journal of European Economic History*, 11, 1982.

Summers, R., Kravis, I.B., and Heston, A., "International comparison of real product and its composition: 1950–1977," *Review of Income and Wealth*, 26, 1980.

Unger, R.W., "Scheepvaart in de Noordelijke Nederlanden," *AGN* 6, 1979.

Verlinden, C., "Amsterdam," in Fanfani, A., ed. *Cittá mercanti dottrine nell economia Europea del IV al XVIII secolo*, Milan, Giuffré, 1964.

de Vrankrijker, A.C.J., *Geschiedenis van de belastingen*, Bussum, Fibula–Van Dishoeck, 1969.

deVries, Jan, *The Dutch Rural Economy in the Golden Age*, 1500–1700, New Haven, Yale University Press, 1974.

"An inquiry into the behavior of wages in the Dutch Republic and the Southern Netherlands from 1580 to 1800," in Aymard, M., ed. *Dutch Capitalism and World Capitalism*, Cambridge, Cambridge University Press, 1982.

"The decline and rise of the Dutch economy, 1675–1900," *Research in Economic History*, Supplement 3, 1984.

de Vries, Johan, *De achteruitgang der Republik in de 18e eeuw*, Amsterdam, 1959.

Wallerstein, I., "Dutch hegemony in the seventeenth century world economy," in Aymard, M., ed., *Dutch Capitalism and World Capitalism*, Cambridge, Cambridge, University Press, 1982.

Wätjen, H., *Die Niederländer im Mittelmeergebiet zur Zeit threr höchsten Machtstellung*, Berlin, Curtuns, 1909.

Westermann, J.C., "Statistische gegevens over den handel van Amsterdam in de zeventiende eeuw," *Tijdschrift voor Geschiedenis*, 61, 1948.

van der Woude, "Demografische outwikkeling van de Norderlijke Nederlanden 1500–1800," in *Allgemeene Geschiedenis der Nederlanden*, vol. 5.

# Index

*(Italicized page numbers indicate material in tables.)*